CAMBRIDGE TEXTBOOKS IN LINGUISTICS

General editors: S. R. ANDERSON, J. BRESNAN, B. COMRIE,
W. DRESSLER, C. EWEN, R. HUDDLESTON, R. LASS,
D. LIGHTFOOT, J. LYONS, P. H. MATTHEWS, R. POSNER,
S. ROMAINE, N. V. SMITH, N. VINCENT

In this series:

P. H. MATTHEWS *Morphology* Second edition
B. COMRIE *Aspect*
R. M. KEMPSON *Semantic Theory*
T. BYNON *Historical Linguistics*
J. ALLWOOD, L.-G. ANDERSON and Ö. DAHL *Logic in Linguistics*
D. B. FRY *The Physics of Speech*
R. A. HUDSON *Sociolinguistics* Second edition
A. J. ELLIOT *Child Language*
P. H. MATTHEWS *Syntax*
A. REDFORD *Transformational Syntax*
L. BAUER *English Word-Formation*
S. C. LEVINSON *Pragmatics*
G. BROWN and G. YULE *Discourse Analysis*
R. HUDDLESTON *Introduction to the Grammar of English*
R. LASS *Phonology*
A. COMRIE *Tense*
W. KLEIN *Second Language Acquisition*
A. J. WOODS, P. FLETCHER and A. HUGHES *Statistics in Language Studies*
D. A. CRUSE *Lexical Semantics*
A. RADFORD *Transformational Grammar*
M. GARMAN *Psycholinguistics*
G. G. CORBETT *Gender*
H. J. GIEGERICH *English Phonology*
R. CANN *Formal Semantics*
J. LAVER *Principles of Phonetics*
F. R. PALMER *Grammatical Roles and Relations*
M. A. JONES *Foundations of French Syntax*
A. RADFORD *Syntactic Theory and the Structure of English: A Minimalist Approach*
R. D. VAN VALIN, JR, and R. J. LAPOLLA *Syntax: Structure, Meaning and Function*
A. DURANTI *Linguistic Anthropology*
A. CRUTTENDEN *Intonation* Second edition
J. K. CHAMBERS and P. TRUDGILL *Dialectology* Second edition
C. LYONS *Definiteness*
R. KAGER *Optimality Theory*
J. A. HOLM *An Introduction to Pidgins and Creoles*
C. G. CORBETT *Number*
C. J. EWEN and H. VAN DER HULST *The Phonological Structure of Words*
F. R. PALMER *Mood and Modality* Second edition
B. J. BLAKE *Case* Second edition
E. GUSSMAN *Phonology: Analysis and Theory*
M. YIP *Tone*
W. CROFT *Typology and Universals* Second edition
F. COULMAS *Writing Systems: an Introduction to their Linguistic Analysis*
P. J. HOPPER and E. C. TRAUGOTT *Grammaticalization* Second edition
L. WHITE *Second Language Acquisition and Universal Grammar*
I. PLAG *Word-formation in English*
W. CROFT and D. A. CRUSE *Cognitive Linguistics*
A. SIEWIERSKA *Person*
A. RADFORD *Minimalist Syntax: Exploring the Structure of English*
D. BÜRING *Binding Theory*

Cognitive Linguistics

WILLIAM CROFT

University of Manchester

and

D. ALAN CRUSE

University of Manchester

CAMBRIDGE
UNIVERSITY PRESS

CAMBRIDGE UNIVERSITY PRESS
Cambridge, New York, Melbourne, Madrid, Cape Town, Singapore, São Paulo

Cambridge University Press
The Edinburgh Building, Cambridge, CB2 8RU, UK

Published in the United States of America by Cambridge University Press, New York

www.cambridge.org
Information on this title: www.cambridge.org/9780521667708

First published 2004
Fourth printing 2007

Printed in the United Kingdom at the University Press, Cambridge

A catalogue record for this book is available from the British Library

ISBN-13 978-0-521-66114-0 hardback
ISBN-13 978-0-521-66770-8 paperback

Contents

List of figures   *page* xii
List of tables   xiii
Preface   xv

1 Introduction: what is cognitive linguistics?   1

Part I: A conceptual approach to linguistic analysis

**2 Frames, domains, spaces: the organization of conceptual
structure**   7
  2.1   Arguments for frame semantics   7
  2.2   Concepts: profile-frame organization   14
  2.3   Some consequences of the profile-frame/domain distinction   16
  2.4   Extensions of the basic profile-frame/domain distinction   22
      2.4.1 Locational and configurational profiles   22
      2.4.2 Scope of predication   23
      2.4.3 Relationships between domains   24
  2.5   Domains and idealized cognitive models   28
  2.6   Mental spaces   32

3 Conceptualization and construal operations   40
  3.1   Introduction   40
  3.2   Attention/salience   46
      3.2.1 Selection   47
      3.2.2 Scope of attention (dominion)   50
      3.2.3 Scalar adjustment   51
      3.2.4 Dynamic attention   53
  3.3   Judgement/comparison   54
      3.3.1 Categorization   54
      3.3.2 Metaphor   55
      3.3.3 Figure-ground alignment   56
  3.4   Perspective/situatedness   58
      3.4.1 Viewpoint   59

		3.4.2	Deixis	59
		3.4.3	Subjectivity	62
	3.5	Constitution/Gestalt		63
		3.5.1	Structural schematization	63
		3.5.2	Force dynamics	66
		3.5.3	Relationality (entity/interconnection)	67
	3.6	Conclusion		69

4   Categories, concepts and meanings   74

4.1   Introduction   74
4.2   The classical model of category structure   76
4.3   The prototype model of category structure   77
    4.3.1   Graded centrality   77
    4.3.2   The representation of conceptual categories   81
    4.3.3   Levels of categorization   82
    4.3.4   Shortcomings of prototype theory   87
    4.3.5   The frame-based account of prototype effects   91
4.4   A dynamic construal approach to conceptual categories   92
    4.4.1   Category boundaries   93
    4.4.2   Frames   95
    4.4.3   Levels of categorization   96
4.5   The dynamic construal of meaning   97
    4.5.1   Contextualized interpretation   98
    4.5.2   Purport   100
    4.5.3   Constraints   101
    4.5.4   Construal   103
4.6   Structural and logical aspects of meaning   104
4.7   Part I: Concluding remarks   105

Part II: Cognitive approaches to lexical semantics

5   Polysemy: the construal of sense boundaries   109

5.1   Introduction   109
5.2   Full sense boundaries   110
    5.2.1   Homonymy and polysemy   111
    5.2.2   Entrenchment   111
    5.2.3   Boundary effects   112
    5.2.4   The nature of full sense units   115
5.3   Sub-sense units with near-sense properties   116
    5.3.1   Facets   116
    5.3.2   Microsenses   126
    5.3.3   Ways-of-seeing   137
    5.3.4   Semantic components and low-autonomy active zones   138

| | 5.3.5 | Contextual modulation | 140 |
| 5.4 | Autonomy: summary | | 140 |

6 A dynamic construal approach to sense relations I:
hyponymy and meronymy   141

6.1	Hyponymy		141
	6.1.1	Introductory	141
	6.1.2	Hyponymy and context	143
	6.1.3	Relations between lexical items	146
	6.1.4	Taxonymy	147
6.2	Lexical aspects of the part-whole relation		150
	6.2.1	The part-whole relation	151
	6.2.2	Meronymy	159

7 A dynamic construal approach to sense relations II:
antonymy and complementarity   164

7.1	Oppositeness		164
	7.1.1	Aspects of the construal of oppositeness	164
	7.1.2	Main varieties of opposite	165
	7.1.3	Goodness-of-exemplar in opposites	166
7.2	Complementarity		167
	7.2.1	Gradable vs. non-gradable construal of properties	167
	7.2.2	Profiling against domains	167
7.3	Antonymy		169
	7.3.1	A survey of antonym types	169
	7.3.2	Monoscalar systems: polar antonyms	172
	7.3.3	Bi-scalar systems	181
7.4	Variable construal of antonyms and complementaries		185
	7.4.1	Absolute vs. relative construal	185
	7.4.2	Scale features	189
7.5	Conclusion		192

8 Metaphor   193

8.1	Figurative language		193
8.2	The conceptual theory of metaphor		194
	8.2.1	Introduction	194
	8.2.2	Issues in the conceptual theory of metaphor	198
8.3	Novel metaphor		204
	8.3.1	The life history of a metaphor	204
	8.3.2	How do we recognize metaphors?	206
	8.3.3	Blending Theory and novel metaphors	207
	8.3.4	Context sensitivity	209
	8.3.5	Asymmetry of vehicle and target	210

8.4		Metaphor and simile	211
	8.4.1	Two types of simile	211
	8.4.2	Theories of the relation between simile and metaphor	211
	8.4.3	Metaphor-simile combinations	215
8.5		Metaphor and metonymy	216
	8.5.1	Characterizing metonymy	216
	8.5.2	Metaphor-metonymy relations	217
	8.5.3	Types of indeterminacy	219
8.6		Conclusion	220

Part III: Cognitive approaches to grammatical form

9   From idioms to construction grammar

		From idioms to construction grammar	225
9.1		Introduction	225
9.2		The problem of idioms	229
9.3		Idioms as constructions	236
9.4		From constructions to construction grammar	247

10   An overview of construction grammars

		An overview of construction grammars	257
10.1		Essentials of construction grammar theories	257
	10.1.1	Grammatical representation: the anatomy of a construction	257
	10.1.2	The organization of constructional knowledge	262
10.2		Some current theories of construction grammar	265
	10.2.1	Construction Grammar (Fillmore, Kay et al.)	266
	10.2.2	Lakoff (1987) and Goldberg (1995)	272
	10.2.3	Cognitive Grammar as a construction grammar	278
	10.2.4	Radical Construction Grammar	283
10.3		Conclusion	290

11   The usage-based model

		The usage-based model	291
11.1		Grammatical representation and process	291
11.2		The usage-based model in morphology	292
	11.2.1	Entrenchment and representation of word forms	292
	11.2.2	Regularity, productivity and default status	295
	11.2.3	Product-oriented schemas	300
	11.2.4	Network organization of word forms	302
	11.2.5	Conclusion	307
11.3		The usage-based model in syntax	308
	11.3.1	Type/token frequency, productivity and entrenchment	308
	11.3.2	Product-oriented syntactic schemas	313

	11.3.3	Relevance and the organization of construction networks	318
	11.3.4	The acquisition of syntax and syntactic change	323
11.4	Conclusion		326

12 Conclusion: cognitive linguistics and beyond   328

References   330
Author index   344
Subject index   347

Figures

2.1	RADIUS and CIRCLE	*page* 15
2.2	NIECE	23
2.3	Domain structure underlying the concept of the letter T	26
2.4	Specific and nonspecific indefinites	35
2.5	Mental space diagram for example (29)	36
4.1	Boundaries of AIRPLANE, GLIDER and HANG GLIDER	90
7.1	A simplified monoscalar system	170
7.2	A disjunct equipollent system	170
7.3	A parallel equipollent system	170
7.4	An overlapping system	171
7.5	A full monoscalar system	173
10.1	The symbolic structure of a construction	258
10.2	The relation between form and function in a componential syntactic theory	258
10.3	The relation between form and function in construction grammar	259
10.4	Simplified generative grammar and construction grammar representations of *Heather sings*	260
10.5	Elements, components and units of a construction	261

Tables

3.1 Linguistic construal operations as instances of general
    cognitive processes   *page* 46
9.1 Types of idioms compared to regular syntactic expressions   236
9.2 The syntax-lexicon continuum   255

Preface

This book provides an overview of the basic principles and methods of cognitive linguistics, in particular as they are applied to semantic and syntactic issues. It is intended to be used as a textbook for a course on cognitive linguistics for advanced undergraduates and postgraduate students, as well as functioning as an introduction to this approach to language for linguists and researchers in neighboring disciplines. Parts I and II may also function as a textbook for a course on cognitive semantics, supplemented by case studies from the cognitive linguistic literature. Part III may also function as introductory reading for a course on construction grammar, followed by readings from the literature that delve into the details of particular theories of construction grammar and the analyses of particular constructions.

The chapters of the book were independently written, but jointly discussed. Croft is responsible for chapters 1–3 and 9–12, and Cruse for chapters 4–8 (this fact will no doubt be obvious to the reader). Cruse also contributed to §3.2.1, and Croft to §8.2. Although we have written our chapters independently, the book represents a single coherent perspective on cognitive linguistics. We agree on all of the major points, and most of the minor ones; what minor disagreements remain do not compromise the integrity of the analysis as a whole.

Croft would like to thank members of the linguistics and psychology departments at the Max Planck Institute for Evolutionary Anthropology, Leipzig, Germany, and Jóhanna Barðdal, Chuck Fillmore, Laura Janda, Paul Kay and Ron Langacker for their comments on earlier versions of Part III, and Liliana Albertazzi and the participants in the Workshop on 'Which Semantics?,' Bolzano, Italy, 1995 for their comments on topics dealt with in Part I. Cruse would like to thank Liliana Albertazzi and fellow-participants (George Lakoff, Ron Langacker and Len Talmy) at the Summer School on Cognitive Semantics, Bolzano, Italy, 1999; Arie Verhagen and the students at the LOT Winter School, Leiden, Holland, 2002; and members of the Equipe Rhéma, University of Lyon, France, for their comments on various topics dealt with in the book. Last but not least, we both thank the students of successive classes on cognitive linguistics at the University of Manchester, who used materials that eventually became the chapters presented here. Of course, all responsibility for the final product remains with us.

1

Introduction: what is cognitive linguistics?

Cognitive linguistics is taken here to refer to the approach to the study of language that began to emerge in the 1970s and has been increasingly active since the 1980s (now endowed with an international society with biennial conferences and a journal, *Cognitive Linguistics*). A quarter century later, a vast amount of research has been generated under the name of cognitive linguistics. Most of the research has focused on semantics, but a significant proportion also is devoted to syntax and morphology, and there has been cognitive linguistic research into other areas of linguistics such as language acquisition, phonology and historical linguistics. This book can only outline the basic principles of the cognitive linguistic approach and some of its more important results and implications for the study of language. In this chapter, we briefly describe the major hypotheses of cognitive linguistics (as we see them), and how we will develop these hypotheses in the rest of the book.

We see three major hypotheses as guiding the cognitive linguistic approach to language:

* language is not an autonomous cognitive faculty
* grammar is conceptualization
* knowledge of language emerges from language use

These three hypotheses represent a response by the pioneering figures in cognitive linguistics to the dominant approaches to syntax and semantics at the time, namely generative grammar and truth-conditional (logical) semantics. The first principle is opposed to generative grammar's well-known hypothesis that language is an autonomous (indeed, innate) cognitive faculty or module, separated from nonlinguistic cognitive abilities. The second principle is opposed to truth-conditional semantics, in which a semantic metalanguage is evaluated in terms of truth and falsity relative to the world (or, more precisely, a model of the world). The third principle is opposed to reductionist tendencies in both generative grammar and truth-conditional semantics, in which maximally abstract and general representations of grammatical form and meaning are sought and many grammatical and semantic phenomena are assigned to the 'periphery'.

Generative grammar and truth-conditional semantics are of course still vigorous research paradigms today, and so cognitive linguists continue to present arguments for their basic hypotheses as well as exploring more specific empirical questions of syntax and semantics within the cognitive linguistic paradigm. Some of these arguments will be presented in the course of this book. Here we describe in somewhat more detail the content of these three hypotheses and how they are manifested in subsequent chapters.

The first hypothesis is that language is not an autonomous cognitive faculty. The basic corollaries of this hypothesis are that the representation of linguistic knowledge is essentially the same as the representation of other conceptual structures, and that the processes in which that knowledge is used are not fundamentally different from cognitive abilities that human beings use outside the domain of language.

The first corollary is essentially that linguistic knowledge – knowledge of meaning and form – is basically conceptual structure. It is probably not difficult to accept the hypothesis that semantic representation is basically conceptual (though what that entails is a matter of debate; see below). But cognitive linguists argue that syntactic, morphological and phonological representation is also basically conceptual. This might appear counterintuitive at first: sounds are physical entities, and ultimately so are utterances and their formal structure. But sounds and utterances must be comprehended and produced, and both of those processes involve the mind. Sounds and utterances are the input and output of cognitive processes that govern speaking and understanding.

The second corollary is that the cognitive processes that govern language use, in particular the construction and communication of meaning by language, are in principle the same as other cognitive abilities. That is, the organization and retrieval of linguistic knowledge is not significantly different from the organization and retrieval of other knowledge in the mind, and the cognitive abilities that we apply to speaking and understanding language are not significantly different from those applied to other cognitive tasks, such as visual perception, reasoning or motor activity. Language is a distinct human cognitive ability, to be sure. From a cognitive perspective, language is the real-time perception and production of a temporal sequence of discrete, structured symbolic units. This particular configuration of cognitive abilities is probably unique to language, but the component cognitive skills required are not.

This position is sometimes taken as a denial of an innate human capacity for language. This is not the case; it is only a denial of an autonomous, special-purpose innate human capacity for language. It is of course reasonable to assume that there is a significant innate component to general human cognitive abilities, and that some of those innate properties give rise to human linguistic abilities that no other species apparently has. However, innateness of cognitive abilities has not been a chief concern of cognitive linguists, who are more concerned with demonstrating the role of general cognitive abilities in language.

The hypothesis that language is not an autonomous cognitive faculty has had two major implications for cognitive linguistic research. Much cognitive linguistic research has been devoted to elucidating conceptual structure and cognitive abilities as they are seen to apply to language, in the effort to demonstrate that language can be adequately modeled using just these general conceptual structures and cognitive abilities. Part I of this book is devoted to explicating cognitive linguistic models of cognitive structure and abilities (see also chapter 11).

Second, cognitive linguists appeal at least in principle to models in cognitive psychology, in particular models of memory, perception, attention and categorization. Psychological models of memory have inspired linguistic models of the organization of linguistic knowledge into frames/domains (chapter 2), and grammatical knowledge in networks linked by taxonomic and other relations (see chapters 10–11 in Part III). Psychological models of attention and perception, especially Gestalt psychology, have led to the explication of many conceptualization processes in semantics (chapter 3, and see also the next paragraph). Finally, psychological models of categorization, in particular prototypes and graded centrality, and more recent models of category structure, have had perhaps the greatest influence on both semantic and grammatical category analysis in cognitive linguistics (chapter 3; see, e.g., Lakoff 1987, Taylor 1989[1997]).

The second major hypothesis of the cognitive linguistic approach is embodied in Langacker's slogan 'grammar is conceptualization.' This slogan refers to a more specific hypothesis about conceptual structure, namely that conceptual structure cannot be reduced to a simple truth-conditional correspondence with the world. A major aspect of human cognitive ability is the conceptualization of the experience to be communicated (and also the conceptualization of the linguistic knowledge we possess). A major theme of the chapters in Part I of this book is that all aspects of conceptual structure are subject to construal, including the structure of categories (chapter 4) and the organization of knowledge (i.e., conceptual structures; chapter 2). In particular, it is argued that grammatical inflections and grammatical constructions play a major role in construing the experience to be communicated in specific ways (chapter 3). Part II of this book also explores and defends the conceptualization hypothesis for a wide range of lexical semantic phenomena, including topics widely discussed in cognitive linguistics (polysemy and metaphor) and lexical semantic topics that have not generally been examined by cognitive linguists (namely lexical relations such as antonymy, meronomy and hyponymy).

The third major hypothesis of the cognitive linguistic approach is that knowledge of language emerges from language use. That is, categories and structures in semantics, syntax, morphology and phonology are built up from our cognition of specific utterances on specific occasions of use. This inductive process of abstraction and schematization does not lose the conventionalized subtleties and differences found among even highly specific grammatical constructions and word meanings.

As we noted above, this hypothesis is a response to approaches to syntax and semantics in which highly general and abstract schemas and categories, sometimes claimed to be innately given, are assumed to govern the organization of linguistic knowledge, and apparently idiosyncratic or anomalous patterns are relegated to the periphery. Instead, cognitive linguists argue that the detailed analysis of subtle variations in syntactic behavior and semantic interpretation give rise to a different model of grammatical representation that accommodates idiosyncratic as well as highly general patterns of linguistic behavior (see, e.g., the arguments in chapter 9). In semantics, this model is manifested in Fillmore's semantics of understanding (chapter 2), and Cruse's dynamic construal approach to categorization (chapter 4 and Part II; see also Croft 2000:99–114). In syntax, this hypothesis has given rise directly to construction grammar as a new theory of syntax, and the usage-based model, developed in greatest detail for morphology and phonology. These models of syntax and morphology are described in Part III of this book.

PART I

A conceptual approach to linguistic analysis

2

Frames, domains, spaces: the organization of conceptual structure

2.1 Arguments for frame semantics

What is it that words denote, or **symbolize** as cognitive linguists usually put it? A simple assumption that has guided much research in semantics is that words denote **concepts**, units of meaning. Concepts symbolized by words such as *stallion* and *mare* can be compared and contrasted with one another. Comparisons of words is the approach taken by **structural semantics**, which analyzes types of semantic relations among words, including hyponymy and antonymy. Some approaches to (lexical) semantics have proposed that word concepts such as STALLION and MARE[1] are not atomic. Many concepts can be broken down into **semantic features**, so that STALLION is [EQUINE, MALE], and MARE is [EQUINE, FEMALE]. Finally, in the logical tradition that underlies much work in semantics, concepts are ultimately defined by their **truth conditions**: the conditions under which one can say that a concept does, or does not, appropriately apply to a situation in the world.

In this widespread approach to semantics, it is recognized that concepts do not simply float around randomly in the mind. First, there are the relations between words and their corresponding concepts described by structural semantics. But there has been a strong feeling that concepts are organized in another way as well. Certain concepts 'belong together' because they are associated in experience. To use a classic example (Schank and Abelson 1977), a RESTAURANT is not merely a service institution; it has associated with it a number of concepts such as CUSTOMER, WAITER, ORDERING, EATING, BILL. These concepts are not related to RESTAURANT by hyponymy, meronymy, antonymy or other structural semantic relations; they are related to RESTAURANT by ordinary human experience. The concept of RESTAURANT is closely tied to the other concepts, and cannot be isolated from the other concepts.

---

[1] We follow the practice of Fillmore (1982a) and Langacker (1987) in using lower-case italics to represent the word form, and capitals to represent the concept underlying the word meaning.

The need for another means for organizing concepts has been felt by researchers in cognitive psychology and artificial intelligence as well as in various branches of linguistics, and has led to a variety of similar proposals, each typically with its own name. Among these names are: frame, schema, script, global pattern, pseudo-text, cognitive model, experiential gestalt, base, scene (Fillmore 1985:223, n. 4). The most influential version of this proposal in cognitive linguistics has been the model of **frame semantics** developed by Fillmore. We present Fillmore's theory and arguments in this section, and turn to extensions of Fillmore's ideas by other cognitive linguists in later sections.[2]

Fillmore views frames not as an additional means for organizing concepts, but as a fundamental rethinking of the goals of linguistic semantics. Fillmore describes his frame semantic model as a model of the semantics of **understanding**, in contrast to a truth-conditional semantics: the full, rich understanding that a speaker intends to convey in a text and that a hearer constructs for that text. Fillmore argues that in the analysis of linguistic meaning, understanding is the primary data; truth-value judgments and judgments of semantic relations such as synonymy and implication are derivative and theory-driven (Fillmore 1985:235). Fillmore's frame semantics brings linguistic semantics back to that primary data and does not exclude any of it from consideration.

Fillmore uses a tool metaphor to describe the understanding process (Fillmore 1982a:112): a speaker produces words and constructions in a text as tools for a particular activity, namely to evoke a particular understanding; the hearer's task is to figure out the activity those tools were intended for, namely to invoke that understanding. That is, words and constructions evoke an understanding, or more specifically a frame; a hearer invokes a frame upon hearing an utterance in order to understand it.

Fillmore uses a wide range of examples to demonstrate that there are significant phenomena in linguistic semantics that cannot easily be captured in a model of structural semantics, semantic features and/or truth-conditional semantics. We survey his arguments here.

The analysis of semantic features is often justified on the basis of lexical sets that appear to be analyzable in terms of a simple set of features. For example, the lexical set in (1) can be analyzed in terms of the features [MALE/FEMALE], [ADULT/YOUNG], and [UNMARRIED]:

(1)   [MALE]   [FEMALE]
        MAN   WOMAN   [ADULT]
        BOY   GIRL   [YOUNG]
        BACHELOR   SPINSTER   [UNMARRIED]

Yet our understanding of these concepts is more complex than this paradigm of feature constrasts implies. The relation between *man/boy* and *woman/girl* is not the same: for many people, the term *girl* is used for female humans at a significantly higher age than the term *boy* is used for male humans (Fillmore 1982a:126). Moreover, the attitudes towards the sexes that this linguistic behavior is assumed to evoke has led to changes in the relationship and hypercorrection such that the term *woman* is attested as being applied even to an eight-year-old girl (ibid., 127). In a frame semantic analysis, *man, boy, woman* and *girl* evoke frames that include not just the biological sexual distinction but also differences in attitudes and behavior towards the sexes that would explain the traditional asymmetry in the use of *boy/girl* and the more recent change in the use of *woman*, including its hypercorrective use. Likewise, the difference between our understanding of *bachelor* and our understanding of *spinster* involves much more than a simple feature [MALE/FEMALE] (ibid., 131).

Many lexical contrasts contain semantic asymmetries that cannot be captured by features (except in an ad hoc fashion), but lend themselves easily to a frame semantic account. For example, the opposing terms used for the vertical extent of an erect human being are *tall* and *short*, for vertical distance from a bottom baseline (e.g. a branch of a tree) they are *high* and *low*, but for the vertical dimension of a building they are *tall* and *low* (Fillmore 1977a:71). It would be difficult if not impossible to come up with a unitary feature definition of *tall* that captured its different contexts of use from *high*, and did the same for *short* vs. *low*. Instead, one can simply describe the frames for humans, buildings and other objects, and specify which words are used for vertical extent or distance in that frame.

Similarly, no simple unitary definitions would capture the contrast between the adjectives *live* and *alive* given in (2)–(4) (Fillmore 1977a:76–77):

(2)   a. Those are live lobsters.
        b. Those lobsters are alive.

(3)   a. Her manner is very alive.
        b. She has a very alive manner.

(4)   a. His performance was live.
        b. He gave a live performance.

Moreover, one cannot define the features in terms of applicability to a semantic class, such that the sense illustrated in (2a–b) applies to living things; this would give an incorrect understanding to the theatre advertizing *live naked girls* than the one intended (presumably, as opposed to naked girls on a film screen, not dead naked girls; ibid.). In a frame semantic analysis, *live* and *alive* are simply associated in different ways to three different frames: life in (2), personality in (3), and mode of performance in (4). In other cases, there are outright lexical splits, such as *brother/brothers* and *brother/brethren*, which represent a split in frames including different plural forms; a unitary definition of *brother* would miss the frame contrast (ibid., 76).

Fillmore notes that his frame semantic model shares significant properties with lexical (semantic) field theory (Fillmore 1985:225–26; 1992:76–77). Lexical field theory groups together words that are associated in experience, not unlike frame semantics. However, lexical field theory differs from frame semantics in that words are defined relative to other words in the same lexical field, whereas in frame semantics, words are defined directly with respect to the frame. For example, in lexical field theory, one would observe that *large* in the field of sizes of packages of soapflakes is in contrast with *jumbo, economy giant* and *family size* and hence describes the smallest size in the field, unlike uses of *large* in other lexical fields (Fillmore 1985:227).

In frame semantics, the same observation can easily be captured: *large* labels the smallest size in the SOAPFLAKES frame. But lexical field theory predicts that the meaning of a word in a field can only be defined in contrast to neighboring words in the field. Lexical field theory has difficulties if there are no neighboring words, or a speaker does not know the neighboring words: it predicts that the term has a different meaning. Fillmore notes that while German has a word for the sides of a right angle triangle other than the *Hypotenuse*, namely *Kathete*, most English speakers do not have such a word (ibid., 228–29). Yet the understanding of English *hypotenuse* and German *Hypotenuse* is the same, provided the speaker understands what a right angle triangle is. This is not a problem in frame semantics, where the word concept is linked directly to the frame, in this case the RIGHT ANGLE TRIANGLE frame.

Another argument in favor of a frame-based approach to lexical semantics are words whose corresponding concepts inherently refer to other concepts extrinsic to the concept denoted by the word. Some word concepts refer to a prior history of the entity denoted. A *scar* is not just a feature of the surface of someone's skin, but the healing state of a wound; a *widow* is a woman who was once married but whose husband has died (Fillmore 1977a:73). Other word concepts, especially for properties and actions, cannot be understood without understanding something about the participant in the action or possessor of the properties: one cannot understand *gallop* without knowing about the body of a horse, or *hungry* without understanding the physiology of living things (ibid., 73–74). This is true of object concepts as well: *lap* cannot be understood except in reference to a person's posture and the function of one's lap in supporting another object (ibid.).

Another clear class of examples that requires reference to extrinsic entities are deictic expressions that evoke the speech act situation (Fillmore 1982a:117). For example, the past tense situates an event in a point or interval or time relative to the speech act situation. The speech act situation, including its time of occurrence, functions as the frame against which past time reference is profiled. Likewise, all other deictic words and inflections, such as person deixis (*I, you, he/she/it, we, they* and person-based agreement inflections) and spatial deixis (*this, that, here, there*), evoke the speech act situation. Other types of grammatical words and inflections also have meanings evoking the speech act situation. For example, the definite articles *the* and *a* define the identity of the noun referent relative to the mutual knowledge of speaker and hearer (*the* basically indicates mutually known, *a* not mutually known, in most contexts). The meanings of *the* and *a* evoke the speech act situation because they make reference to the mental states of speaker and hearer (see also §3.4).

Above all, many word concepts cannot be understood apart from the intentions of the participants or the social and cultural institutions and behavior in which the action, state or thing is situated. For example, the concept VEGETARIAN only makes sense in the frame of a culture in which meat-eating is common; the concepts STRIKE or BORROW can only be understood in the frame of a culture in which such actions occur (Fillmore 1982a:120). Even something as simple as an *apple core* evokes a frame describing a particular way of eating apples: 'an apple-core is that part of the apple that somebody who eats apples the way most of us do has left uneaten' (Fillmore 1977a:73).

Another respect in which a word meaning makes reference to extrinsic entities is that a word allows the speaker and hearer to focus their attention on only part of an entire frame; no one word gives the full structure of the frame. The classic example is the commercial transaction frame (Fillmore 1977a:58–59; 1977b); but a much clearer case is the RISK frame (Fillmore and Atkins 1992). Fillmore and Atkins identify the following elements of the RISK frame: Chance (uncertainty about the future), Harm, Victim (of the Harm), Valued Object (potentially endangered by the risk), Situation (which gives rise to the risk), Deed (that brings about the Situation), Actor (of the Deed), (Intended) Gain (by the Actor in taking a risk), Purpose (of the Actor in the Deed), Beneficiary and Motivation (for the Actor). The verb *risk* occurs in many syntactic constructions, some of which are exemplified in (5a–e), but none of them include all or even most of the elements of the RISK frame (Fillmore & Atkins 1992: 83, 87, 89, 94, 96; all but the first are corpus examples):

(5)   a. You've (*Actor/Victim*) risked your health (*Valued Object*) for a few cheap thrills (*Gain*).
       b. Others (*Actor/Victim*) had risked all (*Valued Object*) in the war (*Situation*).
       c. She (*Actor/Victim*) had risked so much (*Valued Object*) for the sake of vanity (*Motivation*).
       d. Men (*Actor/Victim*) were not inclined to risk scalping (*Harm*) for the sake of settlers they had never seen (*Beneficiary*).
       e. I (*Actor/Victim*) didn't dare risk a pause (*Deed*) to let that sink in (*Purpose*).

In a frame semantic analysis, any of the uses of *risk* evokes the entire RISK frame, even if only part of that frame is overtly focused on by the construction in which *risk* is used.

The semantics of understanding also allows Fillmore to account for linguistic facts that do not lend themselves to a truth-functional analysis. For example, the collocations in (6) could be reversed as in (7) without producing semantic anomaly (Fillmore 1977a:75–76):

(6)   a. A dog was barking.
        b. A hound was baying.
(7)   a. A dog was baying.
        b. A hound was barking.

In other words, the difference between (6) and (7) cannot be accounted for by semantic constraints. But the examples in (6a–b) sound much more natural because the noun and the verb in each sentence both evoke the same frame.

Likewise, a truth-conditional semantics cannot capture many aspects of our understanding of (8) (Fillmore 1985:230–31):

(8)   My dad wasted most of the morning on the bus.

Fillmore notes that choosing *father* or *dad* (without the possessive) would express a different relationship between the speaker and the speaker's father; *the morning* is understood to be defined against the frame of the working day (i.e, around 8am to noon) rather than the calendar day (midnight to noon); *waste* frames the use of time very differently from *spend*; and *on the bus* frames the speaker's location in terms of the bus being in service, rather than simply a physical container (which would be evoked by *in the bus*).

A truth-conditional model also cannot account for the anomaly of frames that are appropriate at one time of utterance but not at another because the world has changed in the meantime. Fillmore uses the contrived example in (9), noting that it could be said in 1984 but not in, say, 1919 (Fillmore 1985:238–39):

(9)   During World War I, Ronald Reagan's birth mother dropped his analog watch into the sound hole of the acoustic guitar.

Such a sentence could be uttered in 1984, because World War II had occurred, allowing the 1914–18 war to be renamed World War I; medical technology had allowed the dissociation of the birth mother from the genetic mother (who donates the egg); and electric guitars and digital watches had been invented. None of these framings of the objects, persons or events was available in 1919, and so (9) would be an impossible utterance at that time, even if true retrospectively.

Finally, frame semantics offers a natural account of a number of problematic phenomena that seem to be caught between semantics and pragmatics, including the nature of text coherence. A large class of presuppositional phenomena appear to be tied to specific words, such as *regret* in (10) (Fillmore 1985:249):

(10)   John regretted signing the letter.

Example (10) denotes (or **entails**) a particular mental state of John, namely his feeling of regret, but (in one analysis) is said to **presuppose** that John did sign the letter. The problem for truth-conditional semantics is that if John did not sign the letter, (9) has no truth conditions. In order to preserve truth conditions one may shunt the presupposition problem off to pragmatics. This seems odd since the presupposition is associated with a particular word and its meaning, which is semantic. But presuppositions display a further type of peculiar behavior, in negative sentences such as (11):

(11)   John didn't regret signing the letter.

In one interpretation, the entailment is negated – John does not have any regrets – but the presupposition is not – John signed the letter. However, there is another interpretation of (11), namely that John did not regret signing the letter because he did not sign it (Fillmore 1985:251).

Fillmore argues that the behavior of presuppositions can be easily accounted for in a frame semantic analysis. The concept REGRET includes in its frame the accomplishment of an action towards which the regretter has his/her regrets. If the action is absent from the frame, understanding of the positive sentence fails. Negation, on the other hand, can negate either the concept denoted or the frame itself. Negating the state of affairs in the frame preserves the rest of the frame, including the action that could have led to the regrets. This is the first interpretation of (11) described above. Negating the entire frame, on the other hand, also negates the action that could have led to the regrets. This is the second interpretation of (11): the speaker denies the framing of the situation as including the action of John having signed the letter.

We may compare (11) to other examples of frame negation, such as the one in (12) (Fillmore 1985:245, from Wilson 1975:138):

(12)   You didn't spare me a day at the seaside: you deprived me of one.

In (12), the speaker denies the positively evaluated framing of the action as sparing her, and replaces it with the negatively evaluated framing of depriving her.

Finally, the semantics of understanding plays a major role in text understanding. For example, the well-known example of initial definite reference, e.g. *the carburetor* in (13) (described as 'bridging' by Clark and Haviland [1977] and 'evoked' by Prince [1981a]), are in fact due to the frame evoked by the first sentence (Fillmore 1977a:75):

(13)   I had trouble with the car yesterday. The carburetor was dirty.

The car in the first sentence evokes a frame that allows the hearer to identify which carburetor of the millions in the world the speaker was referring to. But frame semantics contributes more than the resolution of definite reference to the analysis of the coherence of texts. Fillmore contrasts (13) with (14) (ibid.):

(14)   I had trouble with the car yesterday. The ashtray was dirty.

The second sentence in (14) is incoherent with the first, even though the definite reference can be resolved (most cars have ashtrays). The reason for this is that there is nothing evoked in the frame of *having trouble with the car* that has anything to do with the ashtray – unlike (13), because dirty carburetors do cause problems for cars.

Fillmore's arguments present a wide range of data that justify the introduction of frames to the analysis of linguistic semantics, and the replacement of a truth-conditional semantics with a semantics of understanding. In the following sections, we lay out more systematically the frame semantic model and follow its further development in cognitive linguistics.

2.2   Concepts: profile-frame organization

In the preceding section, we described the frame as a coherent region of human knowledge, or as a coherent region of conceptual space. The question immediately arises: How does one identify a coherent region of conceptual space, differentiating it from other regions? An a priori approach to this question, using one's own intuitions to identify frames, would be highly subjective. A more empirical approach to this question is to identify frames based on the words and constructions of a human language such as English. This approach is taken by Langacker (1987), which we will use as our starting point.

Langacker illustrates his approach to the problem with the meaning of the word *radius*. The word form *radius* symbolizes (denotes) the **concept** RADIUS. We begin here by assuming that concepts correspond to meanings of linguistic units (words, complex expressions or constructions). One may also assume that concepts exist that do not correspond to linguistic meanings. However, one would have the same problems trying to identify concepts independent of linguistic meanings as trying to identify frames independent of linguistic meanings, namely the lack of an empirical basis for doing so. For this reason, we will restrict ourselves to concepts corresponding to actual linguistic meanings in this chapter.

The first sense for *radius* in the American Heritage Dictionary is 'a line segment that joins the center of a circle with any point on its circumference.' A RADIUS is a line segment, but not any line segment: the line segment is defined relative to the structure of the circle. In other words, one can understand RADIUS only against a background understanding of the concept CIRCLE, which can be geometrically illustrated as in Figure 2.1.

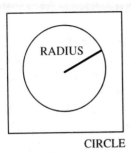

CIRCLE

Figure 2.1 *RADIUS and CIRCLE*

In other words, the concepts RADIUS and CIRCLE are intimately related, and this relationship must be represented in conceptual structure. Langacker describes the relationship between RADIUS and CIRCLE as one of a concept **profile** against a **base**. The profile refers to the concept symbolized by the word in question. The base is that knowledge or conceptual structure that is presupposed by the profiled concept. Langacker also uses the term **domain** for the base (this term is also used in Lakoff 1987). This is identical to Fillmore's frame (§2.1): 'by the term "frame" I have in mind any system of concepts related in such a way that to understand any one of them you have to understand the whole structure in which it fits' (Fillmore 1982a:111). The term 'profile' has also come to be used as a verb to describe the relationship between word form and word meaning (profile+base): e.g. *radius* profiles a particular line segment in the CIRCLE base/domain/frame.

A concept profile is insufficient to define a word concept, because it presupposes other knowledge in its definition, namely its base. But a single base, such as CIRCLE, is a complex conceptual structure that includes a wide range of concept profiles, such as RADIUS, ARC, CENTER, DIAMETER, CHORD and so on. Hence the base alone is insufficient to define a linguistic concept either. The conclusion that follows from this is that THE MEANING OF A LINGUISTIC UNIT MUST SPECIFY BOTH THE PROFILE AND ITS BASE. This is identical to Fillmore's conclusion regarding concept frames.

The fact that a base supports multiple concept profiles is what makes the base a **domain**, in the intuitive sense: several different concept profiles have it as a base. We can now define a domain as A SEMANTIC STRUCTURE THAT FUNCTIONS AS THE BASE FOR AT LEAST ONE CONCEPT PROFILE (typically, many profiles). As Taylor (1989[1997]:84) notes, 'In principle, any conceptualization or knowledge configuration, no matter how simple or complex, can serve as the cognitive domain for the characterization of meanings.' We may now say that the domain CIRCLE includes the concepts of an arc, a diameter, a radius, a chord and so on.

The canonical example of a profile-base relation is the part-whole relation: all agree that a concept such as ARM cannot be defined without reference to BODY. A similar class of concepts are kin terms such as *daughter*. The concept DAUGHTER presupposes the concept PARENT, and the particular type of kin relationship that holds between them. The concept NIECE presupposes other kinship concepts, and more complex kin relationships. In other words, the base against which a profile is defined can be more complex than just the whole of which some entity is a part. In some cases, one cannot always find a single simple word to describe the base: for NIECE, perhaps the best description of the base is KINSHIP SYSTEM, or some part of that system (see §2.4).

But it is not only relational nouns that represent a concept profile against a base, as we saw in §2.1. Consider another example, the word *weekend* (Fillmore 1985:223–24). The concept WEEKEND can only be understood against a whole background system of the calendrical cycle, defined partly by natural phenomena (the sequence of day and night) and cultural conventions (the seven-day week cycle, and its division into working days and nonworking days). Likewise, the concept BUY can only be understood against a background knowledge of the commercial transaction situation. Different aspects of the commercial transaction are profiled by BUY, SELL, PAY, COST and so forth. Such domains/frames cannot be readily represented in a geometric form in the way that RADIUS and CIRCLE are represented in Figure 2.1, although schematic diagrams are often resorted to in cognitive linguistics in order to represent the complex interconnectedness of concepts in domains or frames.

In fact, no concept exists autonomously: all are understood to fit into our general knowledge of the world in one way or another. What matters for semantic analysis is the profile-base relation, and the relationships between bases and domains. Some of the corollaries of this analysis of word meaning into profile and base/frame/domain will be explored in the following section.

2.3   Some consequences of the profile-frame/domain distinction

The terms frame (Fillmore), base (Langacker) and domain (Fillmore, Lakoff, Langacker) all appear to identify the same theoretical framework, as described in the preceding sections. Fillmore describes this framework as frame semantics, and this term has entered into more general usage among cognitive linguists. However, the terms frame and domain continue to compete for usage, and base is also used among cognitive grammarians. We will use the terms frame and domain interchangeably here. Nevertheless, there are still other terms that have been proposed to describe types of semantic analyses that bear a strong affinity to frame semantics. We mention three influential theories here, which originated in artificial intelligence (scripts), cognitive psychology (the 'theory theory') and sociology (communities).

The examples of frames given above appear to be largely static in character. But this is not necessary: a frame is any coherent body of knowledge presupposed by a word concept. In particular, frames can include dynamic concepts, that is, extending through time. For example, PURIFIED presupposes in its frame a prior impure state of the entity which is then changed by some process; in contrast, PURE does not presuppose anything about prior states and processes. Of course, process terms such as RUN or BUY presuppose a sequence of events and prior and posterior states. The term **script** is often used for a frame/domain with a sequence of events, following Schank and Abelson (1977). They use the term to describe a canonical sequence of events presupposed by a social activity such as going to a restaurant. We subsume scripts under frames/domains.

Another theoretical construct that can be understood as a type of frame or domain is the so-called 'theory theory' of categorization found in cognitive psychology. Advocates of the theory theory argue that our understanding of categories such as HORSE or HAMMER is based not on perceptual features but on theories of biological kinds and artifacts respectively (Murphy and Medin 1985). For instance, we have at least a folk theory of biological kinds that indicates that individuals of the same category (e.g. HORSE) are members of that category by virtue of descent and reproduction, and perceptual similarity of horses (and the distinctness of individuals of other species) are a result of those basic biological patterns. Likewise, hammers are defined by the fact that they are manufactured by human beings for a particular function, and perceptual similarity of hammers (and the distinctness of other kinds of artifacts) are a result of their intended function. In frame semantic terms, the base for HORSE includes the 'theory' of biological kinds and the base for HAMMER includes the 'theory' of artifacts (see Fillmore 1986a:54).

Fillmore also uses the notion of framing to describe differences in the community or social domain of use of a word (Fillmore 1982a:127–29). For example, he notes that in the legal domain, that is, the community that engages in legal activity, the concepts of MURDER and INNOCENT differ from those concepts used outside that domain/community. In the legal domain, MURDER is profiled in a frame/domain where it contrasts with MANSLAUGHTER, but outside that domain, MURDER is profiled in a domain lacking that contrast. In the legal

domain, INNOCENCE is profiled against a frame in which innocence and guilt are
the result of judgements in a trial (and in fact, guilt can be established only after
the completion of the trial). Outside that domain, INNOCENT is profiled against a
frame in which innocence and guilt are defined by whether the person in question
committed the crime or not. Other concepts such as FLIP STRENGTH exist only
in a specialized community, in this case publishers of pornography (the interested
reader may turn to Fillmore 1982a:12 for further details). Hence, frame semantics
is being extended to describe differences that appear to be defined on social rather
than conceptual grounds. But there is a link between the two. Communities are
defined by the social activities that bind the members together. Clark argues that
communities involve the possession of shared expertise among their members: the
specialized knowledge that is acquired by engaging in the activities that define the
community (Clark 1996:102–4). This shared expertise is the conceptual structure
that is found in the frame/domains of the concepts symbolized by the specialized
vocabulary used by members of the community.

The distinction between profile and frame/domain is a useful tool for analyzing a
number of interesting semantic questions. In particular, some distinctions in word
meaning apply not to the profiled concept – what is usually thought of as 'the
definition' of a word – but to its frame/domain.

For example, some concepts appear to denote the same thing in the world but
profile it against a different frame. For example, LAND and GROUND denote
(profile) what seems to be the 'same thing,' but against different frames: LAND
describes the dry surface of the earth in contrast with SEA, while GROUND describes the dry surface of the earth in contrast with AIR (Fillmore 1982a:121).
The frame chosen by one word or another allows one to make different inferences:
Fillmore notes that a bird that *spends its life on land* does not go in the water, but
a bird that *spends its life on the ground* does not fly (ibid.). Langacker offers the
example of ROE and CAVIAR, both being fish eggs: ROE is profiled against the
frame/domain of the reproductive cycle of fish, while CAVIAR is profiled against
the frame/domain of food preparation/consumption (Langacker 1987:164–65).
Another example is FLESH, profiled against the frame/domain of the body's
anatomy, vs. MEAT, profiled against the frame/domain of food. The semantic
difference is reflected in the collocations *flesh and bones*, describing an emaciated
body, and *meat and potatoes*, describing a bland but filling type of meal (contrast
meat and bones and *flesh and potatoes*).

The alternative framing of the same profile is particularly common with terms
that are evaluative in character. For example, STINGY profiles one end of a scale,
the opposite of which is GENEROUS; while THRIFTY appears to profile the
same end of the same scale, and its opposite end is profiled by WASTEFUL
(Fillmore 1982a:125). The difference is the orientation of the associated evaluative

scale: the evaluation of STINGY-GENEROUS is the inverse of that for THRIFTY-WASTEFUL. Of course, a speaker may choose to frame someone as either STINGY or THRIFTY. In other words, how an experience is framed is a matter of **construal**: it depends on how the speaker conceptualizes the experience to be communicated, for the understanding of the hearer. This is only one example of the construals that pervade human conceptualization of experience (see chapter 3).

Another type of evaluative framing effect is more indirect, as in the example FETUS vs. UNBORN BABY, terms used by opposing sides of the debate on abortion. FETUS profiles the entity in question against a more general MAMMAL frame: any mammal's unborn progeny may be called a *fetus*. This frame makes abortion appear less morally repugnant, since it is widely accepted in society that animals can be killed for certain purposes. The complex phrase UNBORN BABY exploits two frames. BABY profiles the same entity against the more specific HUMAN frame: we prototypically use *baby* only for human offspring. Both BABY and UNBORN profile the entity against its projected later lifestage, namely after birth. These frames make abortion appear more repugnant, since killing humans is accepted only under quite restricted circumstances (e.g. war and self-defense), and all agree that once a fetus is born, it is a human being. The difference in framing the entity denoted by *fetus* or *unborn baby* therefore orientates (or biases, to frame it differently!) the hearer towards the political stance on abortion adopted by the speaker.

The above examples all illustrate different words that profile the same concept but in subtly different frames. There are also examples where a single word is usually analyzed as polysemous – having distinct albeit related meanings – but where those meaning differences are more due to differences in frame rather than differences in profile. For example, a word such as *mouth* describes roughly the same concept profile but with different frames:

(15)   *mouth*: BODY, BOTTLE, CAVE, RIVER

In the examples of frames for *mouth* in (15), *mouth* can be thought of as denoting the same type of profile, namely the opening to a container (however, a cave may have several openings to the earth's surface, and the container of a river is defined by both the riverbed and gravity). The word *mouth* is generally considered to be polysemous, that is, it has a sense for each of the profile-base pairings (senses that may not share the same word in other languages). In other words, the profile alone is insufficient in defining the senses of *mouth*.

The profile-frame/domain distinction is particularly useful in understanding the nature of semantic differences between words and their apparent translation equivalents in different languages. The profile-frame/domain distinction may shed light on some aspects of why translation is difficult and often unsuccessful.

One can find frame-based semantic contrasts across languages that are similar to those found within a single language such as LAND/GROUND. Fillmore contrasts the English word concept LUKEWARM with the Japanese word concept NURUI. Both concepts profile the state 'at room temperature,' but for English speakers LUKEWARM is used for liquids that are ideally hot or ideally cold, whereas for some Japanese speakers NURUI is used only for liquids that are ideally hot (Fillmore 1982a:121).

Sometimes linguistic differences across languages represent differences in how much information is specified in the frame, rather than something about the inherent structure of the profiled concept. English *river* profiles a more or less permanent flow of water in a natural channel, presupposing a frame specifying the relevant topographical features. French contrasts *rivière* and *fleuve*. The concepts for both French words is essentially the same as the concept for the English word – a natural flowing waterway – but the frame is more specific than the English frame for each word: *fleuve* specifies in addition that it is a major waterway that flows into the sea, unlike *rivière*. Hence a translation of *fleuve* as *river* is partly accurate (the profile), but not completely so (its frame). Another example is English *eat*, which profiles the process of consuming food. German contrasts *essen* and *fressen*: both describe the process of consuming food also, but the former specifies that the eater is human and the latter that the eater is an animal (nonhuman). This is a framing effect and is therefore subject to construal (§3.3). That is, one can use the term *fressen* to describe the action of a human being, but it frames that action much differently than *essen*, leading to a construal of the action as being animal-like (crude, sloppy, etc.).

The nature of word meaning across languages is sometimes obscured by analysts who do not distinguish between profile and frame in their word definitions. For example, some languages are described as having words that correspond to whole sentences in English. Two candidate examples are given in (16)–(17), the first from a native American language and the second from a European language:

(16)   Alabama *ispaspaakáhmit* 'to be shaped into a patty, shaped like a biscuit (said of the shape of the mixture of brains and moss used for curing hides)' (Sylestine et al. 1993:203)

(17)   Swedish *tura* – 'sitting on the boat going back and forth between Helsingborg and Helsingør' (Karina Vamling, pers. comm.)

By distinguishing profile from frame/domain, we may give a more straightforward semantic analysis. The concepts profiled are pretty simple: *ispaspaakáhmit* profiles a shape and *tura* profiles sitting. But the frames in which the concepts are situated are very specific (in [17], staying on the boat means paying only one fare and drinking duty-free alcohol). A similar English example would be *genuflect*. *Genuflect* profiles more or less the same concept as *kneel*, a bodily movement – but in a highly specific frame, namely Catholic religious practice. But even less culturally specific word concepts can be fruitfully divided into profile and frame. A *radius* profiles a line segment; the difference between *radius* and *line segment* is found in their frames.

The profile-frame distinction also allows for a natural analysis of words in languages that have been described as 'untranslatable' in a more profound way than the examples of *fleuve* or *fressen* given above. For example, Geertz gives a lengthy explication of Javanese *rasa*, part of which is quoted below:

> *Rasa* has two primary meanings: 'feeling' and 'meaning'. As 'feeling' it is one of the traditional Javanese five senses – seeing, hearing, talking, smelling and feeling, and it includes within itself three aspects of 'feeling' that our view of the five senses separates: taste on the tongue, touch on the body, and emotional 'feeling' within the 'heart', like sadness and happiness. The taste of a banana is its *rasa*; a hunch is a *rasa*; a pain is a *rasa*; and so is a passion. As 'meaning', *rasa* is applied to words in a letter, in a poem, or even in common speech to indicate the between-the-lines type of indirection and allusive suggestion that is so important in Javanese communication and social intercourse. And it is given the same application to behavioral acts generally: to indicate the implicit import, the connotative 'feeling' of dance movements, polite gestures, and so forth. But in this second, semantic sense, it also means 'ultimate significance' – the deepest meaning at which one arrives by dint of mystical effort and whose clarification resolves all the ambiguities of mundane existence [etc.]. (Geertz 1973: 134–35)

Basically, understanding the meaning of *rasa* presupposes understanding large portions of Javanese culture and worldview. In frame semantic terms, the concept RASA presupposes a frame consisting of much of Javanese culture. Examples of this type can also be found closer to home. For example, a translator dealing with a twentieth-century German philosophical work, writes about the term *Bildung*: '*Bildung* is translated by "culture" and related forms such as "cultivation", "cultivated" . . . The term has the flavor of the late-eighteenth and nineteenth centuries and played a key role throughout German-speaking Europe' (Gadamer 1989:xii). That is, BILDUNG is profiled against a frame of the culture of the German intellectual elite stretching back almost two centuries.

In other words, the reason that words such as *rasa* and *Bildung* are 'untranslatable' is because of the culture-specific character of the frame/base against which the concept is profiled. Translating *rasa* as *feeling* or *meaning*, or *Bildung* as *culture*, approximates the profile of the concept but does not have the same frame at all.

2.4   Extensions of the basic profile-frame/domain distinction

The distinction between profile and domain/frame is a fundamental one in the theory of semantics used in cognitive linguistics. It has nevertheless proved to be insufficient in itself to capture a number of important semantic phenomena, and the basic theory has been elaborated in several directions.

2.4.1   *Locational and configurational profiles*

One extension of the frame semantic model recognizes two different kinds of profiles. Consider again the SPACE domain. A concept like RECTANGLE is profiled in the SPACE domain. Note that an octagon is an octagon wherever it is located in space. What matters for the profile of RECTANGLE is simply the number and configuration of line segments forming the sides. The profile for RECTANGLE contrasts with the profile of a spatial concept such as HERE. HERE profiles a location in SPACE, one that is defined with respect to the position of the speaker. You cannot move the profiled location without changing the concept. The same constraint applies to a concept like MOUNT TAMALPAIS. This concept also profiles a location in SPACE; another mountain in another location is not, nor ever will be, MOUNT TAMALPAIS (in contrast to MOUNTAIN, which is a topographical configuration that can be located anywhere). These are two different kinds of profiles: RECTANGLE has a **configurational** profile and HERE or MOUNT TAMALPAIS has a **locational** profile (Langacker 1987:153; Clausner and Croft 1999:7–13).[3]

Not every frame/domain can support both kinds of profiles. Color words, for example, specify regions in the HUE scale; if one moves to a different location on the HUE scale, then the concept changes, for example from RED to YELLOW. But there is no configurational profile on the HUE scale. This is not a fact about all one-dimensional scalar domains. For example, the domain of (musical) PITCH has both locational and configurational profiles. For example, particular notes such as C-SHARP, or more precisely one specific note such as C#″ (the C-sharp an augmented octave above middle C), profiles a single location on the pitch scale. However, a musical interval such as OCTAVE has a configurational profile: an OCTAVE is an octave wherever it occurs as long as the pitch interval is correct (Clausner and Croft 1999:10). More generally, measurable one-dimensional scalar domains such as PITCH, LENGTH and so on allow for both locational and configurational

---

[3] Langacker argues that the locational-configurational distinction applies to domains, but Clausner and Croft demonstrate that the same domain can support locational and configurational profiles.

profiles. Antonymic adjectives such as TALL/SHORT (see chapter 7) profile a particular location or direction on a scalar domain. Units of measurement on the scale, such as INCH or FOOT, profile configurations: an inch is the same interval no matter the locations subsumed under the measured interval.

cf I AR on scientific language

2.4.2   Scope of predication

In §2.2, we used the example of NIECE, demonstrating that its proper definition presupposes the system of kinship relations. But we do not need the entire kinship system in order to understand the concept NIECE. Only a small part of it is necessary as represented in Figure 2.2 (the gender-neutral square symbol is used because the intervening kin for NIECE may be male or female).

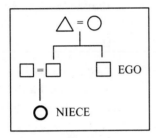

Figure 2.2 *NIECE*

The relevant part of the kinship system for defining NIECE is called the **scope of predication** for the concept (Langacker 1987:118–19; renamed immediate scope [Langacker 1999:49]).

An example of different scopes of predication can be found in the behavior of human body parts such as the following parts of the arm (Langacker 1987:119): KNUCKLE ⊂ FINGER ⊂ HAND ⊂ ARM ⊂ BODY. Each one has its immediate successor as its scope of predication. Possessive constructions referring to wholes within the scope of predication are acceptable, but if the whole is beyond the scope of predication, then the sentence is odd (Langacker 1987:119; but see §6.2.1.7):

(18)   a. A body has two arms.
        b. A hand has five fingers.
        c. A finger has three knuckles and a fingernail.
        d. ?An arm has five fingers.
        e. ??A body has twenty-eight knuckles.

Nested scopes of predications can be generalized to nesting of frames/domains in general.

2.4.3   Relationships between domains

Much more complex is the elaboration of the relationships among domains – not surprisingly, since this touches on the organization of human knowledge in the mind.

An important fact about profiles and frames/domains is that one can have successive chains of profile-frame relations. The concept RADIUS can only be understood in terms of CIRCLE, as noted above. But the concept CIRCLE can itself only be understood in terms of (two-dimensional) SPACE. That is, the word *circle* profiles CIRCLE against the SPACE frame. In other words, a concept that functions as the frame/domain for other concepts is itself a profile for another conceptual frame/domain. In other words, whether a conceptual structure is the profile or frame/domain is a matter of construal (see §§2.3, 3.2).

The chain of profile-frame relations does eventually bottom out, when we reach directly embodied human experience. SPACE is a good candidate for a directly embodied human experience. Langacker calls domains rooted in directly embodied human experience **basic domains** (Langacker 1987:148); he calls nonbasic domains **abstract domains**. A major theme of Lakoff and Johnson's cognitive linguistic research is that even our most abstract knowledge is ultimately grounded in directly embodied human experience (Lakoff and Johnson 1980, chapter 12; Johnson 1987; Lakoff and Johnson 1999). Other examples of basic domains besides SPACE are MATERIAL, TIME, FORCE and a host of perceptual and bodily sensations (COLOR, HARDNESS, LOUDNESS, HUNGER, PAIN etc.). There are also emotional and other mental states and processes, and also social properties, relations and processes, that do not presuppose other domains. Exactly which mental and social domains are basic depends on one's theory of mind and social interaction, and so we will not make any specific proposals here.

The relation between an abstract domain and the basic domain it presupposes is not a taxonomic relation (or, as Langacker calls such relations, a **schematic** one). It is a relationship of concept to background assumption or presupposition. This distinction is sometimes obscured by the English language. For example, the word *shape* as a mass noun stands for the domain, but as a count noun (*a shape*) it is a more general or schematic concept subsuming [CIRCLE], [SQUARE], [TRIANGLE] and so on. A more general or schematic concept is not the domain for the particular concept; in fact, a schematic concept is itself profiled in the same domain as its instantiation. As will be seen below, it is not always easy to distinguish a taxonomic relation from a profile-domain relation.

Langacker argues that some domains involve more than one **dimension** (Langacker 1987:150–51). An obvious case is space, which involves three dimensions (some concepts such as CIRCLE need only two dimensions for their definition; others such as LINE need only one). Many physical qualities that are grounded in the experience of sensory perception, such as TEMPERATURE and PITCH, are one-dimensional. Others, such as COLOR, can be divided into HUE, BRIGHTNESS and SATURATION. Generally, dimensions of a domain are all simultaneously presupposed by concepts profiled in that domain. This is the critical point: a concept may presuppose several different dimensions at once.

In fact, a concept may presuppose (be profiled in) several different domains. For example, a human being must be defined relative to the domains of physical objects, living things and volitional agents (and several other domains, e.g. emotion). The combination of domains simultaneously presupposed by a concept such as HUMAN BEING is called a **domain matrix**. Langacker makes the important point that there is in principle only a difference of degree between dimensions of a domain and domains in a matrix (Langacker 1987:152). In practice, we are more likely to call a semantic structure a domain if there are a substantial number of concepts profiled relative to that structure. If there are few if any concepts profiled relative to that structure alone, but instead there are concepts profiled relative to that structure and another one, then those structures are likely to be called two dimensions of a single domain. The term 'domain' implies a degree of cognitive independence not found in a dimension (see also §5.3.1).

The domain structure presupposed by a concept can be extremely complex. Let us now consider how one would define what seems to be a kind of physical object, the letter T. It is directly defined as a letter of the alphabet; its base (domain) is hence the alphabet. The alphabet is itself an abstract domain presupposing the notion of a writing system – it is not just an instance of a writing system, since the latter involves not just a set of symbols such as an alphabet but also the means of putting them together, including the direction of letters on a page, spaces for words and so on. The domain of writing systems in turn presupposes the activity of writing. The activity of writing must be defined in terms of human communication, which presupposes the notion of meaning – perhaps a basic domain, since the symbolic relation appears not to be reducible to some other relation – and visual sensations, since writing is communication via visually perceived inscriptions, rather than auditorily or through gestures. And since writing is an activity, the domains of time and force or causation (both basic domains; see §3.5) are also involved in the domain matrix of writing, since the letter T is the product of an activity. Since writing is a human activity, it presupposes the involvement of human beings. Human beings are living things with mental abilities, such as volition, intention, cognition and emotion (themselves dimensions of the mental domain or better domains in the matrix of the domain of the mind). Living things in turn are physical objects endowed with life. Physical objects possess material existence and are spatial entities (although material objects always have spatial extent, spatial objects like geometric figures can exist without material embodiment).

A diagram exhibiting all of the basic-abstract domain relations presupposed in defining the concept of the letter T is given in Figure 2.3 (based on Croft 1993[2002]:170, Fig. 2.1; the profiled concept is given in boldface, and the basic domains are given in capitals).

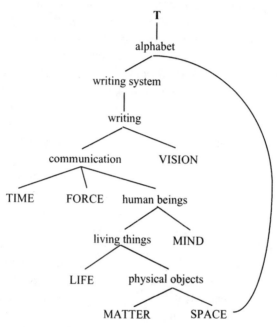

Figure 2.3 *Domain structure underlying the concept of the letter T*

From this, it can be seen that it is incorrect to describe the concept of the letter T simply as belonging to the domain of writing, as a typical informal theory of domains would most likely have it. The vast majority of concepts belong to abstract domains, which are themselves profiled in complex domain matrices, often also abstract and so ultimately presuppose a large array of basic domains that can be called a **domain structure** (Croft 1993[2002]:169; this corresponds to Langacker's **maximal scope** [Langacker 1999:49]).

It is not easy to distinguish profile-base relations from taxonomic/schematic relations (that is, type vs. instance). For example, is writing an instance of human communication, or is writing an instance of an activity that can only be understood in terms of the goals of human communication? Figure 2.3 assumes that the latter is a more accurate description. Likewise, since writing is an instance of human activity, human activity does not appear as its domain, but the various domains that it presupposes – time, change, force, volition – do appear, because anything presupposed by a human activity will be presupposed by any instance of it.

It is also difficult to determine direct vs. indirect reference to a domain. The definition of an arc does not directly presuppose two-dimensional space, but rather it presupposes a circle which in turn presupposes two-dimensional space. Thus, an arc is not directly a two-dimensional object per se, but only such by virtue of being a part of a circle. Likewise, the letter T is not directly a shape, but only such by virtue of being a letter of the alphabet. But in fact, is the letter T a shape by virtue of being a letter of the alphabet, or by virtue of being the physical product of the activity of writing? Figure 2.3 assumes that it is best described as the former, since the set of symbols is a set of shapes.

Another similar problem in this example is the location of the domain of mental ability. The activity of writing is a volitional, intentional activity, so it presupposes the domain of mental ability. But mental ability is presupposed by writing because writing presupposes human involvement, and the human involvement involves volition and intention. Determining the exact structure of the array of domains upon which a profiled concept is based requires a careful working out of the definitions of concepts.

A further complication in the relation between profiles and domain matrices is that a word sometimes profiles a concept in only one of the domains in the domain matrix, or even just a domain deeply nested in the domain structure. The contrast can be illustrated by the concepts PERSON and BODY. PERSON is profiled against the abstract domain of HUMAN BEING (along with MAN, WOMAN etc.). The concept of HUMAN BEING is in turn profiled against the domain matrix of LIVING THING + MIND: human beings are living things with certain mental states and abilities (recall the classical definition of man as a rational animal). LIVING THING is in turn profiled against the domains of PHYSICAL OBJECT and LIFE: living things are physical objects endowed with life. The concept BODY represents a person's physical reality (alive or dead). Its base is nevertheless still the abstract domain of HUMAN BEING (or more precisely ANIMAL), but it profiles just the PHYSICAL OBJECT domain in the domain structure underlying HUMAN BEINGS. Contrast BODY with SOUL, which profiles a nonphysical domain of a human being, what we have called MIND for convenience; or with CORPSE, which profiles the PHYSICAL OBJECT domain but also profiles a particular region in the LIFE domain, namely DEAD.

2.5   Domains and idealized cognitive models

An important insight of Fillmore and Lakoff in their early work on frames/domains is that the knowledge represented in the frame is itself a conceptualization of experience that often does not match the reality. The example most cited to illustrate this point in the cognitive literature (not just linguistics but also philosophy, psychology and artificial intelligence) is the concept of BACHELOR (Fillmore 1975:128–29; 1977a:68–70). A simple conceptual analysis of BACHELOR is an ADULT UNMARRIED MALE. This definition may suit most normal cases. But there are a number of cases where speakers react with uncertainty as to whether the person involved is a bachelor or not:

(19)   a. The Pope
         b. Tarzan
         c. An adult male living with his girlfriend
         d. A male homosexual
         e. A male homosexual living with his boyfriend
         f. A seventeen-year-old living on his own, running his own Internet firm, and dating several women. [cf. a seventeen-year-old living with his parents and going to school, who virtually all agree is not a bachelor]

The apparent problem with the simple definition of BACHELOR as ADULT UNMARRIED MALE is not that the definition is too simple (but see below). There is a sense in which the meaning of *bachelor* really is just 'adult unmarried male'. It is just that the concept BACHELOR is profiled against a frame that does not accommodate the variety of actual social statuses found in the real world (Fillmore 1977a:69; 1982a:117–18). The frame for BACHELOR represents an idealized version of the world that simply does not include all possible real-world situations. Lakoff calls such a frame an **idealized cognitive model** (**ICM**; Lakoff 1987, chapter 4).

The analysis proposed in the preceding paragraph makes it look as if the information in the frame for the idealized cognitive model – just ADULT UNMARRIED MALE – is simpler than the reality that often does not match the idealization. But it is not. The ICM for BACHELOR, or rather the ICMs for ADULT, UNMARRIED and MALE have to include much more information than is usually associated with those labels. The ICM for ADULT must include reference to living arrangements, relationships to parents, and occupational activity (see [19b] and [19f]). The ICM for UNMARRIED must include a life history sequence in which adolescence is followed by an absence of lasting sexual relationships and then followed by marriage, without taking vows of celibacy (see [19a] and [19c]). The ICM for MALE must also include sexual orientation (with an eye to reproduction; see [19d] and

[19e]). In other words, the ICMs for BACHELOR are going to be as detailed and as hedged as reality in order to describe the 'ideal' life history and lifestyle that is implied by BACHELOR.

Searle (1979) argues that in fact the frame for any word concept is going to be infinitely complex. Searle is interested in what he calls the background assumptions for defining the literal meaning of words; in frame semantic terms, the background assumptions are the frame(s) for understanding the literal meaning of a linguistic expression. Searle argues that the sort of background knowledge that is relevant to a linguistic expression's meaning cannot be enumerated in such a way that all contexts of use can be predicted. That is, a basically infinite set of background assumptions are required to characterize the literal meaning of an utterance, and hence its appropriate use in context. Consider the following example (Searle 1979:127):

(20)   Give me a hamburger, medium rare, with ketchup and mustard, but easy on the relish.

We assume we understand what the meaning of this request is; we invoke a background frame of fast food restaurants, the ordering and serving of food, how a hamburger is cooked and garnished, and so on. But there is more to it than that:

> Suppose for example that the hamburger is brought to me encased in a cubic yard of solid lucite plastic so rigid that it takes a jack hammer to bust it open, or suppose the hamburger is a mile wide and is 'delivered' to me by smashing down the wall of the restaurant and sliding the edge of it in. (Searle 1979:127)

These situations are admittedly unlikely to be encountered in real life, in the way that unmarried men living with their girlfriends or homosexual men commonly are encountered. Nevertheless, in the frame for ordering a hamburger we would want to represent the assumptions that it is not supposed to be too large, nor encased in solid lucite plastic, nor any of an indefinitely large number of other things that one could do to a hamburger.

Langacker makes a similar observation with a similar type of example, given in (21) (Langacker 1988:16):

(21)   He is barely keeping his head above the water.

We may think we know what this sentence means, but

> imagine a race over the ocean by helicopter, where the contestants must transport a severed head, suspended by a rope from the helicopter, from the starting line to the finish; a contestant is disqualified if the head he is carrying ever dips below the water's surface. (Langacker 1988:16–17)

In other words, we have to bring to bear our full knowledge of the way the world is or, more accurately, the way we expect the world to be, in order to describe the precise meaning of an utterance.

Another way of saying this – the more common way of saying it in cognitive linguistics – is that we have to call on our **encyclopedic** knowledge in order to properly understand a concept. Some semanticists have argued that only a small subset of our knowledge of a concept needs to be represented as the linguistic meaning of a word; this is known as the **dictionary** view of linguistic meaning. But the frame semantic model of linguistic meaning highlights the failings of the dictionary view (Fillmore 1982a:134; 1985:233). The dictionary view fails because it generally describes only the concept profile, or at best a very simplified version of the concept frame implicit in a concept profile (see Haiman 1980 for further arguments; see also Quine 1951[1961]). Once one begins to specify the conceptual structure of the frame that supports the concept profile for a word or linguistic expression, the semantic structure quickly expands to encompass the total (encyclopedic) knowledge that speakers have about the concept symbolized by the word or construction.

Of course, encyclopedic knowledge is all interconnected in our minds. If the meaning of a word includes the frame as well as the profile, then one must abandon the concept of word meanings as small discrete chunks of conceptual structure. Langacker proposes an alternative model of the meaning of a word as an **access node** into the knowledge network (Langacker 1987:161–64):

> The entity designated by a symbolic unit can therefore be thought of as a **point of access** to a network. The semantic value of a symbolic unit is given by the open-ended set of relations . . . in which this **access node** participates. Each of these relations is a cognitive routine, and because they share at least one component the activation of one routine facilitates (but does not always necessitate) the activation of another. (Langacker 1987:163)

A word meaning is therefore a perspective on our knowledge of the world, as seen through the concept profiled by the word. This view of word meaning is not that different from the view of a conceptual category in cognitive psychology as a means of accessing further information about the individual categorized. This view of word meaning also highlights how choosing a word is a way of construing the relationship between the experience being communicated and the interlocutors' existing knowledge.

In the example of the ICM for the word *bachelor*, the deviations from the ICM were all examples in which it is not clear whether *bachelor* is applicable to those cases at all. For other words, a modifier is appended to the word to indicate deviation from the ICM. For example, Lakoff describes the ICM for *mother* as involving a cluster of several different ICMs (Lakoff 1987:74–76):

(22) BIRTH: the person giving birth is the mother
 GENETIC: the female who contributed the genetic material is the mother
 NURTURANCE: the female adult who nurtures and raises a child is the mother of that child
 MARITAL: the wife of the father is the mother
 GENEALOGICAL: the closest female ancestor is the mother

The cluster ICM (as Lakoff names it) is essentially a domain matrix. Thanks both to modern medicine and to traditional social arrangements, the real world has many cases where only parts of the cluster model for MOTHER applies to particular individuals. These deviations from the cluster ICM are indicated by conventional compounds and adjective + noun expressions:

(23) a. *stepmother*: fits the NURTURANCE and MARITAL models but none of the others
 b. *foster mother*: fits the NURTURANCE model but none of the others
 c. *birth mother*: fits the BIRTH model but none, or not all, of the others
 d. *genetic mother*: fits the GENETIC model but not all of the others
 e. *unwed mother*: fits (probably) all but the MARITAL model [etc.]

Nevertheless, one might still obtain varying results if asking of individuals falling under any of the categories in (23) whether she is the 'real mother' of the child (see chapter 5).

In other cases, there is clearly an ICM but linguistic convention has allowed the word, unmodified, to describe situations that lack some of the properties of the ICM. Fillmore gives the example of the ICM for *breakfast*, which has as its frame a cycle of meals, and profiles 'the one which is eaten early in the day, after a period of sleep, and for it to consist of a somewhat unique menu' (Fillmore 1982a:118). But you can work through the night and have eggs, toast and so on at sunup and call it *breakfast*; you can sleep till 3pm, get up and have eggs, toast and so on and call it *breakfast*; and you can sleep through the night and in the morning have chocolate cream pie and a martini and call it *breakfast* (ibid., 118–19). Each of these cases lacks one feature of the ICM for BREAKFAST. One can also call a meal *breakfast* that lacks both 'early in the day' and 'after a period of sleep' too: restaurants exist that serve *breakfast all day* (ibid.; the menu feature appears to be more important than the other two).

Another example similar to BREAKFAST is the ICM for *lie* (Coleman and Kay 1981). The ICM for LIE, such that a speaker S telling an addressee A the proposition P is a lie, is:

(24)   a. P is false.
       b. S believes P to be false.
       c. In uttering P, S intends to deceive A.

Coleman and Kay performed an experiment with stories designed to test every combination of the features listed in (24), and found that, in general, the situations with more of the three properties (24a/b/c) tended to be described by experimental subjects more often as lies than situations with fewer of the properties. Two situations (at least) have conventional expressions that indicate their deviation from the ICM. Polite *social lies* such as saying *What a lovely party!* or *How nice to see you!* can be said in circumstances in which (24a/b) hold but (24c) does not. The other situation can be illustrated with the exchange in (25) (Coleman and Kay 1981:29):

(25)   John: Where are you going?
       Mary: [out to buy John's birthday present] We're out of paprika.

In the situation in (25), (24a/b) do not hold but (24c) does (just the opposite of social lies); in this situation an English speaker could say that Mary *is being economical with the truth.*

In the case of *breakfast* and *lie,* the word profile extends to a range of situations whose features vary. Nevertheless, there appears to be agreement as to the situation that counts as the ICM for these words. ICMs thus give rise to judgements of graded centrality to members of a category, a phenomenon that is usually described as prototype effects (see Lakoff 1987 and chapter 4).

2.6   Mental spaces

Semantic frames/domains represent one of the two major organizing principles for conceptual structure. The other important organizing principle is the one illustrated by the examples in (26):

(26)   a. Gina bought a sports car.
       b. Giorgio believes that Gina bought a sports car.
       c. Paolo believes that Gina bought a pickup truck.
       d. Gina wants to buy a sports car.
       e. Gina will buy a sports car.
       f. If Gina buys a sports car, then she will drive to Paris.

In (26a), a situation is asserted (profiled), evoking the frame/domain of commercial transactions. In (26b), the same situation is represented, but as a belief rather than a fact. Example (26c) demonstrates that such beliefs may be at variance with the facts, and with other beliefs. In (27d), the same apparent situation is also represented, but it has a different status: the event has not taken place, it is only something in Gina's mind. In fact, even the sports car may exist only in Gina's mind. Example (26e) is more similar to (26d) than (26a), even if it is a prediction about the real world: the event has not taken place. Finally, in example (26f) the event is again hypothetical, and so is the event described in the consequent clause.

In a truth-conditional semantics, (26a) is unproblematic, but (26b–f) are. The situation 'Gina has bought a sports car' is false in (26d–e), but not necessarily false in (26b–d) or even (26g). One must be able to distinguish between the status of situations depending on whether they are true in the real world, or whether they are only true in someone's beliefs or desires, or true at another time in the real world.

In a truth-conditional semantics, the standard way of representing the status of situations is as possible worlds: there is the real world, and then there are worlds with situations that are possible but not (necessarily) actual. Possible worlds are then identified with a person's beliefs or wishes or some other mental attitude. Possible worlds pose metaphysical problems for many people, however. Do possible worlds exist? If so – or especially if not – where are they?

Fauconnier (1985, 1997; see also Fauconnier and Sweetser 1996) proposes an alternative model of representing the status of knowledge that is metaphysically more attractive and allows for elegant solutions to a number of problems in semantic and pragmatic analysis. Fauconnier replaces the notion of a possible world with that of a **mental space**, and argues that the mental space is a cognitive structure. That is, the allocation of a situation to 'Gina's desire,' 'Paolo's belief' or 'The hypothetical situation' is done in the mind of the speaker (and hearer), not in some as yet unclear metaphysical location. Fauconnier then proposes a set of principles for the interpretation of utterances and the assignment of situations to the appropriate mental space. We briefly present Fauconnier's model and a number of examples here; the reader should consult his work for detailed arguments in favor of his model over truth-conditional approaches to the same phenomena.

Utterances such as (26a) are normally construed as situating events or states in a **base space** (Fauconnier 1997:38–39), normally the present reality (more precisely, the mutually known world of the interlocutors; in Fauconnier 1985 this is called the reality space). Utterances such as (27b–f) have elements that Fauconnier describes as **space builders**: included in their meaning is the setting up of a new space different from the base space and linked to it. Space builders include a wide range of semantic phenomena corresponding not only to possible worlds in logical semantics but also a variety of other operators, including temporal expressions ([27a]; see Fauconnier 1985:29–30, 33–34; Fauconnier 1997, chapter 3), image or 'picture noun' contexts ([27b]; Fauconnier 1985:10–12), fictional situations ([27c]; ibid., 73–81), games and other systems ([27d]; ibid, 31), negation and disjunction ([27e–f]; ibid., 92, 96–98) and the separate cases in quantification ([27g]; see Fauconnier 1986):

(27)   a. In 1770, France was a monarchy.
        b. In the photo, she has black hair.
        c. In the movie, Ian McKellen is Gandalf.
        d. In this game, aces are low.
        e. I don't have a car.
        f. Either you take a cab or you walk home.
        g. Every guest got a receipt.

All of these examples have in common the building of a mental space in which a situation is held to be 'true' in that space only. More generally, we can say that just as words and constructions evoke semantic frames/domains, words and constructions also build spaces; at the very least, they 'build' or evoke the base space. The relevant word or construction then conventionally specifies that the asserted situation holds in the appropriate space.

Between the base space and any built space, there must be a mapping of the elements found in each space. Many interesting and puzzling semantic and pragmatic phenomena are a product of the possible mappings between spaces. We may divide the phenomena found in the mapping into two parts. First, what do the named elements of the built space (e.g. *Gina* and *sports car*) correspond to, if anything, in the base space? Second, what conceptual structures from the base space also occur in the built space(s), and vice versa? We begin with the first question.

In (26d), it seems straightforward to say that the person named *Gina* in the desire space built by *Gina wants . . .* is mapped onto Gina in the base space. But the object described as *a sports car* may or may not correspond to anything in the base space: Gina may have seen a particular car on the lot, or she may not have any specific car in mind. This is the distinction between a specific and nonspecific reading, respectively, of *a sports car* in (26d). The specific and nonspecific readings are represented in Figure 2.4.

Fauconnier crucially distinguishes between **roles** and **values** in mappings between spaces. A role is a linguistic description describing a category; a value is an individual that can be described by that category. Roles can be a category or type with various instances or tokens; *sports car* is such a role, since there are many instances (values) of sports cars. A role can also be a category that is filled by a single individual at one time but by different individuals over time; *the President of the United States* is an example of such a role. Roles and values are specific to a single mental space, and all counterpart relations between roles and values in different spaces must be established cognitively by the interlocutors.

specific reading   nonspecific reading

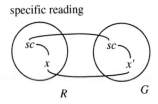

sc: sports car (role)
R: reality space
G: Gina's want space

Figure 2.4 *Specific and nonspecific indefinites*

Figure 2.4 easily represents the difference between the specific and nonspecific readings. In the specific reading of (26d), the value x' of *a sports car* in Gina's want space G has a counterpart value x in reality (the car she saw on the lot). In the nonspecific reading, there is no counterpart value in reality: she imagines a sports car she wants, but has not identified it with any existing car.

One of Fauconnier's central insights is that many puzzling semantic phenomena are the result of the fact that a value in one space can be described by the role its counterpart in another space has, even if that role is invalid for the value in the first space. This is the **Access Principle** (Fauconnier 1997:41; it is called the ID Principle in Fauconnier 1985:3). For example, (28) is not contradictory (Fauconnier 1985:29):

(28)   In 1929, the lady with white hair was blonde.

The value in the 1929 temporal space – the blonde girl – is being described with a role, *lady with white hair*, from the base space (the current reality).

Armed with the distinctions between mental spaces, between roles and values within spaces and across spaces, and the Access Principle, Fauconnier goes on to explain a wide range of semantic and pragmatic phenomena using these distinctions. Only a selection of these can be described here.

The phenomenon described as referential opacity is illustrated in 29:

(29)   Oedipus wants to marry his mother.

In the Greek myth, (29) is true under one reading (*his mother* = 'the person you and I know is Oedipus' mother') but false under another (*his mother* = 'the person Oedipus believes is his mother'). This distinction is due to the fact that Oedipus does not know that Jocasta is his mother. In mental space terms, the individual value named *Jocasta* does not fill the role *his mother* in Oedipus' belief space, although she does in reality space; see Figure 2.5 (adapted from Fauconnier 1985:49).

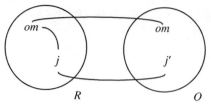

om: Oedipus' mother (role)
j: Jocasta (value in R)
j': Jocasta (value in O)
R: reality space
O: Oedipus' belief space

Figure 2.5 *Mental space diagram for example (29)*

In the true reading of (29), the description *his mother* for *j* in R is used for the value *j'* in O by the Access Principle. The false reading of (29) uses the description *his mother* in O, but it does not apply to *j'* in O. (A similar analysis can be applied to referential/attributive ambiguities; Fauconnier 1985:159–60.)

Only a few further examples can be given of how Fauconnier's model handles a variety of complex reference and identity phenomena (Fauconnier 1985:45, 36, 32, 39, 31, 155):

(30)   a. Rose is blonde, but George thinks she's a redhead.
        b. Hitchcock saw himself in that movie.
        c. I didn't buy a car. Otherwise, I would drive it to work.
        d. Your car is always different.
        e. If I were a millionaire, my VW would be a Rolls.
        f. Hesperus [the Morning Star] is Phosphorus [the Evening Star].

In (30a–b), the pronoun identifies a value in a built space (George's beliefs, the movie) by referring to its counterpart in the base space (the blonde Rose, Hitchcock). In (30c), the pronoun refers to a value in a negative space which has no counterpart in reality (*otherwise . . . would* evokes the same negative space; see example [32] below). In (30d), *your car* refers to a role and the predicate describes its changes in value over a sequence of temporal spaces. In (30e), the value filling the role *a Rolls* in the counterfactual space is identified with the value filling the role *my VW* in reality. In (30f), a classic philosophy example, two distinct values in the prior reality space are identified as one value in the current reality space.

The second set of phenomena that Fauconnier explores is what conceptual structures from the base space also occur in the built space(s), and vice versa. For example, in (26d), how much of our knowledge of reality should be attributed to the hypothetical space? Obviously, one cannot attribute to the hypothetical space the real-world fact that Gina has not bought a sports car; that is precisely what is asserted in the hypothetical space. On the other hand, at least other information about Gina, and about sports cars, not to mention much other knowledge about the world, may be attributed to the hypothetical space.

Fauconnier first addresses the question of presuppositions (Fauconnier 1985, chapter 3). As noted in §2.1, presuppositions are situations that are part of the frame of a concept, but are not asserted. The question is, what is the relationship of presuppositions in a built space to those in the base space? For example, consider the sentences in (31) (Fauconnier 1985:89–90):

(31)   a. If Max has gone to the meeting, then Max's children are alone.
         b. If Max has children, Max's children are American.

The phrase *Max's children* presupposes that Max has children; that is, a referring expression presupposes the existence of its referent(s). The traditional pragmatic analysis is that one must determine the presupposition of the whole sentence from the presuppositions of its parts (presupposition projection; see, e.g., Levinson 1985:191–225). In (31a), the presupposition that Max has children 'projects' to the base space. But in (31b), it does not project because it is asserted in the antecedent clause: Max may or may not have children in the base space (reality).

Fauconnier instead introduces the principle of presupposition **float**: 'informally: a presupposition floats up [from a built space to its base space] until it meets itself or its opposite' (Fauconnier 1997:61). In example (31a), the built space presupposes that Max has children but does not assert it. Hence the presupposition can float to the base space. In example (31b), however, the built space asserts that Max has children, and hence the presupposition cannot float beyond it to the base space.

Two more complicated examples are given in (32)–(33) (Fauconnier 1985:95, 93):

(32)   It is possible that John has children, and it is possible that John's children are away.
(33)   Luke believes it's raining and hopes that it will stop raining.

Examples (32)–(33) demonstrate that space builders may build the same space or related nonreal mental spaces. In (32), *it is possible* in the second conjunct can be construed as evoking the same possibility space that was built in the first conjunct. In this case, the presupposition that John has children is asserted in the hypothetical space in the first conjunct and therefore it does not float to the base space. Example (33) demonstrates that certain built spaces are related in privileged ways that allow presuppositions to float (see also McCawley 1981[1993]:415–30). A hope for some situation can be built on one's beliefs. Hence the presupposition that it is raining in the second clause of (33) is built on the assertion in the first clause (and therefore does not float to the base space). Reversing the relation between the two spaces fails, because beliefs cannot be built on hopes:

(34)   ??Luke hopes that it is raining and believes that it will stop raining.

Fauconnier then turns to the question of counterfactual conditionals, as in (35) (Fauconnier 1985, chapter 4; 1997, chapter 4):

(35)   If Boris had not come, Olga would have come anyway.

A counterfactual conditional builds a space in which the antecedent clause (Boris does not come) is explicitly the opposite of the base space (Boris did come). Again, the question is, what structures in the base space are also found in the built space? Fauconnier argues that previous, truth-conditional approaches to counterfactuals transfer as much of the structure of the base space as possible to the counterfactual space (Fauconnier 1985:118). Fauconnier instead advocates an analysis in which only the structure relevant for the counterfactual reasoning is transferred to the counterfactual space. He argues that the great flexibility of counterfactuals precludes transferring too much of the structure of the base space to the counterfactual space; compare (36a–d) (ibid.):

(36)   a. If Napoleon had been the son of Alexander, he would have been Macedonian.
        b. If Napoleon had been the son of Alexander, he would have won the battle of Waterloo.
        c. If Napoleon had been the son of Alexander, he would not have been Napoleon.
        d. If Napoleon had been the son of Alexander, Alexander would have been Corsican.

Fauconnier writes:

> It would not make sense to evaluate the 'absolute' truth of any of these statements, but they can all be used to make some point, which requires only very partial structuring of *H* [the counterfactual space] . . . such examples suggest that there is no general *linguistic* algorithm for going from *R* [the base space] to *H*. (Fauconnier 1985:118)

In Fauconnier's more recent work (Fauconnier 1997, chapter 6; Fauconnier and Turner 2002; see also Coulson 2000), he and Turner have emphasized the fact that information from two different spaces, such as those in the counterfactual conditionals in (36a–d), is **blended** in the resulting space, and that this blending process occurs in a much wider range of contexts than counterfactual conditionals. For example, (37) blends elements of a voyage by the catamaran *Great America II* from Boston to San Francisco in 1993 with a voyage by the clipper *Northern Light* on the same route in 1853 (Fauconnier 1997:155–56; see Fauconnier and Turner 1994):

(37)   At this point, *Great America II* is barely maintaining a 4.5 day lead over *Northern Light*.

Obviously, *Northern Light* is nowhere to be seen in 1993, but the blend of the 1853 temporal space and the 1993 temporal space in (37) 'makes a point' about the progress of *Great America II*. In Fauconnier and Turner's blending theory, example (37) evokes four mental spaces: two **input spaces** (in [37], the 1853 and 1993 temporal spaces); a **generic space**, which abstracts the commonalities from the two spaces (the route of travel, distance traversed, time taken etc.) and thereby defines the cross-space mapping between the elements in the two input spaces; and a **blended space**, which creates a novel expressive effect, in this case an image of a race between the current boat and a boat from the nineteenth century. Fauconnier and Turner (2002) argue that blending is a process of space mapping that pervades human reasoning, and explore the phenomenon of blending in a wide range of phenomena, most notably metaphor.

At this point, blending theory has moved quite a distance from mental space theory. Mental space theory illustrates how utterances evoke not just semantic frames but also spaces representing the status of our knowledge (beliefs, desires, hypotheticals, counterfactuals) relative to reality, how language uses links between different spaces in referring to individuals, and how knowledge can float between spaces. Blending theory has shifted the focus to how information from two spaces, construed broadly to include domains, is combined to produce novel conceptual structures. This aspect of blending theory is discussed with respect to metaphor in §8.3.3. In this chapter we have focused on the fact that the original mental space theory describes a significant dimension for the structuring of our conceptual knowledge orthogonal to semantic frames/domains, and offers solutions to many semantic and pragmatic problems in addition to those illustrated in this section.

3

Conceptualization and construal operations

3.1   Introduction

In chapter 1, we noted that one of the basic hypotheses of cognitive linguistics is that, in Langacker's words, semantics is conceptualization. This hypothesis challenges the view that semantics is purely truth-conditional. We have already seen in chapter 2 examples of semantic interpretations of linguistic expressions that go beyond truth-conditional semantics. Situations can be framed in different ways – e.g., *my dad* vs. *dad* vs. *father* and *waste time* vs. *spend time* in *My dad wasted most of the morning on the bus* (see §2.1) – and these ways convey to the hearer different conceptualizations of the relationship between the speaker and the speaker's father, of the positive or negative quality of the situation being described, and even of the nature of the situation being described (characterizing time in terms of money).

Framing is pervasive in language: as we argued in chapter 2, all linguistic units evoke a semantic frame. Yet framing is but one example of the ubiquity of conceptualization in linguistic expression. All aspects of the grammatical expression of a situation involve conceptualization in one way or another, including inflectional and derivational morphology and even the basic parts of speech. Whenever we utter a sentence, we unconsciously structure every aspect of the experience we intend to convey. The purpose of this chapter is to describe the range of conceptualization processes or **construal operations** that human beings employ in language.

The role of conceptualization in language is clearest when a single language provides alternative expressions for what appears to be truth-functionally equivalent situations. The example of framing given above contrasts different lexical expressions – *dad/father* and *spend/waste* – that otherwise appear to be truth-functionally equivalent. (We deliberately hedge on the phrase 'truth-functionally equivalent' because it often turns out that there are some situations that so favor one conceptualization over another that the other expression is unacceptable and so the two expressions are not always judged as truth-functionally equivalent.) But it is equally easy to find examples of inflectional and derivational contrasts between otherwise approximately truth-functionally equivalent expressions:

(1)   a. leaves on the tree
      b. foliage-Ø on the tree
(2)   a. Conor lives in New York City.
      b. Conor **is** li**ving** in New York City.
(3)   a. The chimney is **above** the window.
      b. The window is **below** the chimney.
(4)   a. Something **moved** in the grass.
      b. There was a **movement** in the grass.
(5)   a. The car brushed the bicycle.
      b. The bicycle **was** brush**ed by** the car.
(6)   a. **There was Sam** sitting on the floor.
      b. **Sam was** sitting on the floor.

Examples (1a–b) and (2a–b) differ in the choice of nominal and verbal inflection, (1a–b) by plural count noun and mass noun, and (2a–b) by the choice of a simple vs. a progressive form. Examples (3a–b) differ in the choice of a function word, in this case a preposition, and a reversal of subject and prepositional complement choice. Examples (4a–b) differ derivationally in part of speech, between a verb and its derived noun. Examples (5a–b) and (6a–b) differ in the grammatical construction used to describe the scene, active vs. passive voice in (5) and presentational vs. ordinary declarative in (6). All of these sentences seem to be truth-functionally equivalent. But English is not being unnecessarily profligate here: the a and b members offer a different conceptualization of the experience in every case. These and other examples will be explicated in the following sections.

Similar evidence is found in cases when the same word can be used with two different inflections, derivations or constructions, and there are subtle but definite conventional truth-functional differences in the two uses:

(7)   a. We have chocolate-Ø for dessert.
       b. We have chocolates for dessert.
(8)   a. Ira **is** a nuisance.
       b. Ira, stop **being** a nuisance!
(9)   a. Timmy is **in front of** the tree.
       b. Timmy is **behind** the tree.
(10)   a. Jill is **fussy**.
       b. Jill is **a fussbudget**. (Bolinger 1980:79)
(11)   a. The dog chewed the bone.
       b. The dog chewed **on** the bone.

In (7a), the mass noun refers to a substance, but in (7b), the same noun as a count noun refers to an object which is covered with the substance but may or may not be filled with the same substance. In (8a), the simple present describes a behavioral trait of Ira's, while (8b) describes a particular activity of his. Examples (9a) and (9b) differ in Timmy's position relative to the speaker and the tree; to make (9a) and (9b) truth-functionally equivalent, the speaker would have to move to the other side of the tree. Example (10a) describes a behavioral trait of Jill, but (10b) describes the same trait as a constant (and annoying) aspect of Jill's personality. In example (11a), the object role of *the bone* indicates that the bone itself is being affected by the dog's action, but in (11b), the oblique role indicates that it is only meat and gristle on the bone that is being affected.

The examples in (7)–(11) are equally indicative of the role of construal in language as the examples in (1)–(6). The truth-functional differences in (7)–(11) are indicative of favored conceptualizations that have led to the extension of a particular construal to a situation that does not (easily) allow for alternative construals. For example, the fact that certain sweets come in individuated units allows for a construal of the substance noun *chocolate* as a count noun (compare *I'd like an orange juice, please*), and *chocolate* as a count noun is extended to other such sweets where only the (perceptually salient) outer surface is made of chocolate. But both *a chocolate* and *an orange juice* share the construal as an individuated unit, even if the link to the substance is more tenuous in the former case. In fact, in cognitive linguistics conceptualization is the fundamental semantic phenomenon; whether alternative construals give rise to differences in truth conditions or not is a derivative semantic fact.

In some cases where construal is accompanied by a truth-functional semantic shift in meaning, English allows speakers to express the construal-plus-shift overtly, as in:

(12)   Stop **acting like** a nuisance!
(13)   I'd like a **glass of** orange juice, please.

Example (12) uses the process verb *act* and a manner construction to denote the activity and (13) uses a container word *glass* and the partitive construction to denote the individuated amount of juice. This is not always possible in English; for example, *a chocolate* does not have an obvious overt expression of its individuation, and there is no simple overt expression of the different types of chewing actions in (11a–b).

Other languages require overt expression of construal-plus-shift, in contrast to English. For example, Vietnamese cannot simply use a mass noun in a count noun construction or vice versa, as English does in (7); and Russian requires overt marking in the following examples were English does not:

(14)   a. soloma   'straw' [mass]
         b. solom-**ink**-a   'a straw' [count (American English)]
(15)   a. On kričal.   'He cried/was crying' [multiple times]
         b. On krik-**nu**-l.   'He cried' [once]

In (14b), Russian requires the singulative suffix *-ink* before the gender-case inflection *-a* in order to use the mass noun stem *solom-* in a count construction; English simply uses *straw* in either construction (with a concomitant truth-conditional semantic shift). In (15b), Russian requires the semelfactive suffix *-nu* before the past inflection *-l* in order to use the extended-activity verb stem *krik-* in the once-only construal; English simply uses *cry* in the simple past or the past progressive (with the relevant semantic shift).

Thus, there is cross-linguistic and language-internal variation as to whether construal plus truth-conditional semantic shift is expressed covertly or overtly. We will call the former **coercion** and the latter **conversion**.[1] We see no significant difference between coercion and conversion in conceptual semantic terms; in both cases, the truth-conditional semantic shift that accompanies the construal is conventionalized in the language, and cannot be assumed to carry over to other languages or even other words in the same language. In both cases, what we are interested in is the construal process itself, and this is a part of both conversion and coercion.

There are many construal operations that have been identified by cognitive linguists, and by other linguists who take a conceptualist approach to linguistic semantics. There have also been various proposals for grouping together construal operations that appear to be related. The two most comprehensive classifications are those of Talmy and Langacker. Talmy proposes a four-way classification under the name of **imaging systems** (Talmy 1977, 1978a, 1988a,b), given in (16):[2]

(16)   I. Structural Schematization
         II. Deployment of Perspective
         III. Distribution of Attention
         IV. Force Dynamics

Langacker surveys a wide range of construal operations under the rubric of **focal adjustments** (Langacker 1987, §3.3); his classification of focal adjustments

---

[1] There is no uniformity in terminology in the literature, unfortunately: 'coercion,' 'conversion' and 'shift' have all been used for the covert case.

[2] Talmy somewhat alters this classification in the version found in Talmy (2000), and changes their name to **schematic systems**. The first three categories are basically the same (the first is renamed configurational structure), while force dynamics is dropped entirely and a system called 'Domain', consisting solely of the domains of space and time, is added. The 'Domain' category includes the construals represented by noun and verb (see §§3.2, 3.5). We believe that force dynamics should be retained as a construal system; see Table 3.1.

is given in (17):

(17)   I. Selection
       II. Perspective
           A. Figure/Ground
           B. Viewpoint
           C. Deixis
           D. Subjectivity/Objectivity
      III. Abstraction

Talmy's and Langacker's classifications have a number of features in common: for example, both have categories of perspective, and Talmy's attentional imaging system includes Langacker's selection and abstraction focal adjustments. These classifications are not comprehensive, however. Fillmore's framing is a construal operation, for example, but does not obviously fall under the categories in either Talmy's or Langacker's classifications. Lakoff and Johnson's (1980) theory of metaphor is an example of another widespread type of linguistic conceptualization that is not discussed explicitly by either Langacker or Talmy. Langacker himself makes use of other construal operations, such as scanning, comparison and the entity/interconnection distinction, that he does not include in his classification of focal adjustments.

There is another theoretical construct in cognitive linguistics which imposes a conceptualization of experience, namely **image schemas** (Lakoff 1987; Johnson 1987; Lakoff and Turner 1989; Johnson 1987; Clausner and Croft 1999). Image schemas are defined as schematic versions of images. **Images** are representations of specific, embodied experiences (see Fillmore 1975:123; 1977a:73–74). Domains that give rise to images are described as **embodied** (Lakoff 1987:267; Johnson 1987:19–23) or grounded (Lakoff and Turner 1989:113). These domains are all basic domains as defined in §2.4. Image schemas are not specific images but are **schematic**. They represent schematic patterns arising from imagistic domains, such as containers, paths, links, forces, and balance that recur in a variety of embodied domains and structure our bodily experience (Lakoff 1987:453; Johnson 1987:29). Image schemas are also not specific to a particular sensory modality (Lakoff 1987:267; Johnson 1987:24–25). Image schemas structure our bodily experience (Talmy 1972, 1977, 1983), and they structure our non-bodily experience as well, via metaphor (Lakoff 1987:453; Johnson 1987:29; see chapter 8). This definition clarifies the seemingly contradictory description of image schemas sometimes found: image schemas are 'abstract' in one sense of that word – they are schematic – but not 'abstract' in another sense of that word – they are embodied.

An inventory of image schemas drawn from Johnson 1987 and Lakoff and Turner 1989 is given in (18) (based on Clausner and Croft 1999:15; the headings and items in italics were added by Clausner and Croft).

(18) *SPACE*   UP-DOWN, FRONT-BACK, *LEFT-RIGHT*,
                           NEAR-FAR, CENTER-PERIPHERY, CONTACT
      SCALE   PATH
      CONTAINER   CONTAINMENT, IN-OUT, SURFACE,
                           FULL-EMPTY, *CONTENT*
      FORCE   BALANCE, COUNTERFORCE, COMPULSION,
                           RESTRAINT, ENABLEMENT, BLOCKAGE,
                           DIVERSION, ATTRACTION
      UNITY/MULTIPLICITY MERGING, COLLECTION, SPLITTING,
                           ITERATION, PART-WHOLE, MASS-COUNT,
                           LINK
      IDENTITY   MATCHING, SUPERIMPOSITION
      EXISTENCE   REMOVAL, BOUNDED SPACE, CYCLE,
                           OBJECT, PROCESS

Image schemas are also construals of experience, though they exhibit some of the characteristics of domains as well (see §3.5).

In this chapter, we present all of the construal operations and image schemas discussed by cognitive linguists under a new classification.[3] This classification is given in Table 3.1 on page 46.

A chief aim of this classification is to demonstrate the close relationship between construal operations proposed by linguists and psychological processes proposed by cognitive psychologists and phenomenologists. If linguistic construal operations are truly cognitive, then they should be related to, or identical with, general cognitive processes that are postulated by psychologists. In fact, most if not all of these construal operations are special cases of general cognitive processes described in psychology and phenomenology. This view follows from the basic hypothesis of cognitive linguistics that language is an instance of general cognitive abilities.

The classification of construal operations in Table 3.1 is not intended to be a reduction of construal operations to just four processes. The various construal operations listed under the four headings are all distinct cognitive processes. The analysis we propose is that the various construal operations are manifestations of the four basic cognitive abilities in different aspects of experience. The remainder of this chapter describes and illustrates the construal operations under these four headings.

---

[3] An earlier version of this classification is presented in Croft and Wood 2000.

Table 3.1 *Linguistic construal operations as instances of general cognitive processes*

I. Attention/salience
   A. Selection
      1. Profiling
      2. Metonymy
   B. Scope (dominion)
      1. Scope of predication
      2. Search domains
      3. Accessibility
   C. Scalar adjustment
      1. Quantitative (abstraction)
      2. Qualitative (schematization)
   D. Dynamic
      1. Fictive motion
      2. Summary/sequential scanning
II. Judgement/comparison (including identity image schemas)
   A. Categorization (framing)
   B. Metaphor
   C. Figure/ground
III. Perspective/situatedness
   A. Viewpoint
      1. Vantage point
      2. Orientation
   B. Deixis
      1. Spatiotemporal (including spatial image schemas)
      2. Epistemic (common ground)
      3. Empathy
   C. Subjectivity/objectivity
IV. Constitution/Gestalt (including most other image schemas)
   A. Structural schematization
      1. Individuation (boundedness, unity/multiplicity, etc.)
      2. Topological/geometric schematization (container, etc.)
      3. Scale
   B. Force dynamics
   C. Relationality (entity/interconnection)

3.2   Attention/salience

The process of **attention** is a well-known basic phenomenon in cognitive psychology. Attention appears to be closest to what Chafe (1994:26–30) calls the focus of consciousness. Attention comes in degrees and is usually modeled in terms of degree of activation of conceptual structures in a neural network model of the mind. The phenomenon of attention focuses on the human cognitive ability involved, but there are also natural properties of phenomena in the perceived world that lend themselves to being attended to by human beings, and these properties are said to enhance those phenomena's **salience** to human beings' attention.

Attention is a complex psychological ability whose different aspects can be most easily illustrated by visual ability: one can select one object or another to focus one's attention on; focus of attention is surrounded by a scope of attention; one can take a more coarse-grained or more fine-grained view of a scene; and one can fix one's gaze on a scene or move one's eye over it. These four aspects of attention are found across all domains of thought.

3.2.1   Selection

The focal adjustment of **selection** is our ability to attend to parts of our experience that are relevant to the purpose at hand and ignore aspects of our experience that are irrelevant. The phenomenon of profiling a concept in a semantic frame, described in detail in chapter 2, is an example of selection. In most cases, different words in a semantic frame or domain focus our attention on the different elements in the frame, for example *radius, arc, circumference* in the CIRCLE frame. In other cases, derivational morphology shifts the profile, as in *writer*, whose *-er* suffix shifts the profile of *write* from process to agent. The participant that the *-er* suffix selects is not fixed to a single participant role but depends on salience, manifest both in conventionalized forms such as *stapler* (the instrument) or in novel forms such as *clapper* (Jane T., describing a lamp that turns on when you clap your hands).

Selection of the profile by a single underived word stem is also flexible and subject to construal. For example, many English nouns are also used as verbs (Clark and Clark 1979): *pan* can be construed as profiling either a metal object or a process in the GOLDSEEKING frame. Both the process and the metal object are salient in this frame, hence the choice of one word for both. Likewise, British English speakers can construe *bin* as profiling either a wastebasket or the action of tossing something into the wastebasket.

Such examples are not usually analyzed as examples of construal since the profile is of course central to a word's meaning and any shift in profile has truth-functional consequences. However, two semantic processes that involve subtler and/or more systematic shifts in profile lend themselves to a construal analysis.

The first example is the highlighting of different **facets** (see chapter 5) or domains in a domain matrix, as in (19)–(22):

(19)   a. Where is the Sunday Times? (physical object or tome)
        b. Have you read the Sunday Times? (semantic content or text)

(20)   a. Paris is a beautiful city. (location)
        b. Paris closed the Boulevard St. Michel. (government)
        c. Paris elected the Green candidate as mayor. (population)

(21)   a. The *Chronicle* costs a dollar. (tome)
        b. The *Chronicle* called for his resignation. (editor)
        c. The *Chronicle* went bankrupt. (company)

(22)   a. The window is dirty. (pane)
        b. She came in through the bathroom window. (opening)

A newspaper, book or other embodied text is simultaneously a physical tome and a meaningful text. But (19a) selects the physical object facet and (19b) only the text facet. The range of possible profiled facets for a word can be quite wide. For example, (20c) selects the voting members of the population, but *All Paris turned out to see the king* selects a wider (but still incomplete) set of the population. The government in (20b) is the city government; but *Paris opposes any reform of the Common Agricultural Policy* profiles the national government by virtue of Paris being the capital of France. It is not clear whether different facets count as different senses; see §5.3.1 for further discussion.

The second example is the phenomenon of **metonymy**. Metonymy is, loosely, the use of a word to denote a concept other than its 'literal' denotation. Examples of metonymy include the following (Nunberg 1995:115; Langacker 1991b:189):

(23)   That french fries is getting impatient.
(24)   They played lots of Mozart.
(25)   She heard the piano.
(26)   I'm in the phone book.

A cognitive linguistic analysis of metonymy is the ability of a speaker to select a different contextually salient concept profile in a domain or domain matrix than the one usually symbolized by the word. In (23)–(24), it is the nouns (*french fries* and *Mozart*) whose concept profiles are shifted. The evidence for this analysis is found in the grammar of the sentences. In (23), although *french fries* is plural, the demonstrative modifying it and the verb are singular, indicating that *french fries* is profiling the single individual who has ordered french fries. In (24), although *Mozart* is countable, the quantifier modifying it is used with mass nouns, indicating that *Mozart* is profiling the abstract uncountable music of Mozart.

In (25)–(26), however, Langacker argues that it is the verbs whose concept profiles are shifted. This shift in verb concept profile is an example of what Langacker describes as an **active zone** analysis. In an active zone analysis the relational predication – a verb, adjective, adverb or preposition – adjusts its meaning to accommodate its semantic argument, and incorporates the 'literal' argument as its

active zone. Thus, in (25) the meaning of *heard* is 'S BJ heard the sound of O BJ' –
compare *She heard the sound of the piano* – and the active zone in the verb meaning
is the sound emitted by the object referent. In (26) the meaning of *be in (the phone
book)* is 'S BJ's name is printed in L OC', and the active zone is a name and its
relation to the subject referent.

Langacker argues that the difference between (27a–c) is due to alternative construals of the adjective, not a syntactic alternation:

(27)   a. To play Monopoly is fun.
         b. Monopoly is fun to play.
         c. Monopoly is fun.

In transformational analyses, *be fun* in (27b) is semantically identical to *be fun* in
(27a), and (27b) is syntactically derived by a movement of *Monopoly* to the main
clause subject position ('Tough-movement'). In Langacker's analysis, (27b) is not
syntactically derived from (27a). Instead, *be fun* in (27b) is semantically distinct
from *be fun* in (27a); (27a) takes an entity as its subject and has the activity carried
out on the subject referent as its active zone. Support for the active zone analysis
is suggested by (27c): the clause from which the subject would be moved in the
syntactic analysis is absent, and yet (27c) is acceptable, with an interpretation of
be fun as in (27b).

The active zone analysis of (25)–(26) is the opposite of the traditional metonymy
analysis, in which it is the noun phrase that shifts profile (*the piano* to *the sound
of the piano*, *I* to *my name*). The verb (adjective, preposition) semantic shift is
quite different from the usual examples of metonymy on verb phrases, where, for
example, *go to the bathroom* is metonymic for 'perform certain bodily functions',
and *pick up the phone* in *If you want to find out, you've only got to pick up the phone*
is metonymic for a more complex activity. In these latter examples, the profile is
shifted from one event to an associated event in the same semantic frame. The
semantic shift of the relational predicate in the active zone analysis for (25)–(26)
serves a different function.

Nunberg (1995) argues for a distinction between noun and verb semantic shift
(the latter equivalent to the active zone analysis), or 'predicate transfer' as he calls
it, using evidence from grammatical behavior such as that cited above for (23)–
(24). Nunberg argues that one advantage of the active zone analysis is that in a
sentence such as *Roth is Jewish and widely read*, one can account for the lack of
zeugma by analyzing *widely read* as taking the author as subject, not his books;
hence the subjects are truly coreferential (Nunberg 1995:122–23); but see §5.3.1
for an alternative analysis of the same phenomenon in facets.

Whichever is the best analysis for examples such as (25)–(26), the phenomenon
of profile shift (semantic shift) appears to be a function of salience. Langacker

notes that in (25)–(26), and (27b–c) as well, the effect of the semantic shift is to allow a more salient entity to be the semantic as well as syntactic argument of the verb (*I* instead of *my name*, *the piano* instead of *the sound of the piano*, *Monopoly* instead of *to play Monopoly*; Langacker 1991b:193). Nunberg argues that the primary 'pragmatic' constraint on predicate transfer is the noteworthiness of the relationship of the predicate to its argument in the context – in cognitive linguistic terms, its salience in the semantic frame. For example, *I'm in the Whitney Museum* (said by an artist about her painting) confers a noteworthy property to the artist of being represented in a major museum; the same artist saying *??I'm in the second crate on the right* does not (Nunberg 1995:113). Nunberg also notes that noteworthiness is subject to construal: a jealous painter might say *Those daubers get one-person shows while I'm relegated to a crate in the basement* (ibid., 129, n. 7).

3.2.2   Scope of attention (dominion)

The second aspect of attention is that the focus of attention – what is selected – is surrounded by a **scope** of attention, that is, a periphery of consciousness where entities are **accessible** to attention (Chafe 1994:29). We saw an example of scope of attention in §2.4, example (18e), repeated in (28):

(28)   ??A body has twenty-eight knuckles.

In the scope of predication, the domains immediately presupposed by a profiled concept are accessible in a way that more indirectly presupposed domains are not (see §2.4, example [18]). This is a matter of construal; the scope of predication can shift in the appropriate context as in (29):

(29)   A: We've found every bit of the body, sir – even the knuckles.
       B: How many did you find?
       A: Twenty-seven, sir.
       B: Come on, now! How many knuckles does a body have?
       A: Oh, you're right, sir. Twenty-eight.

Another example of a grammatical constraint that makes reference to the scope of attention has to do with a combination of locative expressions specifying a location:

(30)   The money is in the kitchen, under the counter, in the lefthand cabinet, on the top shelf, behind the meat grinder.

Each locative expression profiles an entity in the scope defined by the preceding locative expression (i.e., the locative expression defines successively narrower **search domains**; Langacker 1987:286). Scrambling the order of locative expressions creates cognitive chaos:

(31)   The money is on the top shelf, in the kitchen, under the counter, behind the meat
         grinder, in the lefthand cabinet.

Yet another example of scope of attention is the notion of **accessibility** of a referent in discourse (Ariel 1990; Gundel et al. 1993; Chafe 1994). Consider the passage given in (32), from the Pear Stories narratives (Chafe 1980):

(32)   And then definitely when he's up there,
         . . a kid comes by on a bicycle.
         From the direction where the goat man left,
         okay?
         A–nd . . u–m the bicycle's way too big for the kid.
         I'm giving you all **these details**.
         I don't know if you want **them**.

A third person pronoun such as *them* construes the referent as being in the focus of attention of the hearer, which is appropriate in (32) because the details have just been mentioned. However, when *details* is first uttered, the details are not in the focus of attention – they have not been mentioned as such – but they are in the scope of attention – the description in the preceding intonation units has been about the details of the film. The choice of the proximal demonstrative adjective *these details* construes the details as being in the hearer's scope of attention but not in focus (Gundel et al. 1993:275).

Langacker proposes a highly generalized concept of scope in terms of the **dominion** made accessible by a **reference point** which functions as the (initial) focus of attention (Langacker 1999, chapter 6). Langacker argues that reference point and dominion constitute the construal underlying the possessive construction: the 'possessor' in examples such as *my watch, your anxiety* and *Lincoln's assassination* functions as a reference point to establish a dominion in which the appropriate referent of the head noun can be selected. Langacker also extends his analysis to metonymy. For example, in (20c) above, the speaker focuses the hearer's attention on the city of Paris by using *Paris*. Paris then functions as a reference point whose scope or dominion includes its inhabitants; the inhabitants of Paris are therefore accessible as the subject referent for the predicate. Choosing *The people of Paris* instead of *Paris* in (20c) would construe the situation differently, putting the people in the focus of attention instead of in the dominion of another focus.

3.2.3   Scalar adjustment

The third aspect of attention is an adjustment of the scale of attention. It can be illustrated with a visual example (Talmy 1983:238):

(33)   a. She ran across the field.
         b. She ran through the field.

Examples (33a–b) could describe the same scene, but (33b) invites the hearer to attend to the thickness of the vegetation in the field by using a preposition requiring a three-dimensional volume; (33a) instead construes the field as a two-dimensional surface without thickness. To describe the conceptualization involved here, a metaphor of magnification or **granularity** is often used. Example (33a) offers a **coarse-grained** view of the field, seen as if from a distance so that the thickness of whatever covers the field is invisible to us. Example (33b) offers a **fine-grained** view of the field, as if our view was magnified to reveal its thickness. Examples (34a–c) provide a more elaborate example of granularity:

(34)   a. We drove along the road.
         b. A squirrel ran across the road.
         c. The construction workers dug through the road.

In (34a), the road is viewed at such a coarse grain that it is conceptualized as a line, which provides a path for movement. In (34b–c), the same difference in granularity is found as in (33a–b): in (34b) the road is construed as a two-dimensional surface that can be traversed, and in (34c), the road is construed as a three-dimensional volume whose depth in this case can be an obstacle. At a coarse-grained view, the road's width and depth are reduced and lost, and the road is merely one-dimensional. At a more fine-grained view, or a greater magnification, the width of the road becomes visible, so to speak, and at a still finer-grained view/magnification, the depth becomes visible as well.

Examples (33)–(34) illustrate **quantitative scalar adjustment**:[4] a construal of an object by adjusting the granularity of the scalar dimensions, in this case the three spatial dimensions. Scalar adjustment is found in other measurable dimensions as well. For example, part of the difference in the construals of (2a–b) and (8a–b) in §3.1 is due to temporal scalar adjustment. In both cases, the progressive evokes a finer-grained scale than the simple present. In (8a), Ira's nuisance extends over a long period of time, possibly his entire lifetime; but in (8b), Ira's nuisance extends only over a brief time, that of his objectionable activity. In (2a), Conor's time in New York is conceived of as permanent, or at least construed as long-term, while in (2b), it is construed as short-term or temporary in the context of his lifetime.

Langacker also includes what he calls **schematization** under the same category. Schematization, that is, viewing something by means of a more encompassing

---

[4] Langacker calls this 'abstraction,' but that term is used for such a wide range of theoretical concepts, even in cognitive linguistics, that we choose a more precise term here.

category, is a **qualitative** scalar adjustment: rather than losing a measurable scale or dimension, one loses irrelevant properties. For instance, *triangle* specifies the number of sides of the shape, but the more schematic *polygon*, which could be used to describe the same shape, is vague as to the number of sides it possesses (Langacker 1987:135). A word or construction that is vague rather than ambiguous with respect to a semantic property is an example of schematization. Possessing an indeterminate or nonrestrictive property is not the same as lacking the property: polygons have sides, even if the concept of a polygon is indeterminate with respect to that feature. Schematization is a phenomenon of attention: the concept of a polygon ignores the number of sides to any particular subtype of polygon, in contrast to the concept of a triangle. One can also find differences in schematization in frames as well as profiles. To take an example from §2.3, the frame for the English word *eat* is vague as to whether the eater is human or animal, unlike German *essen* and *fressen*. More generally, the choice of words at different levels of categorization (see chapter 4) to refer to an object will construe the object at different levels of schematization.

3.2.4   Dynamic attention

Focus, scope and scale of attention are all static construals of a scene. The fourth aspect of attention is that it can be dynamic: one's attention can move across a scene. That this is a matter of conceptualization, not just a fact about the world, can be seen in (35) (see Talmy 2000, chapter 2):

(35)   The road winds through the valley and then climbs over the high mountains.

The road is not actually going anywhere, but it is conceptualized as if it is: the mind's eye, so to speak, represents one as going along the road. Talmy describes this as **fictive motion**, because it is a construal of a static scene in dynamic terms. Of course, most of the time speakers construe static scenes statically and dynamic scenes dynamically; this underlies the distinction between state and process in predicates (see §3.6). But example (35) and many similar examples demonstrate that this semantic property is subject to construal.

Langacker also makes use of the static/dynamic attentional contrast in construal, but for a different phenomenon. One of the basic conceptual distinctions between predicates (prototypically verbs) and arguments or modifiers (nouns and adjectives), according to Langacker, is the mode of **scanning** of the scene. Langacker distinguishes **summary scanning**, a holistic conceptualization of a scene in its entirety, and **sequential scanning**, a scanning of a scene in conceived time, which is not the same as objective time (Langacker 1987:144–45, 248–49). For example, when a verb predicates an action as in *Boston Bridge collapsed*, the event is scanned sequentially, over time. In contrast, when the verb is nominalized in a referring expression such as *the collapse of Boston Bridge*, the event is construed summarily as a whole unit without being scanned through time, even though the event occurred objectively through an interval of time (compare *move* vs. *movement* in examples [4a–b] in §3.1). Summary scanning is the norm for nouns denoting objects when used as referring expressions, such as *the tree* or *the lamp*, and for modifiers such as *tall* in *the tall tree*.

Summary/sequential scanning is not the same as fictive motion. Fictive motion represents the state/process construal, but summary/sequential scanning underlies the difference between sentence predication and nonpredicated states of affairs. For Langacker, *The road is in the valley* involves sequential scanning because it is predicated, but *The road winding through the valley* involves summary scanning because the (fictive) motion of the road is not predicated.

3.3   Judgement/comparison

Kant describes **judgement**, which he considers a fundamental cognitive faculty, as a particular kind of **comparison**: 'judgement in general is the faculty of thinking the particular as contained under the universal' (Kant 1790[1952]:18). Husserl, generalizing over the Western philosophical tradition from Aristotle onwards, gives judgement the more general meaning of a comparison between two entities: 'the most general characteristic of the predicative judgement is that *it has two members*: a "substrate" (*hypokeimenon*), about which something is affirmed, and that which is affirmed of it (*kategoroumenon*)' (Husserl 1948[1973]:14, emphasis original). Langacker also considers comparison to be a fundamental cognitive operation (Langacker 1987:103–5). Thus we may link the fundamental philosophical concept of judgement to the cognitive psychological process of comparison.

3.3.1   *Categorization*

Perhaps the most fundamental judgement of comparison is categorization, which was described in terms of framing in chapter 2. The act of **categorization** – applying a word, morpheme or construction to a particular experience to be communicated – involves comparison of the experience in question to prior experiences and judging it to belong to the class of prior experiences to which the linguistic expression has been applied. There are many ways in which a situation can be compared and judged to be like a prior experience. As we saw in §2.3, the choice of a linguistic category based on comparison to a prior situation frames – construes – the current situation in different ways, as in *fetus* vs. *unborn baby* or *thrifty* vs. *stingy*. In addition to the flexibility of framing a situation by comparing it to one or another prior situation, speakers also have the flexibility of comparing the current situation to a prior one and in effect redefining the frame. For example, upon entering a holding pattern over Milan airport, a pilot said *We'll be on the path they call a racetrack; that's essentially a circle with two straight sides* – a significant reconceptualization of the category CIRCLE.

Langacker describes the comparison process between the current situation and the category to which it is assigned as **sanction** (Langacker 1987:66–71). He recognizes a gradient between **full sanction** – unproblematic subsumption of the new situation – and **partial sanction** – a more creative extension of the category to the current situation. Categorization involves schematization (§3.2) as well as judgement: in comparing the new experience to prior ones and categorizing it in one way over another, we attend to some characteristics and ignore others. The pervasiveness of construal in the process of categorization has already been discussed in chapter 2 and will be described in detail in chapter 4.

3.3.2   Metaphor

Another construal operation widely discussed in cognitive linguistics, **metaphor**, also involves judgement or comparison. Metaphor involves a relationship between a **source domain**, the source of the literal meaning of the metaphorical expression, and a **target domain**, the domain of the experience actually being described by the metaphor. For example, to *waste time* involves comparing TIME (the target domain) to MONEY (the source domain) in the metaphor represented by the Lakoffian formula TIME IS MONEY (Lakoff and Johnson 1980). Time is construed as a valuable asset that is possessed by human beings and can be 'used' in the same way that money is.

The choice of metaphor to describe a situation in a particular domain construes the structure of that domain in a particular way that differs depending on the metaphor chosen. For example, the metaphor in *stockmarket crash* construes the low level of the market as abnormal, the result of defective operation, whereas a high (or rising) market is normal. On the other hand, *stockmarket correction* construes the low level of the market as normal, its correct level, whereas the high level is abnormal.

The exact relationship between the source and target domains in a metaphorical expression is a matter of debate within cognitive linguistics. Metaphor, like categorization, is sufficiently important for conceptualization to merit its own chapter in this book (chapter 8), and is discussed in greater detail there.

3.3.3   *Figure-ground alignment*

A third example of comparison as a linguistic construal is **figure-ground** alignment. Figure-ground alignment appears to be strongly influenced by objective properties of the scene, although they can be overridden in various ways (that is, it is subject to construal). The figure-ground distinction is derived from Gestalt psychology (e.g. Koffka 1935, ch. 5), introduced into cognitive linguistics by Talmy (Talmy 1972, 1983, 2000).

Talmy uses the figure-ground relation to account for the expression of spatial relations in natural language. All spatial relations in language – both location (36) or motion (37) – are expressed by specifying the position of one object, the **figure**, relative to another object, the **ground** (sometimes more than one ground object, as in [38]–[39]):

(36)   The book [*figure*] is on the floor [*ground*].
(37)   Sheila [*figure*] went into the house [*ground*].
(38)   The Isaac CDs [*figure*] are between Compère [*ground*] and Josquin [*ground*].
(39)   Greg [*figure*] drove from San Rafael [*ground*] to Trinidad [*ground*] in five hours.

The figure and ground are asymmetrical. Although *near* is a spatially symmetrical preposition, (40b) sounds odd compared to (40a) (Talmy 2000:314):

(40)   a. The bike is near the house.
        b. ??The house is near the bike.

Likewise, there is no preposition that functions as the inverse of *in* in (41a) (from Leonard Talmy), because the figure-ground orientation is quite unnatural:

(41)   a. There's a crocodile in the water.
        b. ??There's water 'being-a-suspending-medium-for' the crocodile.

Talmy identifies the following properties of objects that favor figure or ground construal, in the narrower domain of spatial relations (based on Talmy 1983:230–31; see Talmy 2000:315–16):

(42) | *Figure* | *Ground* |
        | --- | --- |
        | location less known | location more known |
        | smaller | larger |
        | more mobile | more stationary |
        | structurally simpler | structurally more complex |
        | more salient | more backgrounded |
        | more recently in awareness | earlier on scene/in memory |

Nevertheless, figure-ground relations can be manipulated. The same object can function as figure in one context and ground in another, as in (43a–b); and the favoring contexts can also be overridden for the opposite figure-ground construal, with appropriate contextualization, as in (44):

(43)   a. **The cat** [*figure*] is on the table [*ground*].
       b. I found a flea [*figure*] on **the cat** [*ground*].
(44)   [*The speaker is composing a scene for a photograph:*]
       I want the house [*figure*] to be behind Susan [*ground*]!

Figure-ground relations are found in other domains, including relations between events (Talmy 1978; Croft 2001, chapter 9). The main (figure)-subordinate (ground) event relation is construed asymmetrically in (45a), compared to the symmetrical coordinate event relation in (45b):

(45)   a. I read while she sewed.
       b. I read and she sewed.

The event in the ground/subordinate clause is conceptualized as the basis or ground – i.e., a cause or precondition – for the event in the figure/main clause. Figure-ground asymmetry may lead to outright anomaly, as in example (46) (Talmy 2000:325):

(46)   a. He dreamed while he slept.
       b. *He slept while he dreamed.

The two events could be coextensive, but since dreaming is contingent on sleeping, sleeping must function as the ground and therefore (46a) is acceptable while (46b) is not.

For most figure-ground subordinators, there is no natural inverse for the figure-ground relation specified by the subordinator (Talmy 2000:326):

(47)   a. She slept until he arrived.
       b. ??He arrived 'immediately-and-causally-before-the-end-of' her sleeping.
(48)   a. We stayed home because he had arrived.
       b. ??He arrived 'to-the-occasioning-of-(the-decision-of)' our
         staying home.

In a few cases, it is syntactically simple to construct both a semantic relation and its inverse, for example *before* and *after*. However, there is a difference in construal depending on the choice of event as figure ([49a–b], from Croft 2001:331):

(49)   a. After Tom resigned, all hell broke loose.
       b. Tom resigned before all hell broke loose.

In (49a), Tom's resignation is presumed to let loose the forces of chaos; whereas in (49b), Tom succeeded in cutting out when he saw what was happening (or perhaps before the consequences of his actions became apparent to everyone).

Similarly, simultaneous subordinators such as *when* are temporally symmetrical, but inappropriate choice of figure and ground events leads to conceptual peculiarity (compare [50b] to [50a], from Croft 2001:330):

(50)   a. When Jerry was chair of the department, everything was all right.
        b. ??When everything was all right, Jerry was chair of the department.

In (50a), the healthy state of affairs is presumed to be due to Jerry's chairmanship. Example (50b) on the other hand is odd, making Jerry look like an opportunist who has the extraordinary ability to take advantage of a healthy state of affairs to assume the chairmanship of the department.

Figure-ground alignment is an example of comparison in that the two elements of the scene are compared to each other; but unlike categorization and metaphor, the judgement is one of contrast rather than similarity. Langacker also explicitly links figure-ground to comparison, arguing that the typical figure-ground alignment falls out of his model of comparison as cognitive events of scanning a scene (Langacker 1987:121–22).[5]

3.4   Perspective/situatedness

Perspective, especially deixis, is perhaps the most obvious and most commented upon of the construal operations. Particularly for spatial descriptions, perspective is essential, and its dependence on the relative position and viewpoint of the speaker is well known. But perspective is also found in nonspatial domains: we have a perspective based on our knowledge, belief and attitudes as well as our spatiotemporal location. The closest cognitive property to perspective taken broadly is probably the philosophical notion of our **situatedness** in the world in a particular location – where location must be construed broadly to include temporal, epistemic and cultural context as well as spatial location. This broad interpretation of location is related to what the phenomenological philosopher Heidegger calls Being-in-the-world. Heidegger argues that Being-in-the-world is more than simple spatial inclusion; rather, it is the fundamental situatedness of existence in

---

[5] Despite this, Langacker subsumes figure-ground under perspective among his focal adjustments. In fact, Langacker himself gives an argument to show that figure-ground alignment is conceptually independent of foreground-background perspective (see §3.4 below). Langacker also argues that figure-ground is conceptually distinct from focus of attention, which suggests that the figure-ground distinction does not belong under the general category of attention either (pace Talmy 1988a:195; Talmy does not include figure-ground in the schematic systems in Talmy 2000).

Langacker makes greater use of the concepts **trajector** and **landmark**. A trajector is defined as the figure in a relational profile (Langacker 1987:217; see §3.5 for the definition of relationality); landmarks function as grounds to the trajector.

all respects (Heidegger 1927[1962]:79–80; cf. Dreyfus 1991:40–45). That is, we are always already in a situation and construing it from some perspective.

3.4.1   Viewpoint

It is easiest to begin illustrating perspectival construals with spatial examples. Langacker proposes **viewpoint** as a focal adjustment with two subtypes: vantage point and orientation (Langacker 1987:122–26). **Vantage point** was illustrated in (9a–b) in §3.1: the description of Timmy's position as being *in front of the tree* or *behind the tree* depends on the vantage point of the speaker.[6] A particular vantage point imposes a foreground-background alignment on a scene (ibid., 124–25).[7] Alternative construals of Timmy's position are achieved simply by the speaker moving to another position – that is, the linguistically expressed spatial relation is dependent on the speaker's situatedness. Vantage point is sensitive to construal; in (51), it is the vantage point of the addressee (at the relevant future time) that is used to interpret *behind*:

(51)   Follow my instructions carefully. Enter the woods by the south gate. Follow the path until you come to the big oak tree. You will find the box behind it.

Orientation refers to the vertical dimension, defined by a person's canonical upright position. One example of orientation is the choice of *above* and *below* in (3a–b) in §3.1 (along with a switch in figure-ground alignment): the actual chimney-window orientation described in (3a–b) is relative to the canonical orientation of the speaker. Alternative construals for orientation are much rarer, since we rarely go around standing on our heads or hanging from our feet.

3.4.2   Deixis

Deixis is the phenomenon of using elements of the subject's situatedness – more specifically, the subject qua speaker in a speech event – to designate something in the scene. Deixis has been widely studied (see, e.g., Levinson 1983, chapter 2), and we focus on deixis as construal here. Person deixis – the pronouns

[6] This analysis applies only to the **situational** use of *in front of/behind*. In sentences such as (9a–b), the choice of preposition is determined purely situationally, by the relative positions of speaker, Timmy and tree. In a sentence such as *The cat is in front of the house*, there is available another interpretation in which the house has an **inherent** orientation such that the side with the main entrance is the front side, regardless of the speaker's relative position. The remarks in this paragraph refer only to the purely situational interpretation.

[7] A number of linguists have argued that clausal subordination represents a foreground-background distinction, but it appears to be better analyzed as a figure-ground distinction (Talmy 1978, 2000; Reinhart 1984; Croft 2001).

I, you, he/she/it, we and *they* – are only defined relative to who is speaking, and this variation is an example of alternative construals defined by the speech act situation (§2.1). Likewise, deictic demonstratives such as *this* and *that*, and deictic time reference such as present and past tense, are only defined relative to the location and time of the speech event.

In addition to the relativity of spatiotemporal reference to the situation or perspective of the speech event, it is possible to construe another time and place as the deictic center. Examples (52a) and (52b) are construed with a deictic point of view at a place and time in the narrative; (52c) is bizarre because the point of view clashes with the reported information (Fillmore 1982b:262–63):

(52)   a. He was coming up the steps. There was a broad smile on his face.
       b. He was going up the steps. There was a wad of bubblegum on the seat of his pants.
       c. He was coming up the steps. There was a wad of bubblegum on the seat of his pants.

Likewise, the use of the so-called narrative present in (53b), or the 'sportcaster's present' in (54b), presents a construal of the time of the linguistic event, which has the effect of bringing the reported event conceptually closer to the listener (this construal also involves a 'moving' deictic center, moving with each reported event):

(53)   a. He came up behind me, I stopped suddenly, and he rammed into me.
       b. He comes up behind me, I stop suddenly, and he rams into me.
(54)   a. He hit the ball and the first baseman missed it.
       b. He hits the ball – the first baseman misses it . . .

In other words, deictic elements often display two layers of conceptualization: one relative to the situatedness of the speech act participants, and another construal that displaces the actual situatedness of the interlocutors to another time and place.

The situatedness of the speech act participants affects the structure of utterances in another, more profound way. The formulation of utterances is dependent on the shared knowledge, belief and attitudes of the interlocutors, what is often called the interlocutors' **common ground** (e.g. Clark 1996; Langacker [1987:127] calls it the epistemic ground). As Clark points out in many different contexts, what we choose to express in utterances and how we express it is determined to a great extent by what we assume is or is not part of the common ground; the common ground provides us with an epistemic perspective situating the speaker and the hearer.

The simplest example of epistemic perspective is the use of the definite and indefinite articles. Examples (55a–b) represent an alternative construal of what the hearer knows:

(55)   a. Did you see a hedgehog?
         b. Did you see the hedgehog?

Example (55a) construes the hedgehog as unknown to the hearer, while (55b) construes it as part of their common ground. The construal in (55b) could also be used in a context when the hearer in fact does not know about the hedgehog, as a way of surprising the hearer with the discovery by manipulating the epistemic deictic construal.

But in fact the wholesale structuring of clauses is determined by the epistemic perspective of common ground. This structuring often goes under the name of information structure or information packaging (Lambrecht 1994). Examples (6a–b) in §3.1 illustrate alternative construals of a scene based on a difference in information structure. The presentational sentence in (6a) (a subtype of what are also called thetic or sentence-focus structures; Lambrecht 1994:177) presents all of the information as part of the assertion directed to the hearer. The ordinary topic-comment (categorical or predicate-focus) sentence in (6b) presents the subject referent as part of a presupposition of current interest (and therefore part of the interlocutors' common ground) and only the predicate as part of the assertion (Lambrecht 1994:121). In fact, information structure is one of the clearest syntactic examples of alternative construals of what is the same scene from a truth-conditional point of view.

Another example of perspectival construal that has been discussed more by pragmatically oriented linguists than by cognitive linguists is the notion of **empathy** (Kuno and Kaburaki 1977). By empathy, Kuno and Kaburaki mean the participant in the reported event whose perspective is taken by the speaker. Empathy is perspectival and as such is subject to alternative construals. Kuno and Kaburaki argue that empathy is involved in the semantics of a number of grammatical constructions. For example, the choice of describing Bill as *John's brother*, that is, as a person anchored by his relation to John, instead of as *Bill* independent of John, implies that the speaker empathizes more with John than Bill. Likewise, choosing the passive *Bill was hit by John*, instead of the active *John hit Bill*, implies speaker empathy with the subject referent, namely Bill (compare [5a–b] in §3.1). Example (56c) is therefore odd compared to (56a–b), because of a clash in construed empathy: the speaker uses a description of Bill that implies empathy with John, combined with a grammatical voice that implies empathy with Bill (Kuno 1987:203–6):

(56)   a. Then John$_i$ hit his$_i$ brother.
         b. Then Bill was hit by John/his brother.
         c. ??Then John's brother$_i$ was hit by him$_i$.

Some linguists have argued that the distinction between the grammatical re-lations of subject and object is one of deixis or empathy. DeLancey (1981), in his analysis of split ergativity and subjecthood, argues that the unmarked subject category involves construing the orientation of the speaker towards the temporal and causal beginning of the event. On the other hand, Langacker (1991a:305–17) defines subjecthood in terms of the most prominent figure, which combines the construal operations of attention (most prominent) and judgement (figure). Whichever is the correct analysis – and it is possible that different languages use different construals for subjecthood – the point is that fundamental grammatical categories such as subject, which are treated as 'meaningless' in some syntactic theories, represent a construal of the referent in the situation described by the ut-terance, and the construal analysis can predict patterns of (un)acceptability such as that found in (56a–c).

3.4.3   Subjectivity

The last construal operation under perspective in Table 3.1 is Langacker's notion of **subjectivity/objectivity**. This refers to how one conceptualizes a scene that includes the speaker herself/himself. Two simple if restricted examples illus-trate the alternative construals (Langacker 1987:131):

(57)   [*said by mother to child:*]
         a. Don't lie to me!
         b. Don't lie to your mother!

Example (57a) represents the more common **subjective** construal of the speaker using a deictic personal pronoun, defining her identity relative to the speech act situation. Example (57b) involves **objectification**: the speaker describes herself in terms independent of the speech act situation.

It is also possible to **subjectify** reference to an entity (Langacker 1987:132):

(58)   That's me in the top row. [*said when examining a photograph*]

In (58), an entity that is not the speaker, namely the physical image in the pho-tograph, is described using a deictic expression (*me*), as is in fact common in so-called picture noun contexts (see also §2.6). Another, more common example of subjectification is the construal implied when using certain spatial expressions that can leave a ground object unexpressed (Langacker 1991b:326, 328):

(59)   a. Vanessa is sitting across the table from Veronica.
         b. Vanessa is sitting across the table from me.
         c. Vanessa is sitting across the table.

Example (59c) is an instance of subjectification of the *across* phrase: (59c) can only refer to the situation where Vanessa is sitting across the table from the speaker (unlike [59a]), yet explicit reference to the speech act participant is absent (unlike [59b]). Langacker argues that many grammatical expressions, and also the process of grammaticalization in language change, crucially involve subjectification (Langacker 1991b, chapter 10; 1998); unfortunately, space prevents us from presenting Langacker's analyses here.

Perspectival construals all result from our being in the world in a particular location and manner. From a purely bodily point of view, we are in a particular spatial location in the world (vantage point) and in a canonical upright orientation. From a communicative perspective, we are situated as participants in the speech event, which defines our spatial and temporal location and our roles in the speech event (deixis). Our roles in the speech event, however, also define the status of the situation to be communicated in speaking (epistemic deixis), our attitude towards it (empathy), and our presentation of ourselves in that situation (subjectivity).

3.5   Constitution/Gestalt

The construal operations to be described in this section represent the conceptualization of the very structure of the entities in a scene. These construal operations represent the most basic level of **constituting** experience and giving it structure or a **Gestalt**, as described by Gestalt psychologists (Koffka 1935; Wertheimer 1923[1950]) and phenomenologists such as Husserl (who uses the term 'constitution' in a similar context; see Husserl 1948[1973]). For example, many of the principles of Gestalt psychology such as proximity, bounding and good continuation are analyses of how human minds construe a single complex object from seemingly fragmented perceptual sensations. In cognitive linguistics, the most detailed discussion of constitutive construals is by Talmy, under his imaging systems of structural schematization (Talmy 1988a) and force dynamics (Talmy 1988b; both revised and expanded in Talmy 2000). In addition, most of the image schemas described by Lakoff, Johnson and Turner are construals of the structure of entities.

3.5.1   *Structural schematization*

Structural schematization describes the conceptualization of the topological, meronomic and geometrical structure of entities and their component parts. The subgrouping in Table 3.1 attempts to classify the wide range of structural schematizations (for a more complete inventory, see Talmy 2000:47–68). The first subgroup, **individuation**, includes whether or not entities are individuated (bound-edness), and if so, their unity and relation to their parts, and their multiplicity if more than one individual is construed.

Such basic structural properties of entities are manifested in the choice of a count noun, mass noun or pluralia tanta form for nouns, and aspectual inflections for verbs. Even these properties are a matter of construal. For example, boundedness is not simply a spatial or material property. A *person, star* and *island* represent individuals bounded spatiotemporally; but a *team, constellation* and *archipelago* are also bounded entities (count nouns) where the speaker has construed them as whole units with distinct parts; even nothingness can be bounded as in *hole* or *intermission* (Langacker 1987:200–1).

In many cases there are alternative expressions for what appear to be the same entities that differ in their construal of structure (see especially Wierzbicka 1985). Examples (1a–b) in §3.1, the count noun *leaves* vs. the mass noun *foliage*, is one case. *Foliage* construes the entity as a relatively homogeneous substance, without clear boundaries (a mass of foliage can be borne on several trees). *Leaf* construes the entity as a bounded individual, which in turn is part of a single tree; *leaves* multiplies the individual, making it truth-conditionally comparable to *foliage* in the right contexts. Either construal is available through the lexicon of English. There is also a quantitative scalar adjustment involved: *leaves* evokes a more fine-grained construal than *foliage*. Similarly, *chocolate* as a mass noun is a homogeneous, unbounded substance, while *a chocolate* is a bounded individual with internal structure, the characteristic construal of a count noun (conventionalized in this case; see [7a–b]). Again, the mass noun represents a more coarse-grained scalar adjustment. Countability also interacts with qualitative scalar adjustment: *chair* construes the entity as individuated and of a specific type; *furniture* construes it as an abstract mass along with tables, sofas, beds and so on in a coarse-grained schematization.

The bounded/unbounded structural schematization also applies to states and processes, as in (8a–b) from §3.1 (Croft 1998a, in prep.). The simple tense/aspect in *Ira is a nuisance* construes Ira's behavior as a temporally unbounded behavioral trait of Ira that abstracts away from individual instances of nuisance behavior on Ira's part. On the other hand, the progressive in *Ira, stop being a nuisance!* provides a finer-grained scalar adjustment that construes an individual bounded action of Ira's.

Image schemas such as containers or surfaces represent a construal of a more specific **topological** or **geometric** structure of objects. Herskovits 1986 provides a detailed and insightful construal analysis of geometric structure, only two examples from which can we present here. There are natural construals of objects that lend themselves to being containers or flat objects, such as *in the box* or *on the carpet*;

but there are also many examples of alternative construals of objects (Herskovits 1986:76):

(60)   a. There is milk in the bowl.
         b. There is dust on the bowl.

If there is a lot of dust or a few drops of milk, the actual spatial configuration of figure and ground in (60a) and (60b) is not that much different. But since the function of bowls is to contain potable liquids, the bowl is construed as a container with *in* in (60a), and since dust is thought of as an extraneous substance, the bowl is construed as a surface with *on* in (60b).

The geometric construal of an object often requires selective attention (Herskovits 1986:65, 67):

(61)   a. She is under the tree.
         b. The cat is under the table.
         c. One could see the shiny silver carp under the water.

In (61a), she is unlikely to be under the ground or inside the trunk (though such a construal is possible if, say, the suspect is leading the detective to the location of the body of the murder victim). The usual construal selects only the lower surface of the foliage as the underside of the object. In (61b), selection ignores the table legs, and scalar adjustment reduces the tabletop to a two-dimensional surface. In (61c), selection (driven by encyclopedic knowledge) profiles only the top surface of the water to specify the figure-ground relationship (and all of these examples are construed relative to the speaker's canonical upright orientation, of course).

Another image schema that imposes a structure, this time more typically associated with properties, is the **scale** image schema, which provides a gradable dimension to a domain, which may or may not be measurable. The ways in which an entity is construed as possessing a scale or multiple scales are described in detail in §7.4. Here we simply note that the same domain may be construed with a scale (in contrast to a polar construal, as in [62a–b] and [63a–b]), or construed as calibratable, as in (64), a domain not usually considered measurable:

(62)   a. Sally's pregnant.
         b. Sally's very pregnant.
(63)   a. Here is a used washing machine.
         b. Let me offer you this slightly used washing machine for only
            $300!
(64)   a. This Sauternes has a fragrant bouquet.
         b. The bouquet of the Fargues is twice as fragrant as that of the Climens.

3.5.2   Force dynamics

A second major category of constitutive construals is the **force dynamic** model of the conceptualization of events (Talmy 1976, 1988b, 2000). The force dynamic model is a generalization of the notion of causation, in which processes are conceptualized as involving different kinds of forces acting in different ways upon the participants of the event. The examples in (65) illustrate some of the force-dynamic patterns that Talmy analyzes:

(65)   a. I kicked the ball.
         b. I held the ball.
         c. I dropped the ball.

Example (65a) represents the prototypical causative type: an antagonist (the causer) forces an agonist (the causee – the ball) that tends towards rest to move. Example (65b) extends the notion of causation to maintaining a rest state: the antagonist resists the agonist's tendency to move. Example (65c) further extends to notion of causation to enablement: the antagonist acts in a way that allows the agonist to exert its tendency towards motion.

Croft (1991, 1998b, in prep.) argues that the force-dynamic structure of events largely determines the encoding of subject, object and oblique arguments of predicates. For instance, the choice of *for* in *I baked brownies for Mary* vs. *with* in *I beat the eggs with a fork* is determined by the fact that Mary is the endpoint, the beneficiary of the baking event, while the fork acts upon the eggs and is therefore an intermediate participant in the force-dynamic chain. The difference in degree of affectedness of *chew the bone* and *chew on the bone* in (11a–b) in §3.1 is a (conventionalized) consequence of the alternative construals of the degree of affectedness of the bone evoked by the object-oblique contrast.

Different choices of verbs, or different voice forms, or different argument-linking constructions, express different conceptualizations of the force-dynamic structure of the event. For example, (66a) construes the situation as force-dynamically neutral (being a static situation), but (66b) construes the situation as having a force-dynamic value of resisting the effects of some (unspecified) force-applying process.

(66)   a. The bowl was on the table.
         b. The bowl stayed on the table.

The alternative transitive and intransitive constructions in (67a–b) construe the event as externally caused or as self-contained (which allows [67b] to be used if no external agent or force is manifest as well as when the speaker wishes only to construe the event as such):

(67)   a. She opened the door.
        b. The door opened.

Force and resistance play a role in the construal of semantic domains other than causation. For example, Talmy (1988b) and Sweetser (1990, chapter 3) argue that deontic modals such as *may* and *must* in (68a–b) construe the deontic modality as letting causation or the absence of resistance ([68a]; compare [65c]) vs. the application of force ([68b]; compare [65a]):

(68)   a. You may leave.
        b. You must leave.

Sweetser extends this analysis metaphorically to the epistemic meanings of the modals in (69):

(69)   a. She may be ill.
        b. She must be ill.

May in (69a) indicates the absence of resistance from concluding that the proposition *She is ill* is true, while *must* in (69b) forces one to the conclusion that *She is ill* is true.

3.5.3   Relationality (entity/interconnection)

Finally, an even more fundamental constitutive property of entities is subject to construal. Many semanticists distinguish between **relational** and **nonrelational** entities. A relational entity inherently implies the existence of another entity. For example, an adjectival concept such as ROUND cannot be conceived of without reference to something that is round, and a verbal concept such as RUN cannot be conceived of without reference to a runner. A nonrelational entity can be so conceived: for example, a nominal concept such as TABLE can be conceived of without reference to another entity.

Langacker argues that the difference between nouns ('things' in his conceptual terminology) and adjectives or verbs is that the latter are relational and the former are not (Langacker 1987:214–17). Thus, in Langacker's conceptual scheme, verbs ('processes') are construed as relational and sequentially scanned (see §3.2); adjectives and other modifiers ('atemporal relations') are construed as relational but summarily scanned; and nouns ('things') are construed as nonrelational and summarily scanned.

Langacker's definition of relationality rests on his definition of things/nounhood. He argues that nounhood construes a concept as a region or 'set of interconnected entities' (Langacker 1987:198); entities are nonrelational. Contrasting nonrelational things with relational concepts, Langacker describes a relational concept as profiling the interconnections between entities while a noun profiles the entities that are interconnected (ibid., 216). For example, one can think of the (nonrelational) noun *circle* as profiling the points (entities) that make up the circle, while the (relational) adjective *round* profiles the interconnections that define the circle's curvature.

Langacker's definition of relational vs. nonrelational suggests that a construal as an entity (or set of entities) is a better definition of nounhood than functioning as a region. A verbal or adjectival concept such as *round* involves a region also, but profiles its interconnections instead of its entities. Moreover, Langacker's example of *circle* vs. *round* also reveals that entity and interconnection are not givens, but instead involve conceptualization. The noun *roundness* does not profile the points/entities making up a round thing; it does not mean the same thing as *circle*, or even *round object*. Instead, *roundness* construes the shape as an entity, rather than as interconnections as the adjective *round* does. In fact, Langacker notes that anything can be construed as an entity, including interconnections (ibid., 198). Conversely, a predicate nominal construction like *be a circle* – which in many other languages is simply the word 'circle' inflected more or less like a verbal predicate – construes the set of entities as an interconnection, namely the relation of being an instance of the type defined by the noun (Croft 1991:69–70).

Examples (10a–b) in §3.1 illustrate the entity-interconnection construal. *Jill is fussy* construes the trait as relational, and thus introduces a degree of separation between the behavioral trait and the person (expressed as subject). *Be a fussbudget* construes the trait as nonrelational, and therefore saying that *Jill is a fussbudget* can only be construed as membership of a category of persons who are defined by this behavioral trait. Hence (10b) makes out Jill as a more problematic child than does (10a).

Constitutive construal operations are somewhat different from the construal operations resulting from the cognitive abilities of attention, comparison and perspective. Constitutive construal operations provide a structure to the experience being communicated. As such, they are not unlike domains, as has been noted for image schemas, most of which are constitutive construal operations (Clausner and Croft 1999:16–25). There are many words denoting concepts that must be profiled in an image-schematic domain, such as *more, very, in, part, alike, force* (see §2.2; in fact, such words make up Parts I and II of *Roget's Thesaurus*). Image schemas also have a complex internal structure, like domains:

> . . . image schematic gestalts have considerable internal structure – they are not undifferentiated. On the contrary, it is the organization of their structure that makes them experientially basic meaningful patterns in our experience and

understanding. The schema for these gestalts have parts and dimensions that stand
in various relationships that allow us to make sense of our experience. (Johnson
1987:61)

Johnson notes that many image schemas are experienced together and describes
this as a superposition of schemas, using the example of things we co-experience
as both near us and central to our vantage point vs. things far away and peripheral:
'The CENTER-PERIPHERY schema is almost never experienced in an isolated or
self-contained fashion . . . Given a center and a periphery, we will also experience
the NEAR-FAR schema as stretching along our perceptual or conceptual perspective' (Johnson 1987:125). The superimposition of image schemas is identical to
the combination of domains in a domain matrix. In fact, image-schematic domains
are usually combined in a matrix with ordinary domains. For example, our experience of degrees of weight combines the SCALE image schema(tic domain) with
another basic domain, WEIGHT. It is very difficult to separate WEIGHT and
SCALE, but in this respect, WEIGHT and SCALE represent the tightest relationship between domains in a domain matrix, that is, what Langacker describes as
dimensions of a domain (see §2.4).

The analysis of (constitutive) image schemas as image-schematic domains is
not incompatible with their function as construal operations, because domains
themselves are construals, framing the experience to be communicated in a certain
way. What makes image schemas worthy of separate treatment here is their pervasiveness in experience: to be communicated, our experience must be construed
in terms of basic structure, scales and force dynamics.

3.6   Conclusion

As the preceding discussion demonstrates, any sentence involves a myriad
of construals of the experience to be communicated. Everything from the choice
of words and their part of speech to the various inflections and constructions that
make up the grammatical structure of an utterance involves conceptualization.
Even fundamental conceptual properties such as the categorization of experiences
and their basic structure is subject to construal. This fact raises two questions, one
more technical and one more philosophical.

The more technical question is: how do the construal operations interact? Two
general observations can be made about the interaction of construal operations.
The first is that construal operations can be nested or iterated (Talmy 2000: 84–
88; Herskovits 1986:57–59; Langacker 1987:138–46). Talmy illustrates nesting
with the examples of a gradually built up set of structural schematizations in (70)

(Talmy 2000:84):

(70)   a. The beacon flashed (as I glanced over).
        b. The beacon kept flashing.
        c. The beacon flashed five times in a row.
        d. The beacon kept flashing five times at a stretch.
        e. The beacon flashed five times at a stretch for three hours.

In (70a), *flash* is construed as a single individuated event. In (70b), the event is construed as iterated. In (70c), the iterated event is bounded by the number of iterations; (70d) iterates the bounded iterated event of (70c), and (70e) bounds the iterated complex event of (70d).

Herskovits represents nested geometric construal operations as semantic functions, as in (71) (Herskovits 1986:59–60):

(71)   a. The bird is in the bush.
        b. Included(Part(Place(Bird)), Interior(Outline(VisiblePart(Place (Bush)))))

The formula in (71b) describes the most natural construal of (71a): a scene in which (at least) part of the spatial region occupied by the bird is included – the meaning of *in* – in the interior space defined by the outline of the visible part of the spatial region occupied by the bush.

The second general observation is that the layers of construal operations must yield a conceptually unified construal of the meaning of the utterance (Croft 1993[2002]:163, 194–99). Croft argues that all of the concepts in a single clause must be construed as part of a single unified domain.[8] Examples (72)–(73), for example, must be construed wholly in the domain of emotion and semantic content respectively; this requires a metaphorical construal of the spatial preposition *in* in (72) and a metonymic construal of the human proper name *Proust* in (73) (ibid., 195):

(72)   She's in a good mood.
(73)   Proust is tough to read.

In (72)–(73), the alternative construal of one word in the clause (*in, Proust*) is driven by the normal or 'literal' construal of another word or phrase in the clause (*mood, read*). However, all that matters is that the entire clause is construed in a single domain. It is possible that alternative construals are available for the entire

---

[8] In the original 1993 paper, Croft argues that only immediate clause dependents must be conceptually unified; the internal structure of argument phrases may be unified around a different domain. Nunberg's analysis of metonymy suggests that even argument phrases must conform to the unity of domain (Nunberg 1995; see also §3.2.1).

clause, leading to ambiguity as in (74), or a construal that is outside the 'literal' meanings of any of the words, as in (75) (Croft 1993[2002]:198, 199):

(74)   This book is heavy. (*physically weighty or emotionally powerful*)
(75)   The newspaper went under. (*construed in the domain of business activity*)

The conceptual unity of domain is only one of three conceptual unities that a clause must obey. The referents in a clause must be construed as belonging to a single place and time in a mental space (Fauconnier 1985; Croft 1993[2002]:200). Thus in (76), the hearer must construe the referent of *her sister* to exist in Margaret's belief space (whether or not Margaret has a sister in reality, or whether or not the description *her sister* applies to the referent in Margaret's belief space), and must construe the referent of *a car* to exist in the same space (again, whether or not a specific car fitting the description exists in reality):

(76)   Margaret believes that her sister bought a car.

The referents in a clause must also conform to a single instantiation of the event plus participants (Croft 1993[2002]:201). This unity of selection accounts for the interaction between verbal aspect, noun countability and adverbial construals, as in (77)–(78):

(77)   a. Sally drinks wine.
         b. Sally spilled wine on the carpet.
(78)   a. Dan wrote the letters in two hours.
         b. Dan wrote letters for two hours.

In (77a), the situation is construed as generic (hence unbounded and not referring to a specific event); so *wine* must be construed as referring to the type. In (77b), the situation is construed as specific and bounded, so *wine* must be construed as referring to a specific bounded amount of the liquid. In (78a), the situation is construed as bounded by the definite noun phrase and the compatible adverbial phrase *in two hours*; so *write* is construed as bounded (telic). In (78b), the situation is construed as unbounded and specific by the adverbial phrase *for two hours*, so the unbounded bare plural *letters* is construed as specific (not generic as in *I hate to write letters*), and *write* is construed as specific and unbounded.

The more philosophical question that construal raises is, what is the relationship between language, thought and experience? Are there any constraints on the relationship, and in which direction do the constraints operate: from language to thought to experience, or the reverse direction, or both?

In a number of places in this chapter, we have referred to the typical construal of a particular experience: for example, pregnancy is typically construed as not gradable, a smaller, movable object is typically construed as figure, an action is typically scanned sequentially, and so on. The nature of our experience in many instances favors certain construals over others. It is these widespread typical or **default** construals that have led semanticists to posit a more rigid model of the mapping from linguistic meaning to experience. Cognitive linguists emphasize that flexibility is necessary for understanding conceptualization, and this flexibility is due to the nature of the human mind as it engages with the world. But experience does constrain human conceptualization to some degree, rendering some construals difficult and others almost impossible.

It appears that the pervasive role of conceptualization in linguistic expression entails a relativistic approach to the relation between language and thought: the way we conceive our experience is determined by the grammatical structure of our language. This strongly relativistic formulation is not generally found in cognitive linguistics, however.

Langacker argues that language-specific semantic structure must be distinguished from a universal conceptual structure (Langacker 1976). Langacker rejects the claim that 'semantic structure can, in some unclear but hopefully straightforward way, be related directly to thought and cognition, i.e. the structures manipulated in cognition are essentially the same as the semantic structures underlying sentences' (ibid.). In discussing an example from Whorf, who compares the English *He invites people for a feast* to its nearest Nootka equivalent, which literally translates into something like 'He goes for eaters of cooked (food)' (ibid., 342–44), Langacker suggests that both could be expressing the same cognitive experience, but employ different semantic structures to express the experience. As Lakoff puts it, 'experience does not *determine* conceptual systems, [it] only *motivates* them' (Lakoff 1987:310).

Langacker calls language-specific semantic structures **conventional imagery**. The semantic representations of Cognitive Grammar, many examples of which have been used in this chapter, are intended to describe this conventional imagery, not the presumably universal cognitive structures that these conventional images construe. Langacker uses the example of the expression of bodily states (Langacker 1976:345) to illustrate his approach: English speakers say 'I am cold', whereas French speakers say literally 'I have cold' and Modern Hebrew speakers say 'It is cold to me.' In Langacker's view, 'these expressions differ semantically even though they refer to the same experience, for they employ different images to structure the same basic conceptual content' (Langacker 1987:47).

The question remains as to the status of these conventional images in thought. Langacker suggests that it is relatively ephemeral:

> When we use a particular construction or grammatical morpheme, we thereby select a particular image to structure the conceived situation for communicative

purposes. Because languages differ in their grammatical structure, they differ in the imagery that speakers employ when conforming to linguistic convention. The relativistic view does not per se imply that lexicogrammatical structure imposes any significant constraints on our thought process – in fact I suspect it to be rather superficial (cf. Langacker 1976). The symbolic resources of a language generally provide an array of alternative images for describing a given scene, and we shift from one to another with great facility, often within the confines of a single sentence. The conventional imagery invoked for linguistic expression is a fleeting thing that neither defines nor constrains the contents of our thoughts (Langacker 1991b:12).

Slobin (1991) suggests a somewhat similar view, which he describes as 'thinking for speaking': the conceptualization of experience found in grammar is relevant for communication, but not necessarily relevant for other cognitive activities.

However, not all construals are conventional; there are many cases of novel language use that will represent novel construals, and all conventional construals began as novel. Even some conventional construals are still perceived as 'loaded.' Croft (2001, chapter 3) suggests a stronger role for active construal which he calls the **conventional universalist** position. When a grammatical structure is used for the first time (or the first few times) to construe an experience, it does influence the way speakers think of that experience. But as the extension of that grammatical expression to the new experience becomes conventionalized – that is, it becomes the normal or even the only way to talk about the experience – then the original construal no longer constrains how speakers think of that experience. Evidence for the conventional universalist position includes the fact that the extended construction displays grammatical behavior incompatible with the original construal but applicable to the experience being communicated. For example, in French the expression of bodily states is construed as possession; compare (79a) to (79b):

(79)   a. J'ai froid. 'I am cold' [lit. 'I have cold']
         b. J'ai une voiture. 'I have a car.'

But bodily states can be construed as gradable, which is incompatible with possession (Croft 2001:115):

(80)   a. J'ai très froid. 'I am very cold' [lit. 'I have very cold']
         b. *J'ai très une voiture. [lit. 'I have very a car']

Construal is a central aspect of language and its relation to thought; but it is constrained by convention as well as by the experience itself. This hypothesis guides the approach to categorization in the next chapter.

4

Categories, concepts and meanings

4.1   Introduction

The act of categorization is one of the most basic human cognitive activities. Categorization involves the apprehension of some individual entity, some particular of experience, as an instance of something conceived more abstractly that also encompasses other actual and potential instantiations. For instance, a specific animal can be construed as an instantiation of the species DOG, a specific patch of color as a manifestation of the property RED, and so on. We shall call this abstract mental construct a **conceptual category**. Conceptual categories can be regarded as cognitive tools, and are usually credited with a number of general functions:

(a) *Learning*. Experiences never recur exactly: our ability to learn from past experience would be severely impaired if we could not relate the present to similar aspects of past experience, that is, by putting them into the same conceptual categories.

(b) *Planning*. The formulation of goals and plans to achieve them also requires knowledge to be disassociated from individuals and packaged into concepts characterizing categories of entities.

(c) *Communication*. Language works in terms of generalities, that is, in terms of categories. Any linguistic expression, however detailed, in the end represents only a category of referents.

(d) *Economy*. Knowledge does not (all) need to be related to individual members: a significant amount can be stored in relation to groups of individuals. New knowledge gained on the basis of interaction with one or more individuals can be easily generalized to other members of category. Conversely, knowing, on the basis of a limited number of criteria, that an individual belongs to a particular category, can give access to a much wider range of information about that individual.

There is an important distinction to be made between generic concepts like CAT and TERRORIST, and individual concepts like TONY BLAIR and CLEOPATRA. The process of categorization presupposes a more basic one, namely, that of classifying particular experiences as experiences of one and the same individual entity. In both cases a Gestalt is formed, but they are different sorts of Gestalt. Both are construals, in our sense. An adult human has knowledge about thousands of individual items, not just persons, but also objects, places and so on. A large proportion of things communicated about and consciously entertained are individual in nature: consciousness is largely inhabited by individuals. Generic concepts mostly function to identify and/or characterize individuals. A particular individual concept is also a bundle of knowledge, perhaps very rich, perhaps sketchy in the extreme. An individual concept is not itself a final construal, as it is capable of almost unlimited modulation, particularly via the descriptive content of definite referring expressions (e.g. *that shifty-looking character standing beside the piano*). Such content has a dual function: it contributes to the narrowing down of the search space in which the referent is located, and it modulates the eventual construal of the individual concept. Most experimental work and theorizing, both in cognitive psychology and cognitive linguistics, has been concerned with generic concepts rather than individual concepts.

Conceptual categories can be viewed from several different perspectives, which, although connected, should be clearly distinguished. We shall be mainly concerned with three of these. Firstly, conceptual categories can be viewed as collections of individuals. The properties of collections are distinct from the properties of the individuals that constitute them. The two properties that will concern us most are, first, category boundaries, and second, graded centrality, that is, the fact that a category typically has a core tapering to a periphery. Secondly, we can look at a conceptual category from the point of view of the individuals that make up the category: how can we characterize them, and how can we distinguish them from members of other categories? Thirdly, there is the question of the level of categorization. This is partly a matter of inclusiveness – some categories include others as subcategories – and hence is a relative property, but as we shall see, there are grounds for proposing absolute levels with definable characteristics. We shall treat level of categorization as being determined by the type and quantity of information in the characterization of members of the category.

The view of conceptual categories as fixed cognitive entities with stable associations with linguistic expressions has been, and still is, the dominant one in cognitive psychology and linguistics. However, more recently, a dynamic picture of concepts is emerging, in which they are viewed as being created at the moment of use. On this view, all aspects of conceptual categories are subject to construal. This is the view that will be adopted in this book, alongside a parallel view of word meaning. Before expounding the **dynamic construal** approach, we first survey the theories of conceptual structure that have had the greatest influence on the development of cognitive linguistics.

4.2   The classical model of category structure

The so-called classical model of conceptual categories defines them in terms of a set of necessary and sufficient features. The features are necessary in that no entity that does not possess the full set is a member of the category, and they are sufficient in that possession of all the features guarantees membership. Thus, the category COLT may be defined by the features [EQUINE], [MALE], [YOUNG]. This basic idea is of great antiquity, but the immediate inspiration for its adoption by psychologists such as Collins and Quillian (1969) was its use in structuralist semantics, and later by Katz and Fodor (1963). In the Katz and Fodor system, some features were binary and others not. Binary features had only two values, present or absent. For instance, the definition of FILLY would differ from that of COLT in the value of the feature denoting sex: COLT would be [EQUINE], [MALE+], [ADULT−], whereas FILLY would be [EQUINE], [MALE−], [ADULT−]; MARE would be defined by the features [EQUINE], [MALE−], [ADULT+], and STALLION by [EQUINE], [MALE+], [ADULT+]. Non-binary features such as [EQUINE] belonged to sets of 'antonymous n-tuples,' only one of which may be present in any individual (that is to say, a combination of features such as [EQUINE], [CANINE], [FELINE] would be impossible). This picture of category structure is typically accompanied by the 'nesting assumption' (Hahn and Chater 1997:47), which states that a subordinate concept, such as ROBIN, contains as part of its definition the features defining a superordinate concept such as BIRD (in construction grammar, this is called 'inheritance' – see §10.2.1). Collins and Quillian (1969) incorporated the feature definition of concepts, together with the nesting assumption, in their proposal for a hierarchical model of semantic memory.

The classical model establishes a clear and rigid boundary to a category. Inclusion relations between categories are also captured, but no account is possible of absolute levels of categorization (see below). It is important to note that a classical definition of an entity is not a full description of it or its place in the world: one has only to think of one's experience and knowledge of, say, a kitten, in comparison with the definition [FELINE][DOMESTIC+][ADULT−].

The difficulties faced by the classical model of conceptual categories are many. Three frequently cited shortcomings have provided the major motivation for the development of alternative theories. Firstly, for many everyday concepts, as Wittgenstein pointed out with his well-known example of GAME, adequate definitions in terms of necessary and sufficient features are simply not available. Furthermore, as Fillmore (1975) pointed out in connection with the noun *bachelor*, even for those concepts that seem to have definitions, the definitions typically hold only within a specific domain (see discussion of *bachelor* in §2.5). Secondly, what is here called 'graded centrality' constitutes a problem; that is, the fact that some members of a category are judged 'better', or 'more representative' of the category than others: in a classical category, all members are equal. Thirdly, the classical model can offer no account of why category boundaries, in practice, seem to be vague and variable (they are frequently described as 'fuzzy', but our account will be somewhat different). A model of category structure is supposed to provide a basis for an account of how we use categories in remembering, planning, reasoning and so on. A classical definition is not a very efficient vehicle for this purpose, because the information it contains is too sparse.

Several theories of the nature of natural categories have been proposed, mostly in the psychological literature, but the theory that has had the most influence on the development of cognitive linguistics is undoubtedly prototype theory, to which we now turn.

4.3   The prototype model of category structure

The pioneering experimental and theoretical work on prototype theory was carried out by Rosch and her co-workers (see Rosch 1973, 1978; Rosch and Mervis 1975), although this built on earlier insights, notably Wittgenstein 1953 and Brown 1958.

4.3.1   Graded centrality

Not all members of a category have the same status within the category. People have intuitions that some category members are better examples of the category than others. Members that are judged to be the best examples of a category can be considered to be the most central in the category. There has been a considerable amount of experimental work by cognitive psychologists on the notion of **Goodness-Of-Exemplar** (henceforward **GOE**). The most basic experimental procedure is simply to present subjects with a category and a list of putative members of the category and to ask them to assign to each member a numerical score from 1 to 7 according to how good an example it is, with 1 designating a very good example, and 7 a very poor example or not an example at all. Subjects reportedly have no difficulty grasping what is required of them. Furthermore, provided the subjects are drawn from a more-or-less uniform speech community, the results cluster strongly around particular values (in other words, subjects are not responding at random). Combining the results from a large number of subjects allows the identification of the best examples of categories: these are typically referred to as the **prototypes** or **prototypical members** of the category. So, for instance, if the category was VEGETABLE, the ratings of various items (by British subjects) might be as follows (these scores represent the ratings of one of the authors):

	GOE rating
LEEK, CARROT	1
BROCCOLI, PARSNIP	2
CELERY, BEETROOT	3
AUBERGINE, COURGETTE	4
PARSLEY, BASIL	5
RHUBARB	6
LEMON	7

GOE ratings may be strongly culture dependent. (Familiarity is undoubtedly a factor influencing GOE scores, but the scores cannot be reduced to familiarity.) For instance, in a British context (say, a typical class of undergraduates), DATE typically receives a GOE score of 3–5 relative to the category of FRUIT, but an audience of Jordanians accorded it an almost unanimous 1.

The significance of GOE scores is enhanced by experiments showing that they correlate to a significant degree with a number of independent properties. The following is a selection of these properties ('a high GOE score' means one that is close to 1).

(i) *Frequency and order of mention.* When subjects are asked to list as many examples of a given category as possible, usually within a time limit, the overall frequency of mention of an item shows a strong correlation with its GOE score, while the average position of an item in lists correlates inversely with GOE.

(ii) *Order of learning.* By and large, children learn prototypical members of categories before more peripheral members. (This may, however, simply be a function of the frequency of words addressed to them.)

(iii) *Family resemblance.* Items with a high GOE rating have a higher degree of **family resemblance** (measured by sharing of features) to other category members than items with low GOE ratings, and a lower degree of resemblance to members of other categories.

(iv) *Verification speed.* In typical experiments, subjects see two words flashed onto a screen. Their task is to answer as quickly as possible 'Yes' if the second word denotes a member of the category designated by the first word, and 'No' if it does not (e.g. VEGETABLE: CARROT, VEHICLE: CHAIR). The subjects' speed of response is measured. It is found that responses are faster to items with a higher GOE score.

(v) *Priming.* Priming experiments frequently use the **lexical decision task**: subjects are presented with a string of letters and have to say as quickly as possible whether or not the string forms a word. Presenting a semantically related word, or the same word, before a test item has the effect of speeding up subjects' responses: this phenomenon is known as **priming**. The relevant case here is when the prime is a category name, like FRUIT. The degree of speeding up is the priming effect. The priming effect correlates with the GOE score of the category member, that is, for Britons, FRUIT will speed up the response to APPLE to a greater degree than the response to, for instance, DATE.

Psycholinguistic variables such as verification speed and priming are regarded as particularly significant correlates of GOE because they are not under conscious control and therefore can be claimed to reveal underlying properties of categories.

There has been some dispute in the literature regarding the relationship between the GOE of an item and its **degree of membership** (henceforward **DOM**) in the category. Some say that, in giving GOE scores, subjects are in fact giving DOM scores. However, this is misleading. What they were asked to do was to rate items as to how good they were as members of particular categories. Saying that they were giving DOM ratings is a subsequent interpretation. Those who object to the equation of GOE and DOM (for instance, Lakoff [1987:45], Pulman [1983], Cruse [1992b]), point to examples like OSTRICH in the category BIRD. There is no doubt, they say, that an ostrich is a fully paid-up member of the BIRD category, but also undeniably has a low GOE, hence the two parameters must be independent. Ungerer and Schmid (1996) claim not to see a problem, but they do not throw any light on the matter. Taylor (1989[1997]) claims that both assessments of OSTRICH are DOM judgements, but they are made with respect to differently construed categories. An ostrich is judged a full member relative to an 'expert' category, which has clear membership criteria; the graded membership judgement is made relative to the everyday category BIRD, which does not have clear membership criteria. This is ingenious, and we are sympathetic to the appeal to different construals of categories denoted by the same lexical item, but Taylor's account does not stand up to close scrutiny.

The first point to make is that yes/no judgements and graded judgements co-exist as alternative construals in many semantic domains. Take, for example, the case of *dead* and *alive*. The domain of what might be called 'vital status' is often construed dichotomously: saying *John is dead* normally commits one to the truth of *John is not alive*. But also possible to say *John is more alive than Mary*. This does not change the domain, but reconstrues it as a gradable scale. The same is true of category membership. In the case of BIRD (whether construed as an expert category or an everyday one), anything on the right side of the boundary is *in the category*, but at the same time, variable centrality allows a gradable construal of some things as *more in the category* than others, hence there is some legitimacy in interpreting GOE as DOM.

At the same time, there is something counterintuitive about saying that an ostrich is, say, only 30% a bird, and perhaps the term DOM should be reserved for a distinctive property. We may think of a category as a container (i.e., a result of the imposition of the Lakoffian CONTAINER image-schema on a domain). What would we normally understand by a description of an object as *30% in a container*? Surely something like a teddy bear that is partly in and partly out of the toy box, rather than one that is nearer the side of the box than the middle? There is a category equivalent of this picture. When we say that, for instance, a priest is *to some extent a social worker*, we are effectively placing him part-in, part-out of the category (cf. Lakoff 1973). That is to say, we are construing the categories PRIEST and SOCIAL WORKER as partially overlapping. This is surely a more useful conception of DOM. (NB: the view expressed here regarding DOM is significantly different from that in Cruse 1992.)

Two problems may be signaled here in connection with GOE experiments and results. One concerns the meaning attributed, in the context of the experiments, to expressions such as *How good is X as an example of category Y?* How, exactly, is *How good?* interpreted? Used in actual contexts, *good* and *better* do not normally give rise to communicative problems. For instance, the goodness of a dog, if thought of as a pet for a young child, is different from what it would be if it was thought of as providing security for a house, or as contributing to the life of a farm. This does not destroy the notion of GOE, but suggests that truly significant results would require specific construals of both the categories being judged and the meaning of *good*. Various at least partially distinct notions of goodness can be teased out (see, for instance, Lakoff 1987:84–90). The following are the main types:

(i) *Typicality/representativeness*. This indicates how accurate/useful an idea of a category one would get from familiarity with only one subcategory. This dimension has a clear relation to frequency. Lakoff points out that we are much more likely to generalize properties from typical to non-typical members than vice versa. In certain cases, a known individual member may be assumed to be typical of a class (for instance, if a person has limited experience of the class).

(ii) *Closeness to an ideal*. This is related to what in Cruse 1990 was called 'quality.' The example given there was that of emeralds. The most highly valued emeralds have a deep, intense color, and are without flaws; but these are also the most rare (and the bigger, the rarer), so they are in no way typical. As Lakoff points out, ideals operate in many domains. They may be represented by a set of abstract properties, as in the case of emeralds, or they may be centered around an individual (called by Lakoff a 'paragon').

(iii) *Stereotypicality*. This is interestingly different from typicality, but a fully convincing explanation of the difference is not yet available. Lakoff's account

(1987:85–6) is suggestive, but not fully explanatory. Lakoff says that the use of typicality is usually unconscious and automatic, whereas the use of stereotypes is conscious: this is plausible. He also says that stereotypes change, but typicality is constant over a person's lifetime. However, typicality changes as reality changes (think of a typical car or computer or camera), whereas a stereotype can persist in the face of change. Stereotypes are also typically associated with evaluative features.

There is another problem. A lot of the classical experiments deal with sub-categories as category members, rather than individuals: for example, subjects are given a category such as FRUIT, and a range of fruit types such as APPLE, STRAWBERRY, MANGO, PASSION FRUIT, DATE, OLIVE and so on for GOE scoring. Other experiments involve individuals: for instance, the work on proto-typical colors by Rosch (Heider 1971, 1972, and Berlin and Kay 1969) and others; also experiments with young children typically use individual items, not category names. It does make a difference. Using categories as examples of other categories suppresses properties that can enter into the notion of goodness. This is true of quality as described above. Another example is the property of well-formedness: it is all very well saying that an apple is the best example of a fruit, but what if it is a rotten apple? As far as individuals are concerned, well-formedness is yet another variety of goodness.

4.3.2   The representation of conceptual categories

Prototype theory comes in two main versions (according to the psychol-ogist Hampton 1997). In both versions, the linked notions of graded centrality and best examples occupy a central place. (Linguists tend not to distinguish clearly between the two versions.) One version represents a concept in terms of a list of the attributes of category members. This resembles a classical definition except that the features of a prototype representation are not required to be necessary and sufficient (although neither of these is necessarily ruled out for individual features). The centrality of an item in the category depends on how many of the relevant set of features it possesses: the more it possesses, the better an example of the category it will be. A feature is justified if, other things being equal, its presence leads to a higher GOE rating. In some versions, features can be weighted according to their contribution to centrality, and such versions will set an overall weighting score as a qualification for category membership. It is possible that no existing member of a category possesses all the prototype features. In such a case, the core of the category is represented by the member or members with the highest feature count (the actual prototype will then be an idealization represented by the full set of features).

Another version of prototype theory depends on the notion of similarity. A concept can be thought of as represented by an ideal exemplar, and membership and centrality of other items can be defined in terms of their similarity to the prototype. Hampton emphasizes that the two versions of prototype theory are not equivalent. Simple concepts, such as those involving color or shape, for instance, are better served by the similarity approach, whereas complex concepts, such as BIRD or VEHICLE, can best be handled by the feature-list model (see Hampton 1997:88). The feature-list version of prototype theory accounts for Wittgensteinian categories such as GAME, for which there is no definition in terms of necessary and sufficient features, but which show family resemblance relations. The fact that there are no necessary and sufficient features is also consistent with the fact that when subjects are asked to supply attributes that characterize a category, they do not confine themselves to attributes possessed by all members of the category, but also give features that a significant majority possess. Hampton says that both versions of the theory give a satisfactory account of the existence of borderline cases. However, it is difficult to see why a system where category membership depends on the presence of X features out of a list of Y will generate more borderline instances than one where membership depends on the presence of Y features out of a list of Y. On the other hand, one can see how a similarity-based system will throw up borderline cases, especially if the similarity dimensions vary continuously.

4.3.3   Levels of categorization

Prototype theory also provides an account of levels of categorization. Categories occur at different levels of inclusiveness, with more specific ones nested within more inclusive ones:

(1)   a. vehicle – *car* – hatchback
           b. fruit – *apple* – Granny Smith
           c. living thing – creature – animal – *dog* – spaniel
           d. object – implement – cutlery – *knife* – bread knife
           e. object – item of furniture – *table* – card table

Normally, one level of specificity in each set, called the **basic** (Rosch et al. 1976) or **generic** (Berlin et al. 1973) level of specificity, has a special status, and importance. (The basic level items in [1] are printed in bold italic.) Apart from the basic level, two further levels of specificity with different characteristics are usually identified: **superordinate level** and **subordinate level**. These are not defined simply by their position in the chain – there are substantive characteristics that distinguish one level from another. (For an extended discussion of hierarchical structure in concepts, see Murphy and Lassaline 1997.)

4.3.3.1   Basic level categories

The principal distinguishing characteristics of basic level items are as follows:

(i)   It is the most inclusive level at which there are characteristic patterns of behavioral interaction.

To appreciate this point, imagine one is asked to mime how one behaves with, say, a dog: this is not too difficult, most people would mime, for instance, patting and stroking the dog. But suppose one were asked to mime how one behaves with an animal: this is very difficult unless one knows what kind of animal it is. The same is true of *furniture* relative to *chair*, and *spoon* relative to *cutlery*.

(ii)   The most inclusive level for which a clear visual image can be formed.

A similar effect can be observed if one is asked to visualize a member of a category: it is easy to form a mental image of a non-specific dog, chair or apple, but virtually impossible to do so for animal, furniture or fruit, without being specific. It is also the level at which picture-word matching is most rapid.

(iii)   The most inclusive level at which part-whole information is represented.

This includes relations between parts. For most superordinate artifactual categories, such as TOOL, CUTLERY, CLOTHES or FURNITURE, there is no common part-whole structure for members. Biological superordinate categories show more regularity in part-whole structure, but there is much less commonality in the relations between the parts.

(iv)   The level used for everyday neutral reference.

A chain of specificity, like those illustrated in (1) above, provides a range of terms potentially usable for reference to an individual entity. Thus a particular dog can be simultaneously a spaniel, a dog and an animal. However, unless there is a specific communicative need, the basic level term will be used for reference (see Cruse 1977 for more details):

(2)   A: I can hear something outside.
          B: It's just a dog/?spaniel/?animal

Basic level terms (i.e., terms whose default construals are basic level categories) are often felt by speakers to be the 'real' name of the referent. Cross-linguistic studies have shown that they tend to be shorter than terms at other levels, normally monomorphemic, and are original in the sense of not being borrowed by metaphorical extension from other domains (Berlin et al. 1973). They are also more frequently used by parents in talk to children, and thus, not surprisingly, they are the first words children learn.

(v)   Individual items are more rapidly categorized as members of basic level categories than as members of superordinate or subordinate categories.

A spaniel, say, in a photograph, will be more rapidly categorized as a dog, than as an animal or a spaniel.

All these properties can plausibly be seen as consequences of what Murphy and Lassaline (1997:106–7) call the 'differentiation explanation' for basic level properties. Basic level categories represent the best categories into which the immediate superordinate category can be divided, in terms of:

the degree of difference between members of the category and members of neighboring categories.

internal homogeneity, i.e., the degree to which members of the category resemble one another.

informativeness, i.e., how much additional information can be accessed over and above what the superordinate term gives access to.

Consider the terms *animal*, *dog* and *spaniel*. The category ANIMAL is satisfactorily distinct from neighboring categories such as BIRD, FISH and INSECT, and is also informative, but the degree of resemblance between members is less than for the category DOG. The category SPANIEL has a high degree of resemblance between members, but distinctiveness from members of neighboring categories and extra informativeness are low. The category DOG scores highly on all criteria.

4.3.3.2   Superordinate level categories

Superordinate categories have the following characteristics (NB: the term 'superordinate' is not here used in the purely relational sense of 'hyperonymic'):

(i)   Superordinate categories are less good categories than basic level categories, because although members are relatively distinct from members of neighboring categories, within-category resemblance is relatively low.

(ii)   Superordinate categories have fewer defining attributes than basic level categories.

In experiments by Rosch et al. (1976), where subjects were asked to list the attributes of basic level items in a superordinate category, few attributes were generated that could serve as defining attributes of the superordinate category. However, as suggested in Cruse 1992b, this is perhaps not the best way to elicit attributes of superordinate categories. The most salient attributes of a category are those that differentiate it from other members of its default contrast set. The salient features of a horse are those that distinguish a horse from other animals. Subjects asked to list the attributes of a horse are unlikely to produce 'has bones,' 'breathes' and so on, because these are shared by other members of the contrast set; they are more likely to mention 'can be ridden,' 'has a mane,' 'has a long tail,' 'neighs,' and so on. The only way to get significant attributes of ANIMAL is to set up contrasts with categories such as FISH, PLANT, INSECT. The same is true of FURNITURE: it is no use looking at informants' responses to *chair, table* and the like. More revealing would be to ask what features distinguish items of furniture from, say, curtains, carpets, appliances, fireplaces and windows. Thinking of furniture in this way suggests that items of furniture are prototypically hard (unlike carpets), mobile (unlike fireplaces) and are places where things happen (unlike appliances, which are for doing things with). (For a similar, but independent, analysis of the category FURNITURE, see Bolinger 1992). However, it remains true that characteristic features of superordinate categories are fewer, and, as a consequence, family resemblance relations are less marked.

(iii)   Immediate superordinates of basic level categories often have a single-attribute relation to a higher superordinate category (think of FOOTWEAR in relation to SANDAL, UNDERWEAR in relation to VEST).

(iv)   Linguistically, names for superordinate categories are often mass nouns when basic level terms are count nouns.

Examples of this are *crockery* (*cups* and *plates*), *cutlery* (*spoons* and *forks*), *furniture* (*tables* and *chairs*), *footwear* (*boots* and *shoes*), *(computer) hardware* (*hard disks* and *modems*). Less frequently mentioned are cases where the converse is true: the superordinate is a count noun and the basic level term a mass noun: *metals* (*iron* and *copper*), *beverages* (*beer* and *wine*), *spices* (*pepper* and *coriander*). There is never a discrepancy in this respect between basic-level and subordinate-level terms. Superordinate terms are also frequently morphologically complex and/or polysyllabic.

4.3.3.3   Subordinate level categories

Subordinate level categories have the following characteristics:

(i)   They are less good categories than basic level, because although members have high mutual resemblance, they have low distinctiveness from members of neighboring categories.

(ii)   They are much less informative relative to their immediate hyperonymic category, hence, when subjects are asked to list distinctive attributes, the lists differ very little from the lists given for the hyperonymic basic level items.

(iii)   They are frequently polymorphemic, the most common pattern being modifier-head (e.g. *teaspoon, rocking-chair*).

This is taken by, for example, Ungerer and Schmid (1996) to indicate that they are distinguished from basic level by a single property, rather than encyclopedically (e.g. *teaspoon, rocking-chair*). However, a distinction needs to be made between naming practices and conceptual content: the 'single property' is a matter of naming, while there are virtually always unencoded encyclopedic distinctive characteristics. For instance, although *spaniel* is a single-morpheme word, and *long-tailed tit* is a complex expression incorporating a single property (the possession of a long tail), the extra specificity in each case over the basic level category is encyclopedic.

The above account is close to the account given by cognitive psychologists such as Murphy and Lassaline (1997). Anthropological linguists have also made extensive studies of the hierarchical organization of categories (see, for instance, Brown 2002). Their approach differs in many ways from that of the psychologists. Firstly, they have a strong cross-linguistic orientation. Secondly, the most extensive studies have been of biological kinds (a distinction is usually made between 'folk-classifications' and 'expert systems': most studies are of the former): some (e.g. Atran 1990) claim that only biological kinds are truly hierarchized, and among biological kind concepts only 'general purpose' categories such as animal, dog, spaniel, beech, copper beech, bush and so on are hierarchized, but not utilitarian categories such as vegetable, weed or pet. Thirdly, they recognize a greater 'depth' of hierarchization, and use different terms for the levels. The following is an example (the equivalent psychological categories are given in brackets):

(3)   beginner   *plant*
       life form   *bush*   (= superordinate level)
       generic   *rose*   (= basic level)
       specific   *hybrid tea* (= subordinate level)
       varietal   *Peace*

The properties attributed to the generic level do not significantly add to what was said above concerning the basic level. The remarkable constancy of hierarchical structuring across a wide variety and degree of complexity of cultures suggests that it is a cognitive universal and probably innate. There is a dispute among anthropologists as to the underlying motive force for the evolution of classificatory systems. One school holds that it is driven mainly by utilitarian considerations: the categories evolved because they were an aid to survival. The other school holds that the evolution of the systems for classifying biological kinds is driven by intellectual curiosity. There are a number of reasons for the latter claim. The systems are remarkably similar across the world, even though the cultures and their environments differ markedly; many cases are found of distinctions that have no utilitarian value in the culture that uses them; they tend to coincide to a high degree with scientific classifications. Brown (2002), while acknowledging the force of these arguments, points out nonetheless that hunter-gatherer societies typically have far fewer categories than settled agrarian societies, and suggests that there is a functional reason for this. Small agrarian communities are typically larger than hunter-gatherer communities, and when harvests fail, it is very important for them to have access to alternative food sources, hence a detailed knowledge has survival value. Hunter-gatherer societies, on the other hand, are typically much smaller, and their essentially mobile lifestyle makes them much less dependent on food available in a particular locality; hence detailed knowledge of local flora and fauna is of less value.

4.3.4 Shortcomings of prototype theory

A number of problems have been pointed out in connection with prototype theory. Only the major ones are presented here.

4.3.4.1 Simplistic nature of feature list

A major criticism of the prototype model of category structure is that a simple feature list, even with a relaxation of the requirement that features be necessary and sufficient, is far too simplistic. Even more sophisticated versions such as Barsalou's (1992b) model, based on frames (in the sense of structured lists of dimensions and values), fail to capture the full range of properties linked in complex chains of association and causation involved in a typical 'rich' concept such as a natural kind concept. There are various aspects to this excessive simplicity. One is that it cannot handle context sensitivity. Studies have shown that what is chosen as the best example of a category can be influenced by indicating a context for the judgement (Barsalou 1987). Labov (1973) also showed that the boundaries between adjacent categories can be affected by adding contextual features. Another concerns the relation between the number of features present and GOE. This relation is not a simple one of counting how many features are present. There is also interaction between the features: the effect of the presence of one feature depends on the presence and values of other features. To give a very simple example, the feature WOODEN lowers the GOE of a spoon if it is small, but not if it is large. There must be thousands of interactions like this, some involving several features simultaneously.

4.3.4.2 The 'odd number paradox'

The 'odd number paradox' has also been put forward as a problem for prototype theory. Armstrong et al. (1983) found that people will grade ODD NUMBERS for centrality, even though the category ODD NUMBER has a clear definition in terms of necessary and sufficient features. Their proposed solution, the so-called 'dual representation' hypothesis, combines the prototype approach and the classical approach (Smith et al. 1974). The idea is that concepts have two representations, which have different functions. There is a 'core' representation, which has basically the form of a classical definition. This representation will govern the logical properties of the concept. The other representation is some sort of prototype system which prioritizes the most typical features, and whose function is to allow rapid categorization of instances encountered. With this set-up, the odd-number effect ceases to be a puzzle. However, this conjunction of two theories inherits most of the problems of both of them: in particular, it reinstates a major problem of the classical theory that prototype theory was intended to solve, namely, the fact that for a great many everyday concepts there is no available core definition.

4.3.4.3 Problems with features

There is a problem that afflicts all models of conceptual structure that traffic in features. What are they, and where do they come from? In most accounts they seem to be simply other concepts. In other words, concepts are just points in a concept network. This is curiously reminiscent of the structuralist characterization of word meaning (see, for instance, Lyons 1963, 1968). But in that case, the conceptual system is hermetically sealed off from the world, and it is difficult to see what explanatory power it can have in terms of human mental activity. To be really explanatory, the features will have to be 'grounded in a subsymbolic level' (Hampton 1997:91), that is, will have to be, or be shown to relate systematically to, non-linguistic features drawn from perception, action, intention and so forth. Hampton points out an even more vicious circularity. If we map BIRD onto HEAD by means of a 'has a' link, we will lose a lot of information if we do not make it clear that the head in question is not, say, an elephant's head, but a bird's head.

4.3.4.4 Contrasting categories

Contrasting categories such as CAT, DOG, LION, CAMEL and so on pose a problem for prototype theory. There is really no explanation for the mutual exclusion relation that holds between them. Such an explanation is logically impossible unless we incorporate into prototype representations features with negative weighting (so, for instance, 'has soft fur,' 'purrs when stroked,' 'moves by hopping,' 'larger than average human,' 'has scales' would all have negative weighting for *dog*). It does not appear that this strategy has ever been followed.

4.3.4.5   Boundaries in prototype theory

Prototype theorists have paid insufficient attention to the question of category boundaries and their location, and the same is true of many cognitive linguists. In the following quote Langacker appears to deny the existence of boundaries: 'There is no fixed limit on how far something can depart from the prototype and still be assimilated to the class, if the categorizer is perceptive or clever enough to find some point of resemblance to typical instances' (Langacker 1991:266).

Lakoff acknowledges their existence, but devotes little space to discussing them. (Hampton [1991] is one of the few psychologists to propose a version of the prototype model in which category boundaries are explicitly recognized.) However, a boundary is arguably the most basic of all the properties of a category. A category is like a container: one of its major functions is to divide the objects in the world into those things that are in it and those things that are not in it. This function cannot be fulfilled without a boundary.

The notion of category boundary hardly needs detailed justification. If A says *That is an X* and B says *No, it isn't*, then either they perceive the referent of *that* differently or they disagree as to the location of the boundary of the category X. Certain adjectives such as *artificial*, as in *artificial cream*, and *fake* as in *a fake Monet*, indicate that the referent does not fall into the category designated by the noun; *regular* as in Lakoff's (1973) *Mark Spitz is a regular fish* (Mark Spitz was an Olympic swimmer), for appropriate interpretation, requires the hearer to realize that Mark Spitz is not, in fact, a fish.[1]

Apparently well-formed but nonetheless unacceptable inference patterns like the following can only be explained in terms of boundary location:

(4)   a. A car seat is a kind of seat.
       b. A seat is an item of furniture.
       c. ?A car seat is an item of furniture.

One explanation (due to Hampton – a slightly different account is given in chapter 6) is that for *An X is a Y* to be acceptable, it is enough that a prototypical X should fall within the category Y; it is not necessary for all X's to fall within the category. Hence, the pattern of acceptability seen in (4) can be explained by the disposition of boundaries in Figure 4.1 (heavily shaded areas denote prototype cores):

[1] It should be emphasized that the existence of a boundary does not entail the existence of a 'core definition' with necessary and sufficient criteria, as proposed in what Hampton (1997:93) calls the 'binary view' put forward by Smith et al. (1974).

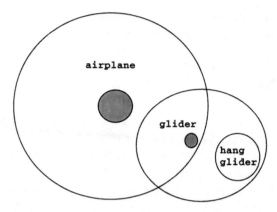

Figure 4.1 *Boundaries of AIRPLANE, GLIDER and HANG GLIDER*

Here, the prototype of GLIDER falls within the category boundary of AIR-PLANE, but HANG GLIDER falls outside it.

There is a psycholinguistic correlate of the position of a boundary, involving speed of response to a categorization task. If subjects are asked whether or not an item belongs to a given category, the speed of response depends on how near the item is to the category boundary: the closer it is, the slower will be the response. Hence, in (5), the **bold** items will be responded to slowest:

(5)   (FRUIT) apple . . . . . . **tomato** . . . . . . potato
        (VEHICLE) car . . . . . . **bicycle** . . . . . . chair
        (WORD) hand . . . . . . **malk** . . . . . . pkhq

Another indication of marginal status is the following. Take the case of SHOE as a member of the category CLOTHES. One would not hesitate to say of a suitcase that contained underwear, shirts, socks, jackets and trousers, but nothing else, that it 'contained only clothes.' However, one would hesitate to say of a suitcase full of shoes, that it contained only clothes; on the other hand, there would be no such hesitation if the contents were all shirts. This is arguably a function of the marginal status of shoes in the category of clothes compared with shirts. It appears that we construe the category CLOTHES differently, that is, more generously, when confronted with a variety of types of clothes, including marginal ones; when confronted with a collection of shoes, we construe the categories CLOTHES and SHOES as mutually excluding.

The location of the boundary of a category is independent of its prototype, that is to say, two categories may have the same prototype but different boundaries; likewise, two categories may have the same boundaries but different prototypes. Take the French word *corde* and its default English translation *rope*. A questioning of native speakers of the two languages suggests that the prototypes of the two categories are very close: both put forward the same sorts of thing as best examples. However, their boundaries differ. *Le Petit Larousse* defines *ficelle* ('string') as 'une corde mince'; a parallel definition of *string* as 'a thin rope,' would seem very odd. That is to say, *ficelle* falls within the (default) boundary of the category CORDE, but *string* falls outside the boundary of the category ROPE. The converse case, of identical boundary but different core, is perhaps exemplified by *courage* and *bravery* in English. It would be hard to think of an act that was a manifestation of courage but not of bravery, or vice versa. But their core regions are arguably distinguishable. Student informants were asked to give a relative rating of (6a) and (6b) as (i) an example of a brave act and (ii) an example of a courageous act.

(6)   a. A person jumps into a fast-flowing river in an attempt to save someone who has fallen in.

         b. A person risks his/her career and livelihood by exposing malpractice and injustice at the heart of government.

There was substantial agreement that (6a) was the better example of bravery and (6b) the better example of courage.

A fundamental problem with boundaries is that they do not arise naturally from a prototype representation. Even in Hampton's version of the model, the boundaries are simply stipulated in an arbitrary fashion. Prototype theorists typically say that natural conceptual categories have fuzzy boundaries. Indeed, this is one of the main arguments against the classical model. Claimed pointers to fuzziness are, for instance, the fact that different subjects make different judgements as to the location of boundaries, and the same subject will make different judgements under different contextual conditions. Even the psycholinguistic experiment quoted above yields a borderline region rather than a sharp line. However, it should be pointed out that even a fuzzy boundary has a location. The notion of a fuzzy boundary will be critically examined below.

4.3.5   The frame-based account of prototype effects

A simple list of features is inadequate as a representation of a conceptual category. The notion of frame as described in chapter 2 offers a more satisfactory picture of a concept as a complexly structured body of interconnected knowledge. This picture allows a more flexible account of such matters as graded centrality. Graded centrality can be seen as a matter of the goodness of fit between the perceived features of some individual, and one or more aspects of the frame that characterizes an ideal individual in a category.

Three ways in which this occurs can be identified. First, there is the question of the convergence between the individual and the profiled region of the frame. Take the case of *car* and *tractor* within the category of VEHICLE. Most informants award *car* a somewhat higher GOE score than *tractor*. The reason appears to be that the ideal vehicle is designed for travel along roads, rather than across fields, hence there is a better fit between CAR and VEHICLE than between TRACTOR and VEHICLE. The second type of graded centrality involves items that do have a traditional definition, like *bachelor*. In this case, graded centrality can arise from similarity between the ideal background domain and the actual background of the individual. As we have seen, the definition operates against a set of cultural background assumptions concerning marriageability: the reason we regard a (Roman Catholic) priest as not a very good example of a bachelor, even though he satisfies the basic definition, is that our background assumptions about priests do not fit our assumptions about an 'ideal' bachelor. A third case is when a concept is characterized by a cluster of ICMs, as in the case of MOTHER (§2.5). Here, the ICMs behave like features, in that the more of the members in the ideal cluster are present in a particular instance, the more central the instance is within the category.

4.4   A dynamic construal approach to conceptual categories

Most views on the nature of categories have had in common a belief in a constant underlying mental representation of some kind for each category. However, more recently, a new approach to categories has emerged that challenges this assumption. For instance, Smith and Samuelson pass a harsh judgement on the 'fixed categories' assumption: 'These foundational ideas of stable categories and stable concepts, however, have led to little progress. Instead, a steady succession of theories of concepts have been offered, rejected, resurrected and rejected again' (Smith and Samuelson 1997:163).

Smith and Samuelson quote a number of experimental results in support of a proposal that the notion of fixed categories with permanent representations is a myth. Among these are Barsalou's (1983) experiments involving ad hoc categories with no conventional names, like 'things on a desk that could be used to pound in a nail,' or, 'things to take on a picnic.' Subjects readily formed new and contextually coherent categories that showed the same characteristics as established categories, including graded centrality and characteristic features. They propose instead, that categories are inherently variable, and created on-line as and when needed. This general line of approach is endorsed by Whittlesea (1997), who argues that there is no hard evidence for the existence of a separate system of abstracted knowledge, and that the alleged properties of fixed concepts can be given other explanations.

According to Smith and Samuelson, the elements out of which a concept is created are past history, recent history, current input. On the topic of past history, that is to say, accumulated memories of previous experiences, they point out that each experience has a permanent effect on our 'ways of knowing,' and further have this to say:

> Critically, the accrual of these long-term changes provides a source of stability in a continually changing system. If there are statistical regularities, patterns, in our experiences that recur over and over again, then as each moment of knowing is laid on the preceding moments, weak tendencies to behave and to think in certain ways will become strong tendencies – sometimes so strong that they will not be easily perturbed and thus might seem fixed. (Smith and Samuelson 1997:175–6)

What is recorded on each past experience will include such things as salient contextual factors, perceived and inferred relations (causal and other) with other things, accompanying language and so on. The second element is immediately preceding mental activity. They adduce the ubiquitous effect of priming as an example of this. More particularly for concept formation they claim:

> [T]here is a pull for coherence from one thought to the next one, for the meaning of an event to depend on its place in a stream of events. If we think first about eating and then about frogs we will think differently than if we think first about ponds and then about frogs. (ibid.)

The final element is a construal of immediate context, including linguistic, perceptual, social, psychological aspects, including current goals and plans, inferences and expected outcomes, perceived causal relations and so on.

Let us now look briefly at how this dynamic view of concepts impinges on the three key features of concepts, namely, boundaries, frames and levels.

4.4.1   Category boundaries

It is not difficult to find examples of different placement of category boundaries in construals of a word in different contexts. Take the example of *pet* in English. Nowadays, there are electronic devices that mimic certain characteristics of animals, except that they are less demanding and less messy: they are sometimes called *cyberpets*. Suppose we ask whether these objects are pets or not:

(7)   Is a cyberpet a pet?

When this question is put to a typical class of undergraduates, a typical result is that a minority, but a significant minority, answer *Yes*, while the majority say *No*. This is, of course, a typical 'fuzzy' result. Now suppose the question in (8) is asked:

(8)   Is a cyberpet a real pet?

The response this time is overwhelmingly *No*, because the word *real* encourages a particular construal of the position of the category boundary. On the other hand, suppose a scene is set such as the following: an educational psychologist, say, is advising the parents of a child with behavioral problems, and says (9):

(9)   I advise you to get her some kind of pet – even an electronic one might be beneficial.

In this case, no one in a typical class finds anything anomalous in the psychologist's utterance, even though *pet* is used to include the electronic variety. The expressions *some kind of* and *even* in the context encourage us to construe a broader category of pets.

Another example is *dog* in (10)–(12):

(10)   A dog has four legs.

At first sight this seems an obvious truth. But what about dogs that have lost one or more legs in an accident? It seems that when we interpret (10), we construe the category of dogs to include only well-formed dogs. Yet another construal of the boundaries of the category of dogs is illustrated in (11):

(11)   Dogs are mammals.

Here we construe a category appropriate to biological discourse, which includes three-legged dogs and wild dogs. Consider also cases like (12):

(12)   A dog makes an excellent companion for an old person.

Here we construe a category appropriate to human social behavior, which includes only pet dogs.

As a final example, consider the construals of *bird* in (13) and (14):

(13)   I wish I could fly like a bird.
(14)   We get lots of birds in our garden.

For (13), we must exclude flightless birds and injured birds incapable of flight from our construal of *bird*. In (14) we are constrained to interpret *bird* (if uttered by an inhabitant of a typical Manchester suburb) as 'most familiar type of small garden bird,' on the assumption that no one would expect to see ostriches or eagles in their garden.

As we have seen, one of the perceived inadequacies of the classical model of category structure was that it entailed sharp boundaries, whereas natural categories were claimed to have fuzzy boundaries. However, the notion of a fuzzy boundary needs reexamining. Claimed pointers to fuzziness are, for instance, the fact that different subjects make different judgements as to the location of boundaries, and the same subject will make different judgements under different contextual conditions. But all the evidence for fuzziness involves reactions to isolated lexical items, rather than construals in specific contexts. While the category boundary construed in response to a lexical item can vary with context, there is no reason to suppose that there is anything fuzzy about the different construed boundaries. A boundary is a line of demarcation between 'inside' and 'outside.' According to the dynamic construal approach, it is in principle sharp. However, we can have various degrees of knowledge about a boundary. For instance, we may only know that it is located within a certain range of possibilities. Uncertainty as to location is perfectly compatible with the sharpness of a boundary.

Consider the boundary between 'alive' and 'dead.' The decision criteria vary according to context and according to what we are talking about. In the case of human beings, the boundary is a matter of dispute. Consider, too, the 'human being' boundary in connection with the debates on abortion. In both these cases, the location of the boundary is a matter of dispute and uncertainty, but is not vague, certainly not to the disputants. The debate presupposes that there is a dichotomous construal with a determinate boundary. Very often a boundary construal serves only to categorize specific individuals as inside a category or not, that is, only a local boundary needs to be construed rather than a complete delimitation of the category. Lakoff (1987) makes a special case for the fuzziness of categories such as TALL MAN, which involve a graded property. However, on the dynamic construal approach, contextualized occurrences even of categories of this type involve a specific construed reference point on the relevant scale (see chapter 8 for more detailed discussion).

In conclusion, it is arguable that we do not need the notion of fuzzy boundary: everything can be accounted for by variable construal of a normal, that is, determinate, boundary.

4.4.2 Frames

Frames/ICMs (in some cases cluster ICMs) are presented by Fillmore and Lakoff as more-or-less invariant structures having a stable association with lexical items, which allow for variable boundary construal, presumably in terms of the goodness-of-fit required between perceived reality and aspects of the frame. However, although the frame may be relatively more stable than the boundaries, the dynamic construal approach allows also for variable construal of the frame itself. The experiments of Barsalou, reported above, where ad hoc categories are formed that have all the characteristics of established categories, suggest that frames may be construed on-line. Also, the type of variation shown by the category DOG in *dogs and other pets* and *Dogs are mammals* seems more convincingly explained by a modulation of the frame, rather than an adjustment in the degree of fit with a constant underlying the DOG frame. In any case, whether or not frames are subject to construal, the mechanism of boundary placement is still in need of elucidation.

4.4.3   Levels of categorization

Given that level status is a function of content and relations between contents, it would not be surprising if variation in level construal were to be observed between speakers, and within the usage of a given speaker at different times and in different contexts.

It is not difficult to find cases where different speakers apparently assign items to different levels. Take the case of categories associated with the word *bird*. For some speakers, *bird* denotes a category at superordinate level which we may call AVES. This has ANIMAL, FISH, INSECT and so on as sister categories, and as subcategories at basic level we will find SPARROW, THRUSH, BLACKBIRD and so on. For other speakers, the default denotation of *bird* is a basic level category that contains familiar garden birds, which has as sister categories not only CAT and DOG, but also less familiar birds such as TURKEY, OSTRICH and EAGLE (Jolicoeur et al. 1984). Individual bird species such as THRUSH and BLACKBIRD are subcategories of BIRD at subordinate level. The first picture makes more sense biologically, as the species are aligned at basic level. But many speakers argue strongly that, for them, the difference between, say, a sparrow and a thrush is 'more like' that between a collie and a spaniel, than like that between a cat and a dog. Speakers for whom the default construal of *bird* is BIRD presumably also have a construal of *bird* as AVES. Equally, speakers (like the present author) for whom *thrush* denotes a basic level category, and whose default construal of *bird* is AVES are capable of operating with the other system, if the occasion demands.

Now, the question is: What is the difference between the basic level THRUSH and the subordinate level THRUSH? It seems that an important factor is richness of content, in terms of knowledge, memories, connections and so forth. Basic level categories ideally have rich content and clear differentiation from sisters. While a competent naturalist will have a relatively rich representation of items such as blue-tit, swallow, thrush and so on, town-dwellers may well know the names, but very little else about the different birds, so they will not form satisfactory basic level items: the names will be little more than placeholders for potential knowledge.

They may be able to form an image of a generic (garden) bird, but not have enough experience or knowledge to be able to visualize individual species; their patterns of behavior will be very much the same towards all garden birds. Insofar as they have both a superordinate level and a basic level construal of *bird*, these will not be different level construals of the same category, but two different categories that fit at two levels.

What happens in the case of a speaker who can operate with two different systems? Consider the case of a dog-breeder who in his work environment exhibits basic level characteristic behavior in respect of categories such as SPANIEL, COLLIE, ALSATIAN, TERRIER. What happens when he converses with a non-specialist? Presumably many, at least, will adjust themselves cognitively to the new situation, and revert to the societal default construal of the terms. But do they actually change their categories? Or do they simply construe a new level for them? If they actually restructure the categories, for instance by backgrounding aspects of knowledge that are highly relevant in a professional setting, then they are effectively creating new conceptual categories. It would seem reasonable to assume that level cannot be construed independently of content, that is to say, any observed movement up or down a taxonomic hierarchy will be a consequence of different construals of the category denoted by a lexical item.

4.5   The dynamic construal of meaning

A major requirement of a satisfactory account of the relation between words and meanings is to integrate in a coherent picture both the appearance of determinate structural properties in the lexicon and, at the same time, the apparently infinite flexibility of meaning in context. A fairly standard way of attempting this is to locate structure in the lexicon (or at least infer it from lexical entries) and account for variability by means of pragmatic rules and principles. In this book, an alternative approach is explored, whereby neither meanings nor structural relations are specified in the lexicon, but are construed 'on-line,' in actual situations of use. This is not a new idea. It was first suggested within linguistics by Moore and Carling (1982), and it is not uncommon now among cognitive linguists (for instance Lakoff and Sweetser [1994] and Croft [2000]); there are also parallel proposals regarding concepts within cognitive psychology, as we have seen. But proponents of this approach in the past have typically not applied it to the sorts of problems that engaged the attention of structural linguists, such as sense relations, lexical fields, componential analysis and so on (polysemy has been extensively studied, but arguably such studies pay insufficient attention to structural features such as sense boundaries). It is not of course denied that the linguistic expressions provide a vital component of the raw material required for the construal of meaning. But, as we shall see, they represent only one component among several. On this view, words do not really have meanings, nor do sentences have meanings: meanings are something that we construe, using the properties of linguistic elements as partial clues, alongside non-linguistic knowledge, information available from context, knowledge and conjectures regarding the state of mind of hearers and so on.

Our account of word meaning will incorporate, albeit in an adapted form, the basic insights of the dynamic construal picture of conceptual categories. It should be borne in mind, however, that concepts are not necessarily equatable with contextually construed meanings, or, as we shall call them, **interpretations**. Consider the following sentences:

(15)   Dogs are not allowed in this building.
(16)   I like cats, but I can't stand dogs.

In any situated use of these sentences, the interpretation of *dog* will be the same as the concept DOG construed in the same context. However, cases like this, although widespread, are probably in the minority. Take sentence (17), said in reference to the family dog, whom someone forgot to feed at mid-day:

(17)   Oh, look: that poor animal hasn't had anything to eat since this morning!

Here we can say that the word *animal* causes the construal of an appropriate conceptual category ANIMAL. However, the fully construed meaning involves an individual concept, namely the family dog, which is itself further construed in response to contextual factors (which include, among many others, the fact that the word *animal* was used in the referring expression, rather than the word *dog*). Even without statistical evidence, it seems a safe guess that the bulk of everyday communication ultimately concerns individual things or people, rather than classes of individuals.

There are four basic notions in the present account of meaning, namely, contextualized interpretation, purport, constraints and construal and they will be discussed in that order.

4.5.1   Contextualized interpretation

There is something special about a word actually used in a living context. As Wittgenstein says, 'Every sign by itself seems dead. What gives it life? In use it is alive. Is life breathed into it there? – Or is the use its life?' (Wittgenstein, quoted in *The Guardian*, September 7, 2001).

We shall say that 'life' is breathed into a sign when it is given a contextualized interpretation. An isolated sign certainly has semantically relevant properties,

semantic potential, and these properties have an influence on eventual interpretations, but they are to be distinguished from the interpretations themselves. (Any
attenuated intuitions of meaning that we get from isolated words can be attributed
to default construals of some kind.) Let us look at a couple of concrete examples
that illustrate this point (the following examples are taken from the novel *The
Breaker*, by Minette Walters):

(18)   Bertie was lying on the doorstep in the sunshine as Ingram drew the jeep to a halt
         beside his gate . . . The dog raised his shaggy head and thumped his tail on the
         mat before rising leisurely to his feet and yawning.
(19)   Bibi . . . sat cross-legged on the floor at Tony's feet . . . nervously [she] raised her
         head.

It is not necessary to dwell on these passages in detail. They are cited simply to
draw attention to the 'deadness' of the individual signs, in contrast to the vividness
of the interpretations we construct. Think of what a dictionary entry will tell us
about the meanings of, for instance, *thump, raise, rise*, and compare this with the
detailed picture the words evoke in the passages quoted. And contrast *raise* in *the
dog raised his shaggy head* and *nervously she raised her head*. These are different
actions, not simply because one is performed by a dog and the other by a girl:
the dog's head actually moves to a higher position relative to the ground; the girl
merely tilts her head so as to look upwards.

Of course, when we construe these scenes, we draw on our stored knowledge
of the behavior of girls and dogs in different circumstances: if Bibi had been lying
face-down on the floor with her chin on a book, say, and someone had asked to see
the book, then the head-raising referred to in *Bibi raised her head* would have been
much closer to that referred to in *The dog raised his head*. Clearly these subtleties
are not inherent in the word *raise*, but they are part of construed meaning in context,
and are construed as a direct result of the occurrence of the word *raise* (cf. the
discussion of Fillmore's semantics of understanding in §2.1).

When we encounter a piece of language in the course of normal communication,
there is an instant of comprehension, a kind of crystallization of the perception of
meaning – we know what somebody has said (or written etc.). This is similar to
our recognition of a familiar face, or when we realize that what we are seeing is a
dog and so on. In the case of the face, we do not merely recognize whose face it
is, but at the same instant we see perhaps that the person is tired, or worried, and
the hair is windblown and so on. On further reflection, we might infer what the
person has been doing, or what the cause of worry is. The processing can continue
indefinitely, but there is nonetheless a prior moment of recognition.

Something similar happens when we encounter a piece of language. We recognize in an instant what has been said, but we can go on working out consequences

and further inferences indefinitely. It is what constitutes the focus of our attention at the moment of understanding that is referred to here as the interpretation of an expression. Phenomenologically, it is a fairly clear-cut event. It will be useful to distinguish pre-crystallization processes, processes preceding and leading up to crystallization, and post-crystallization processes. In many approaches to meaning, there is a determinate starting point for the process of constructing an interpretation, but an indeterminate end point. For example, in Relevance Theory (Sperber and Wilson 1986), the starting point is an explicature, and the end point (insofar as there is one) is an indeterminate series of implicatures of diminishing strengths. The present model of comprehension has an indeterminate starting point (a purport) and a determinate end point.

An interpretation resembles a picture in that it is not susceptible of finite characterization in terms of semantic features, or whatever. Any features are themselves construals. Of course, a meaning must in some sense have a finite neural representation, but the elements out of which the representation is composed are more like the pixels underlying a picture on a computer screen: the resulting experienced picture is a Gestalt and so is an interpretation. The nature of this experience is still mysterious.

Notice that the above characterization focuses on the hearer. Presumably there is something in the mind of the speaker which precedes the utterance, but there is a sense in which a speaker does not know what they have said until they process their own utterance. A major task for the speaker is to devise an utterance that will lead to the desired interpretation forming in the hearer's mind.

4.5.2   Purport

Each lexical item (word form) is associated with a body of conceptual content that is here given the name **purport**. Purport is part of the raw material contributed by the word to processes of construal of an interpretation (the other part being a set of conventional constraints). A purport does not correspond to any specific interpretation, even an abstract one, nor does a word, in general, have a stable association with specific conceptual categories. At the same time, there is an intuitive sense of coherence among most of the uses of a word. This can undoubtedly be partly explained by the constant association between word form and purport.

Purport may consist of a relatively coherent body of content, or it may display relatively disjunct parts (as in traditional 'homonymy'); or, indeed any intermediate degree of coherence or lack of it. (We do not say of a word such as *bank*, which has a disjunct purport, that it has two [or more] purports. There is not a great deal of harm in saying this for extreme cases, except that it obscures the fact that there is a continuum of 'disjunctness' on which these cases occupy extreme positions.)

Purport is not to be thought of as a variety of construed meaning. Purport is to interpretation as egg is to omelette, or flour to bread: it is of a different ontological category. Purport is an ingredient of meaning, not a constituent. It cannot be explained, in general, as an abstract, or superordinate meaning, which becomes specified in context. Interpretations are not contextual specifications of purports, they are transformations.

Purport is some function of previous experiences of (construed) occurrences of the word in specific situations. As such, it is continually developing: every experience of the use of a word modifies the word's purport to some degree.

4.5.3 Constraints

Of course, the construal of interpretations is not unconstrained: the constraints are many and varied. They vary in strength and may reinforce one another or cancel one another out (for examples of conflicting constraints, see the discussion of facets and microsenses in chapter 5). They can also be overcome by cognitive effort, but the stronger the constraint, the greater the cognitive effort required to impose a construal that defies the constraint. They also vary in their stability under change of context. I have classified constraints informally under a number of headings.

4.5.3.1 Human cognitive capacities

One very basic type of constraint is represented by the nature of the human cognitive system. I am thinking here both of positive aspects, such as the universal tendency to impose a figure-ground structure, or other Gestalt principles, such as closure and so on, as well as of negative aspects such as memory and attentional limitations.

4.5.3.2 Nature of reality

Another type of constraint is what we shall naively call 'the nature of reality.' Some aspects of experience naturally lend themselves more readily to construal in certain respects and less readily to construal in other respects. To take a simple example, we have the choice when speaking of attributes, to construe them either as being present or absent, or as being present to varying degrees. Take, for example, the state of being married: this is much easier to construe as a dichotomy (*married:single*) than as a matter of degree (*very married, slightly married*). On the other hand, if we are thinking of linear spatial extent, this is much easier to construe as a gradable scale than as a dichotomy. For similar reasons, it is difficult not to construe a sense boundary between the two meanings of *bank*, and this has something to do with the raw/brute reality concerning river banks and money banks.

4.5.3.3 Convention

Another very important constraint is convention: how the society in which we live habitually construes situations and uses words, and so on (see Lewis 1969, Clark 1996 and Croft 2000 for the theory of convention and its limits). There are two aspects of convention. One is the mapping between word forms and regions of conceptual content. This in itself constitutes a constraint: the principal source of difference in semantic potential between one word and another arises from difference in associated purport. The other aspect of convention is a limitation of the possibilities of construal of a particular purport. Certain construals, because of the strength of the constraints, will acquire a special default status, and extra cognitive effort will be required to impose a different construal. Conventional constraints are frequently context sensitive, that is to say, given a particular purport in a particular context (or, more likely, a context-type) conventional constraints may favor certain construals over others.

4.5.3.4 Context

Last, but not least, there are contextual constraints. These, in general, correspond to what Clark (1996) calls **common ground**.

(a)   *Linguistic context*

This is one component (the **actional basis**) of what Clark calls **personal common ground**. We can distinguish three aspects:

(i) Previous discourse, that is, what has been said immediately prior to a given utterance, obviously constitutes a powerful source of constraints.

(ii) Immediate linguistic environment: the phrase or sentence in which a word appears strongly constrains its construal. To give an obvious example, we would tend to interpret *bank* differently in (20) and (21), simply because of the immediate linguistic context:

(20)   We moored the boat to the bank.
(21)   I've got no money – I'll call in at the bank on the way home.

(iii) Type of discourse: under this heading are included such matters as genre (whether we are dealing with a poem, novel, textbook, newspaper report, personal letter, friendly conversation, police interrogation etc.), register (whether formal or informal, if formal, whether technical or non-technical, if informal, whether jocular etc.) and field of discourse (legal, ecclesiastical, sporting, political etc.).

(b) *Physical context*

Also important is what the participants can see, hear and so on in their immediate surroundings. This corresponds to Clark's **perceptual basis** for personal common ground.

(c) *Social context*

This refers to the kind of situation the participants are in and the social relations between them (including power relations). These can strongly influence construal.

(d) *Stored knowledge*

All utterances are processed against the background of a vast store of remembered experiences and knowledge, which is capable of affecting the likelihood of particular construals. For instance, in the case of *bank* above, our interpretation of (21) will be different if we know that the speaker is an eccentric recluse, and keeps his money in a box in the bank of a river. Items (iii) and (iv) are components of Clark's **communal common ground**.

4.5.4 Construal

Construal, in the sense introduced by Langacker, is the central notion in this account of lexical semantics. It is by means of a series of processes of construal that an essentially non-semantic purport is transformed into fully contextualized meanings. For a detailed discussion of construal processes see chapter 3.

4.5.4.1 Chains of construal and pre-meanings

As pictured here, the process of construing a meaning is not accomplished in a single stage, but is a result of a series of elementary processes, some of which are serially ordered, others proceeding in parallel. In many cases, as we shall see, stages in the construal process intermediate between purport and interpretation may have important semantic properties. Such intermediate stages will be referred to as **pre-meanings**. For instance, the construal of boundaries creates pre-meanings that have logical properties and that are independent of subsequent or concomitant construal processes (see, for instance, the discussion of autonomous sense units in chapter 5, and category inclusion in chapter 6).

4.5.4.2 Default construals

Conventional constraints play a vital role in stabilizing language usage within a speech community, indeed, of making communication possible. They are represented in the minds of individual speakers, but their origin lies outside the individual, in the speech community. Different conventional constraints vary in strength. A weak constraint will yield no more than a favorite, or most likely construal, which can be easily overridden by contextual constraints; a strong constraint will require heavy countervailing pressure to be overcome. Different aspects of construal may be independently subject to conventional constraints: the result of a constraint will rarely be a fully construed meaning, and is much more likely to be a pre-meaning involving, say, only a boundary placement and leaving scope for further enrichment by construal. Conventional constraints are not necessarily independent of context: some may operate only in certain context types. They can also operate at different levels of specificity, with narrow scope constraints refining the work of wider scope constraints. Some constraints will be defeasible, but will govern some aspect of construal if there is insufficient or no indication from the context as to required construal. The outcomes of these constraints will function as default construals. Default construals can also be context dependent. It is probably default construals that give the illusion of fixity of meaning.

4.6   Structural and logical aspects of meaning

One of the main aims of the dynamic construal approach to word meaning is to achieve a unified account of both hard and soft aspects of word meaning, both flexibility and rigidity, and to locate the origins of these at first sight contradictory properties. The 'hard' properties include sense relations such as hyponymy, incompatibility, meronymy and antonymy, and the existence of structured lexical sets (word fields), as well as logical properties such as entailment. For instance, it is generally accepted that *It's a dog* entails *It's an animal*. But what does this mean? And how can it be the case if *dog* and *animal* do not have fixed meanings? It will be argued here that such properties properly belong to pre-meanings resulting from the construal of boundaries, principally, and scales and reference points. Confident assertions regarding entailment in decontextualized sentences can be attributed to default construals of boundaries. Hence, flexibility comes from the nature of purport and the sensitivity of construal processes to contextual factors; conventional constraints ensure that contextual variability remains within certain limits. Rigidity comes from the operation of image schemas such as the container schema and the scale schema. Boundary construal can also account for the appearance of componentiality in word meaning, without the necessity of assuming that semantic features are permanent elements of the meaning of a word.

The principle of compositionality states that the meaning of a complex expression is a compositional function of the meanings of its parts. The view of word meaning expounded in this book obviously has repercussions on the interpretation of this principle and its validity. The first point to make is that if the 'parts' are taken to be words, then since, on the present approach, words do not have meanings, then the principle is uninterpretable. However, we could take 'meanings' to be 'construed meanings,' in which case we need to consider a slightly revised version of the principle:

(22)   The construed meaning of a complex expression is a compositional function of the construed meanings of its parts.

This, too, is untenable, however, as it does not allow an adequate role for context in the construal of the meaning of the complex. The principle could be further modified to take account of this:

(23)   The meaning of a complex expression is the result of a construal process one of the inputs to which are the construals of its constituent parts.

This allows context to act at two levels: the initial construal of the word meanings, and at the level of the whole expression. But this is a long way from the original principle of compositionality. It is more reminiscent of cookery. Is cookery a compositional art? Certainly, the final result is determined by (a) the ingredients and (b) the processes applied, so there is an element of compositionality. But it is not what the proponents of the principle usually have in mind. If we think of global construals, then they are almost certainly compositional only in the cookery sense. But there may be aspects of meaning that do obey the classical principle, at least up to a point. Logical properties are determined by boundary placements, so perhaps the pre-meanings created by boundary construals behave in the classical way? This seems plausible: when we construe *red hats*, we construe a category of red things and a category of hats, and it seems inescapable that the resulting category will be the intersection of these two categories. This is only valid, however, for class membership: we have no guarantee, for instance, that the result will be either prototypical hats nor that their color will be a prototypical red. In other words, for certain aspects of meaning, at certain levels of construal, classical compositionality holds, but not for all aspects or levels.

4.7   Part I: Concluding remarks

With this chapter we conclude the exposition of the basic principles and key concepts underlying the enterprise of cognitive linguistics as we see it. In the chapters that follow, these principles and concepts will be refined, expanded and further illustrated through their application, first, to aspects of word meaning in Part II, and second, to grammar in Part III. We aim to show that the cognitive approach to language not only opens up new aspects of language, but also addresses the traditional concerns of grammarians and semanticists in a more satisfying fashion.

PART II

Cognitive approaches to
lexical semantics

5

Polysemy: the construal of sense boundaries

5.1   Introduction

Polysemy is understood here in a broad sense as variation in the construal of a word on different occasions of use. It will be treated here as a matter of isolating different parts of the total meaning potential of a word in different circumstances. The process of isolating a portion of meaning potential will be viewed as the creation of a sense boundary delimiting an autonomous unit of sense. For instance, in (1), the meaning 'river bank' is as it were fenced off from the rest of the word's potential, and presented as the only functionally relevant portion. The fact that *bank* can also refer to a financial institution is suppressed:

(1)   John moored the boat to the bank.

The operative factor in this case is of course the immediate linguistic context. Polysemy is interpreted in this chapter somewhat more broadly than the traditional lexicographic acceptation involving distinct, established senses, but it includes the traditional view as a special, perhaps in some ways prototypical, case.

On the present account, bounded sense units are not a property of lexical items as such; rather, they are construed at the moment of use. (The notion of sense boundaries that are sharp, but subject to construal, distinguishes the present account from that of Cruse 2000, and also from accounts such as Deane 1988 and Geeraerts 1993, which question the existence of boundaries.) When we retrieve a word from the mental lexicon, it does not come with a full set of ready-made sense divisions. What we get is a purport, together with a set of conventional constraints. However, in particular cases there may be powerful stable constraints favoring the construal of certain sense units. If the permanent constraints are pushing very strongly in one direction, a correspondingly strong countervailing pressure will be necessary to go against them; if the permanent constraints are weak, whether a boundary is construed or not will depend on other, mainly contextual, factors. We can portray the total meaning potential of a word as a region in conceptual space, and each individual interpretation as a point therein. Understood in this way, the meaning potential of a word is typically not a uniform continuum: the interpretations tend to cluster in groups showing different degrees of salience and cohesiveness, and between the groups there are relatively sparsely inhabited regions.

The phenomenon can be illustrated briefly using the well-known example of *bank* in English. There are various uses of this word related to the notion of the collection and custody of money or some other commodity, as in *a high street bank, The World Bank, a blood bank, a sperm bank, a data bank* and so on. These form a cluster. There is an intuitively clear discontinuity separating all these from, for instance, *We moored the boat to the bank, The banks of the stream were covered with brambles, He slid down the bank into the water, I know a bank whereon the wild thyme blows* (Shakespeare) and *Ye banks and braes o' bonny Doon* (Burns). This forms a natural 'fault line' which facilitates the construal of a boundary. Within the 'custodial' cluster we can find subclusters. One such cluster has to do with the custody of money. Even this has subclusters. The exact significance of *bank* in terms of images evoked, implicatures and so on is different in *She works in a bank, I must hurry – I want to get to the bank before it closes* and *I got an unpleasant letter from my bank this morning.*

The distinct sense units that fall under the heading of polysemy are not, in general, interpretations as these were defined in chapter 4: mostly they are what were called pre-meanings, that is, units that appear somewhat further upstream in the construal process than full-fledged interpretations. Recall that an interpretation may be the result of a chain of construal processes: a pre-meaning is still subject to further construal. It is, however, more elaborated than 'raw' purport. Pre-meanings can appear at different stages in the construal chain, the result being that one set of pre-meanings can be nested inside a larger pre-meaning, and several stages of nesting can occur. (This is not to suggest that all the units construable from a single purport can be arranged in a single hierarchy.)

There are several aspects to the partitioning of word meaning. One is the nature of the distinct units that appear; another is the nature of the differentiating factors separating adjacent units; a third is the nature of the boundary – what are the consequences of the boundary and how does it reveal itself? All these aspects are important and interesting. We shall start by considering full sense boundaries and the units they delimit.

5.2   Full sense boundaries

Full sense boundaries delimit the sort of sense units that include those that are the stock-in-trade of traditional dictionaries. For us, the class is wider: traditional dictionaries include only those sense units that are well entrenched in the language and are strongly supported by conventional constraints; however, the same characteristics can be found in nonce construals.

5.2.1   Homonymy and polysemy

It is usual for dictionaries to make a distinction between homonymy and polysemy in the ordering of entries on the page: homonymous senses are given separate main headings, that is to say, they are treated as separate words that have, accidentally, the same spelling and/or sound. Polysemic senses are listed under a single main heading and are treated as 'different meanings of the same word.' The distinction between polysemy and homonymy will not figure prominently in the present account, because it has few, if any, consequences in terms of boundary effects, or the nature of the delimited units.

The distinction can be viewed either diachronically or synchronically. The more traditional distinction is the diachronic one: homonymous units are derived from distinct lexical sources, and their orthographical/phonological identity is due either to the loss of an original distinction due to language change, or to borrowing, whereas polysemic units are derived from the same lexical source, being the result of processes of extension such as metaphor and metonymy.

The diachronic distinction between homonymy and polysemy is a yes/no matter, and is a question of historical fact, resolvable in principle, if not always in practice. The synchronic distinction is less firmly based, and is a matter of degree. The question is whether there is a felt semantic relationship between two interpretations of a word or not. The question can be more precisely formulated (but still not very precisely) as follows: is one interpretation a plausible semantic extension of the other? There are several problems with this characterization. One is that there are degrees of plausibility: where do we draw the line? Another, perhaps more serious, is what exactly 'plausible' means. There is a difference between (i) 'I can sense a connection between the two meanings,' (ii) 'I understand your explanation of how one meaning gave rise to the other' and (iii) 'If I had never met meaning B before, only meaning A, I would understand the word in sense B if I encountered it in a suitable context.'

5.2.2   Entrenchment

The interests of lexicographers are necessarily focused on aspects of word meaning that are strongly supported by stable, mainly conventional constraints, and that have attained some sort of default status. They are more likely to recognize gross distinctions than subtle ones. This is not a criticism. The possible readings of any word are nondenumerable. A dictionary can only offer a finite list, so a high degree of selectivity is inevitable. In the absence of clear criteria, it is also inevitable that different dictionaries will make different distinctions, especially where more subtle distinctions, or ones less clearly licensed by convention are concerned. As far as the present discussion is concerned, there is no difference between entrenched readings and nonce readings in respect of boundary properties or the nature of delimited units.

5.2.3   Boundary effects

A sense boundary reveals its presence in a variety of ways. These can be viewed as different kinds of autonomy of the delimited units. By **autonomy** is meant the ability of a unit to behave independently of other units that might be construed in the same context.

5.2.3.1   Antagonism: attentional autonomy

The feature that distinguishes full sense units from other types of unit is antagonism. Basically this means that two units are mutually exclusive as foci of attention. They are in competition, and if one is at the focus of attention, the other is excluded. This can be clearly felt in the following examples:

(2)   We finally reached the bank. (margin of river, financial institution)
(3)   Mary was wearing a light coat. (light in color, light in weight)
(4)   He studies moles. (animals, skin defects, industrial spies)
(5)   If you don't do something about those roses, they will die. (bushes, flowers)

There are two main consequences of antagonism. The first is the well-known identity constraint:

(6)   Mary was wearing a light coat; so was Jane.

There are strong constraints favoring the construal of two autonomous pre-meanings, namely, 'light in color' and 'light in weight.' Because the two readings of *light* are antagonistic, we are strongly constrained to construe the same reading of *light* in both conjuncts. Two points may be noted here. The first is that the identity constraint is not absolute: it is possible to construe (6) with different readings for *light* in the two conjuncts, but it requires more cognitive work, and the penalty is a sense of wordplay. The second point is that if we construct the sentence without verb-phrase anaphora, while there is still arguably some pressure to use a single reading of *light*, it is much weaker:

(7)   Mary was wearing a light coat; Jane was wearing a light coat, too.

The second consequence of antagonism appears when two antagonistic readings are simultaneously evoked in connection with a single occurrence of a word. The effect is variously referred to as punning, zeugma or syllepsis. (For some scholars these are not identical, but they all have the same source. We shall not pursue the differences here.) It is intuitively instantly recognizable, creating a species of cognitive tension and often a comical effect, and is presumably due to competition between the readings:

(8)   John and his driving license expired last Thursday.
(9)   Dogs can become pregnant at twelve months, but usually live longer than bitches.

The so-called 'zeugma test' has been criticized on the grounds that it does not give consistent results, in that cases occur where an identical semantic contrast will in some contexts produce zeugma and in other contexts will not, and, most damagingly, contexts can be found where even the prototypical examples of alleged ambiguity will not yield zeugma. One type of example is illustrated in (10):

(10)   (*B is doing a crossword puzzle*)
         A: The answer to 21 across is *bank*.
         B: But the clue doesn't say anything about money.
         A: True, but not all banks are money banks, you know.

The first occurrence of *bank* in A's response to B is not felt by most people to be zeugmatic, although it ought to be, if *bank* is truly ambiguous and the zeugma test is reliable (so the argument goes). It ought to be clear that this is no problem for the approach adopted here. Whether or not a sense boundary appears in particular cases is a matter of construal: 'consistency' would only be expected if the boundary was an inherent property of the word, which our approach denies. Now, in the case of *bank*, there are certainly strong conventional constraints favoring the construal of a boundary, which means that in the majority of contexts a boundary will be construed. However, in (10), no boundary is construed (the two readings are 'unified' – see discussion below), and the above occurrence of *bank* is not ambiguous. This occurs only in a very small range of context types. (Incidentally, any two meanings can be unified in this way.) However, the fact that it occurs does not constitute a valid reason for questioning the validity of the test.

5.2.3.2   Relational autonomy

Antagonism is indicative of the most marked level of autonomy. There are other symptoms, but these also appear at lower levels of autonomy and are therefore not diagnostic for full sense boundaries. One of these symptoms is the possession by two readings of distinct sets of sense relations. This feature is complicated by the fact that sense relations are themselves basically context-sensitive construals; for this reason, the more stable the relations are, and the more supported by conventional constraints, the stronger the evidence they provide for the autonomy of readings, and hence for the presence of a boundary. An example is *light* in (11):

(11)   Mary is wearing a light coat.

Here *light* has two distinct antonyms, *dark* and *heavy*. Cases such as *light* are to be distinguished from cases such as *old*. *Old* might be held to have two distinct antonyms in *an old car* (*new*) and *an old man* (*young*). However, there are good reasons for viewing *new* and *young* as jointly constituting the antonym of *old*. *New* and *old* have a common meaning component 'has been in existence a relatively short time' which forms a satisfactory antonymic partner to an interpretation that covers the range of possibilities for *old*, namely, 'has been in existence a relatively long time.' The unity of *old* is supported by the lack of zeugma in (12):

(12)   John's car is almost as old as he is.

When the relationships in question are of a taxonomic or meronomic variety, what is important is that purportedly autonomous readings should belong to different lexical fields. The two pre-meanings of *bank* are good examples. Thus, *bank* in *the bank of the river* has *source*, *bed* and *mouth* as co-meronyms, but no obvious hyponyms or hyperonyms, whereas in *the bank in the High Street*, it has co-hyponyms like *building society* and *insurance company*, and *financial institution* as a hyperonym; as for meronyms, they would presumably be different departments of the bank.

5.2.3.3 Compositional autonomy

Compositional autonomy will assume greater importance in connection with lower levels of autonomy, but it also applies clearly to units delimited by full sense boundaries. It refers to the fact that in a compositional process – for instance the modification of a noun by an adjective – one of the participating elements will engage with, or take as its scope, only a portion of the meaning of the other. That portion will be said to display compositional autonomy, and it will be assumed that a boundary has been drawn between it and the rest of the meaning.

The workings of compositional autonomy are very obvious in the case of units delimited by full sense boundaries. For instance, in *a steep bank*, the adjective *steep* in effect ignores completely the meaning 'financial institution' – it is as if it did not exist; likewise, in *a high-street bank*, the meaning 'edge of river' is cut off and plays no part.

5.2.4   The nature of full sense units

A question that arises in connection with full sense units is this: What is it about them that makes them antagonistic? An obvious, but not quite adequate, answer is that they are typically very different semantically. They tend, for instance, to have few components in common, to belong to different domains, to be of different ontological types and so on. The most prototypical cases show semantic distance on one or more of these dimensions, and generally speaking, the greater the semantic distance between two readings, the more likely they are to be antagonistic. However, this is not the whole story, because some very close readings are antagonistic. Take the case of *month*, which maps onto two sense units, each clearly defined, each referring to a period of time: 'period of four weeks' and 'calendar month.' When we use the word *month*, we must have one or other of these units in mind: *a month's supply of tablets* normally means 28 days; *the first three months of the year* would almost certainly be construed as referring to calendar months. It would hardly be possible to find an ambiguous word whose component units were closer.

A more revealing approach (but which is still in some ways mysterious) is to say that antagonistic readings are readings that resist unification. There are three relevant modes of unification: (i) the assimilation of two items as parts of the same whole; (ii) the inclusion of two classes as subclasses of a superordinate class; (iii) englobement – the encompassing of two disparate items as components of a global Gestalt. On this view, full senses are readings that strongly resist any kind of unification. Take the case of *bank*. It is hard to think of the different sorts of bank as parts of a whole, or as united into a global Gestalt. We might think of a very general category to which they both belong, such as 'entity,' or even 'location,' but this is not good enough, because it does not distinguish banks from non-banks. Actually, it is possible to unify the two readings of *bank*, in a very restricted range of contexts (which is why we cannot say that antagonistic readings can never be unified). Recall the example cited above, which most speakers do not find anomalous:

(13)   Not all banks are money banks.

The first mention of *bank* here represents a unification of the two units. The context in this case enjoins us to find a distinctive unifying property for the two kinds of bank. As it happens, this is not too difficult, although it requires a conceptual shift to a metalinguistic level. The unifying factor is that both concepts are designated/mapped onto by the same word form.

5.3   Sub-sense units with near-sense properties

We have taken antagonism between sense units to be indicative of the highest degree of autonomy. However, there also exist sense units that resemble full senses in many ways, but do not display antagonism, or do so only in restricted contexts (in the same way that full senses can only be unified in restricted contexts). The fact that these cases do not show antagonism means that the units in question can be unified. The different types can be conveniently classified on the basis of the type of unification involved. Units that have a significant degree of autonomy, but can be unified into a superordinate category will be termed 'microsenses' (the present account is based mainly on Cruse 2002a); units that have a significant degree of autonomy, but can be unified to form a global Gestalt, will be termed 'facets' (see Cruse 2000a, 2000b, especially the latter). These appear to be the only possibilities. Although parts of a whole can function independently for compositional purposes (see below), there do not seem to be any part-whole counterparts to microsenses.

5.3.1   Facets

Facets are distinguishable components of a global whole, but they are not capable of being subsumed under a hyperonym.

5.3.1.1   Introduction

Although facets display a significant degree of autonomy, they are not generally considered to represent polysemy in the traditional sense; for instance, they are rarely given separate definitions in dictionaries. Prototypical examples of words with facets are the readings of *bank* (in the 'financial' sense) and *book*:

(14)   *bank* = [PREMISES]   The bank was blown up.
            [PERSONNEL]   It's a friendly bank.
            [INSTITUTION]   The bank was founded in 1597.

(15)   *book* = [TOME]   a red book
            [TEXT]   an interesting book

The items in (16) illustrate cases of words possessing facets analogous to [TOME] and [TEXT]:

(16)   a. *letter*:   a crumpled letter
                a moving letter

        b. *CD*:   an indestructible CD
                a beautiful CD

c. *film*:   a 16mm film
            a sad film

d. *speech*: a deafening speech
            an incomprehensible speech

Sentences (17a–c) illustrate three facets of *Britain*:

(17)   a. Britain today lies under one meter of snow. [LAND]
        b. Britain is today mourning the death of the Royal corgi. [PEOPLE]
        c. Britain declares war on North Korea. [STATE]

Other possible examples of facets are: *mother* [CARE-GIVER], [BIRTH-GIVER], and *chicken* [BIRD], [FOOD].

It should be borne in mind that facets as such are not meanings, but pre-meanings, and are both the result of construal processes and at the same time the subject of further construal. I shall illustrate the properties of facets using the [TOME] and [TEXT] facets of *book*. (In Cruse 2000b evidence was presented for the existence of a third facet of 'book,' which might be characterized as [PHYSICAL TEXT] [picked out by such predicates as 'badly printed'/ 'poor lay-out,' 'in Cyrillic,' 'hard on the eyes' etc.], and which differs from the [TOME] facet in being, for instance, two-dimensional, rather than three-dimensional etc. While only a few facets may be strongly favored by conventional constraints, in principle there is no reason to believe that the facets of a sense constitute a determinate set.)

5.3.1.2 Autonomy in facets

The facets of *book* show their autonomy clearly in two of the three main ways discussed above:

(a)   *Relational autonomy*

Facets show full relational independence, in that each facet may partic-ipate in its own sense relations, independently of other facets. For instance, in most contexts, the hyponyms of *book* form two parallel taxonomies, but there is no relationship between the two taxonomies:

(18)   Some of the books we read were novels and the others were biographies.

In (18), *book* is construed as the facet [TEXT], which stands in a hyperonymic relation to the incompatible hyponyms *novel* and *biography*.

(19)   Some of the books were paperbacks, most were hardbacks.

In (19), *book* is construed as the facet [TOME], which stands in a hyperonymic relation to the incompatible hyponyms *paperback* and *hardback*.

(20)   *Some of the books [GLOBAL] were hardbacks, the rest were novels.

As (20) illustrates, *novel* and *hardback* do not coordinate in a context that expects items to be construed as incompatibles within a single domain. The normality of generic decontextualized statements such as (21a) and (21b) shows that the potentiality for the construal of facets for *book* is well supported by conventional constraints:

(21)   a. A novel is a kind of book.
         b. A paperback is a kind of book.

(b)   Compositional autonomy

Predicates can apply to facets independently:

(22)   a red book; a dusty book

In these phrases, the adjective modifies only the [TOME] facet of *book*. In (23), on the other hand, the adjectives modify only the [TEXT] facet:

(23)   an exciting book; a difficult book

This in itself is only a relatively weak indication of autonomy. More striking is the ambiguity of a phrase with no ambiguous words and no syntactic ambiguity. Any predicate that can apply to either facet separately gives rise to an ambiguity not attributable either to lexis or syntax:

(24)   a. two books
         b. two books in one
         c. a new book
         d. a long book

Example (24a) can designate either two copies of the same text (i.e. two 'tomes') or two texts; (24b) is interesting because the numerals *two* and *one*, respectively, modify different facets (yet there is no zeugma); *a new book* may be a new copy of a very ancient text, or a copy (whether in pristine condition or not) of a recently composed text; *a long book* may be one with lots of words in it, or it may have a non-canonical physical shape (notice that *two long books* or *two new books* have to be long or new in the same way).

In an appropriate context, a question containing *book* can be truthfully answered both in the affirmative and the negative, that is to say, responses can be relative to one facet to the exclusion of the other. Consider (25):

(25)   Do you like the book?

Out of context this is likely to be interpreted as referring to the [TEXT] facet only, but it is not difficult to envisage a scenario in which it could be construed as referring equally to the [TOME] facet. In such a case, the potential exists for both *Yes* and *No* to be true answers.

(c)   Autonomous 'cores'

An interesting manifestation of autonomy is worth mentioning. Consider (26) and (27):

(26)   I'm not interested in the contents, etc., I'm interested in the book itself.
(27)   I'm not interested in the binding, etc., I'm interested in the book itself.

Both (26) and (27) are normally interpretable and involve different readings of *the book itself*, namely, [TOME] in (26) and [TEXT] in (27). This will be taken to indicate that *book* has two 'cores'. Compare, however, the same procedure applied to *novel*:

(28)   ?I'm not interested in the plot, etc., I'm interested in the novel itself.
(29)   I'm not interested in the binding, etc., I'm interested in the novel itself.

It seems that it is easy to isolate the [TEXT] facet of *novel*, but more difficult to construe an autonomous [TOME] facet. This is also suggested by the relative oddness (at least in the absence of more specific context) of *a red novel, a dusty novel, a shiny novel*, compared with *a red book, a dusty book* and *a shiny book* (we shall return to the 'novel problem' below).

(d)   Some miscellaneous aspects of autonomy

A textless tome and a tomeless text can both be designated by *book*:

(30)   I've got a book to write the minutes of the meeting in.
(31)   A: How's your book going?
          B: Oh, it's all in here [pointing to head], but I haven't written anything down yet.

This, and the independent countability of facets can be taken as an indication of a certain degree of referential distinctness.

Also, each facet can have independent metaphorical extensions. In order to interpret (32), it is only necessary to access the [TOME] facet:

(32)   a book of matches

Finally, each facet can have an independent proper name. *Middlemarch* is the name of a text, not of a physical object, nor yet of a text-physical object complex.

(e)   Attentional autonomy in facets

It is extremely hard to demonstrate attentional autonomy with facets. In most situations where zeugma might be expected (if facets were full senses), it does not arise:

(33)   It's a very helpful book, but rather heavy to carry around.

One possible case, however, is (34):

(34)   ?John wrote a red book.

What is written is the text, but what is red is the physical object, and combining the two seems to be cognitively difficult. It is not clear what the conditions are for the appearance of zeugma here, since it does not appear to be present in (35):

(35)   John wrote that red book on the top shelf over there.

However, in the vast majority of contexts, simultaneous activation of distinct facets does not lead to zeugma.

5.3.1.3   Unifying facets

On the above evidence, one might be tempted to say that the facets of *book* are separate senses, related to separate concepts. However, the distinctness of facets is sometimes overestimated. For instance, the *Oxford Advanced Learner's Dictionary* gives two separate entries for the facets of *book*: they are listed as *1(a)* and *1(b)*, and are thus not distinguished from senses. It was argued in Cruse 1986 that they were separate senses. However, there is evidence that there exists a global sense 'book,' corresponding to a global concept BOOK, which represents a unification of the two facets, and which justifies the claim that the facets do not have the full status of lexical senses. A summary of this evidence follows. (Notice that facets cannot be unified as hyponyms of a hyperonymic category: there is no category that subsumes 'tomes' and 'texts.' Nor are they parts of a whole in the normal sense.)

(a)   Prototypical co-occurrence

If we think of *book* as a basic-level item, it is clear that the prototype has both facets: although either can exist without the other, partnerless facets are, to say the least, peripheral. Naive subjects learn about the dual nature of book with initial surprise (but ready acceptance, nonetheless).

(b)   Joint compositional properties

One aspect of joint compositional properties is that there are predicates that attach themselves to both facets simultaneously:

(36)   to publish a book

It is not possible to publish something that does not comprise both a text and some physical manifestation.

Another aspect of joint compositional properties has already been mentioned, namely, serial composition without zeugma. In other words, facets do not show antagonism in circumstances where senses would:

(37)   This is a very interesting book, but it is awfully heavy to carry around.

In (37), *interesting* modifies the [TEXT] facet, and *heavy to carry around* the [TOME] facet.

(c)   Joint lexical relations

The global reading (which includes both facets) has its own sense relations. An example of this is the hyperonym/hyponym relation between *publication* and *book* (also, between *educational establishment* and *school*, and *tourist accommodation* and *hotel*, and the incompatibility relation between *building society* and *bank*).

(d)   Global reference

Definite noun phrases such as *the red book*, or *that friendly hotel* arguably refer to the relevant global entity, rather than purely to the facet targeted by the adjective.

(e)   Joint extensions

There are extensions of sense that require both facets to be taken into account for them to be intelligible:

(38)   I can read him like an open book.

To interpret *read* in (38), we must access our knowledge of how texts are processed; to interpret *open*, we need to access knowledge of books as physical objects.

(f)   Joint nameability

The Lindisfarne Gospels (a medieval text) is the name of a global [TEXT]+[TOME] entity.

5.3.1.4   Why are facets not full senses?

In the case of *bank*, the conceptual representation provides strong pressure for a split reading, and in the case of *teacher* in (39) and (40), which exhibits none of the symptoms of autonomy, the conceptual representation provides strong pressure for a unified reading.

(39)   Our teacher is on maternity leave. (construed as 'female teacher')
(40)   Our teacher is on paternity leave. (construed as 'male teacher')

In the case of *book*, it appears that the stable constraints do not push us strongly in either direction, so we are (relatively) free to construe the facets either as autonomous or as unified in response to other constraints, such as contextual or communicative ones. This is not so much because conceptual constraints are absent, or inoperative, but because they act in contrary directions, effectively canceling one another out.

One obvious factor pointing toward an autonomous manifestation of facets is 'conceptual/semantic distance.' As we have already noted, the more similar two readings are, other things being equal, the easier it will be to unify them, and the more difficult to construe a boundary between them; conversely, the more different they are, the more difficult it will be (generally speaking) to unify them and the easier it will be to construe them as autonomous. Clearly, a difference of basic ontological type, for instance, 'concrete' vs. 'abstract,' represents a substantial semantic distance, and will be expected to constitute a constraint opposing unification. The facets of *book*, and those of every multifaceted word that have been identified, are of distinct ontological types, and therefore it is no surprise that they show autonomous tendencies.

The problem with facets is rather one of explaining why they are so easily unified, given their conceptual distinctness. One possibility is that there is a counterconstraint operative here. First of all, the facets typically co-occur in a range of significant contexts – in fact, they prototypically co-occur; secondly, they do not *simply* co-occur, rather, they operate in a kind of functional symbiosis. The only reason for having the [TOME] is to concretely manifest the [TEXT]; the text is useless without some physical manifestation. In Langackerian terms, we can say that they are *jointly* profiled against a single domain matrix. This acts as a strong constraint favoring unity. So, in the case of facets, we have significant constraints favoring a unified construal and constraints favoring the construal of a boundary. When this state of affairs obtains, whether a boundary is construed or not in particular circumstances will depend on other factors. For instance, in (28) and (29) above, the linguistic context motivates the hearer strongly to look for a reading excluded by the first conjunct, i.e. to construe a boundary.

5.3.1.5 The novel problem

Let us turn now briefly to the *novel* problem. Why is it that, out of context, *a red book* is normal, but *a red novel* is somewhat odd? It seems that construing a [TOME] facet for *novel* is difficult. There are certain usages that at first sight seem to point to the existence of a [TOME] reading for novel (in that they are normal even out of context):

(41)   a. A novel of some three hundred pages
         b. A thick novel with many colored illustrations
         c. A paperback novel

However, these are not really counterexamples to the general inaccessibility of the [TOME] reading, because the physical features can be construed as giving information about the text of the novel (cf. Kleiber 1996). But even *a red novel* can be normalized in a sufficiently (and appropriately) elaborated context (a special intonation is required to get the correct reading):

(42)   All the novels are on the right and the travel books are on the left. Incidentally, I want to show you something – pass me that red novel on the top shelf.

Cases like (43) are presumably similar (cf. example 1 in Fauconnier 1994:143):

(43)   A: Pass me the Keats and the Wordsworth: Keats is red and Wordsworth is green.
         B: I can see a blue Keats, but not a red one.

These examples are convincing enough, but are hard to invent and clearly require special contextual justification. But there are still facts about *novel* that need to be explained. For instance, as mentioned earlier, why are the following odd out of context, while the equivalent expressions with *book* are not?:

(44)   a. ?a red novel
         b. ?a dirty novel (in the physical sense)/?This novel is dirty
         c. ?a dusty novel

Furthermore, certain contexts that are clearly ambiguous with *book* require a considerable cognitive effort to see as ambiguous with *novel*:

(45)   a new novel
         two novels

Perhaps most strikingly, as has been already noted, the *X itself* construction has two readings with *book*, but only one with *novel*:

(46)   I'm not interested in the typography or the cover design, I'm interested in the novel itself.
(47)   ?I'm not interested in the plot or the characters, I'm interested in the novel itself.

At the very least, we can say that the [TOME] reading of *novel*, in spite of the fact that it informs a good deal of our everyday interaction with novels, for one reason or another, is much more difficult to construe than that of *book*.

Why, then, does *novel* behave in a different way from *book*? One approach to answering this question is to look at features of meaning that distinguish items that behave like *book* from those that behave like *novel*. It might be argued, for instance, that what is distinctive about a novel is its text, not its physical format; one might even say that the immediate default contrasts of *novel* are other literary genres, like *poem* or *short story*. In the case of *book*, on the other hand, the facets are perhaps more equally balanced. There are two sorts of contrast: first, with other everyday physical objects such as *clock*, *vase*, *ornament* or *in-tray*, and second, with other text-types, such as *newspaper*, *magazine*, *brochure*, *directory*.

There is a certain intuitive plausibility about this explanation, but on close examination, the matter is much more complex. Take the case of *dictionary*. The most distinctive property of a dictionary is the text it contains. Yet *dictionary* behaves not like *novel* but like *book* in that, for instance, *two dictionaries* is ambiguous between 'two different dictionary-texts' and 'two copies of the same text.' At this point one might point out that while a novel does not have a distinctive format, a dictionary does, at least prototypically, and this might account for the higher salience of the [TOME] facet. There are two objections to this. One is that there are other book-like entities with distinctive formats that behave like *novel*: one of these is *thesis*, which at least in a British university has a highly distinctive format. Yet *two theses* can only mean two different texts, and not two copies of the same thesis. The other objection is that novels do prototypically have a distinctive format, or at least there are possible book formats that are unlikely to be novels: think of the characteristic large-format art books, or atlases.

A different line of argument is to say that there is no *novel* problem: *novel* behaves as one might expect. The problem lies with *dictionary* in that it unexpectedly behaves like *book* in spite of being defined by its contents. At this point, the example of *bible* is perhaps relevant: a bible is defined by its contents, but *two bibles* normally refers to two copies of the same text. This is presumably because the text of a bible is (in everyday experience) unique – there are no others of the same type. There is some plausibility in the suggestion that, to an ordinary person, the same is true of 'The Dictionary.' That is to say, there is a naive assumption that there is only one text, and this forces a [TOME] interpretation of plurality (something similar would occur with, for instance, two David Copperfields). (The fact that one says *Look it up in the dictionary* at least as readily as *Look it up in a dictionary* is confirmatory evidence.)

There is still a problem, though. Consider the following cases:

(48)   a. a tall secretary
        b. a burly barman
        c. a fair-haired professor of linguistics

Just as *novel* is defined by its text, *secretary*, *barman* and *professor of linguistics* are defined by their jobs, yet there appears to be no prohibition on the use of 'irrelevant' adjectives, as there is with *novel* and *thesis*. (It may be that this is an aspect of the wider problem of restrictions on active zones: why, for instance, can we say *Mary is fair*, meaning that she has fair hair, but not ?*Mary is blue* [without elaborate contextualization], meaning that she has blue eyes?)

5.3.1.6 Near neighbors of facets

Many word meanings represent an association between ontologically distinct components, and it is in the domain of such associations that facets appear. However, the degree of integration of the components varies, and it appears that the construal of facets is favored by an intermediate degree of integration. Where there is a lower degree of integration, the components behave more like full senses, and where integration is higher, the facets lose their autonomy. Consider the notion of a punch on the nose. Here we have an action (concrete) associated with a sensation (mental). However, signs of facethood are absent, since *intense*, for instance, which is normal with *pain*, is not normal with *punch on the nose*:

(49)   *an intense punch on the nose

This would be contrary to expectations if action and sensation could be construed as facets. Somewhat more facet-like is *factory*:

(50)   a. The factory was blown up. [PREMISES]
        b. The whole factory came out on strike. [PERSONNEL]
        c. (50%?) The factory that was blown up came out on strike.

However, out of a typical class of student informants, only about half will accept (50c) as normal. In contrast, there is unanimity concerning the normality of (51c):

(51)   a. A red book
        b. A funny book
        c. You'll find that red book on the top shelf very funny.

This suggests that the components of *factory* are less integrated than those of *book*. However, there seem to be cases of dual-nature concepts that are even more integrated than *book*, and that show significantly less facet-like behavior. One example is *woman* (many words referring to human beings are similar). Although informants are intuitively not happy to put *woman* into the same semantic category as *book*, it does shows some signs of facethood (the facets will be referred to as [BODY] and [MIND], for convenience, but this carries no philosophical implications). For instance, there are adjectives that attach themselves to one facet or the other:

(52)   a. A tall woman [BODY]
        b. An intelligent woman [MIND]

There is some evidence of relational autonomy in that, for instance, the meronyms are different; and there are separate classificatory systems for body types and personality types. And consider the following scenario. Suppose we wired Mary up to a computer which mapped accurately every neuronal connection in her brain, producing a replica of her mind that one could communicate with, but unfortunately destroyed the original patterns in the process. We would then have a body and a mind. Which one would be the 'real' Mary? Arguably, one could refer to either entity as *Mary*. But other indications of autonomy seem to be weak. For instance, it is hard to find any ambiguous contexts explicable only by appeal to facets; and *woman* (for many informants) fails the *X itself* test:

(53)   I'm not interested in the woman's body, I'm interested in the woman herself.

(54)   ?I'm not interested in the woman's mind or personality or feelings, I'm interested in the woman herself.

Another example concerns the verb *weigh*. This involves a physical action allied to a mental action:

(55)   a. John weighed the potatoes with trembling hands. [PHYSICAL ACTION]
        b. John weighed the potatoes accurately. [MENTAL ACTION]

The integration here shows up in the lack of truth-conditional independence in the two putative facets. In answer to the question *Did John weigh the potatoes?* one can only base one's answer on the global reading; that is to say, it is not sufficient merely, for instance, to put some potatoes onto a scale to be able to truthfully say one has weighed them. Likewise, there is no analogue of a tomeless text, or a textless tome. Nor does, for instance, *John weighed the potatoes calmly* seem ambiguous in the way that *John writes beautifully* is, or even *Did you write the letter?* (i.e. 'Did you compose the text?'/'Did you produce the physical inscription?') It is not being suggested that there is anything unusual about *woman* or *weigh*. There are grounds for believing that it is facets that represent the atypical case. Facets can be viewed as occupying a relatively restricted position in a theoretical space constituted by two dimensions: integration and ontological distinctness, both characterized by variation in degree. With reduced integration, facets are simply polysemic senses related by metonymy; with increased integration, facets lose their independence. A reduction of ontological distinctness also leads to a loss of autonomy, giving rise to normal sister parts of complex objects or events.

5.3.2 Microsenses

Microsenses are distinct sense units of a word that occur in different contexts and whose default construals stand in a relation of mutual incompatibility at the same hierarchical level, rather like, for instance, the names of animals such as *cat, dog, sheep, cow, pig, horse*. Typical examples of words with microsenses are *knife* and *card*. Consider how these words are understood in the following contexts:

(56)   John called the waiter over to his table and complained that he had not been given a knife and fork.

(57)   The attacker threatened the couple with a knife.

(58)   I got a card the other day from Ralph, who's on holiday in Tenerife.

(59)   Let me give you my card; let me know as soon as you have any news.

These are to be contrasted with the readings of *knife* and *card* that appear in (60) and (61), respectively, which are hyperonymic to the readings in (56)–(59) above:

(60)   You can buy any kind of knife there.

(61)   The box was full of cards of various sorts.

Words like *knife* and *card* have a hyperonymic reading and a cluster of hyponymous readings, whose default construals are sister incompatibles. All of these units exhibit a significant degree of autonomy. It is the specific units, which are here termed **microsenses**, that do the bulk of the 'semantic work' of the lexeme. The hyperonymic construal has a secondary role. It requires positive contextual pressure for activation: it is never the default selection (for instance, in [60] and [61] *any kind of* and *of various sorts* are contextual triggers for the hyperonymic reading). Furthermore, it is relatively ill-defined, and does not have an established place in any lexical field. The words *knife* and *card* show what may be termed **default specificity**, that is, when we encounter them, our first assumption is that one of the specific construals is intended, and we look for evidence as to which one.

A natural reaction at this point is to say that this is a purely pragmatic matter – the different construals of *knife* and *card* in the above examples are no different from those of *friend* in (62) and (63) (i.e. 'female friend' and 'male friend,' respectively):

(62)   My best friend married my brother.

(63)   My best friend married my sister.

However, there are significant differences. Firstly, in (62) and (63) we see merely different contextual construals of a purport that is essentially neutral with respect to sex. The readings 'female friend' and 'male friend' do not exhibit autonomy. The neutral purport is inferentially enriched in different ways in (62) and (63) in response to the contextual elements *married my brother* and *married my sister*. In the absence of contextual pressure, the neutral reading of *friend* will be construed. This type of construal, which does not involve the creation of autonomous intermediate units of sense, will be termed **contextual modulation**. Microsenses, on the other hand, constitute autonomous sense units, and their hyperonymic reading requires contextual pressure.

In order to substantiate the above claims regarding the special status of microsenses it is necessary to lay out the arguments in detail. First we need to establish that microsenses are not merely contextual modulations; then we need to distinguish them from both full senses and facets.

5.3.2.1 Why microsenses are not contextual modulations

The argument that microsenses are not contextual modulations has two strands: the first involves evidence that the specific readings have too much autonomy, and the second involves evidence that the hyperonymic reading does not have default status.

Evidence for the autonomy of the specific construals comes from a number of sources. First, they can show relational autonomy, in that each has its own independent set of sense relations. The microsenses of *knife*, for instance, give rise to construals belonging to different taxonomies, and which therefore have different hyperonyms, hyponyms and co-hyponyms:

(64)   cutlery: **knife**, fork, spoon
        weapon: **knife**, gun, cosh, grenade
        instrument: **knife**, scalpel, forceps
        (garden) tool: **knife**, spade, fork, trowel, rake
        (DIY) tool: **knife**, screwdriver, hammer, plane

A second indication of the salient individuality of microsenses is that they exhibit truth-conditional autonomy. An indication of this is when a yes/no question can be truthfully answered *No*, based on one microsense, when the hyperonymic reading, or another microsense, would require a positive answer. The following are examples:

(65)   Mother: (*at table; Johnny is playing with his meat with his fingers*): Use your knife to cut your meat, Johnny.
        Johnny: (*who has a pen-knife in his pocket, but no knife of the proper sort*) I haven't got one.
(66)   Tom: (*who has a football under his arm*): Let's play tennis.
        Billy: Have you got a ball?
        Tom: No, I thought YOU had one.

Of course it is the case here that context makes clear what sort of ball is relevant, and this means that if there were no appropriate microsense available for selection, contextual modulation would lead us to much the same meaning. It is important to emphasize, however, that truth-conditional autonomy is not an automatic property of contextually enriched readings. For instance, in (67), although context makes clear what sort of car would be appropriate, B's answer cannot be based on the contextually specified reading:

(67)   A: (*There are 6 people to transport*) Do you have a car?
       B: (*Who has a 2CV*) *No.
          Yes, but it's too small to take us all.

Microsenses also give rise to an identity constraint. There is a palpable pressure to interpret the second conjunct in each of the following sentences with the same reading of the word in bold as was chosen for the first conjunct:

(68)   a. John sent a **card**; so did Mary.
       b. John has some **equipment**; so has Bill.
       c. John needs a **knife**; so does Bill.

The constraint appears to be stronger in some cases than others: this may be a reflection of degree of autonomy. But the contrast with (69a) and (69b), where there is no constraint, is clear:

(69)   a. John has a cousin; so has Mary.
       b. John has a car; so has Mary.

An important aspect of the individuality of microsenses is that they function as basic level items in their home domains. For instance, at table, *knife* is a basic level item, alongside *spoon*, *fork* and so on (the relevant reading of *fork* is also a microsense), and displays all the characteristic properties of basic level items. This is not any sort of knife, but the specific variety that falls under the hyperonym *cutlery* (at least in British English). Although there are other sorts of knives, in the appropriate context there is no need for a specifying epithet: and, indeed, most speakers would be hard put to supply one. In contrast to microsenses, there are no cases where contextually modulated readings like those in (62) and (63) function as basic level items.

The hyperonymic readings of microsense complexes (i.e. the combination of hyperonym plus a set of microsenses) are distinct in a number of ways from those of contextual modulations. One of the most striking properties of hyperonyms which subsume a set of microsenses is their default specificity. Words like *knife*, *card* and *equipment* have a strong preference for specific use, and this renders them odd (to varying degrees) in a minimal context:

(70)   a. Do you have any equipment?
       b. Do you possess a card?
       c. Do you have a knife?

The examples in (70) may be contrasted with those in (71):

(71)   a. Do you have any children?
        b. Do you have a car?

In (71a-b) there is no pressure for specificity, and they are not (automatically) anomalous in contexts that do not sanction a more specific interpretation. A corollary of the property of default specificity is that the hyperonymic readings of words such as *knife* require overt contextual pressure for their activation: the mere absence of specifying pressure is not enough. Thus, although the questions in (70) are to some degree odd, those in (72) and (73) are not:[1]

(72)   Do you have a knife/card/ball of any kind?
(73)   a knife wound; a knife-sharpener

The hyperonyms of sets of microsenses seem to correspond to somewhat non-prototypical concepts. For instance, they do not seem to have clear relational properties, or at least not readily accessible ones. In spite of the fact that a knife is intuitively an everyday object, speakers are notably hesitant in suggesting either a hyperonym or other member of the same contrast set that applies to all knives, whereas they have no problem with, say, *dog* or, indeed, with one of the microsenses of *knife*. Furthermore, in terms of the distinction between subordinate level, basic level and superordinate level conceptual categories, the hyperonymic reading of *knife* seems to be associated with the latter type of category. There are resemblances between the inclusive category KNIFE and typical superordinate level categories such as FURNITURE. For instance, both have a rather schematic, impoverished nature, which is different from the rich content of typical basic level categories. Also, they are not associated with clear visual images or patterns of behavioral interaction.

It is a curious fact that, while (linguistically untrained) speakers readily accept the dual nature of multifaceted words like *book*, they are reluctant to accept the composite nature of *knife*. It seems that the unity of the concept is more salient than

---

[1] The account of default specificity given in Cruse 2000a is not quite correct. There it was suggested that questions like those in (70) are odd if the context does not sanction the selection of one of the microsenses. However, it was also suggested that there are situational contexts, for instance camping, for which there is no corresponding microsense. It would seem to follow from this that questions like those in (70) are invariably odd in such contexts. However, this is not true: (i) seems normal:

(i)   (*in a camping context*) I need to cut this rope. Do you have a knife?

Relevance considerations here narrow down the range of suitable knives: they have to be capable of cutting the rope in question. But this looks like contextual modulation rather than the selection of a microsense. It seems therefore that the default specificity constraint is satisfied by any sort of specification, whether or not it involves a microsense, and it is the unrestricted reading of the hyperonym that requires overt contextual justification.

its components. Speakers readily offer unified dictionary-type definitions such as 'an implement with a handle and a blade used for cutting.' However, the initial intuitive plausibility of this definition diminishes slightly on closer examination. Firstly, it does not differentiate knives from saws, chisels and other cutting implements, and secondly, it contains several words with microsenses just like those of *knife*, so it must be interpreted as something like: 'an implement with a knife-type blade and a knife-type handle, used for knife-style cutting'; in other words, we need to know what a knife is before we can make intuitively satisfying sense of the definition.

5.3.2.2   Why microsenses are not full senses or facets

Microsenses are not distinct senses because they are unifiable under a hyperonym, and are therefore not, by the usual criteria, antagonistic. The reason microsenses are not facets is because facets are of different ontological types and cannot be subsumed under a hyperonym.

5.3.2.3   Microsenses and facets compared

Microsenses are in some ways a kind of converse of facets in that, whereas for facets, the difference of ontological type would lead us to expect them to be autonomous, but the default construal is in fact a unified one, in the case of microsenses, their close similarity would be expected to produce unified readings but, in fact, it is the specific readings that are in some sense the default case. Hence, for microsenses, we need to identify a strong countervailing constraint favoring the placement of boundaries. The answer once again seems to be the domains in which the microsenses operate. The notion of domain was invoked to unify facets, whereas with microsenses, it is the different domains in which the microsenses operate that confer distinctness. Thus, semantic distance between readings may be counterbalanced by a strong tendency toward joint relevance, whereas semantic closeness can be counterbalanced by distinctness of habitual contexts. (Remember that in the case of both facets and microsenses, the countervailing constraints are sufficiently closely balanced for contextual constraints to have a significant effect.)

5.3.2.4   A Langackerian explanation for microsense behavior

Two main lines of explanation will be explored here. The first is broadly Langackerian in spirit (cf. Tuggy 1993). Within this framework there are two possible approaches to microsense complexes, which are not necessarily contradictory. The first approach is based on different levels of entrenchment (which will be taken to be equivalent to the strength of conventional constraints) for the hyperonymic reading and the specific readings, as illustrated in (74):

(74) **cousin:**   hyperonym: heavily entrenched; rich
                                      specifics: pragmatically generated

        knife: hyperonym: lightly entrenched; sparse
                                        specifics: heavily entrenched; rich

   card (paper vs. plastic):   hyperonym: pragmatically generated
                                        specifics: heavily entrenched

        bank: hyperonym: non-existent
                                        specifics: heavily entrenched

There is a graded shift of emphasis from hyperonym to hyponym(s); although only four stages are shown, the scale is to be thought of as continuous. The representation of *card* needs further comment. The distinction between the different sorts of 'paper' cards would be like that of *knife*. What is illustrated in (74) is the distinction between paper and plastic cards. Many speakers report that they find it difficult to interpret sentences like (75) to include both types:

(75)   The box contained various types of cards.

However, plastic and paper cards can be united in special contexts such as (76):

(76)   The box contained a variety of plastic and other sorts of cards.

A distinction is being made here between hyperonymic readings that must be 'overtly licensed' by the context (as with *knife*) and those that must be 'contextually coerced' (as with *card*); the latter are considered not to be entrenched, but pragmatically generated. (Again, of course, we are dealing with a continuous scale, this time of resistance to unification, and the cutoff point is to some extent arbitrary.)

To what extent can the above picture throw light on the nature of microsense complexes? Let us assume that every occurrence of a use of a word with a particular reading increases that reading's entrenchment, and that increasing entrenchment enhances the permanence, salience and accessibility of the reading.

Clearly, if a range of specific readings is more accessible than the hyperonymic reading, then there will be a preference for a specific reading, if there is one that fits the context. More can be explained if we assume that each reading represents a point in a profile-base chain, or, thinking in terms of the Langackerian notion of domain matrix, a point of intersection of a number of profile-base chains. Now it may be presumed that the profilings against different bases can differ in salience. Since there is a common hyperonym for all the members of a set of microsenses, then they must all have in common a profiling against the same base. But let us suppose that that is not the most salient profiling for any of them: each has a most salient profiling against a different base (thinking of cutlery, weapons, surgical instruments etc.).

This will explain the seeming anomaly of sets of incompatibles sharing the same word form. These readings are not really in competition with one another – the sister units are only half-sisters. It also plausibly motivates their truth-conditional autonomy. If the different microsenses were not domiciled in different domains, it would be difficult to explain why, say, *child* does not develop microsenses corresponding to 'boy' and 'girl,' since it must frequently be used with such reference. It is possible, then, that mere frequency of occurrence is not enough to cause autonomy to develop, but that some other differentiating factor must be present. In the case of microsenses, this extra factor could plausibly be occurrence in different domains; in the case of facets, although they are not differentiated by domain (sister facets tend to occur together), they are differentiated by ontological type.

What does this account fail to explain? Two apparently contradictory things. Firstly, it does not explain why immediate intuition goes for the hyperonymic reading. In other words, people need convincing that the word shows default specificity: unlettered intuition is aware more of the unity of 'knife' than of its plurality. Secondly, given that this is so, what would we expect in a context that does not sanction the selection of one of the specifics? Would we not expect the hyperonymic reading to emerge? But it does not – it only appears when it is overtly sanctioned, that is, one component of default specificity is not accounted for.

There is another way of looking at microsense complexes within an overall Langackerian approach. The above approach implicitly pictures microsenses as developing from an initial unified reading by 'entrenchment + differentiating factor.' Perhaps this might explain the intuition of unity of words like *knife*, but it is not a wholly plausible scenario. A more plausible scenario is that we start with distinct readings that then become united. Langacker's network model works like this (cf. Langacker 1991: 266–71). We start with *knife* being used to designate a particular kind of knife; then this is metaphorically extended to refer to a distinct type of implement, with sufficient resemblance to the original to justify the use of the same word; then a hyperonymic reading develops, which subsumes these two. In this case, without taking differential entrenchment into account, the difference in 'richness' of the resulting concepts may be governed by how much common content can be abstracted from the specific readings. Obviously, if *child* developed this way, then the common abstracted content would be rich, but in the case of *knife*, much less so.

However, the 'bottom-up' scenario fails to explain the intuitive primacy of the hyperonymic reading of *knife*. One possible explanation for this is that metalinguistic functions of language obey different rules to 'actual situated use.' Perhaps for metalinguistic purposes, semantic similarity is the stronger constraint, whereas in everyday use, domain allegiance is more important. Perhaps there is enough semantic commonality in the various microsenses of a word like *knife* to fuel a unified response in reflective metalinguistic use, but not enough to counteract the domain distinctness in normal situated use. If so, then we can count a 'metalinguistic' frame as one of the 'overt contextual sanctions' for a hyperonymic construal.

5.3.2.5 A 'latency' approach

There is another phenomenon, which exhibits a number of resemblances and parallels with the phenomenon of microsenses, but which is not easily assimilated to the above account of microsenses. Since this second phenomenon cannot be sharply distinguished from microsenses, an account of the latter that throws no light on the former is necessarily incomplete. The phenomenon in question is what Matthews (1981:125) calls **latency**.

A prime example of latency is the following:

(77)   Look out, Mary's watching!

Here a specific direct object has to be recovered from context by the hearer. Notice that the identity constraint is operative here:

(78)   John's watching; so is Bill.

This is to be contrasted with, for example (79), where there is no identity constraint:

(79)   John's reading; so is Bill.

Furthermore, different readings have truth-conditional autonomy:

(80)   Is John watching?

In answering (81), one is only obliged to answer with respect to the latent direct object. Suppose the latent element is *us*; then we can answer 'No' to the question, as long as John is not watching us, and it does not matter if he is watching something else. Notice, too, that the autonomy can be overridden in contexts that make the objects explicit; (81) is not zeugmatic:

(81)   John is watching Mary, and Bill, Susan.

This example of latency is of course syntactic in nature, and the latent element is a separate word. Perhaps a little closer to present concerns is the example of *cub*: this has a kind of default specificity, not unlike that of *knife*, which requires us to identify which kind of cub is being talked about, if it is not made explicit. Thus, for example, if an identification cannot be made, the result is odd:

(82)   I was walking through the woods this morning and I spotted a cub.

Similarly (83) is odd if what I saw were a lion cub, a fox cub and a bear cub.

(83)   I saw three cubs this morning.

The identity constraint operates here, too:

(84)   John saw a cub, and so did Mary.

And different readings have independent truth-conditions. The question *Did you see any cubs?* can be truthfully answered *No* if the subject of conversation/common interest is foxes, and the speaker did not see any fox cubs, irrespective of whether he/she saw any other kind of cub. Specifying the type of cub explicitly, removes the restrictions and allows a hyperonymic reading:

(85)   The lioness and the vixen were playing with their cubs.

This sort of behavior is exhibited by a wide range of words, such as *handle*, *wheel*, *cover*, *blade*, *lid*, *leg*, *thigh*, *top*, *patient*, to name but a few. (Is it possible to make sense of *John is a patient*, without knowing whose patient he is? There is no such thing as a patient 'tout court.')

There are some obvious resemblances between these examples of latency and microsenses. As we have seen, with latent elements, we find default specificity, a hyperonymic reading accessible only under contextual pressure, identity constraints, independent truth-conditions. All this looks very much like what we find with microsenses. A possibility, therefore, is that *knife*-type words and words that show latency basically exemplify the same phenomenon. That is to say, microsenses might correspond to deleted specifying expressions that must be recovered from the context before an interpretation can be carried out. This is a different explanation from the one offered above for microsenses, especially if we were thinking in terms of the meaning of *knife* as a single mapping onto a complex concept. It is much closer to pure pragmatics, since there will only be a mapping to the hyperonymic concept, and the detailed readings will be left to contextual constraints, as opposed to being selected from entrenched alternatives (i.e., having a strong conventional component). It would still not be simple contextual modulation, however, because of the obligatory nature of specification.

There are a number of possible objections to the latency analysis for microsenses. First of all, although in some cases an appropriate specifying expression can be found corresponding to a microsense (for instance, *postcard*, *Xmas card* and so on), in many cases there appears to be no readily available qualifier. This is true, for instance, of the *knife* and *fork* used at table and, for many speakers, of the card bearing one's name, address and so on that one gives to people one meets. This seems to argue against saying that when we speak of knives and forks at table we are deleting a specifying epithet. The fully rounded basic-level status of these concepts also seems distinct from the possible interpretations of *cub*. Another objection is the 'openness' of latency. If we leave everything to pragmatics, then the list of possibilities is open-ended, whereas the range of possible readings of *knife*-type words seems to be too highly constrained: for instance, the list of possible implicit qualifiers for *ball* includes *tennis* and *golf*, but excludes *small*, *soft*, *green* and *rubber*.

However, when we look at the cases of latency suggested above, we find that in many cases, at least, the range of choice for specification is not completely open. It is true that the possible direct objects of *watch* in (78) and (79) seem to be unconstrained except by the meaning of *watch* together with pure contextual factors. But other examples vary in the freedom with which the implicit qualifier can be implemented. For instance, for *thigh*, any type of animal that has thighs is possible, and the list is open in the sense that a newly discovered animal would instantly be added to the list, but, for example, *plump* or *long* or *sunburnt* are excluded. For *cub*, the restrictions are even greater: only types of animal are allowed, not *young*, *small*, *brown*, or whatever, and among animals, only certain ones count (not, for example, cat, dog, sheep, horse etc.). These cases begin to look not very different from the case of *ball*, cited earlier as an example of a microsense complex. (There is a curious tie-up, both for *ball* and *cub*, with the notion of 'kind of,' discussed in Cruse 1986, Cruse 2002b and chapter 6: a tennis ball is a kind of ball, but a large ball is not, and the qualifiers of *cub* have to be kinds or types of animal.)

In other words, the more restricted the choice, the more difficult it is to differentiate the latency account from the microsense account. In the case of *sentir* it appears literally impossible to decide. In certain contexts this either means 'to smell' or 'to taste':

(86)   Jean peut sentir l'ail.

This is to all intents and purposes ambiguous: French informants say they have to intend one meaning or the other, one cannot be non-committal. Furthermore, there is a strong identity constraint in (87):

(87)   Jean peut sentir l'ail; Marie aussi.

However, the two readings can coordinate without zeugma, provided the sense modalities are made explicit:

(88)   Jean sentait l'odeur du citron et le goût de l'ail.

So perhaps the best solution is to propose a continuum ranging from the pure latency of *watch*, where the choice of 'filler' is purely pragmatic, through cases like *cub* where the choice is open along one dimension, but constrained in others, to cases like *knife*, where the choice is restricted to a range of entrenched units.

But we are still lacking a satisfactory explanation for the difference between the types.

5.3.3   Ways-of-seeing

What are called here **ways-of-seeing** are derived from what Pustejovsky calls **qualia roles** (Pustejovsky 1995). These are in some ways analogous to thematic roles, but instead of detailing ways arguments may attach to a verb, they govern ways in which predicates can attach themselves to nouns. Pustejovsky proposes four qualia roles:

The **constitutive role**: this describes the internal constitution of the object, and refers to such matters as material, weight, parts and components.

The **formal role**: the features under this heading serve to distinguish the object from other objects within a larger domain, and refer to such matters as orientation, magnitude, shape, color and position.

The **telic role**: this describes the purpose and/or function of the object.

The **agentive role**: the matters referred to here are, for instance, how the object comes into being, whether an artifact, a natural kind, created by whom or what, what causal chain leads up to it, and so on.

Qualia roles are reconceptualized here as ways-of-seeing (henceforth WOS) as follows:

The **part-whole WOS**: views an entity as a whole with parts (e.g. a horse, as viewed by a vet).

The **kind WOS**: views an entity as a kind among other kinds (e.g. a horse as viewed by a zoologist).

The **functional WOS**: views an entity in terms of its interactions with other entities (e.g. a horse as viewed by a jockey).

The **life-history WOS**: views an entity in terms of its life-history, especially its coming into being (e.g. a book as viewed by an author or publisher).

The degree of autonomy of ways-of-seeing is less than that of facets or microsenses. Ways-of-seeing do not correspond to distinct concepts, and they are not referentially distinct: they represent different ways of looking at the same thing. There is some limited evidence of relational autonomy, which is one feature that differentiates them from the active zones considered below. Take the example of *hotel*. This can be viewed as a piece of real estate, in which case it will contrast with houses, offices, factories and so on. Or it can be viewed as a type of accommodation, in which case it will contrast with B & B, Youth Hostel and so on. Ways-of-seeing provide a possible explanation for certain cases of ambiguous phrases with no ambiguous words and univocal syntax, that is to say, they apparently show compositional autonomy:

(89)   a complete soldier
        Part-whole WOS:'a soldier with no body parts missing' (imagine alien visitors to Earth collecting human specimens)
        Kind WOS: 'soldier with all the conventional qualities of a soldier'
(90)   an expensive hotel
        Kind WOS: 'a hotel that is/was expensive to buy'
        Functional WOS: 'a hotel that is expensive to stay at'
        Life-history WOS: 'a hotel that is/was expensive to build'
(91)   a delightful house
        Part-whole WOS: 'a house that is delightful to look at (due to the harmonious distribution of its parts)'
        Functional WOS: 'a house that is delightful to live in'

There are problems in connection with ways-of-seeing. They are less well supported than facets or microsenses. It is not clear, for instance, that autonomy is greater between perspectives than within ways-of-seeing. A number of cases of WOS-like differential construals are difficult to assign unambiguously to one of the proposed possibilities. Also, the number proposed seems to be largely arbitrary. At the same time, something of the sort is clearly needed: there is a need for a construed pre-meaning unit intervening between facets and the purely compositionally relevant features and active zones. It would be entirely consistent with the approach adopted here to refrain from enumerating possible ways-of-seeing, and to treat the above examples merely as particularly salient possibilities, where it is relatively easy to construe a (minor) sense boundary.

5.3.4   Semantic components and low-autonomy active zones

The lowest (positive) degree of autonomy is shown by certain active zones (see §3.2.1) and semantic components: these are units whose sole manifestation of autonomy is compositional; they do not constitute pre-meanings in the full sense. Semantic components are intensional in nature: they are parts of a more inclusive sense which are compositionally active; active zones have an extensional/referential basis: they are parts of something which are isolated for compositional purposes.

As an example of semantic components, take the case of *an overworked stallion*, and the two readings 'overworked in terms of stud duties' and 'overworked in terms of pulling carts.' We may assume an analysis of 'stallion' as [EQUINE][MALE]. One possible explanation for the ambiguity is that there are two possible sense units to which the modifier 'overworked' may be attached:

(92)   ([EQUINE][MALE])(overworked)
        [EQUINE]([MALE](overworked))

That is, the animal is either overworked as a male or as a horse, generally. In other words, a semantic unit [MALE] may be construed as separable, and can function as scope for the predicate [OVERWORKED]. (Notice that the same construal is not so easy for *an overworked husband*.) The two readings can coordinate without zeugma:

(93)   Dobbin is overworked both as a begetter of foals and as a puller of haycarts.

Another example involves negation.

(94)   It is not a mare.

Here the construal of a boundary separating off [FEMALE] would seem to be the default reading, that is, the sentence would normally be taken to mean that the animal in question was a stallion that is, only the feature [FEMALE] is affected by the negation, the feature [EQUINE] being presupposed. However, in a suitable context where femaleness was apparent, the animal might well be a cow, which would involve negation taking the whole of 'mare' as its scope and [FEMALE] being presupposed. In yet another context, what is presupposed might be 'possible birthday presents.'

Possibly similar cases are 'an old friend':

(95)   [HUMAN]   (old)
              |
        [RELATIONSHIP] (old)

Here again, negation would preferentially apply only to the [RELATIONSHIP] component.

(96)   The astronaut entered the atmosphere again.
        either: ([BECOME] [IN]) again
        or: [BECOME] ([IN] again)

(97)   I almost killed him.
        either: almost ([CAUSE][BECOME][DEAD])
        or: [CAUSE][BECOME] (almost [DEAD])

In some approaches to semantics, such semantic components are held to be inherent properties of lexical items, indeed, permanent constituents of their meaning. In the current approach, they are not fixed, but are construed as and when needed. Of course some construals are inherently easier than others, and some are more subject to conventional constraints than others (there is obviously a relation between these two). The delimitation of [MALE] in 'stallion' is so well entrenched that 'mare' is the default construal of 'not a stallion.' But, for instance, it is not difficult to devise a scenario where *not a horse* will not be construed as 'some non-horse animal,' but as 'some non-horse means of transport': the particular situation will determine what is salient, and the possibilities would seem in principle to be open.

Some active zones have the same sort of degree of autonomy as semantic components, that is, they manifest themselves only in compositional terms. Like components, they can give rise to ambiguity, as in *red eyes* ('bloodshot eyes'; 'pupil is red, as in a photograph' [potentially] 'the iris is red') and *a red pencil* ('writes red'; 'red on the outside'). Notice that although the parts of a pencil selected as the domain of relevance of the adjective *red* are readily distinguishable in reality, and can be pointed to (unlike [MALE] and [HORSE] for *stallion*), a definite noun-phrase like *that red pencil*, whichever interpretation is given, does not refer to the part in question, but to the whole pencil.

5.3.5   Contextual modulation

With contextual modulation, as in the 'male cousin' reading in *My cousin married an actress*, we come to the end of the scale of autonomy, the zero point. Different contextual modulations certainly represent different construals and are not in any sense less important communicatively than different microsenses or facets. What distinguishes them from all the other cases we have considered is that they do not require the construal of distinct autonomous pre-meanings as part of the total construal process. The specifying features of different contextual modulations are, as it were, contributed by the context, not selected, or their creation triggered, by context.

5.4   Autonomy: summary

The construal of autonomy in a sense unit is the result of complex interactions among a variety of constraints, and cannot, in general terms, be regarded as having an inherent association with specific lexical items. Although, in specific cases, the strength of contextual constraints may give the illusion of inherentness, the balance between conventional, cognitive and contextual constraints is in fact continuously variable across instances, and an assumption of inherentness does not give a satisfactory general account of variation. At the same time, autonomy itself is a variable, rather than an all-or-nothing property. No adequate account of variable word meaning can afford to ignore the property of autonomy.

6

A dynamic construal approach to sense relations I: hyponymy and meronymy

Sense relations such as hyponymy, incompatibility and antonymy have been a topic of lively interest for lexical semanticists since the structuralist period (see, for instance, Coseriu 1975; Geckeler 1971; Lyons 1963, 1968; Cruse 1986). Although Lyons (1968) declared that all sense relations were context dependent, they have almost universally been treated (including by Lyons himself) as stable properties of individual lexical items.

Cognitive linguists, for the most part, have had very little to say on the topic. In this chapter and the next, we reexamine a number of sense relations from the standpoint of the dynamic construal approach to meaning. Sense relations are treated as semantic relations not between words as such, but between particular contextual construals of words. We hope to show both that sense relations are a worthwhile object of study (even for cognitive linguists) and that the dynamic construal approach can throw new light on their nature. This chapter focuses on hyponymy and meronymy.

6.1   Hyponymy

6.1.1   Introductory

The following are examples of linguistic expressions whose semantic well-formedness depends on hyponymy (X is hyponymous to Y):

(1)   Xs are Ys (**Koalas** are **marsupials**)
(2)   Xs and other Ys (**Koalas** and other **marsupials**)
(3)   Of all Ys, I prefer Xs. (Of all **fruit** I prefer **mangoes**.)
(4)   Is it a Y?
         Yes, it's an X. (Is it a **tit**? Yes, it's a **coal-tit**.)
(5)   There was a marvelous show of Ys: the Xs were particularly good. (There was a marvellous show of **flowers**: the **roses** were particularly good.)

All the above examples involve nouns. A similar relation can be found between items belonging to other parts of speech:

(6)   Did she **hit** him?
        Yes, she **punched** him in the stomach.
(7)   Is your new skirt **red**?
        Yes, it's a **maroon** velvet.

However, pairs of lexical items related by hyponymy are far more frequently found among nouns than among adjectives or verbs.

In principle the relation of hyponymy is a simple one (contrary to the view expressed in Cruse 2002b), and can be seen as an instance of the operation of the Lakoffian container image schema (see, for example, Lakoff 1987:271–73). Hyponymy can be regarded as simple class inclusion:

(8)   a. the class of dogs is a subset of the class of animals
        b. the class of instances of water is a subset of the class of instances of liquid
        c. the class of instances of murdering someone is a subset of the class of instances of killing someone
        d. the class of scarlet things is a subset of the class of red things

The notion of inclusion can also be pursued intensionally. This yields some insights and is more directly related to semantic concerns, since we are dealing with meanings. It therefore promises greater explanatory power, but at the same time raises some problems. To characterize hyponymy intensionally, we need to say something like:

(9)   If X is a hyponym of Y, then the semantic content of Y is a proper subpart of the semantic content of X.

In one sense this is obvious enough. For instance, if we assume that the relation of hyponymy applies to semantically composite expressions as well as to single lexical items (this convention is not universally followed, but it is harmless), then *a red hat* is hyponymous to *a hat* in that the class of red hats is a proper subset of the class of hats. Intensionally, we can see that the meaning 'a red hat' contains as a proper part, the meaning 'hat' (taking a naive view of compositionality). This picture seems readily transferrable to single lexical items such as *stallion* and *horse*: the meaning 'horse' is a proper part of the meaning 'stallion,' which can be analysed as 'horse' + 'male.' (This does not conflict with what was said in chapter 5, as long as 'male' and 'horse' are viewed as potentially autonomous components of a particular construal of 'stallion,' and not as inherent properties of the words.)

One way of testing for meaning inclusion is in terms of entailment relations between sentences (more properly, propositions) containing the relevant lexical items in corresponding structural positions. One formulation, which is not restricted to nouns, goes as follows:

(10)   X is a hyponym of Y iff F(X) entails, but is not entailed by F(Y).

This sort of definition, but not in this exact form, was first put forward by Lyons (1963). Here, F(–) is a sentential function satisfied by X and Y.

Thus, the fact that *It's a dog* unilaterally entails *It's an animal* indicates that *dog* is a hyponym of *animal*. The reasoning behind this definition is obvious. The entailment definition has the advantage that it does not require us to specify what the components A, B and C actually are. Unfortunately, it also has a couple of disadvantages. First, a hyponymous relation between X and Y does not always lead to entailment between F(X) and F(Y) (*Basil became a Catholic* does not entail *Basil became a Christian* – he may have started out as a Baptist). Secondly, entailment between F(X) and F(Y) does not guarantee hyponymy (*The wasp stung John on the knee* entails *The wasp stung John on the leg* – *knee* is not a hyponym of *leg*.) However, there is no reason in principle why these disadvantages cannot be overcome by a more careful formulation of the test.

6.1.2 Hyponymy and context

A difficulty with the notion of hyponymy, which was noted in Cruse 2002b, is that naive subjects classify pairs like *dog:pet* as hyponyms, even though *It's a dog* does not entail *It's a pet*. Furthermore, *dogs and other pets*, which would appear to be diagnostic of hyponymy, is judged fully normal. In Cruse 1986 the relation between *dog* and *pet* was labeled 'para-hyponymy.' Cruse (2002b) argued that a correct definition of hyponymy would be one that matched native speaker intuitions, but he failed to provide such a definition. This difficulty does not arise with the present approach. Since sense relations do not hold between words as such, but between specific construals of words, there is no necessary inconsistency between the normality of *dogs and other pets*, and the lack of entailment between *dog* and *pet*. The frame *Xs and other Ys* induces construals of X and Y such that the former is hyponymous to the latter. The context-dependence of sense relations was strongly emphasized by Lyons (1968), but in fact it played a surprisingly small role in his lexical semantics; here, it is a central feature of the approach. Strictly speaking, the relation of hyponymy depends on only one aspect of construal, namely, the setting of boundaries. Hyponymy could therefore be said to be a relation between pre-meanings.

Contextual variation in boundary placement was illustrated in §5.4.2.1. Here we concentrate on variation with particular relevance to hyponymy.

Relations of meaning between construals of different words in the same discourse are important because they are frequently necessary for both discourse cohesion and the well-formedness of inference patterns. Take a simple example of an expression pattern whose well-formedness depends on a relation of hyponymy, such as *X and other Ys*. Consider the case of *dogs and other pets*, which most speakers find perfectly normal. The claim here is that the construals of *dog* and *pet* in this context are such that *dog* is a hyponym of *pet*, in that the class of dogs is a proper subpart of the class of pets. This is in spite of the fact that most speakers judge that the truth of *This is a dog* does not guarantee the truth of *This is a pet*.

How can these two apparently contrary positions be reconciled? They are reconcilable because two different construals of *dog* are involved. The construal in *This is a dog, therefore it is an animal* involves some sort of default construal of *dog* (and *animal*), either one that emerges in minimal contexts or one that is triggered by the 'logical' domain evoked by the fairly unfamiliar sentence type; the construal in *dogs and other animals*, on the other hand, is strongly constrained by the *X and other Ys* format, which requires the construals of X and Y to be adjusted so that hyponymy holds. The adjustment can affect either X or Y or both: what emerges if there is no other context is the result of the easiest adjustment, that is, involving the most easily accessible construals (there may also be an additional factor of the contextualizability of the result). For instance, the construal of *dog* in *dogs and other pets* is probably more specific than the default zero context construal, but is easily accessible; in *handbags and other weapons*, however, the construal of *weapons* is less specific than the default zero context construal.

Construability is not infinitely flexible. Sufficiently strong conventional constraints can prevent hyponymous construals from emerging. For instance, *dogs and other cats* is virtually unconstruable in any imaginable context (at least it is not literally construable). There are other constraints, too. For instance, *dogs and other dogs* is not acceptable, even though there are readings of *dog* that would satisfy the requirement of hyponymy. This is perhaps because of a constraint that discourages the repetition of a form if a different construal is required.

As defined above, hyponymy is a transitive relation, based on containment, which is also transitive. There are claimed examples of nontransitivity in the literature, which our conception of hyponymy does not permit. The apparent cases of transitivity failure provide interesting examples of different construals of the same word in different contexts. Two such examples are as follows:

(11)   A car seat is a type of seat.
         A seat is an item of furniture
         *A car seat is an item of furniture.

(12)   A hang glider is a type of glider.
         A glider is a type of aeroplane.
         *A hang glider is a type of aeroplane.

These examples are based on informant responses (see Hampton 1991). Hampton's solution to this problem, as has already been noted, is to say that for *X is a type of Y* to be acceptable, it is sufficient for prototypical Xs to fall within the category boundaries of Y. This assumes that X and Y are lexical items, and that they denote fixed conceptual categories. Our account is different, as it assumes that informants' judgements are based on construals in context. We suggest that hearers are predisposed to look for nonanomalous interpretations of input utterances, and hence an utterance of *X is a type of Y* will be judged acceptable if there are easily accessible construals of X and Y such that X is hyponymous to Y. For instance, *A car seat is a type of seat* is judged normal because there is an accessible construal of *seat* that includes car seats. The sentence *A seat is a type of furniture* is judged normal because there is a construal of *seat* (probably the everyday default construal) that excludes car seats, and is hyponymous to *furniture*. Hence, from our point of view, these examples do not illustrate a breakdown in transitivity. A similar account goes for (9). We are not aware of any convincing examples of a genuine breakdown in the transitivity of hyponymy.

Sense relations have traditionally been viewed as relations between items potentially occurring in a fairly strictly defined 'paradigmatic slot.' This viewpoint has cognitive and communicative validity. The choice of any term out of a paradigmatic set carries implicit information about aspects of its meaning that are shared with other possible choices, information about meanings that are excluded, and it opens up a particular range of more specific meanings, any or all of which may be important to the message being transmitted. However, the traditional assumption that words have inherent meanings has the consequence that paradigmatic sets and the interrelations among members have been viewed as relatively stable structures. Here, while the paradigmatic viewpoint is accepted as valid, the items in the paradigm are not lexical items but contextual construals of lexical items, and the relationships are relations between a particular construal of the item actually chosen and potential construals of other items that might have been chosen in that context.

For instance, consider the following exchange (the reader is invited to imaginatively construct a fuller context):

(13)   A: What's that noise?
         B: It's just a dog.

A full understanding of significance of *dog* in B's reply needs at least (a) a construal of a domain of potential noise-producing agents, given the context, (b) a construal of what is excluded (the use of *just* implies that there are potential alternatives to *dog* that would have had more serious consequences) and (c) a construal of the range of possibilities opened up by *dog* in this context. Relations of hyponymy and incompatibility hold between these various construals.

The paradigmatic viewpoint underlies the entailment approach to sense relations, under which relations are defined in terms of truth-conditional relations between F(X) and F(Y). However, we need to carefully reconsider entailment definitions of relations in the light of the present approach. On the traditional approach, *It's a dog* unilaterally entails *It's an animal*, so *dog* is a hyponym of *animal*; on the other hand, *It's a dog* does not entail *It's a pet*, therefore *dog* is not a hyponym of *pet*. On the present approach, these results hold only within a specific context. It may seem that the only context here is *It's a(n) – .* But this may not be correct: simply asking people to make a judgement of whether or not there is entailment creates a particular mind-set that influences the way the lexical items are construed. (It is worth noting that in the case of *It's a dog* and *It's a pet*, students often have to be persuaded to adopt the 'correct' mind-set, otherwise they see entailment where they are not supposed to.)

6.1.3   Relations between lexical items

We have consistently maintained that sense relations hold between contextual construals of lexical items and not between the lexical items as such. However, it has been common practice for decades to speak of relations between words. Are we simply to say that the traditional conception of sense relations was misguided? This does not seem entirely satisfactory. The question therefore arises as to whether there is a way of rescuing the traditional notion of hyponymy as a relation between words.

Two possible ways of establishing hyponymy as a lexical relation suggest themselves. One is to say that there is a special relation between two words A and B if, in any particular context, the construal accorded to A is always hyponymous to the construal accorded to B. This would seem to point to an important relation between words. Intuitively, one might assume that this is the case with *dog* and *animal*. If so, it would mean that some relations between construals of certain lexical items are not context dependent, even though the construals themselves are context dependent. The question is whether such context-independent relations exist. The indications are that, strictly speaking, they do not. Take Lyons' example of *horse* and *mare*: *It's a mare* unilaterally entails *It's a horse*, but in *Our horse has just given birth to a foal* and *Our mare has just given birth to a foal*, *mare* and *horse* are synonyms. In principle, it seems that all traditional hyponymous pairs are capable of yielding this type of result in appropriate contexts. This line of inquiry does not look promising.

Another possibility is to specify relations between words in terms of privileged construals of some kind. Perhaps we can recruit the notion of a default construal here, that is, a construal that appears in a zero context. We might say, for instance, that the word *koala* stands in a particular relation to the word *marsupial*, on the grounds that the default construal of *koala* is hyponymous to the default construal of *marsupial*. This has some plausibility.

What result would this approach lead to in the case of *dog* and *pet*? At this point we encounter a certain indeterminacy in the notion of a default construal. It is arguable that the unmarked notion of 'dog' for the average western city-dweller is the domestic variety, in which case *dog* will have to be considered a bona fide hyponym of *pet*. But is this a truly context-free construal? And if not, is there such a thing? There is another possible approach. The construal of *dog* that includes wild dogs and is thus hyponymous to *animal*, but not to *pet*, has some sort of scientific basis. The arguments for regarding this construal as the default version do not seem particularly strong as it is probably of relatively infrequent occurrence. But perhaps there is a need for what one might term a 'core' construal, which emerges naturally in some way from purport. If we apply this notion to *pet*, it seems clear that the core construal will exclude electronic pets. The fact that the question *Is an electronic pet a real pet?* is interpreted restrictively is evidence for this: *real* plausibly functions to direct our attention to the core. This, however, leaves unanswered the question of the nature of the core.

6.1.4 Taxonymy

Lyons states that taxonomic lexical hierarchies are structured by the relations of hyponymy (class inclusion) and incompatibility (class exclusion). This is true as far as it goes, but it is necessary to make a distinction between two relations of inclusion. The first is the relation that is exemplified in *An X is a Y* (which corresponds to 'simple' hyponymy); the second is the relation for which *An X is a kind/type of Y* is diagnostic, which is more discriminating than hyponymy, and which functions as the 'vertical' relation in a taxonomy. In Cruse 1986, the second relation is called **taxonymy**. It is perhaps noteworthy that Wierzbicka (1996) includes 'a kind of' as one of her semantic primitives, and does not subject it to further analysis; here, an attempt is made to elucidate its nature. (The following discussion draws heavily on Cruse 2002b.)

Taxonomizing is clearly not simply a matter of dividing a larger class into smaller classes. Some logically impeccable subdivisions do not yield good taxonomies:

(14)   ?A stallion/mare/foal is a kind/type of horse.
        (A stallion is a horse.)
(15)   ?A blonde/queen/actress is a kind of woman.
        (An actress is a woman.)
(16)   ?A red/green/blue hat is a kind of hat.
        (A red hat is a hat.)
(17)   A mustang is a kind of horse.
        An ash-blonde is a kind of blonde.
(18)   A Stetson is a kind of hat.

It is obvious that the expression *is a kind/type of* exerts some kind of selectional pressure on pairs of items. It is, of course, possible that being a kind of something else is an arbitrary fact about a word that has to be learned on an individual basis. For instance, *mustang* could have as part of its semantic specification a feature [KIND OF HORSE], whereas *stallion* would not possess this feature. A more interesting possibility is that there is a principle of taxonomic subdivision that allows the relationship of taxonymy to be predicted from the meanings of the related items.

One approach is to think of the nature of the resultant subcategories and their relations to one another, in the light of the purpose of taxonomization. Taxonomy exists to articulate a domain in the most efficient way. This requires 'good' categories that (a) are internally cohesive, (b) are externally distinctive, (c) are maximally informative (cf. the discussion of basic level categories in §4.3.3). In many of the instances where a good hyponym is not a good taxonym of a hyperonym, there is a straightforward definition of the hyponym in terms of the hyperonym plus a single feature, as in:

(19)   *stallion* = 'male horse'
        kitten = 'young cat'

A significant number of good taxonyms, on the other hand, are not easily definable in terms of their hyperonyms, and require encyclopedic characterization (for instance, the difference between *animal* and *horse* cannot be captured in a single feature). In Cruse 1986 it was suggested that single-feature definitions, in general, are not good taxonyms because they do not create optimal categories. However, there are problems with this analysis. It is not difficult to find cases where a satisfactory taxonomy seems to be founded on a single-property division. Take the case of spoons: these are taxonomized on the basis of what they are used in connection with (*teaspoon, coffee spoon, soup spoon* etc.). It is significant that neither *large spoon, metal spoon, round spoon* nor *deep spoon* is a satisfactory taxonym of *spoon*:

(20)   a. A teaspoon/soup spoon is a type of spoon.
        b. ?A large/metal/round/deep spoon is a kind of spoon.

Perhaps the explanation lies rather in the nature of the features? Some features are conceptually 'simple' (LARGE, ROUND etc.), others are more 'complex' (FUNCTION): perhaps complex features are better able to support taxonomy? What, then, about the subdivision of blondes, which relies on shade of hair color (*An ash-blonde/strawberry blonde is a kind of blonde*)? The fact is, there are reasons to believe that the problem of taxonomy cannot be solved merely by looking at the nature of the subcategories, for the following reasons.

Firstly, take the domain of BLONDES. *Ash-blonde* and *strawberry blonde* are satisfactory taxonyms of *blonde*, but they are by no means the optimal subcategories of BLONDE. We can get much 'better' subcategories than ASH BLONDE and STRAWBERRY BLONDE by dividing the domain into BLONDE HOUSEWIVES, BLONDE DOCTORS, BLONDE TEACHERS, BLONDE LAWYERS and so on, but these are not good taxonyms of *blonde*.

Secondly, suppose that a particular species of bird has a number of varieties and a very marked difference between males and females. In such a case, it is not inconceivable that a male/female division would yield the best categories, in that the males of different varieties resembled one another more than the male and female of a particular variety. However, even if that were the case, a sex-based division would still be taxonomically 'wrong.'

Thirdly, a given category may be a satisfactory subdivision of one superordinate, but not of another. For instance, *?A lumberjack is a kind of man* is not good, but *A lumberjack is a kind of manual worker* is fine. If the crucial factor was the nature of the resultant category, this would be hard to explain.

It is possible that the good category principle has a role to play in the characterization of taxonymy, but it clearly cannot provide a full explanation.

It seems, then, that a satisfactory taxonym must engage in a particular way with a particular aspect of the meaning of the hyperonym. In Cruse 1994, it was suggested that taxonym and hyperonym must share the same *perspective*. The reason *stallion* is not a good taxonym of *horse*, it was argued, is that it has a 'sexual' perspective, while *horse* does not; the reason *blonde* is not a good taxonym of *woman* is that it adopts a 'hair-color' perspective, while *woman* does not. *Ash-blonde*, on the other hand, has the same 'hair-color' perspective as *blonde*, and that is why it is a satisfactory taxonym. This notion of perspective needs to be made more precise; it is not identical to the perspective as defined in §3.4, so to avoid confusion it will be referred to henceforth as **focal orientation**.

Two possible lines of approach may be singled out. The first recruits Langacker's concept of profiling (see §2.2). The proposal is that what is profiled in a taxonym must further specify what is profiled in the hyperonym. From this it will follow that the reason *stallion* and *foal* are not good taxonyms of *horse* is that what they profile, namely, 'male' and 'young', are not specifications of what is profiled in *horse*; a similar explanation holds for *blonde* and *woman*. Likewise, *lumberjack* and *navvy* are not good taxonyms of *man* because their profiles are not specifications of what is profiled in *man*, but they are good taxonyms of *manual worker*, because they specify further and profile what is profiled in *manual worker*, namely, type of work. (It seems likely that there is also a constraint involving the relationship between the domains evoked by taxonym and hyperonym, but it is not at present clear what this is.)

A second suggestion for characterizing the above notion of focal orientation is more tentative, but may be closer to the truth. It is that a good taxonym must have as its **core** a specification of the **core** of the hyperonym. (For present purposes, 'core' is to be thought of intensionally.) Given that the core feature of a *blonde* is the possession of fair hair, it follows that the taxonyms of *blonde* must specify fair hair more restrictively; if it is the core feature of a *manual worker* to perform manual work for money, then a taxonym must specify those activities further; if the core feature of a *spoon* is to fulfill a particular function, then the taxonyms of *spoon* must have as their essence a more specialized function. What, in that case, is the core of *horse*? This is more difficult, but one possibility is its species: intuitively, *mustang* would seem to have a more highly delimited version of the same core.[1]

A question that is pertinent at this point is whether profiled features and core features are the same thing. There are some indications that profile and core are not necessarily the same, and that, when they are different, it is the core that gives the correct prediction with regard to taxonymy. Take the case of *woman*. It seems reasonable to assume that *woman* profiles [FEMALE], and that [HUMAN] functions as base. On the assumption that profiling governs taxonomy, we would predict that the taxonyms of *woman* would specify sexuality more narrowly. Hence, we would expect *lesbian* to be a satisfactory taxonym. But this does not seem to be the case. When asked to suggest types or kinds of women, people tend to offer things like *career woman*, *nest-builder*, *femme fatale* and so on. Now these are not subdivisions of sexuality (although some might have sexual consequences), but of personality or character, and it is not implausible (it is even reassuring!) that these come out as the core of womanhood. (It is harder to think of parallel sex-specific categories for men, but *machotype*, *new man* and *lady's man* are possibilities.)

The notion of core that we have appealed to as an explanation of taxonymy can at present only be offered tentatively, pending a firmer characterization. However, one further point needs to be considered. According to the approach to word meaning adopted here, both the core of a category and the relation of taxonymy should in principle be construals, subject to contextual constraints. Again, a definitive statement cannot at this stage be made, but it does seem that both core and the relation of taxonymy are much less subject to contextual variation than boundary placement.

6.2   Lexical aspects of the part-whole relation

The lexical relation of **meronymy** (sometimes referred to as **partonymy**) presents a number of problems that do not affect hyponymy. It is usually informally

---

[1] In Cruse 2002, what is here called 'core' was referred to as 'essence.'

described as the 'part-whole' relation. However, this is not strictly correct, and a failure to separate the part-whole relation from meronymy leads to a great deal of confusion. Meronymy is a relation between meanings, whereas the part-whole relation links two individual entities. Of course there is an important connection between the two, which will be examined in due course, but the distinction between them must not be lost sight of. Meronymy is also bedeviled by the range of possible construals of the notion of 'part,' some of which are relevant to meronymy and some of which are not. We shall begin by examining the part-whole relation.

6.2.1   The part-whole relation

In this section we shall attempt to distinguish the lexically relevant part-whole relation from neighboring relations, and examine some of its salient characteristics.

6.2.1.1   The portion-whole relation

The part-whole relation may be considered to be a special subvariety of a more general, more basic relation which here will be called the **portion-whole** relation. This relation is illustrated in the following examples (the term 'portion' is used here in a technical sense: it is not claimed that the word *portion* could appear happily in all these sentences):

(21)   A portion of the cake was given to each of the guests.
(22)   Part of the garden was waterlogged.
(23)   Parts of the letter were illegible.
(24)   My portion of the omelette had bits of eggshell in it.
(25)   One section of the house was out of bounds.
(26)   I love this stretch of the river.
(27)   It was a game of two halves.

The basic notion here is the containment of one region or regions (interpreted in the broadest possible manner) within another region. The boundaries of a contained region must be neither identical with, nor must they transgress, the boundary of the containing region. The notion of containment is, of course, a very basic form of construal, which we can assume corresponds to Lakoff's container image schema. For reasons of space, we shall concentrate on central instances and assume that both contained and containing regions are bounded and continuous.

6.2.1.2   Parts and pieces

Consider the following two sentences:

(28)   All the parts of the aeroplane were carefully packed into crates, ready for shipping.
(29)   After the explosion, pieces of the aeroplane were scattered over a wide area.

The most accessible construals of *parts* and *pieces* in these two sentences are distinct. Each unit referred to in (28) falls into one of a limited number of nonarbitrary categories which group together similar items from different wholes, and which are defined by a characteristic set of properties such as shape, size and relationship to the whole aeroplane. We shall designate such items by the term **part**: 'part' is thus a hyponym of 'portion.'

In contrast, the *pieces* referred to in (29) belong to a single category with only one defining property, namely, that they once formed part of a whole aeroplane. The label *aeroplane pieces* can be construed as uniting portions from different aeroplanes into one category, but these pieces do not fall into distinct groups with stable properties that unite similar pieces from different aeroplanes, and they do not have definable relations, other than origin, with the whole entity. (Pieces from a particular type of entity rarely have distinct lexical labels: the example of *shard* comes to mind, but such cases are few and far between.) We shall use **piece** as a technical term alongside *part* to designate portions that do not qualify as parts: 'piece,' too, is thus a hyponym of 'portion.' Although most pieces are not parts, and vice versa, they may be, accidentally, so piece and part are not strictly incompatibles. (The technical term 'piece' covers a wider category than the everyday lexical item *piece*: the waterlogged portions of the garden and the illegible portions of the letter mentioned above are technically pieces.)

The notion of recurrence (identifiability across different wholes) may need to be further restricted. Suppose plates of a certain type always fracture in the same way, yielding recurrent portions. Would they then qualify as parts? Arguably not. Another characteristic of pieces that distinguishes them from parts is that they are not contemporaneous with their canonically constituted wholes: there are no pieces until the whole is destroyed, whereas true parts can be construed even in a well-formed whole. The pieces of the plates that always fracture in the same way, although they can be predicted, have no existence in the unbroken plate. (Even if they were to be admitted into the PART category they would not be prototypical parts, because they have no function relative to the undamaged whole.)

A further feature that distinguishes parts from pieces is what in Cruse 1986 was called 'autonomy.' This is related to the notion of 'spare part.' Parts of artifacts such as machines are often replaceable by functionally equivalent items: in such cases, the replacement counts as, for example, a machine part, even though it has never entered the constitution of a complete machine. (The same is perhaps soon to be true of human body parts.) On the other hand, an exact replica of a piece of a broken plate cannot properly be described as *a piece of the plate*. This property of parts is presumably related to the fact that they prototypically have a species of self-sufficiency, that is, cohesion plus distinctness, as 'objects' in their own right. They are, in other words, subordinate wholes; pieces prototypically lack this self-sufficiency.

6.2.1.3 Factors affecting the GOE of parts

The category PART, like any other natural category, has good and less good exemplars. We may attempt to summarize the main factors that seem likely to contribute to a high GOE for X as a part of Y as follows. (There is a problem with testing for this, since the word *part* has a wide range of construals, only one of which corresponds to PART. A form of expression that may select for PART is *The parts of a Y are A, B, C. . .*):

(i)   The boundary of X does not transgress the boundary of Y.
(ii)   X shares all its substance with Y.

Marbles do not become part of a matchbox by being contained in it. Features (i) and (ii) can be regarded as necessary.

(iii)   The boundaries of X can in principle be demonstrated in a well-formed whole Y.
(iv)   The sharper (more salient) the discontinuity between X and not-X the better the part.
(v)   The greater the internal cohesion of X the better the part.

The discontinuity and cohesion may involve any or all of: shape, texture, color, internal structure, makeup. Detachability and/or independent movability are strong indicators of discontinuity.

(vi)   X has a definable function relative to Y.

What is meant here is function, such as wings for flying or legs for perching in a bird. There is another notion of function that is relative to human users. For instance, the parts of an animal carved out by a butcher may not have distinctive functions for the animal.

(vii)   X is autonomous: exact replicas of X also count as parts.
(viii)   There is type-consistency between X and Y.

The relevant notion of 'type' here is difficult to pin down. One aspect is what is usually called 'ontological type.' There is no agreement on a basic ontology, but the sort of thing referred to by Jackendoff (1983), namely, THING, STATE, PROCESS, EVENT, PROPERTY, TIME, PLACE and so on seem relevant to parts. That is, the parts of a period of time, for instance, should themselves be periods of time; the parts of a thing should be things (rather than, for instance, substances); the parts of an event or a process should be subevents or processes; the parts of an abstract entity should be abstract entities; the parts of a place should be places, and so on.

There is another notion of 'type' that is relevant. There are two broad types of part, called **segmental** and **systemic** parts in Cruse 1986. Segmental parts are clearly spatially delimited and are typically encountered sequentially as the whole is traversed; they may well have heterogeneous internal consistency. Typical examples are the externally visible parts of the body such as arms, legs, head, trunk and so on. Systemic parts are typically spatially interpenetrating, but they are functionally distinct and typically have a greater internal consistency. They are less likely to be perceptually salient. Typical examples in the human body are the nervous system, the vascular system, lymphatic system and the skeleton.

The two types can be observed in other entities besides the human body. A house, for instance, can be divided into segmental parts (rooms) and systemic parts (brickwork, plumbing system, wiring, etc.); a string quartet (to take a non-spatial example) has movements as segmental parts, and first violin, second violin, viola and cello as systemic parallels (notice that we speak of *the second violin part* quite naturally); a similar case could could be made for the scenes and acts of a play (segmental), and the various actors' roles (systemic).

6.2.1.4   Part-whole chains

The part-whole relation generates chains of elements: A is a part of B, B is a part of C, C is a part of D and so on. For instance:

(30)   A finger-tip is a part of a finger.
(31)   A finger is a part of a hand.
(32)   A hand is a part of an arm.
(33)   An arm is a part of a body.

We may say that a constituent element A of a part-whole chain W is an immediate part of another element B, and B an immediate whole of A, if on a particular construal of W there is no element X that is a part of B and of which A is a part. Thus, a finger is an immediate part of a hand, and a hand is an immediate whole of a set of fingers. An immediate whole is the normal scope of predication for its part (§2.4).

6.2.1.5   Ultimate parts and ultimate wholes

A part-whole chain prototypically has a beginning and an end; that is, there is a smallest part, which itself has no construed parts, and there is a largest whole, which is not construed as part of a yet larger whole. A crucial problem is therefore what determines the location of the ends of the chain. It is always possible to think of some portion smaller than the ultimate parts of something: for instance, the fingertips are composed of skin, nerve fibers, capillary blood vessels and so on, and these are composed of various chemical substances that can be further broken down into molecules, atoms, electrons and so on; at the other end of the chain, a body can be part of a family or team, which is part of a population, which is part of the terrestrial biomass and so on. Yet, intuitively, there is a self-contained system beginning with fingertips and ending with the body.

Looking first at ultimate parts, it might well be the case in some instances that no subpart is motivated – there is simply no subregion bounded by a sufficiently salient discontinuity to justify the construal of a boundary. In other cases we can appeal to the notion of type-consistency. One reason why we do not divide fingertips into nerve fibers, capillaries and so on is that they are of the wrong type.

Ultimate wholes pose more puzzling problems. A crucial factor is undoubtedly the existence of a major discontinuity with surroundings, coupled with internal cohesion. However, there are a number of apparent inconsistencies. The following examples arose in the course of class discussions as part of an undergraduate course in lexical semantics. When student informants were questioned about *pan* and *lid*, the majority said that the lid was not part of the pan, but some said they might reconsider their judgement if one or more of the following applied:

(34)   a. the lid was sold as a unit together with the pan
        b. the lid was essential to the functioning of the pan
        c. the lid was attached to the pan by means of a hinge.

When asked about *teapot* and *lid*, however, the majority said that the lid was part of the teapot. If the lid was attached by a hinge, the judgment was unanimous. When asked why the teapot lid was different from the pan lid, the most frequent comment was that it was essential to the functioning of the teapot, and was sold together with it. The screw caps of soft drink bottles and the cork and capsule of a wine bottle were unanimously rejected as parts of the bottle, in spite of the fact that these are arguably essential to function, and bottles are normally sold complete with caps. A possible confounding factor is that they are normally made of different materials from the bottle, which gives rise to a salient discontinuity.

One final type of example will be mentioned. Most informants reject *battery* as a part of *flashlight*, whereas *bulb* is unanimously accepted as a part (there are many similar cases). This is reinforced by the fact that one normally has to buy the batteries separately when one buys a flashlight, but one does not expect to have to buy a bulb separately. Furthermore, the description of a flashlight in a shop will say *battery included* if it is included in the price, but will not say *bulb included*. This is strange, because the battery is contained within the body of the flashlight, and is essential to its functioning.

It appears that a judgement of where the boundaries of an ultimate whole are situated is a result of the interaction of a number of factors, but the details of the interaction are far from clear. It is possible that convention plays a role here.

6.2.1.6   Core parts

Consider the following sentences:

(35)   There were scratches on the hand, but not on the arm itself.
         (The hand is part of the arm.)
(36)   The monitor is faulty, but the computer itself is OK.
         (In the case of an iMac, the monitor is part of the computer.)

The expression *the X itself* selects some sort of core. In the case of the part-whole relation, what seems to be selected is the smallest portion that can be construed as 'a whole X' – any smaller unit Y can only be construed as a part of X (although it can of course be construed as a whole Y): certain (genuine) parts may be stripped off without completely destroying wholeness. We shall call the smallest possible portion of an X that can be construed as a whole X the **core part**. (The term 'core' is deliberately used to suggest a parallel between core parts and the core of a category.) The factors that determine the existence and boundaries of a core part in particular cases are not clear. In the case of the iMac, the fact that most PCs have separate monitors may influence our construal of the iMac. In any case, the core part may be presumed to need adequate motivation as a whole in its own right.

The notion of core part overlaps with, but is not identical with, the 'main functional part,' which can function as active zone in a use of the name of the whole (see Cruse 1986). For instance, *a stainless steel X* is often ambiguous between an X that consists entirely of stainless steel, and one whose main functional part only consists of stainless steel: consider a stainless steel screwdriver/hammer/knife, any of which may have a handle made of some other material. This only applies to certain privileged parts, however: a screwdriver with a tungsten head and a stainless steel handle would not qualify as a stainless steel screwdriver. My intuitions are that the description 'a totally new type of computer' would be valid for an iMac whose central processor had been redesigned, but not for one whose only new component was the monitor portion: in this case, the main functional part and the core part are the same. However, it is not clear that the part of a screwdriver that engages with the screw can be called *the screwdriver itself*, so in this case the main functional part and the core part are distinct.

6.2.1.7   Variable construal and the transitivity of the part-whole relation

In Cruse 1979 and 1986 a distinction was made between 'integral parts' and 'attachments.' These were distinguished as follows:

(i) If *X is a part of Y* and *X is attached to Y* are both normal, then X is an attachment of Y:

(37)   The hand is part of the arm.
(38)   The hand is attached to the arm.

(ii) If *X is a part of Y* is normal, but *X is attached to Y* is not, then X is an integral part of Y:

(39)   The handle is a part of the spoon.
(40)   ?The handle is attached to the spoon.

This distinction was then recruited as part of an explanation for one type of so-called 'transitivity failures' in the part-whole relation, as in:

(41)   a. An arm has a hand.
         b. A hand has fingers.
         c. ?An arm has fingers.

(42)   a. Fingers are parts of a hand.
         b. A hand is a part of an arm.
         c. ?Fingers are part of an arm.

From the point of view of the current approach, both the distinction and the transitivity failures are arguably illusory. Consider, first, the proposed distinction between integral parts and attachments. Notice, first, that there is nothing odd in principle about a part being attached to a sister part: we can say, for instance, without oddness, that the arm is attached to the trunk at the shoulder. Second, there is an easily accessible construal of *arm* that excludes the hand:

(43)   There were burns on the victim's hand, but none on the arm.
(44)   He had a tattoo on his arm (contrasts with *a tattoo on the hand*).
(45)   A broken arm.

Hence, the most obvious explanation of the normality of (38) is that *arm* receives the construal that excludes *hand*. In (37), on the other hand, *arm* receives the inclusive construal. Hence, (37) and (38) contain different construals of *arm*: the hand is attached to arm_1, which is a sister part, but not to arm_2, the whole that includes it. If one makes the effort to construe *arm* in (38) as arm_2, it becomes as anomalous as (40). Turning now to (39) and (40), a slight twist is needed in the explanation. Of course, the handle of the spoon is attached to the 'bowl' of the spoon; the reason (40) is odd, however, is that there is no construal of *spoon* that designates only that part. (This account of the oddness of [41c] and [42c] differs from Langacker's account as presented in §2.4. The two accounts are not necessarily mutually exclusive.)

What about the apparent transitivity failures? It should perhaps first be acknowledged that these are weird sentences: how many of us have encountered them in naturalistic settings? They are also virtually uncontextualized, so one should hesitate before drawing general conclusions from them. The previous explanation was that the relation cannot cross an attachment boundary, that is to say, the parts of an attachment do not count as parts of the whole of which the attachment is part. The evidence for this was extremely limited, not to say contrived. There is, however, an alternative explanation if we assume that the exclusive construal of *arm* is the default (i.e. arm_1), then we can say that (41a) and (42b) exemplify the inclusive construal of *arm* (i.e. arm_2), but that (41c) and (42c) represent the exclusive (default) construal. In support of this account of the 'transitivity failures,' we would claim that (41c) and (42c) improve considerably in normality if one makes the effort to give *arm* the inclusive construal. The general conclusion is that these examples give no grounds for impugning the transitivity of the part-whole relation. However, an explanation is still required of why the inclusive construal is not evoked in (41a) and (42c).

The account of the other transitivity failure given in Cruse 1986 is nearer the mark, but can be more felicitously expressed using the current approach. It concerns the following examples cited originally by Lyons as an unresolved puzzle:

(46)   a. The jacket has sleeves.
        b. The sleeves have cuffs.
        c. The jacket has cuffs.

(47)   a. The house has a door.
        b. The door has a handle.
        c. ?The house has a handle.

There are two issues here: the first concerns the logical validity of the conclusion expressed in (46c) and (47c) based on the respective a and b sentences as premises; the second issue is the normality of (46c) compared with (47c). Let us look first at the logical question. The basic principle is simple: the conclusions are valid if the construals of all terms are consistent between premises and conclusion. This is the case in (46), so the conclusion (46c) is valid. In (47), on the other hand, there is a discrepancy between the construal of *handle* in (47b) and (47c). The word *handle* is typical of those exhibiting microsense behavior: when we hear the word *handle*, in most contexts, unless a hyperonymic construal is explicitly triggered, we look for a subtype of handle that is intended (default specificity), and the resultant subtypes manifest the properties of microsenses. The contextual frame *The X has a handle* elicits an appropriate microsense, that is, 'an X handle.' Hence, *The door has a handle* elicits the construal 'door handle,' while *The house has a handle* elicits the microsense construal 'house handle.' This discrepancy destroys the logical validity of the conclusion. (In [46], 'sleeve cuffs' are identical with 'jacket cuffs.')

The situation with regard to normality is not entirely clear in these examples. Out of context, there is probably a general tendency to a slight oddness if a part-whole statement misses out an intervening term, especially if it is salient, hence we might expect (46c) to be a little hard to contextualize. The reason it is not may be due to another principle, namely that one can always relate parts at any level to the overall whole: thus, for instance, *The human body has fingers* and *fingers are parts of the body* are not so odd as *The arm has fingers*. The normality of (46c) may therefore be due to the fact that *jacket* is construed as the overall whole. The oddness of (47c) is more than we would expect simply from a level-skip: as suggested in Cruse 1986, it is more plausibly explained as being due to the fact that houses do not usually have handles, and it is difficult to imagine what purpose they might serve (Cruse [1986] pointed out that substituting *doll's house* for *house* considerably reduces the oddness, but does nothing for the validity of the conclusion.)

6.2.2   Meronymy

Like every other sense relation, meronymy is viewed here as a relation between contextually construed meanings (or more precisely, by pre-meanings created by boundary construal). However, the relationship is less straightforward than hyponymy, and it is not easy to select the optimum way of expressing it. The problem stems from the fact that the essential relation, the part-whole relation, does not hold between construed classes of elements, but between specific individuals belonging to those classes. Also, the relation itself is subject to construal, unlike the hyponymic relation between two classes. Given two classes, the definition of hyponymy can decide whether hyponymy holds or not: there is no need for a separate construal of the relation. In the case of meronymy, on the other hand, a part-whole relation between two entities is itself a construal, subject to a range of conventional and contextual constraints. So, let us examine the following characterization of meronymy:

(48)   If A is a meronym of B in a particular context, then any member a of the extension of A maps onto a specific member b of the extension of B of which it is construed as a part.

Hence, *finger* is a meronym of *hand* because for every entity properly describable as a finger (in the default construal), there corresponds some entity properly describable as a hand (also in the default construal), of which it is construed as a part. This characterization seems to capture something essential about meronymy.

But it is too restrictive as it stands, because it does not allow for 'spare parts,' which have never participated in any whole (of the relevant sort). We might therefore relax the characterization to admit potential part-whole relations:

(49)   If A is a meronym of B in a particular context, then any member a of the extension of A either maps onto a specific member b of the extension of B of which it is construed as a part, or it potentially stands in the construed relation of part to some actual or potential member of B.

      (Notice that to take account of preserved body parts where the rest of the body has been destroyed, we need to give a 'timeless' interpretation of 'the extension of B.')

This now covers spare parts, but it arguably still misses something essential to meronymy, namely, the construal of partness as an essential element of the construal of the part. Take the case of *lake* and *park*. Many parks have lakes within their boundaries, and in such cases the lake would be construed as 'part of the park.' Furthermore, every lake is potentially a part of some park, so by the second definition, *lake* would qualify as a meronym of *park*. There is, however, a difference between the relation linking *finger* and *hand* and the relation linking *lake* and *park*. In construing *lake* we are under no pressure to construe it as being part of something: in cases where a lake is part of a park, the 'partness' is imposed on the construal as it were from the outside. In the case of *finger*, 'partness of hand' is an essential component of the original construal. Let us call this difference one between an **intrinsic** and an **extrinsic** construal of partness. Then we can say that the relation of meronymy concerns only intrinsic construals of partness:

(50)   If A is a meronym of B in a particular context, then any member a of the extension of A either maps onto a specific member b of the extension of B of which it is construed as a part, or it potentially stands in an intrinsically construed relation of part to some actual or potential member of B.

Notice that this characterization introduces an asymmetry between meronym and holonym. A holonym is characteristically more independent, in that there is no obligatory construal orienting it towards particular meronyms. Of course, the information that says a human body consists of arms, legs and so on is represented in the conceptual system, and is in principle accessible, but does not form a necessary part of every specific construal of *body*. Parts are evoked only under particular types of construal (e.g. under the 'constitutive perspective').

The above characterization has some plausibility when applied to construals of part names. There are good reasons for retaining meronymy as a semantic relation between construals. For instance, certain distinctions can only be made in terms of classes rather than in terms of individual items. This is the case with what in Cruse (1994) is called **range congruence**. Cruse (1986) distinguished the relation between a 'super-meronym' and a 'hypo-holonym' from that between a 'hypo-meronym' and a 'super-holonym.' The first is illustrated by the relation between *nail*, on the one hand, and *toe* and *finger* on the other. Here we have a part name, *nail*, which is related to two different wholes. There is a hyperonymic class of NAILS, which is indifferent to the identity of the wholes:

(51)   Nails had been torn from the victim's fingers and toes.

However, the default use of *nail* denotes a microsense, one for each related whole. Hence, B's answer in (52) is acceptable as true:

(52)   A: (*examining B's hands*) Have you cut your nails this week?
         B: (*who cut his toe-nails the previous day, but had not cut his finger-nails for a long time*) No.

The second relation is illustrated by *body* in relation to *penis* and *vagina*. Here it is the holonym that has the greater 'range': *penis* and *vagina* are parts, but in relation to different subclasses of body. However, in contrast to the first case, there is no evidence whatsoever that there are two microsenses of *body* corresponding to 'man's body' and 'woman's body.' This is interesting, and demands an explanation, but the important thing for present purposes is that it is not a difference at the level of the part-whole relation.

There are, however, difficulties that cast doubt on the utility of meronymy as a **lexical** relation. Let us take the example of the word *lid*. The purport of this word takes us into the conceptual area of containers, access points into containers and means of controlling movement into and out of containers. There seems to be a very strong conventional constraint forcing some sort of construal of incompleteness: a lid is designed for use in conjunction with a container. However, this is not an obligatory construal of partness, since not all lids are parts (cf. bottles, jars, teapots etc.). There is undoubtedly a possibility of construing *lid* in a superordinate sense:

(53)   In this box you'll find a lot of things to put things in, and in the other box, a lot of lids: your job is to sort out which lid goes with which container.

But most commonly, a much narrower construal is required:

(54)   We've lost the lid.

Here, a particular type of container is referred to. Perhaps, then, we should recruit the notion of microsense and say that *lid* has microsenses ('teapot lid,' 'jamjar lid,' 'pan lid' etc.), some of which involve intrinsic construal of partness (cf. Cruse 1986). However, this will not work, because, as was mentioned earlier, whether, for instance, a teapot lid is construed as a part or not depends on factors such as the presence of a hinge, whether sold separately and so on. In other words, we can only be sure of a construal of partness at the level of the individual item. Even the local construal of 'lid type' is not necessarily specified as to partness. (There is no evidence for 'hinged lid' and 'free lid' as distinct microsenses or perspectives.) The same phenomenon can be observed with a wide range of words. The implication seems to be that we cannot in general deal with the part-whole relation except at the level of the individual referent. In (53), for instance, the relation between *container* and *lid* is indeterminate. In other words, the whole notion of meronymy as a lexical relation is dubious.

The picture of meronymy that seems to emerge from the above discussion is the following. There is, first, a very indeterminate purport, then a series of pre-meaning construals that take us nearer and nearer to the target construal, and may involve a commitment to partness at some point before the final construal, but in many cases the part-whole relation cannot be inferred until we reach the level of individual referents.

This is a very awkward picture from the point of view of lexical semantics: there seems little to be said at the lexical level. One conclusion from this might be that meronymy, unlike, say, hyponymy or antonymy, is not a relation between meanings. After all, strictly speaking, the parallel at the individual level of the class-based relation of hyponymy is the part-whole relation, and the strict parallel to incompatibility is a relation between sister parts: incompatibles denote sets with no members in common; co-parts are, in general, parts of the same whole which have no substance in common (provided they are of the same type – segmental parts may share substance with systemic parts). Does this mean that we can dispense with meronymy altogether? There are reasons why this is not an entirely satisfactory proposal.

Perhaps the most cogent arguments in favor of retaining meronymy concern its intuitive appeal, the fact that children learn the names of parts early, the fact that all languages have names for parts of things, and, further, that cross-linguistic generalizations can be made regarding the naming of parts, especially parts of the human body (see Brown 2002 for a survey).

One such generalization concerns the equivalents in various languages for the English *hand*. In many languages this denotes the region of the arm from the fingertips to the elbow. (This is the case of the Modern Greek *to xeri*. However, Greek speakers assure me that it can also be construed to refer to the region from the fingertips to the wrist only, and that there is rarely any confusion.) The generalization is that, where a language has an 'extended' hand, it is highly likely also to have word for 'foot' that designates the region of the leg from the toes to the knee (this is the case with Modern Greek *to podi*). Another generalization, or at least strong tendency, is that extensions from hand to foot are common, extensions from foot to hand are much rarer. Thus, the basic meaning of the French *doigt* is 'finger,' but we also have *doigt de pied* for 'toe' (alongside *orteil*). However, this is not an absolute rule, as the *heel of the hand* is well established in English.

Finally, there is a hard core of word pairs, like *finger* and *hand*, that are extremely difficult not to construe literally with a relation that satisfies our definition (but they are remarkably few in number).

The situation with regard to parts and wholes and their linguistic expression can therefore be summarized as follows:

(i)   The part-whole relation properly applies to individual entities. It is a construal that is subject to variation.

(ii)   The recognition of a relation of meronymy between construals is justified by the existence of a small number of generalizations and distinctions that only apply to classes of parts.

(iii)   Every language has a range of ways of referring to parts of things. Many of these ways involve specialized lexical items, but apart from a very restricted core set of strict lexical meronyms, the relations between these and expressions for whole things are very various.

7

A dynamic construal approach to sense relations II: antonymy and complementarity

7.1 Oppositeness

7.1.1 Aspects of the construal of oppositeness

The notion of oppositeness is well established in everyday language:

(1)   We were traveling in opposite directions.
(2)   I found myself sitting opposite the new Minister for Moral Regeneration.
(3)   John is tall and thin; Pete is just the opposite.
(4)   Mary is extrovert and makes friends easily; Jane is just the opposite.
(5)   He doesn't seem to be interested in the opposite sex.

There are undoubtedly different construals of *opposite* involved here, but intuitively they belong to a family. None of them are metalinguistic. But even speakers innocent of semantic theory have robust intuitions about lexical opposites, and even quite young children rapidly catch on to the idea. Like all sense relations, oppositeness is a matter of construal, and is subject to cognitive, conventional and contextual constraints.

There seem to be two main components in a construal of oppositeness. The first of these is binarity. Opposite meanings are construed as mutually exhausting some domain: within the appropriate domain, there are only two possibilities. Some domains are difficult to construe in any other way. For instance, there are only two directions along a linear path, so *up* and *down*, and *forwards* and *backwards* are natural opposites; likewise, there are only two extreme points on an axis, so *top* and *bottom*, and *front* and *back* are also natural opposites. At a more abstract level, there are only two directions of change between two states, that is, from A to B and from B to A. This confers oppositeness onto *dress:undress*, *tie:untie*, and the like.

These examples have a kind of built-in logical twoness. But a binary opposition does not have to be inherently logically watertight, only locally construed as such. Take the case of *town* and *country* (*urban:rural*), which are often used as a binary opposition. Here a domain something like 'areas of normal residence in a temperate climate' needs to be construed to justify the binarity. The binarity of even an obvious pair of opposites like *male:female* rests on a restricted domain that excludes hermaphrodites, beings with no sex organs (for whatever reason) and so on.

While binarity is undoubtedly an essential feature of oppositeness, it is not, on its own, sufficient. There are many situations where a domain is construed with only two members, but oppositeness seems to be absent. Cruse (1986) mentions *double-decker:single-decker* (as applied to buses); and *monocotyledon:dicotyledon* (a botanical division of the domain of angiosperms – itself one of only two types of seed plant). Another non-opposite two-way division is *food:drink*, in the domain of nutrition. Even *tea:coffee* is a binary choice (within the domain of hot drinks) on an airplane.

What is missing from these examples? Cruse (1986) suggested that the contrast expressed by a pair of true opposites has to be not merely binary, but 'inherently binary'; that is to say, the binarity has to be logically necessary, and not just a contingent fact about the world. But then this, too, was found to be insufficient, as there are logically binary notions that are not good opposites, the main example quoted being *Friday* and *Sunday*, which are the only two days that are one day removed from *Saturday*. (This is of course only one of many binary oppositions that could be invented using the days of the week.) Why are they not opposites? Cruse's suggestion was that their meanings (i.e. Friday and Sunday) do not encode a salient mutual orientation towards *Saturday*, in contrast to, say, *yesterday* and *tomorrow* whose meanings are oriented towards *today*, and which exhibit a certain degree of oppositeness. However, if the approach adopted here is correct, it ought to be possible to devise a situation where such a mutual orientation is induced by contextual constraints, leading to at least some sense of oppositeness. The following is an attempt to do this:

Some important committee regularly meets on Saturdays. An influential caucus holds a pre-meeting on Friday to prepare for the main committee meeting, and a post-meeting on Sunday to discuss the events in the Saturday meeting. For the members of this group, *the Friday meeting* could develop a (weak?) relation of oppositeness to *the Sunday meeting*.

7.1.2   Main varieties of opposite

Several types of opposite can be recognized. (Some of the types described in Cruse 1986 have been shown by informant testing to give rise to only a very weak intuition of oppositeness.) The most salient types are complementaries, antonyms and reversives, together with their morphological derivatives:

complementaries: *dead:alive, open:shut, true:false* (default construals). These
exhaustively bisect some domain into two subdomains.

antonyms: *long:short* etc. These are gradable adjectives or stative verbs and denote degrees of some property that diverge significantly from some reference
value.

reversives: *rise:fall, dress:undress* etc. These are verbs that denote changes in
opposite directions between two states.

Cruse (1986) also has a class of converses like *buy:sell, parent:child* and so
on. Many converses are good opposites, but the position taken here is that their
oppositeness is not a necessary consequence of their being converses, but arises
from other factors (for instance, the oppositeness of the direction of transfer of
goods and money in *buy* and *sell*). They will not be discussed as a class here.

7.1.3   Goodness-of-exemplar in opposites

Certain pairs of lexical items are readily judged to be better opposites
than others, presumably on the basis of default construals. The following would
seem to be some of the relevant factors:

(a)   Intrinsic binarity

This has been discussed above.

(b)   The 'purity' of the opposition

For instance, *male:female* are better opposites than, say, *man:woman*,
which in turn are better than *aunt:uncle*, whereas *convent* and *monastery* are hardly
felt to be opposites at all. The basic opposition underlying all these is MALE vs.
FEMALE, which appears in an 'undiluted,' or 'pure' form in *male:female*; in all
the other pairs mentioned, the basic opposition appears alongside other semantic
material that is, as it were, inert with respect to the opposition, and the more of
this there is, the less salient the opposition.

(c)   Symmetry

For instance, *large* and *tiny* are not such good opposites as *large* and
small (although the sense of oppositeness is not completely absent). One possible reason for this is that *large* and *tiny* are not symmetrically disposed about
the reference point. The residual oppositeness of *large* and *tiny* may be due to
their counterdirectionality: when intensified, they move apart on the scale of
size.

(d)   Matched non-propositional features

The default opposite of *clean* is not *mucky* but *dirty*, and this is because *mucky* is restricted to certain registers, while *clean* has a more general applicability – in this instance, we can say that they evoke different frames. Ideally, non-propositional features such as register and expressivity should be the same for both members of an opposite pair.

7.2   Complementarity

This chapter concentrates on adjectival opposites, of which the main types are complementaries and antonyms. The discussion begins with complementaries.

7.2.1   Gradable vs. non-gradable construal of properties

There are two basic ways of looking at properties, both of which involve basic image schemas. We can either think of properties as present or absent, or we can presuppose presence and think in terms of more or less of them. In the first case, a pair of complementaries will be the most natural linguistic expression; for the second view, we will construe a continuous scale representing values of the property, and linguistic expression will most naturally be by means of a pair of antonyms. Which construal is the most natural, varies from domain to domain. Take the property of 'being married' – you either have it or you don't, and it is odd (but not impossible) to think of one person as 'more married' than another. Therefore the easiest construal of *married:single* is as a pair of complementaries. Or take the domain of spatial extent. It is not very illuminating to think of the presence or absence of something such as length – if something has no length, it most likely does not exist – so 'more or less' is the obvious construal, and opposites in this domain, such as *long:short* are naturally antonyms. However, there are some properties that can plausibly be viewed in either way. Take the domain of 'clean/dirty.' This can be construed either with a binary division or a scale. The pair *clean:dirty* thus show a split personality, behaving at times like complementaries (*It's not clean* implies *It's dirty*), and at times like antonyms (*This shirt is cleaner/dirtier than that one*). Antonyms will be dealt with in detail later: for the moment, let us concentrate on complementaries.

7.2.2   Profiling against domains

Complementaries are construed as both mutually exclusive and mutually exhausting some domain. Hence, if X and Y are adjective complementaries, then if some entity is X, then it is not Y, and if it is not X then it is Y. The notion of domain is essential to the understanding of complementarity. Take the pair *married:single*. We can say that if someone is not married, then they are single, and if they are not single, then they are married. But this relationship is highly dependent on the construed domain within which the two terms are operating. First of all, we need to specify that we are talking about humans: the inference does not work for angels or spiders (or chairs). Second, we must restrict the domain to 'marriageable' persons: the logical relation does not hold for babies (in Western societies at least) or the Pope. Third, we must exclude noncanonical forms of cohabitation. Hence, the logical properties only appear within an appropriately construed domain. In some cases, the appropriate domain is subject to strong conventional constraints, as in the case of the default construals of *dead:alive*: if someone says that John is not dead, it will normally be inferred that John is still alive, that is to say, we are strongly constrained to construe the domain in such a way that the relation of complementarity holds.

The position of the boundary between a pair of complementaries X and Y is an aspect of particular construals. In the case of *dead:alive*, the location of the boundary is sometimes a matter of dispute, including legal dispute, and could well differ in different discourse domains. In everyday language, *John is dead* can usually be taken to mean that John's state is well clear of the zone of uncertainty. It could also, however, function argumentatively to indicate that John was on the wrong side of the speaker's construal of the boundary, that is, as part of a dispute (imagine a discussion as to whether attempts to revive a patient should be abandoned). Notice that if one construes the notion 'life-state' to include zombification and/or the vampiric state, and so on, as well as 'ordinary' death and life, the logical relation of complementarity will not hold.

It is important to bear in mind that complementarity is a relation between construals and not between lexical items: in many cases, properties can be construed either in absolute terms or in gradable terms. In some cases, there is a species of alternation, according to context, between a pair of complementaries and a pair of antonyms; we shall postpone consideration of these until antonyms have been examined in detail. But there also appear to be cases where one term of an opposition is construed as absolute and the other as gradable:

(6)   A: Is John dead?
         B: No, he's very much alive.

Here, *dead* is construed absolutely and *alive* gradably. The two construals of *alive* as gradable or absolute do not seem to amount to a difference between distinct senses. There is, for instance, no zeugma in (7):

(7)   A: Is John alive?
         B: Very much so.

It appears to be possible for the absolute term to function as a zero point on the construed scale for the other term. That is to say, in (6), *dead* is construed as 'zero aliveness.' This does not appear to affect the logical relation between the terms; that is to say, they are still complementaries by the 'not-X entails Y' criterion.

7.3 Antonymy

The following treatment of antonymy is based on Cruse and Togia (1995). Antonyms have the following properties:

(i) They are adjectives or stative verbs
(ii) They denote properties construed as varying in degree
(iii) They are counterdirectional in that one term when intensified denotes a higher value of the relevant property, while the other term when intensified denotes a lower value.

Antonymy is treated here as a relation between construals, and involves the structuring of content domains by means of one of a limited repertory of image schemas. The principal image-schema in this account of antonymy is SCALE, which construes a property in terms of more and less. It will be assumed here (a) that image-schemas vary in schematicity, in that very general ones can be manifested as more specific ones, and (b) that they can join together into complex image-schematic structures. The general notion of opposite probably corresponds to a single image-schema. The different types – complementaries, antonyms, reversives – will correspond to more specific image-schemas. Looking at antonyms in more detail, as we shall see, we need to think in terms of quite complex assemblages of yet more elementary schemas.

The different types of antonymous relation will be presented using default readings of words. However, it must be borne in mind that antonymy is a relation between construals, and particular lexical items can typically be construed differently in different contexts. It should also be borne in mind that much more goes into a local construal of an adjective such as *long* than the selection of the appropriate antonym type: there is also the orientation of the scale relative to the content domain, the identification of an implicit reference point on the scale, and the degree of divergence from the reference point.

7.3.1 A survey of antonym types

7.3.1.1 Monoscalar and biscalar systems

In this section, the basic antonym types are presented. A detailed justification of the types will not be given at this point; some of the justification will become apparent below. The first division is between antonyms that involve a single scale and those that involve two separate scales working in tandem.

A simplified version of a **monoscalar** system is given in Figure 7.1.

Figure 7.1 *A simplified monoscalar system*

The scale denotes a single property, in this case length; the scale has an end point denoting zero value of the property at one end and extends indefinitely in the other direction. One term of the opposition is associated with a higher value of the property and the other term with a lower value. The terms move in opposite directions along the scale when intensified.

There are three basic types of **biscalar** system, depending on the relative disposition of the two scales. In the **equipollent** patterns, the properties of the two scales are fully symmetrical. There are two possibilities here: either the scales are arranged end-to-end, and are completely disjunct, or they are completely overlapping. The **disjunct** type is exemplified by 'hot:cold' in Figure 7.2. Here we have two independent scales which meet at their zero points and extend indefinitely in opposite directions.

Figure 7.2 *A disjunct equipollent system*

The **parallel** type appears to be rarer. Here the two scales run parallel to one another over their whole length (Figure 7.3).

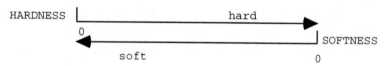

Figure 7.3 *A parallel equipollent system*

In the **overlapping** system, there is partial overlap between the two scales. At the same time, the scales are not equal: there is a major scale (MERIT) and a minor scale (BADNESS), as in Figure 7.4 on page 171.

Figure 7.4 *An overlapping system*

7.3.1.2 Mapping of systems onto content domains

It will be noticed that different antonym pairs have been assigned to the different scalar patterns. Let us assume for the moment that these assignments are correct. The question then arises: is the association between a particular pair and a particular pattern arbitrary? Do we have to learn it? Or is it motivated by general (cognitive or other) principles? It is claimed here that these and other properties of antonyms are strongly motivated. One pointer in this direction is the fact that there is so much cross-linguistic convergence in antonymic properties. Most differences in antonym behavior between nearest translation equivalents in different languages can be attributed to conceptual differences, that is, they are not arbitrary. It seems likely that what linguistic differences there are tend to occur in areas where the conceptual motivation is less strong.

Let us now consider briefly how the different modes of construal show different affinity for different content domains. We shall begin with the monoscalar pattern. The factors favoring this construal include the following:

(i) the salience of properties

A property such that more of it is more salient is preferentially chosen as the basis of a scale (see, however, §7.4.2.1).

(ii) the ease of construal of a determinate end point for the scale

If there is a definite end point, this is preferred as zero value.

(iii) the calibratability of the scaled property

A calibratable property (in terms of conventional units) is preferred to a non-calibratable property as the basis for a scale. Take the case of LENGTH: why do we have a scale of LENGTH rather than a scale of 'SHORTH'? Firstly, more length is generally more salient than more shortness. Secondly there is an end point at the short end, but none at the long end. Thirdly, length is much more easily calibratable than shortness. Hence, a scale of LENGTH is well motivated. Consider, now, the case of SPEED. Firstly, fast moving things are generally more salient than slow moving things. Secondly, there is a clear end point at 'stationary.' Thirdly, both fastness and slowness are easily calibratable. Again, a scale of SPEED is well motivated, although marginally less so than that of LENGTH.

The scales of LENGTH and SPEED may be contrasted with that of DIFFI-CULTY. Firstly, difficult things loom larger than easy things, generally speaking. Secondly, there are two possible end points to the scale, both somewhat vague, namely 'impossibility' and 'no impediment at all.' Thirdly, there are no readily available conventional units for calibration. It can be seen that the motivation for having a basic scale of DIFFICULTY rather than a scale of EASINESS is not over-whelming. It is not surprising, therefore, that (a) English-speaking undergraduates find it relatively hard to decide which way round the scale goes, and (b) some languages (e.g. Modern Greek) actually do it the other way round (that is to say, they have a scale of EASINESS).

Let us now consider why some antonyms operate over a monoscalar system and others over a biscalar system. The answer is that the different image-schematic complexes show different affinities for different content domains. This point can be illustrated with reference to the disjunct equipollent type: why are there two scales and why are they arranged end-to-end? Imagine putting one's hand into (i) a bowl of cold water, (ii) a bowl of tepid water and (iii) a bowl of hot water. You will get a strong temperature sensation in (i), no temperature sensation at all in (ii), and a strong, but different temperature sensation in (iii). In other words, there is a natural zero-temperature sensation in the middle, and two distinct positive temperature sensations – a natural (disjunct) equipollent situation. Given the four patterns to choose from, there is little doubt which fits best. (The two temperature scales are felt to articulate a single coherent domain because basic experience unites them into a single scale: pouring boiling water into cold water makes it first, less and less cold, then tepid, then gradually hotter. There is no such experiential continuity between, for instance, *anger* and *surprise*.) Other natural equipollents are: *like:dislike, proud of:ashamed of, beneficial:harmful*.

Turning now to the overlapping type, the argument for the appropriateness of two scales is once again that we have two distinct notions to quantify: one is merit, and the other is badness. Things can be construed as 'not-good' in two ways: either they lack merit, or they possess a 'positive' badness. Whereas nothing gives us simultaneously a sensation of hot and cold (hence those scales are disjunct), something can exist, for instance, a 25% mark in an exam, that we can choose to see as either lacking merit (i.e. being *poor*), or possessing positive badness (i.e. being *bad*). There is therefore an area of overlap between the two scales. The fact that 'normal' (that is to say, neither good nor poor) corresponds to zero badness, is perhaps evidence of an entrenched optimistic view of life (cf. the 'Polyanna principle'): we are willing to believe of some bad things (say, the 25% mark) that they nonetheless possess some degree of merit; but normality and upwards on the scale of merit is free of badness.

7.3.2   Monoscalar systems: polar antonyms

A detailed examination of the various types of antonym will now be given, beginning with polar antonyms. A full monoscalar system can be represented as in Figure 7.5 (the simpler diagram presented in Figure 7.1 indicated only the absolute scales).

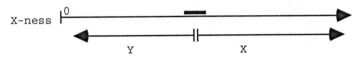

Figure 7.5 *A full monoscalar system*

There are two basic ways of construing a quantity of something: we can either look at it in absolute terms (e.g. *25cm, 1.7 kg*) or we can view it as more or less than some reference value (*a long pencil, a heavy suitcase*). These two ways correspond to what we shall call the absolute scale schema and the relative scale schema respectively. In the diagram, the upper scale is the absolute scale, and the heavy line indicates the reference value (or range) for the relative scale. (Even in the case of a single gradable adjective we need to postulate an absolute and a relative scale, since gradable adjectives are prototypically relative in their basic use.)

7.3.2.1   Subs, supras and the relative scale

The members of a pair of antonyms do not have the same relationship to the absolute scale: one term, when intensified, denotes a higher value of the scaled property, while its partner denotes a lower value. Following Cruse and Togia (1995), these will be called the **supra** and **sub** terms, respectively.

If there is only one term, it will be a supra. Having only a sub term seems intuitively perverse. Why should this be so? Probably because the sub term has a cognitively more complex relationship to the absolute scale than the supra term has, and cognitive complexity has to pay for its keep. This means that supras have the most basic association with the scale: if a nominal denoting the associated scaled property is derived from one of the opposed adjectives, it is always derived from the supra term. Thus we have a scale of LENGTH, not a scale of SHORTNESS, a scale of THICKNESS, not a scale of THINNESS, a scale of DIFFICULTY, not a scale of EASINESS, and so on.

Supras can be recognized by their normality in, for instance, questions of the form *What is its Nom?*, in structures such as *twice as/half as X*, and for many speakers also in *How X is it?* questions. By these criteria, the default reading of *long* is a supra term and that of *short* a sub term. The oddness of (8b), (8d) and (8e) is presumably due to the difficulty of construing *short* as supra (outside of specific contexts):

(8)   a. What is its length?
         b. ?What is its shortness?
         c. twice as long/half as long
         d. ?twice as short/?half as short
         e. ?How short is it? (for some speakers)

Notice that, by the same criteria, the default readings of *good, bad, hot* and *cold* are all supras: this is how we know that they are part of biscalar systems.

(9)   a. twice as good/ half as good
         b. twice as bad/ half as bad
         c. How good was it?
         d. How bad was it?

(The oddness of *What is its goodness/badness* is due to the lack of conventional units of measurement for merit. See §7.4.2.2 below.)

Notice, also, that for some speakers, *twice as short* and *half as short* are synonymous, which is a sign that *short* is being construed as a sub term. No speakers interpret *twice as long* and *half as long* as synonymous.

7.3.2.2   The representation of subs and supras

Now let us consider the question of how to represent the relationship between a supra term and its sub partner. The way they are portrayed in Figure 7.5 makes them look like equipollents. But this is not correct, because there is an asymmetry between the two that is not found in equipollents. The problem is how to represent this asymmetry. In Cruse and Togia 1995, the meanings of *long* and *short* were glossed as follows (with a slight modification):

> *long* = 'noteworthy by virtue of a relative abundance of length'
> *short* = 'noteworthy by virtue of a relative paucity of length'

This is not satisfactory: *abundance* and *paucity* are nominals related to *much* and *little* – in other words, we are explaining one pair of antonyms in terms of another pair, and the essence of antonymy is slipping through the net. There is a way of expressing the relationship without covert resort to antonymy in the definition, in terms of the ordering of points on the scale of length (0 = zero length; R = contextually determined reference point; L = length of object):

> *long*:   0, R, L
> *short*:   0, L, R

We can perhaps put it into words thus:

> *long* = 'noteworthy by virtue of being longer than some contextually determined reference value'
> *short* = 'noteworthy by virtue of some contextually determined reference value being longer'

This shows *short* to be parasitic on *long*, and avoids the risk of surreptitiously incorporating the problem into the solution, but it does not bring out the negative nature of *short*, nor its greater cognitive complexity.

Probably, the essence of the difference between *long* and *short* lies in the fact that 'longness' has a direct correlation with the scale of length, whereas 'shortness' has an inverse correlation, which renders 'short' inherently more complex than 'long', but it is still not clear how this might be encapsulated in a definition.

7.3.2.3   The iconicity problem

There is a curious iconicity paradox in connection with basic relative adjectives such as *long:short, wide:narrow, deep:shallow, high:low* and so on. All definitions of these adjectives in their relative uses presuppose an underlying scale of length, width, depth, height and so on. In other words, the absolute scale appears as conceptually more primitive. Yet the relative adjective is nearly always morphologically simple, and when the name of the underlying property is morphologically related to the adjective it is always morphologically complex.

This at first sight appears to run counter to the principle that morphological complexity mirrors cognitive complexity. One would expect the adjective to be derived from the noun, as in *speed:speedy, weight:weighty, length:lengthy* and so on. Here the iconicity principle is followed, in that the resultant adjective encodes a more complex and subtle notion than the corresponding 'simple' adjective (*fast, heavy, long*). (An apparent exception to the rule is *beauty:beautiful*, but this probably has a historical explanation, in that *beauty* came into the language first. It is worth noting that in French, *beau:beauté* follows the more usual pattern, with a morphologically simple adjective and a complex nominal.)

One possible explanation is that, in applying the iconic pinciple, we should distinguish between structural complexity (in terms of the number of elementary components and their interconnections) and processing complexity (in terms of the cognitive effort involved). Perhaps they are acquired first of all in an unanalyzed, primitive, 'Gestalt' sense, which is basically relative. Maybe in order to develop the full adult system, analysis and restructuring are necessary. Some of the results of the analysis may well be conceptually simpler in some sense than the analysand, but the extra effort that has gone into them is mirrored by the morphological complexity. This has some connection with the fact that superordinate terms, which may be schematic relative to their hyponyms, are nonetheless often morphologically more complex, especially if the latter are basic-level items.

7.3.2.4   Impartiality and committedness

Impartiality can be illustrated in the first instance with comparatives. Although sentence (10) is contradictory, sentence (11) is not, showing that there is no clash between *heavier* and *light*:

(10)   ?This box is quite light, but it is heavy.
(11)   This box is quite light, but it is heavier than that one.

In our terms, *heavier* is impartial with respect to the weight of the referents that form its arguments, in that its use is not constrained to those contexts where *heavy* is appropriate. The same is true of *lighter*, although a slightly more complex test frame is necessary to establish this, as a 'heavy' argument displays a greater affinity for *heavier* than for *lighter* (this factor, labeled 'pull' in Allen 1986, also requires explanation):

(12)   This box is quite heavy, but it's still lighter than the other one, nonetheless.

Committed uses of *heavy* and *light* are illustrated in (13) and (14):

(13)   This box is less heavy than that one.
(14)   This box is not as light as that one.

Other examples of impartiality (the [a] examples) and committedness (the [b] examples) are:

(15)   a. How long is it?
          b. How short is it?
(16)   a. What is its length?
          b. ?What is its shortness?
(17)   a. I was surprised at the length of the programme.
          b. I was surprised at the shortness of the programme.
(18)   a. How clean was the room when you moved in?
          b. I was surprised at how clean the room was/at the cleanness of the room.

For languages other than English, another type of question shows impartiality effects. Compare (19a) and (19b) in French and (20a) and (20b) in Modern Greek:

(19)   a. Elle est longue, ta nouvelle jupe?
          b. Elle est courte, ta nouvelle jupe?
(20)   a. Ine makri to kenurgio su fustani?
             'Is your new skirt long?'
          b. Ine konto to kenurgio su fustani?
             'Is your new skirt short?'

In each case the (a) question is in some sense 'open-minded,' compared to the (b) question, even though the difference has no effect on the nature of the answers to the questions – that is to say, the answer must reflect the truth value of the implicit proposition in each case.

7.3.2.5   The 'Exposure' Principle

It is assumed that any use of an antonymous adjective is either to be given an absolute construal or a relative construal. One broad generalization that can be made is that all absolute construals of either term of a polar antonym pair are impartial. However, as far as relative construals are concerned, sub terms are committed, but supra terms may be impartial or committed. As a working hypothesis, it will be assumed that whether an adjective receives a relative or an absolute construal in a particular context is not haphazard.

In this spirit, we may now survey the various uses of polar antonyms, to see to what extent their partiality can be motivated. One explanatory hypothesis is what is here called the 'Exposure Principle.' First, we need to establish a 'scale of exposure.' In the following, the exposure of the adjective increases from (i) to (v):

(i)   cases of suppletion: *speed, weight, temperature, worse, better*
(ii)   cases of morphological distortion: *length, width, depth*
(iii)   undistorted incorporation in a derived word: *thickness, hardness, diffi-culty, longer, thicker*
(iv)   expressions where the bare adjective occurs in an idiomatic construction: *How long is it?*
(v)   bare adjectives in fully compositional expressions: *It's long, a long piece of string*

The relevance of this scale to the distribution of impartial and committed expressions is captured in the following generalization: the more exposed an adjective the greater its affinity for the relative scale, and the less exposed, the greater its affinity for the absolute scale. So, suppletive forms are maximally likely to be impartial, while bare adjectives in fully compositional expressions are maximally likely to have a relative construal. Why should this be so? One suggestion is that this has to do with the cognitive primitivity of the relative construal: cognitive primitivity is iconically mirrored by constructional transparency.

This first principle only comes into play when there is a choice of forms. If there is only one form, a second principle operates, which limits the application of the first principle, and that is that wherever there is a choice between an impartial reading and a committed reading, but only one available form (i.e. they are in competition), the impartial reading has priority. We shall now illustrate the operation of these principles.

(a)   Comparatives

Both terms of every polar antonym, in all the languages for which data are available, have an impartial comparative form. A committed comparative is also possible in theory, but it would be cognitively more complex, as it involves two reference points rather than just one.

Let us consider first a language such as French, which has only one way of forming the comparative (*plus long*, etc.). This is maximally transparent, which would bias it towards a relative construal on the Exposure Principle. However, this is overruled by the Impartial Priority Principle, with the result that French comparatives are impartial. English is a little more interesting in this respect. Some English adjectives, for example *intelligent*, have only a periphrastic comparative, and in such cases, the periphrastic comparative is impartial:

(21)   Neither of them is very bright, but John is more intelligent than Bill.

But in some cases, we can observe a difference between the interpretation of an inflectional and a periphrastic comparative:

(22)   a. Process X is fast, but it's nonetheless slower than process Y.
         b. ?Process X is fast, but it's nonetheless more slow than process Y.

Here we can see the effect of the exposure scale: *slow* in (22b) is more exposed than in (22a), so (b) is committed and (a) impartial. In English, we can regard the morphological comparative as the default variety, and the periphrastic form in (22b) as somewhat forced. We might therefore expect the morphological variety to attract the priority construal. Hence there are two competing explanations for (22) (although they are not mutually exclusive). A clearer case is provided by Modern Greek, where some adjectives have a more evenly balanced choice between a periphrastic comparative and a morphological comparative. The situation, however, is similar to English: an adjective that has only a periphrastic form is impartial, but where it is in competition with a morphological form, it is the latter that is impartial, and the periphrastic form is committed.

(b)   Quantified comparatives

(23)   X is twice as/half as long as Y.
(24)   ?X is twice as/half as short as Y.

These are quite different to ordinary comparatives. We may assume that any mention of an explicit numeral or numerical quantity predisposes an absolute construal of the adjective, at least partly because only the absolute scale can be calibrated. The oddness of *short* is presumably because there is no conventional way of calibrating shortness. Quantified comparatives can be used with non-calibrated scales (*twice as good, only half as bad*); presumably these are metaphorical extensions from the prototypical calibrated scales. Such extensions are limited as to permissible quantifications: *This stick is three and a half times as long as that one* is normal, but *?Jane is three and a half times as pretty as Sarah* is distinctly odd.

(c)   *Equalities and inequalities*

The expressions *as long as* and *not as long as* are impartial, but *as short as* and *not as short as* are definitely committed:

(25)   a. X is as long as Y/ X is not as long as Y.
         b. X is short, but it is as long as Y.
         c. X is as short as Y.
         d. ?X is long, but it is not as short as Y.

However, although (26) has an impartial reading, (27) does not:

(26)   X is not as long as Y.
(27)   X is less long than Y.

This is in accordance with the Exposure Principle, since *as long as* is an idiom, whereas *less long than* is arguably compositional. However, the difference between *long* and *short* needs further thought. Perhaps it is due to the fact that *as long as* means 'has the same length as,' not 'has the same longness as,' and this only makes sense on the absolute scale; *as short as*, on the other hand, means 'has the same shortness as,' which can only be interpreted with reference to the relative scale, and is therefore committed.

(d)   *What is its NOM?* questions

(28)   What is its length/weight/thickness?
(29)   *What is its shortness/lightness/thinness?
(30)   *What is its goodness/cleanness?
(31)   What is its difficulty/hardness?

Notice that (28) cannot be used to ask *Is it long or short?*, whereas this is a possible meaning of *How long is it? What is its NOM?* seems to demand an absolute quantity as an answer, and since shortness and the like cannot be quantified in this way, that is sufficient reason for the anomaly of (29). The same goes for (30), although here the reason is not that we are dealing with sub terms, but that we are dealing with noncalibrated quantities (see §7.4.2.2). But why is it that this form of question demands a quantity, whereas *How ADJ is it?* does not? A likely answer is that *what?* demands a specific individual entity to be identified. The only way of individuating a quantity of something is by its magnitude. That is fine once we know that we are dealing with, say, the absolute scale of length. But that still leaves the question of why we are limited to the absolute scale of length. One possibility is that it is only on the absolute scale that there is the possibility of a sufficiently definite identification to satisfy the requirements of *what?* In other words, the impressionistic relative scale does not allow anything so definite to be pinned down.

(e)   How X is it? questions

Questions of the form *How X is it?* have two possible interpretations. For instance, *How long is it?* can mean either (i) or (ii):

(i)   'What is its length?' (*How short is it?*)
(ii)   'Is it long or short?' (How short is it?)

Interpretation (i) has no equivalent with *short*, for the reasons discussed above. Interpretation (ii) does have a *short* version, but it is committed. Notice first that the fact that *How long is it?* has a relative construal, whereas *What is its length?* does not, is in accord with the Exposure Principle. But we need to think about why *How long is it?*, on the relative interpretation, is impartial, while *How short is it?* is committed (remembering that *shorter* is impartial). Assuming a general semiotic principle that different forms are preferentially assigned different meanings, then all we have to decide is why *long* is preferred for the impartial sense. The reason for this is perhaps a combination of 'simple before complex' and 'impartial before committed,' yielding the combination 'simple' + 'impartial' as the preferred option.

In Turkish and Modern Greek, the *How*-questions are committed as far as calibrated scales are concerned; impartial questions require *What*-questions. This follows the Exposure Principle, since in these languages, *How*-questions are maximally transparent. This difference with English *How*-questions fits with the fact that in both Greek and Turkish the adjective is more exposed, in that the structure of such questions is not identical to the idiomatic *How Adj is it?* but is fully compositional. For instance in the Turkish *Ne kadar uzun?* ('How long is it?'), the expression *ne kadar* simply means 'how much,' and would occur in the Turkish translation of 'How much money do you have?'. With noncalibratable quantities, *What*-questions are ruled out, and *How*-questions assume the role of impartiality, in accordance with the Impartiality Priority Principle.

(f)   Is it X? questions

(32)   *French*:
         a. Elle est longue, ta nouvelle jupe?
         b. Elle est courte?

(33)   *Modern Greek*:
         a. Ine makris?
            'Is it long?'
         b. Ine kontos?
            'Is it short?'

(34)   *Turkish*:
      a. O uzun mu?
        'Is it long?'
      b. O kısa mı?
        'Is it short?'

Questions of this form containing the supra term (which seem not to occur significantly in English) function in a similar way to the relative construal of *How X is it?*, that is, to ask whether something is long or short. They occur particularly in languages that do not have *How*-questions (e.g. French) or where *How*-questions are committed (e.g. Greek and Turkish). The sub term in each case yields a committed question. In both cases, the relative scale is involved, and the reasons for choosing the supra term to encode the impartial question are presumably the same in both cases, namely, that it is conceptually the simplest.

7.3.3   Bi-scalar systems

Biscalar systems can be diagnosed by the fact that both terms of an antonymic pair are supras. Essentially, biscalar systems incorporate a pair of counterdirectional monoscalar systems. However, in most cases the individual monoscalar components do not exhibit the full range of properties described above. Typically, the supra-supra opposition is the most salient, and the supra-sub oppositions are to a greater or lesser degree backgrounded, in that sub terms are either nonexistent, or their properties are shared among a cluster of highly context-sensitive items.

There are two types of biscalar system, the equipollent type and the overlapping type. These are easily distinguished by their patterns of impartiality and committedness. In the discussion above of monoscalar systems, the notion of partiality was related to the sub-supra distinction. This will henceforth be designated as **scale-partiality** (also **scale-impartiality**, **scale-committedness**). This notion is still relevant to some degree to biscalar systems, but the most salient notion is partiality with regard to the supra-supra distinction, which we shall term **system-partiality** (also **system-impartiality**, **system-committedness**). Equipollent systems are distinguished by the fact that the two terms of the opposition are symmetrical in all their properties. For English, this means that there are no system-impartial uses of either term. In overlapping systems, one term has system-impartial uses, whereas the other term has none.

7.3.3.1   Equipollent antonyms

The outstanding characteristic feature of equipollent antonyms is that the behavior of the two members of a pair is completely symmetrical. In English they are system-committed in all uses, except where there is a morphologically unrelated nominalization, such as *temperature* for *hot:cold*: hence, *hotter, colder, How hot/cold is it?* are all system-committed, but *What is its temperature?* and *I was surprised by its temperature* are both system-impartial.

There are relatively few equipollent pairs in English; the most obvious pair are *hot:cold*, but *happy:sad, sweet:sour, ashamed of:proud of*, and *beneficial:harmful* may be cited. The numbers of pairs in this category seem to vary from language to language. For instance, Cruse has failed (by questioning native speakers) to establish any convincing pairs in Turkish, whereas Togia's observations (1996) indicate that they are relatively common in Modern Greek. We are at present unable to say whether this difference between Turkish and Modern Greek correlates with any other semantic or other characteristic of the two languages.

In the case of *hot:cold*, which may be regarded as the prototypical disjunct equipollents in English, there is evidence that *cool* and *warm*, besides their more salient function as attenuatives of *cold* and *hot* respectively, double up as subs, this time for, respectively, *hot* and *cold*. Thus, (35) and (36) are significantly less anomalous than (37) and (38):

(35)   This pan feels hot, but it feels cooler than that one/still feels cooler than that one, nonetheless.

(36)   This bottle feels cold, but it feels warmer than that one/still feels warmer than that one, nonetheless.

(37)   ?This pan feels hot, but it feels colder than that one/still feels colder than that one, nonetheless.

(38)   ?This bottle feels cold, but it feels hotter than that one/still feels hotter than that one, nonetheless.

The sub term perhaps also occurs in *a cool oven, a cool flame* and *a relatively warm ice age*. Cruse's intuitions are that *This flame is only half as cool as that one* is difficult to process, and resembles *half as short*. Notice, however, that reversing the terms in (35) and (36) leads to anomaly:

(39)   ?This pan feels cool, but it feels hotter than that one/still feels hotter than that one, nonetheless.

(40)   ?This bottle feels warm, but it feels colder than that one/still feels colder than that one, nonetheless.

This suggests that the default readings of *cool* and *warm* are not subs of *hot* and *cold*, and that the sub construal has to be coerced by contextual pressure. Wherever the sub reading is appropriate, either inherently hot/cold items are involved (such as *ice-age, flame*), or there is some other explicit indication that the domain in question is one of hotness or coldness.

Parallel equipollent pairs are even less common than the disjunct type. They seem to occur when (a) there is no property that can be construed as having a zero value in the middle of the scale, (b) each direction of construal is equally motivated and (c) there is no dominant viewpoint, no difference that motivates a 'positive/negative' construal. Hayes (2001) argues that *hard:soft* are plausible candidates, and *dark:light* as applied to colors.

7.3.3.2 Overlapping antonyms

Overlapping antonym oppositions have the following characteristics:

(i) The comparative form of one member is system-impartial (and, because of the disposition of the scales, scale-impartial), while that of the other is system-committed (although scale-impartial):

(41)   John and Bill both got bad marks in the exam, although John's marks were better than Bill's.
(42)   ?John and Bill both got first class marks in the exam; John's marks, however, were worse than Bill's.

(ii) Both members are normal in quantified comparatives; one member is system-impartial ([43] and [44]) and the other system-committed ([45] and [46]):

(43)   Both marks were admittedly bad, but Bill's was twice as good as John's.
(44)   It's true that Bill's wasn't the only bad mark, but it was only half as good as even the other failures.
         (An impartial reading of *half as good* is difficult to construe in [44], but it is possible.)
(45)   ?Both marks were excellent, but Bill's was twice as bad as John's.
(46)   ?Both marks were excellent, but Bill's was only half as bad as John's.

(iii) Both members are normal in *How*-questions; one yields a system-impartial question, the other a system-committed question:

(47)   How good were the results this year?
(48)   How bad were the results this year?

Typical members of this group are: *good:bad, kind:cruel, polite:rude*. Every supra term potentially has a sub partner, but in content areas that lend themselves to one of the biscalar antonymic patterns, the supra-sub opposition may be less salient than the supra-supra opposition. This, however, is not universally the case, and it is at present not clear what circumstances favor one opposition or the other as the most salient.

In English it appears to be the case that supra-supra contrasts have precedence. Take the case of the *good:bad* pair. Each of these has sub partners. The partner of *good* is *poor*. Compare the normality of *?How poor is it?* and *How bad is it?*, and *?twice as poor* and *twice as bad*. (In German, although *schlecht* is a sub partner of *gut*, the *gut:schlecht* opposition is more salient than the supra-supra *gut:schlimm* opposition.) Notice that although *How bad is it?*, *worse* and *twice as bad* are system-committed, they are scale-impartial, since they presuppose no particular value on the 'bad' scale. There is no single sub term for *bad*, but a choice of contextually restricted possibilities, such as *mild* and *slight*: compare *?How mild is your gout?* and *?How slight was your accident?* with *How bad was your gout/accident?*

Although absolute scale-schemas are necessary to explain the scale-impartiality of *better* and *worse*, they are not calibrated, and this gives rise to differences with polars. First, neither member yields a normal nominalization question:

(49)   ?What was the goodness of the film?
(50)   ?What was the cleanness of the room?
(51)   ?What was John's politeness?
         (cf. *What was the length of the rope?*)

Second, *How*-questions have only one interpretation, namely, a relative one. This explains why (52) is normal, but (53) is odd:

(52)   A: The last one was quite short.
         B: How long was it?
         (*Long*, here, gets an absolute reading.)

(53)   ?A: The results were rather poor/bad.
         B: How good were they?
         (B's question only has a relative reading, i.e. 'Were they good or bad/poor?' But A has already given that information, hence the oddness of the question.)

Third, both members are committed in (54)–(56):

(54)   I was surprised by its X-ness.
(55)   I was surprised by John's politeness.
(56)   I was surprised at the room's cleanness.

Given that there are no calibrated quantities with the scales of overlapping antonyms, a relative reading seems adequately motivated.

(iv) Inherentness is a property of overlapping antonyms, and of no other variety. It can be illustrated with *good:bad*. Sentence (57) is quite normal:

(57)   John, Bill and Tom are all pretty hopeless at tennis; John is a little bit better than Bill, while Tom is slightly worse.

This is what we would expect, with *better* showing impartiality. However, while (58) is normal, neither (59) nor (60) is:

(58)   The drought last year was worse than this year.
(59)   ?The drought this year is better than last year.
(60)   ?How good was the drought last year?

It seems that certain items do not collocate with *better* or *How good . . .?*, even though they collocate perfectly normally with *worse*. These items share the property of being normally construed as 'inherently bad': accidents, illnesses, famines, droughts, earthquakes and so on. The inherent badness (or whatever) of some entity is, of course, a construal, and varies with contextual factors. Sentence (61) is more likely in a conversation between two seismologists than between two victims of the disaster in question:

(61)   A: How was the earthquake?
         B: Quite good – better than the last one.

Example (62) provides an example involving *clean* (*clean:dirty* are construed in some contexts as overlapping):

(62)   ?This smudge is cleaner than that one.

A possible explanation of the inherentness effect utilizes the fact that the BAD-NESS scale has only half the extent of the MERIT scale. Perhaps there is a kind of Gricean implicature that the scale on which we place something is the smallest that encompasses all the possibilities for a particular construed domain. Hence, if we say, for instance, *How good was the film?*, we implicate that we are prepared for an answer anywhere on the scale of MERIT. The reason we say *How bad was the famine*, rather than *How good was the famine?*, is because the BADNESS scale encompasses all the expected possibilities for a famine. *How good was the famine* would implicate that we construe the domain of famines as potentially containing good examples.

7.4   Variable construal of antonyms and complementaries

In illustrating the different antonymic patterns available, we have relied heavily on default construals in minimal contexts. In this section we examine the extent of context variability in the construal of pairs of lexical items conventionally regarded as antonymic opposites.

7.4.1   Absolute vs. relative construal

Some opposite pairs behave in some contexts like a pair of complementaries, in other contexts like a pair of antonyms and in yet other contexts as a hybrid opposition in which one term is gradable and the other absolute. A typical example is *clean:dirty*. Example (63) shows them behaving like complementaries:

(63)   I've put the clean shirts in the drawer and the dirty ones in this bag.

Here, a particular domain of shirts is construed as having only two subdivisions, clean ones and dirty ones, and what does not fall under one heading necessarily falls under the other. In (64), on the other hand, dirtiness is construed as a gradable property, and in (65) cleanness is construed as gradable. Most speakers would confidently infer the truth of (65) from the truth of (64), which means that *clean* and *dirty* are behaving like antonyms:

(64)   This shirt is dirtier than that one.
(65)   That shirt is cleaner than this one.

(Notice that both [64] and [65] imply that the shirt in question is at least slightly dirty.) In general, a gradable construal of a property is indicated by the use of the morphological comparative or superlative, or intensifiers such as *more, fairly, quite, rather, extremely* and so on.

In (66), we have a hybrid situation, with *dirty* construed as relative, but *clean* construed as absolute:

(66)   A: How are you getting on with that very dirty pan?
         B: Well, it's almost clean – give me another ten minutes and I'll have it clean.

Hybrid construals are particularly common with expressions of completeness and incompleteness, such as *half* (as in *half clean*), *almost, nearly, practically, completely, quite, utterly*. Notice that *It's neither X nor Y* prevents a dichotomous construal, hence, *It's neither clean nor dirty* is either odd or it coerces a hybrid construal with *dirty* being given a relative construal and *clean* an absolute construal. On this interpretation, *not dirty* receives an interpretation 'not far enough along the *dirty*-scale to deserve the unmodified label *dirty*,' that is to say, 'only slightly dirty.' If this possibility is explicitly ruled out, the expression is virtually unconstruable: **It's neither clean nor even slightly dirty. It's neither dead nor alive* either requires a wider construal of the domain (e.g. *A piece of chalk is neither dead nor alive*), or the envisaging of odd states such as ghosts or vampires; *It's neither possible nor impossible* is very hard to construe at all. The final construal, as always, is a result of interaction between constraints of different kinds and different strengths.

In a hybrid construal, the terms are normally not interchangeable. For instance, *It's neither clean nor dirty* cannot be construed with *dirty* given an absolute construal and *clean* a relative construal. And (66) with the terms reversed not only denotes an odd activity, but is actually not interpretable:

(67)   A: How are you getting on with that clean pan?
         B: Well, it's almost dirty – give me another ten minutes and I'll have it dirty.

The reason for this constraint, which appears to be cognitive, rather than conventional, lies in the nature of the *clean-dirty* opposition. It represents what in

Cruse 1986 was called a privative opposition, that is to say, one in which one term denotes the absence of a property and its partner denotes the presence of the property. In the *clean-dirty* opposition, *clean* denotes the absence of dirt, rather than the converse:

(68)   When something is clean, there is no dirt present.
(69)   ?When something is dirty, there is no cleanness present.

The notion of 'zero dirtiness' is of course a context-dependent construal: we demand different degrees of absolute objective cleanness in different circumstances as a qualification for the label *clean*. Think of a pair of shoes, a kitchen knife, a surgeon's scalpel. In the expression *cleaner than clean*, *cleaner* needs to be interpreted with reference to an absolute scale of cleanness, whereas *clean* denotes the current contextually appropriate reference point.

The reason *clean* has positive polarity (defined as the greater potential for impartial use; cf. *How clean is it?*, which is impartial, while *How dirty is it?* is committed), even though it is an 'absence' term, that is, logically negative, is because there is a strong conventional constraint favoring a positive evaluation. This can be overridden by contextual constraints: after a rugby match on a particularly muddy pitch, a description of the players as *gloriously dirty* is construable; *dirty* as applied to a film or book is frequently given a positive evaluation nowadays – in a recent review, a novel was described as *gloriously filthy*. However, although *dirty* can be construed as positive, where there are sufficiently strong contextual constraints, what seems to be virtually impossible is to construe *dirty* as the zero point of a scale of cleanness.

There is a small number of opposites that behave like *clean* and *dirty*: they display an unusual freedom in respect of construal type. In other cases there is evidence of conventional or cognitive constraints operating. Take the case of *dead:alive*. With these a symmetrical absolute construal is readily accessible:

(70)   A: Is it dead?
        B: No, look, it's breathing – it's still alive.

Also, it is not difficult to construe *alive* as gradable:

(71)   You look rather more alive than you did half an hour ago!

However, *dead* is considerably less comfortable in this context:

(72)   ?You look rather more dead than you did half an hour ago!

Hence, *dead* seems more tied to an absolute construal than *alive* (or, indeed, *clean*). A hybrid construal is fairly normal (notice that it is not *dead* that is being graded here, but 'not-dead-ness'):

(73)   A: You look half-dead.
         B: I feel three-quarters dead.

Figurative uses of *dead* may be less odd when construed as gradable, but this is strictly irrelevant as far as literal construals are concerned:

(74)   Every time I come back to this town it seems even more dead than the last time I was here.

As a final example of absolute/relative alternation, consider *married:single*. These are usually considered quintessential complementaries, and the fact that there are well-defined legal criteria that can be appealed to lends support to this construal:

(75)   I need to ask you a few questions. Are you married or single?

However, as I have noted elsewhere, Iris Murdoch has (76) in one of her novels:

(76)   Jane was very married.

Most speakers find this interpretable, but at the same time feel they are working against palpable constraints in coming to the appropriate construal. Once one accepts this construal, (77) presents no problems:

(77)   Jane is more married than Mary.

But it is much harder to construe (78) as representing the same relation between Jane and Mary as (77):

(78)   Mary is more single than Jane.

That is, (78) cannot be construed as attributing different degrees of 'married-ness' to Jane and Mary. However, (78) is a possible expression of a situation where Jane has a more-or-less steady boyfriend, whereas Mary has several men on the go at any one time, none of whom last very long. In other words, we can construe 'married-ness' as a gradable property, but we cannot construe *single* as sub partner to *married*: we can, however, with some cognitive effort, construe 'married-ness' and 'single-ness' as equipollent partners.

   In contrast, a careful examination of *clean:dirty* in their manifestation as gradable antonyms shows them to belong preferentially to the overlapping type. One indication of this is the element of inherentness, which has already been remarked on:

(79)   This smudge is dirtier than that one.
(80)   ?That smudge is cleaner than that one.

While many lexical items denoting properties can be construed, according to context, as either absolute or gradable, others seem not to have the two possibilities. Particularly interesting are those that are gradable in their default construals. Why is it that, for instance, *cold* can receive an absolute construal, as in (81), whereas *slow*, *light* and *cheap* cannot under any circumstances be interpreted as 'stationary', 'weightless' or 'free', respectively, that is, as zero on the respective scales (as in [82]–[84]):

(81)   Your dinner's almost cold – hurry up and come to table!
         (Here, *cold* represents 'zero hotness,' i.e. room temperature.)
(82)   ?The car was traveling completely slowly.
(83)   ?In space one is completely light.
(84)   ?I didn't pay anything – they were completely cheap.

This is a difficult question. From available examples, it seems that only supra terms can support an absolute construal. However, not all supras have absolute construals: *almost long/heavy/fast. Also necessary is some sort of natural determinate value, frequently also construed as a zero. The reason for the absence of absolute construals for sub terms is not at present obvious. It may have something to do with the fact that they are impressionistic, and do not have a linear relation with the absolute scale. That is to say, to get equal increments of impressionistic shortness, we must, let's say, successively halve the absolute length. That way, zero will be approached asymptotically, but will never be reached. Put another way, the default construal of the SLOW scale has no end. There is a parallel with impressionistic scales of loudness and brightness, which do not have a linear relation to absolute energy level.

Another possibility is that, in those cases mentioned, either the zero point on the scale is of no practical communicative importance (what use have we for the notion of zero length?) or the zero point is preempted by another lexical item (as with *stationary*, *weightless*, *free*). (Of course this could work the other way round: we have a separate lexical item for the zero point because the sub term cannot cover it. This has some intuitive plausibility. More work is needed on this point.)

7.4.2   Scale features

7.4.2.1   Direction of scale and number of scales

Graded properties are normally construed in such a way that an increase in salience is equated with a higher degree of the property, hence we operate with a scale of LENGTH rather than a scale of SHORTH, with *long* as supra and *short* as sub. However, there are contexts where the roles of *long* and *short* appear to be reversed. For instance, (85) and (86) appeared in a newspaper article about the miniaturization of computer components:

(85)   The new device is ten times smaller than anything seen previously.
(86)   'The nanotube transistors are about 350 times smaller than a conventional silicon transistor and faster.' (Guardian On-line Supplement, October 10, 2002, p. 11)

And (87), in the same context, seems normal (although not actually attested):

(87)   A. Every week we produce smaller and smaller chips.
        B. How small do you think you'll be able to get them?
        A: Well, we are not sure, but our best efforts last year were only half as small as this year's.

It seems that in (85)–(87) the scale of linear extent is being construed in the reverse direction from the default construal, as a scale of SMALLNESS rather than a scale of BIGNESS/LARGENESS, with *small* as the supra term. This reversal goes against quite strong cognitive constraints, and would not be possible unless there were definite factors favoring it. In this case there are such factors, namely, the fact that an increase in smallness is correlated with an increase in interestingness, salience, desirability.

Many instances of scale reversal are correlated with a change of antonym type. This is particularly so where the motivation for the reversal is related to evaluativeness. Take the case, discussed earlier, of *easy:difficult*. It is not hard to construe a scale of DIFFICULTY with *difficult* and *easy* as polars, *difficult* as supra, and *How difficult is it?* as an impartial question. But an average class of undergraduates finds it difficult to decide whether *difficult* or *easy* is the supra term, with a significant number opting for *easy*, and an underlying scale of easiness. This seems to be supported by the relative normality out of context of *How easy is it?*

A significant determining factor seems to be whether 'difficulty' is judged negatively or objectively. If 'easy' is positively evaluated, and 'difficult' negatively evaluated, this encourages the movement of *easy:difficult* from the polar construal to the overlapping construal, with both *easy* and *difficult* as supras, but *easy* as the major term (parallel to *good*). A similar alternation in antonym type can be observed with *cheap:expensive* (Hayes 2001). Where these are used simply to indicate price, they behave more like polars, with *cheap* as sub; but where *cheap* has connotations of 'poor quality' and *expensive* of 'high quality,' they behave more like overlapping antonyms, with *cheap* being a (minor) supra term.

A different alternation is found with *thin*, in opposition to *thick* and *fat*. There is no doubt that *thick:thin* are polars, with *thin* as sub term; in other words, there is no scale of thinness, only one of thickness (in the default construal). The majority of native-speaker informants, however, class *fat:thin* as equipollents, out of context. This involves reclassifying *thin* as supra, that is, construing a scale of thinness. The motivation seems to be that there is a societal norm for girth, which is positively evaluated, and significant deviations in either direction are negatively evaluated: the evaluative feature has the effect of encouraging the construal of a scale of thinness (more of the property being more salient).

7.4.2.2 Effects of calibration

The availability or unavailability of conventional units for measuring the degree of a property can make a difference to the way a gradable adjective behaves. Take the case of *strong*. We may speak equally normally of a *strong man* and *a strong solution of a chemical*, and in both cases it would be normal to ask *How strong is the solution?* and *How strong is that man?* However, there is a clear difference in normality between *What is the strength of the solution?* and *?What is the strength of that man?* The reason is that we are not familiar with conventional units for measuring the strength of a man, whereas the strength of a solution can be measured in conventional units. In this case, it might be objected that we are dealing with two autonomous readings of *strong*, since (88) has a definite air of punning:

(88)   ?Mary likes her tea and her men to be very strong.

Perhaps a more convincing example is provided by *strong tea* and *strong beer*. These two coordinate happily without zeugma:

(89)   John likes his tea and his beer to be very strong.

Yet (90) is much more normal than (91), the reason being that the strength of beer is commonly measured in terms of the percentage of alcohol it contains, but there are as yet no units for measuring the strength of tea:

(90)   What is the strength of this beer?
(91)   ?What is the strength of this tea?

It would be difficult to argue that the properties referred to in (90) and (91) are different. The situation is similar in the case of *hard*. There is a scientific scale for expressing the hardness of minerals, so the question *What is the hardness of quartz?* is perfectly well formed in a scientific context. However, although some types of wood are harder than others, the question *What is the hardness of this wood?* is, outside of a specially contrived context, odd. Many other examples could be given.

7.5   Conclusion

The investigations outlined here have shown the complex and varied behavior of antonyms to be remarkably non-arbitrary. In comparison with the other sense relations studied, the role of cognitive constraints is especially prominent.

8

Metaphor

8.1   Figurative language

Prototypical figurative language will be characterized here as language use where, from the speaker's point of view, conventional constraints are deliberately infringed in the service of communication, and from the hearer's point of view, a satisfactory (i.e. relevant) interpretation can only be achieved if conventional constraints on interpretation are overridden by contextual constraints.

What is the motivation for figurative uses of language? Here we need to distinguish the speaker's motivation for using an expression figuratively, and the hearer's motivation for assigning a figurative construal to an expression. Briefly, a speaker uses an expression figuratively when he/she feels that no literal use will produce the same effect. The figurative use may simply be more attention-grabbing, or it might conjure up a complex image not attainable any other way, or it may permit the conveyance of new concepts. As far as the hearer is concerned, the most obvious reason for opting for a figurative construal is the fact that no equally accessible and relevant literal construal is available.

The major types of figurative usage are metaphor and metonymy. Metaphor and metonymy both involve a **vehicle** and a **target**. Metaphor involves an interaction between two domains construed from two regions of purport, and the content of the vehicle domain is an ingredient of the construed target through processes of correspondence and blending. For instance, in (1) (from Patricia Cornwell's *Black Notice*) the speaker's mental processes are presented as having simultaneously the character of thoughts and small sinister creatures:

(1)   A myriad of ugly, dark thoughts clung to my reason and dug in with their claws.

In metonymy, the vehicle's function is merely to identify the target construal. For instance, in (2) there is no combining of the features of cars and humans – the use of *you* is simply an easy route to the intended referent, the car relevantly associated with the addressee:

(2)   Where are you parked?

Metaphor and metonymy have been a major preoccupation of cognitive linguists generally. Metonymy is discussed briefly in §3.2.1; here, the focus is on metaphor.

8.2 The conceptual theory of metaphor

8.2.1 Introduction

Cognitive linguists reject the so-called substitution theory of metaphor, according to which a metaphorical expression replaces some literal expression that has the same meaning. Metaphors ('true' metaphors), in general, are not literally paraphrasable: they have a character that no literal expression has. At the same time, although metaphorical meaning has a special character that distinguishes it from any literal meaning, it has the same range of basic functions as literal meaning. Of course, many metaphorical expressions have a heavy load of expressive meaning, but so do many literal expressions. In other words, metaphorical meaning is not, at least in basic functional respects, a special kind of meaning: it is rather the case that metaphor is the result of a special process for arriving at, or construing, a meaning.

One of the most influential books to emerge from the cognitive linguistic tradition is Lakoff and Johnson's *Metaphors we live by* (Lakoff and Johnson 1980; see also Lakoff and Turner 1989; Lakoff 1987, 1993). Lakoff and his colleagues use evidence from everyday conventional linguistic expressions to infer the existence of metaphorical relations or **mappings** between conceptual domains (in the sense of chapter 2) in the human mind. Lakoff's primary goal in developing the conceptual theory of metaphor is to uncover these metaphorical mappings between domains and how they have guided human reasoning and behavior, as can be seen by his subsequent application of metaphor theory to literature (Lakoff and Turner 1989), philosophy (Johnson 1987; Lakoff and Johnson 1999), mathematics (Lakoff and Núñez 2000) and even politics (Lakoff 1996).

Because of Lakoff's aim to uncover deeply embedded conceptual relations in the mind, for him the ideal metaphorical expressions to analyze are not the widely discussed type of examples in (3), but rather those in (4):

(3)   a. Juliet is the sun. (Shakespeare)
        b. my wife . . . whose waist is an hourglass (from André Breton; Lakoff and Turner 1989:90)

(4)   a. I'll see you at 2 o'clock.
        b. He is in danger.

c. Her anger boiled over.

d. She's had to contend with many obstacles in her life, but she has come a long way since her days in the orphanage.

The expressions in (3) differ from those in (4) in two important respects. First, the expressions in (3) are all of the form *X is Y* where X and Y are both nominal expressions, a quite uncommon type of metaphorical expression in ordinary speech. The expressions in (4) are all common, everyday constructions in which metaphorically used prepositions, verbs and other expressions (typically relational in nature) combine with literal phrases (typically nominals functioning as arguments of the metaphorical relational elements). Hence the metaphorical expressions in (3) are grammatically and semantically quite different from those in (4). This distinction is pertinent because much psycholinguistic research on metaphor (e.g. Gentner 1983, 1988), including research purported to test Lakoff and Johnson's theory (e.g. Glucksberg 2001), is based on the metaphor type illustrated in (3), not (4).

Second, and more important, the metaphors in (3) are novel creations ([3a–b] are both from literary works, for example) while the metaphors in (4) are conventionalized linguistic expressions, another aspect of their common everyday character. Lakoff and Turner distinguish novel metaphors from conventionalized metaphors, calling the former 'image metaphors' (Lakoff and Turner 1989:99; Lakoff 1993:229; see below). Of course, many metaphors do not become conventionalized. But certain metaphors do get conventionalized, and more interesting, the same metaphors tend to become conventionalized independently across languages. There is presumably some reason why certain metaphors are conventionalized again and again across languages, while others are not. Lakoff and colleagues argue that their repeated conventionalization is due to their cognitive significance, which in turn is grounded in human experience (hence the title *Metaphors we live by*). Thus, the main focus of their theory of metaphor is of conventional metaphors, not novel metaphors; we will return to this point at the end of this section.

The central characteristic of Lakoff and Johnson's theory of (conventional) metaphor is that the metaphor is not a property of individual linguistic expressions and their meanings, but of whole conceptual domains. In principle, any concept from the **source domain** – the domain supporting the literal meaning of the expression – can be used to describe a concept in the **target domain** – the domain the sentence is actually about.

For example, the literal meaning of *at* in (4a) is locative in nature, but it has been metaphorically extended to apply also to time. Likewise, *in* in (4b) has a basic locative meaning, and the use in (4) is a metaphorical extension of this: here, a state (danger) is conceived as a container that one can be inside of or outside of. But many other locative expressions can be used to describe time, as in (5), and many container expressions can be used for a wide range of states, as in (6):

(5)   a. We have entered the 21st century.
       b. I finished this in two hours.
       c. They worked through the night.
(6)   a. They're in love.
       b. How do we get out of this mess?
       c. He fell into a deep depression.

Lakoff and Johnson use a formula TARGET DOMAIN IS SOURCE DOMAIN to describe the metaphorical link between the domains. The metaphorical mappings in (4a) and (5) are manifestations of the TIME IS SPACE metaphor, and those in (4b) and 6 of the STATES ARE CONTAINERS metaphor (Lakoff and Johnson 1980:31–32). Likewise, (4c) is a manifestation of the ANGER IS HEAT OF A FLUID metaphor, and (4d), the LOVE IS A JOURNEY metaphor. As Lakoff puts it:

> What constitutes the LOVE IS A JOURNEY metaphor is not any particular word or expression. It is the ontological mapping across conceptual domains, from the source domain of journeys to the target domain of love. The metaphor is not just a matter of language, but of thought and reason. The language is secondary. The mapping is primary, in that it sanctions the use of source domain language and inference patterns for target domain concepts. The mapping is conventional; that is, it is a fixed part of our conceptual system, one of our conventional ways of conceptualising love relationships. (Lakoff 1993:208)

A (conventional) metaphor is therefore a conceptual mapping between two domains. The mapping is asymmetrical, however: the metaphorical expression profiles a conceptual structure in the target domain, not the source domain.

The mapping between source and target domains involves two sorts of correspondences, epistemic and ontological. The ontological correspondences hold between elements of one domain and elements of the other domain; epistemic correspondences are correspondences between relations holding between elements in one domain and relations between elements in the other domain (this includes, for instance, encyclopedic knowledge about the domain). The phenomenon of correspondence will be illustrated using the example of ANGER IS HEAT OF A FLUID (Lakoff 1987:387):

(7) *Ontological correspondences*

source: HEAT OF FLUID	target: ANGER
container	body
heat of fluid	anger
heat scale	anger scale
pressure in container	experienced pressure
agitation of boiling fluid	experienced agitation
limit of container's resistance	limit of person's ability to suppress anger
explosion	loss of control

(8) *Epistemic correspondences*

When fluid in a container is heated beyond a certain limit, pressure increases to point at which container explodes.	When anger increases beyond a certain limit, 'pressure' increases to point at which person loses control.
An explosion is damaging to container and dangerous to bystanders.	Loss of control is damaging to person and dangerous to others.
Explosion can be prevented by applying sufficient force and counterpressure.	Anger can be suppressed by force of will.
Controlled release of pressure may occur, which reduces danger of explosion.	Anger can be released in a controlled way, or vented harmlessly, thus reducing level.

In general, metaphors are conceptual structures, and are not merely linguistic in nature, although, of course, they are normally realized linguistically. The correspondences between domains are represented in the conceptual system, and are fully conventionalized among members of a speech community. An open-ended range of linguistic expressions can tap into the same conceptual structure in both conventional and unconventional ways, and be understood immediately: a conceptual metaphor cannot therefore be reduced to a finite set of linguistic expressions. What Lakoff calls 'elaborations' involve more specific versions of a basic metaphor whose characteristics in the source domain carry over to the target domain. For instance, the difference in intensity between *boil* and *simmer* in reference to a heated liquid carries over to indicate corresponding differences in degree of anger in *to boil with anger* and *to simmer with anger*.

Another consequence of the conceptual nature of metaphor is that certain patterns of reasoning may carry over from the source domain to the target domain. Lakoff calls these 'metaphorical entailments' (it is not clear how metaphorical entailments differ from epistemic correspondences). For instance, with reference to the metaphor *She demolished his argument*, an example of the ARGUMENT IS WAR metaphor: if you destroy all your enemy's weapons, you win the war;

similarly, if you demolish all your opponent's points in an argument, you win the argument.

We may summarize Lakoff's conceptual theory of metaphor as follows:

(i)   It is a theory of recurrently conventionalized expressions in everyday language in which literal and metaphorical elements are intimately combined grammatically.

(ii)   The conventional metaphorical expressions are not a purely linguistic phenomenon, but the manifestation of a conceptual mapping between two semantic domains; hence the mapping is general and productive (and assumed to be characteristic of the human mind).

(iii)   The metaphorical mapping is asymmetrical: the expression is about a situation in one domain (the target domain) using concepts mapped over from another domain (the source domain).

(iv)   The metaphorical mapping can be used for metaphorical reasoning about concepts in the target domain.

8.2.2   *Issues in the conceptual theory of metaphor*

The sketch of Lakoff's conceptual theory of metaphor in the preceding section presents only the major premises of the model. In this section, we will examine some issues about the conceptual theory of metaphor that have led to elaborations of the basic model.

The first issue we describe is the deceptively simple one of how best to describe a particular metaphorical mapping. For example, the expressions in (9) illustrate a metaphor described by Lakoff and Johnson as AN ARGUMENT/THEORY IS A BUILDING (Lakoff and Johnson 1980:46):

(9)   a. We need to construct a strong argument for that.
        b. The argument collapsed.
        c. We need to buttress the theory with solid arguments.

However, other expressions making reference to buildings do not participate in the metaphor (Clausner and Croft 1997:260; Grady 1997:270):

(10)   a. *Is that the basement of your theory?
        b. *That line of reasoning has no plumbing.
        c. *This theory has French windows.

The examples in (10) suggest that the metaphor should be formulated more concisely, that is, using less schematic source and target domains, in such a way that the metaphorical mapping is valid for the concepts in the source and target domains. Clausner and Croft propose the more specific formulation THE CONVINCINGNESS OF AN ARGUMENT IS THE STRUCTURAL INTEGRITY

OF A BUILDING. In some cases, the more schematic metaphorical mapping is replaced by two (or more) distinct specific mappings. Clausner and Croft reformulate Lakoff and Johnson's LOVE IS A PATIENT metaphor (p. 49; examples [11a–b] and [12c] below) as two more specific metaphors, A SOCIAL RELATIONSHIP IS BODILY HEALTH (11) and A SOCIAL RELATIONSHIP IS LIFE ([12]; Clausner and Croft 1997:261–62):

(11)   a. This is a sick relationship.
        b. They have a strong, healthy marriage.
        c. *Their relationship went to the hospital.
(12)   a. The marriage is dead – it can't be revived.
        b. Her selfishness killed the relationship.
        c. His effort to understand her breathed new life into the marriage.

Clausner and Croft also argue that metaphors vary in productivity. Many metaphors, such as THE CONVINCINGNESS OF AN ARGUMENT IS THE STRUCTURAL INTEGRITY OF A BUILDING, appear to be completely productive, once formulated at the appropriate level of schematicity. Other metaphors are only partially productive, in that some expressions are acceptable and others are not. Examples of partially productive metaphors are the revelation idioms:

(13)   spill the beans, let the cat out of the bag, blow the whistle, blow the lid off, loose lips

The expressions in (13) all have as a target domain TO REVEAL A SECRET. But other similar expressions are not conventional in English:

(14)   *spill the peas, *let the cat out of the house

One cannot formulate a single metaphorical mapping at any level of schematicity that would include the expressions in (13) but not the expressions in (14). Yet the expressions in (13) are understood metaphorically. Gibbs and O'Brien (1990) found that the conventional expressions in (13) had coherent mental images associated with them by subjects, while the unacceptable expressions in (14) did not. The fact that the idioms were 'imageable' (Lakoff 1993:211) indicates that there is a metaphorical mapping present; the fact that the nonconventional yet semantically similar expressions in (14) are not consistently imageable indicates that the metaphor is not completely productive. Finally, truly opaque idiomatic expressions such as *kick the bucket* and *by and large* are not interpreted in terms of mapping from a source domain. Clausner and Croft argue that the usage-based model (see chapter 11) can be used to model degree of productivity of metaphorical/idiomatic expressions.

Lakoff and Johnson allow for metaphors to exist at different levels of schematicity, that is, in a taxonomic hierarchy. For example, they posit a schematic metaphor

LOVE IS A JOURNEY, and illustrate three more specific instantiations of the metaphor, LOVE IS A CAR TRIP/TRAIN TRIP/SEA VOYAGE, illustrated in (15)–(17) respectively (Lakoff and Johnson 1980:44–45):

(15)   a. This relationship is a dead-end street.
         b. We're just spinning our wheels.
(16)   a. We've gone off the tracks.
(17)   a. Our marriage is on the rocks.
         b. Their relationship is foundering.

Lakoff (1993:222) further adds that LOVE IS A JOURNEY can be grouped with A CAREER IS A JOURNEY under a more schematic metaphor A PURPOSEFUL LIFE IS A JOURNEY, which in turn is an instance of what he calls the event structure metaphor (roughly, ACTION IS DIRECTED MOTION), which includes the mappings in (18):

(18)   States are locations.
         Changes are movements.
         Causes are forces.
         Actions are self-propelled movements.
         Purposes are destinations.
         Means are paths to destinations.

Grady (1997, 1998) argues for a combination of decomposition of specific metaphors and the subsumption of the parts into highly schematic metaphors that combine with each other. For example, Grady takes the narrowed version of AN ARGUMENT/THEORY IS A BUILDING and analyzes it into the two metaphors ORGANIZATION IS PHYSICAL STRUCTURE and PERSISTING IS REMAINING ERECT (Grady 1997:273). The two metaphor parts are formulated in a schematic fashion in order to capture other metaphors, which Grady argues are part of the same mapping, for example other argument metaphors as in (19) (Grady 1997: 272), and other target domains for structures as in (20) (Grady 1997: 271):

(19)   a. They tore the theory to shreds [FABRIC]
         b. Their theory of a masterpiece of logical construction [WORK OF ART]
(20)   a. The Federal Reserve is the cornerstone of the nation's banking system. [FINANCIAL SYSTEM]
         b. Recent land development has caused the near collapse of the Bay's ecosystem. [ECOSYSTEM]

Grady (1998) presents a similar decomposition of the conduit metaphor (Reddy 1979[1993]).

Grady's and Lakoff's highly schematic analyses raise the question of which metaphors are more basic to human understanding, the more specific or the more schematic ones? To address this question, however, we must first address another issue, namely what conceptual structures are mapped in the metaphor.

Lakoff proposes the Invariance Hypothesis as a constraint on metaphorical mapping (Lakoff 1990:54):

(21)   Invariance Hypothesis: Metaphorical mappings preserve the cognitive topology (that is, image-schematic structure) of the source domain.

Image schemas, as discussed in chapter 3, include much of the basic structuring of experience, such as scales, causation, containment, motion and so on. Lakoff argues in particular that reasoning in the target domain (metaphorical entailments) is governed by the image-schematic structure of the source domain (for example, consider the epistemic correspondences for ANGER IS HEAT OF A FLUID above).

Turner proposes an important constraint on the Invariance Hypothesis:

> In metaphor, we are constrained not to violate the image-schematic structure of the target; this entails that we are constrained not to violate whatever image-schematic structure may be possessed by non-image components of the target. (Turner 1990:252)

Lakoff calls these 'target domain overrides' (1993:216), and illustrates them with *give a kick* and *give an idea*. When you give someone a kick, the person does not 'have' the kick afterward, and when you give someone an idea, you still 'have' the idea. The target domain of transfer of energy or force does not allow that energy to continue to exist after the transmission event, hence that metaphorical entailment does not hold. Likewise, the target domain of knowledge does not imply that knowledge transmitted is lost: that metaphorical entailment does not hold either.

The Invariance Hypothesis and the target domain override raise a fundamental issue about conceptual metaphors: why do they exist in the first place? If the target domain has image-schematic structure already, which can override the metaphor, then why do we have metaphors? Likewise, if we can isolate image-schematic structure, or construct highly schematic metaphors such as ORGANIZATION IS PHYSICAL STRUCTURE, is it not simply a highly schematic conceptual structure that is instantiated in both source and target domains? If so, then is it really a metaphorical mapping, or simply an instantiation of the image-schematic conceptual structure in two different cognitive domains? (This latter view has been propounded by Glucksberg [2001] and Jackendoff and Aaron [1991:328–30].)

Lakoff and Johnson present two counterarguments against these criticisms. First, they argue that, although target domains of metaphors are structured, they are not fully so: 'they are not clearly enough delineated in their own terms to satisfy the purposes of our day-to-day functioning'(Lakoff and Johnson 1980:118). Thus, target domains lack at least some (image-schematic) structure. Lakoff and Johnson argue that the linking of otherwise independent conceptual domains by metaphor in fact *creates* similarity:

> ... the IDEAS ARE FOOD metaphor establishes similarities between ideas and food. Both can be digested, swallowed, devoured, and warmed over, and both can nourish you. These similarities do not exist independently of the metaphor. The concept of swallowing food is independent of the metaphor, but the concept of swallowing ideas arises only by virtue of the metaphor. (Lakoff and Johnson 1980:147–48)

The second counterargument that Lakoff and Johnson present for why conceptual metaphors exist is that there is an asymmetry between source domain and target domain. For example, love is expressed in terms of journeys, but journeys are not expressed in terms of love (Lakoff and Johnson 1980:108). If image-schematic structure were simply a highly schematic concept subsuming the corresponding concepts in the source and target domains, then one would expect metaphorical mappings to go in either direction; but they do not. Even when it appears that there is a bidirectional metaphorical mapping, Lakoff and Turner argue that the two mappings are different:

We can have cases like PEOPLE ARE MACHINES, as in

> At the violet hour, when the eyes and back
> Turn upward from the desk, when the human engine waits
> Like a taxi throbbing, waiting   (Eliot, *The Waste Land*)

> and also the different metaphor MACHINES ARE PEOPLE, as in when we say, 'The computer is punishing me by wiping out my buffer.' But these are two different metaphors, because the mappings go in opposite directions, *and different things get mapped*. In MACHINES ARE PEOPLE, the will and desire of a person are attributed to machines, but in the PEOPLE ARE MACHINES metaphor, there is no mention of will and desire. What is mapped instead is that machines have parts that function in certain ways, such as idling steadily or accelerating, that they may break down and need to be fixed, and so on. (Lakoff and Turner 1989:132, emphasis original)

These two counterarguments are persuasive; but they also imply that the Invariance Hypothesis and the target domain override captures only part of the nature of metaphorical mappings, and perhaps not the most important part. The fact that both people and machines have parts that function (or malfunction) is part of why *human engine* works as a metaphor. But Eliot is certainly conveying more than that with the metaphor, including perhaps the mechanization of twentieth-century life and its dehumanizing effects (not to mention further images created by the simile on the next line).

It is likely that a far richer structure than simply compatible image-schemas is brought into the target domain from the source domain. It also suggests that Lakoff and Johnson's first counterargument – the target domain lacks (image-schematic) structure that is added by the metaphorical mapping from the source domain – makes too sharp a distinction between target domain structure and mapped source domain structure. It implies a minimum of interaction between the target domain structure (already there) and the source domain structure (filling in for the absence of target domain structure). Instead, many metaphor theorists argue for a more interactive relationship between source and target domain structure, involving something like a 'fusion' or 'superimposition' of structure from both domains (Jackendoff and Aaron 1991:334; they also cite Black's [1979] 'interaction' and Ricoeur's [1978] 'reverberation'). Jackendoff and Aaron suggest that the source domain concepts are transformed as well in being metaphorically applied to the target domain (ibid.). It is this intuition that blending theory attempts to capture (see §8.3.3). This interactive relationship of course strengthens the first counterargument: the metaphor brings much more than extra image-schematic structure to the target domain.

The final issue we wish to raise is the relationship between the conventional metaphors that Lakoff centers his attention on and novel metaphor creation. Lakoff and Johnson (1980:52–53) argue that some novel metaphors are extensions of existing conventional metaphors, such as the song lyric *We're driving in the fast lane on the freeway of love* for LOVE IS A JOURNEY (Lakoff 1993:210). Lakoff and Johnson also allow for completely novel metaphors, using as an example LOVE IS A COLLABORATIVE WORK OF ART (Lakoff and Johnson 1980: 139–43). They argue that a novel metaphor of this type can be a systematic mapping between two conceptual domains.

Lakoff and Turner argue that other novel metaphors are more restricted; these are image metaphors. An example they give is *my wife . . . whose waist is an hourglass* ([3b] above; Lakoff and Turner 1989:90). Lakoff and Turner argue that in image metaphors, specific and richly specified mental images are mapped, whereas in conventional image-schematic metaphors, 'there is no rich imagistic detail' (Lakoff and Turner 1989:91). They also argue that image metaphors do not involve the mapping of rich knowledge and inferential structure of conventional image-schematic metaphors (ibid.).

For conventional image-schematic metaphors themselves, Lakoff and Johnson argue that they ultimately originate in human bodily and cultural experience. For example, CONSCIOUS IS UP/UNCONSCIOUS IS DOWN, exemplified by *wake up* and *fall asleep*, are based on the fact that 'humans and most other mammals sleep lying down and stand up when they awaken' (Lakoff and Johnson 1980:15). A cultural example is LABOR IS A (MATERIAL) RESOURCE, in that it can be measured, assigned a value, used and so on. This metaphor arises from the fact that we use material resources for various purposes; by virtue of those purposes the resources have value; and the use of those resources requires labor (Lakoff and Johnson 1980: 65–66).

It seems likely that many conventional metaphors – the kind found in everyday language – have a basis in everyday human experience. However, many novel metaphors do not, and some conventional metaphors do not either, except in terms of very general image schemas such as those described by Grady (1997, 1998). Also, where Lakoff & Johnson discuss truly novel image-schematic metaphors such as LOVE IS A COLLABORATIVE WORK OF ART, and Lakoff and Turner discuss novel image metaphors, they do not describe how a speaker comes up with the new metaphor: they only describe what the structure of the metaphor is. But we have suggested that even conventional metaphor involves a blending of richer structure than just image-schematic structure between source and target domains. It seems plausible that even conventional metaphors draw on the full richness of our encyclopedic knowledge of our bodily and cultural experience, especially when they are first coined. Nor does there appear to be a difference in kind between the 'rich detail' mapped in novel image metaphors and the 'rich knowledge' mapped in conventional image-schematic metaphors. If so, then there is only a difference in degree between conventional metaphors and novel metaphors.

8.3 Novel metaphor

8.3.1 The life history of a metaphor

The Lakoffians make a virtue of concentrating on fully established and conventionalized metaphors. However, it can be argued that, if one wants to get to the heart of metaphor as an interpretive mechanism, one must look at freshly coined examples. These are the only ones all of whose properties are currently available for study: conventionalized metaphors have irrecoverably lost at least some of their original properties. Complex literary metaphors are unsuitable for initial study for different reasons: one must understand the simple before tackling the complex. Easily comprehended fresh metaphors are abundantly available in popular literature, the daily press, on TV and so on.

Several stages can be recognized in the life history of a durable metaphor. When it is first coined, the only way to interpret it is to employ one's innate metaphorical interpretive strategy, which is subject to a wide range of contextual and communicative constraints. Once a metaphor takes hold in a speech community and gets repeated sufficiently often, its character changes. First, its meaning becomes circumscribed relative to the freshly coined metaphor, becoming more determinate; second, it begins to be laid down as an item in the mental lexicon, so that in time, it can be retrieved in the same way as a literal expression; third, it begins a process of semantic drift, which can weaken or obscure its metaphorical origins. At the beginning of its life, even if it is being laid down as an item in the lexicon, speakers are very conscious of its status as a metaphor, and they can recreate easily the metaphorical path of its derivation. As time passes, however, the sense of the expression's metaphorical nature fades and eventually disappears (although it can be brought to life by means of Lakoffian elaborations etc.). Once that happens, the expression is no different from a literal expression, and only etymologists and historians of the language can recreate the path of derivation. At some point along this path of change, the expression acquires a capability to act as a literal basis for further metaphorical extensions, which is not possible for a fresh metaphor.

How does this impinge on the Lakoff account of metaphor? Let us look at some relevant examples. Take the metaphor mentioned by Kövecses (2002:8), SOCIAL ORGANIZATIONS ARE PLANTS. Kövecses gives the following expressions (not in the original order) that are said to exemplify this metaphor:

(22)   They had to prune the workforce.
(23)   Employers reaped enormous benefits from cheap foreign labor.
(24)   He works for the local branch of the bank.
(25)   There is a flourishing black market in software there.

Each of these metaphors is well established in the language, but they are at different stages in their life history. The use of *prune* in (22) still strongly evokes the source domain of arboriculture, together with the therapeutic function of pruning, that is, to remove unnecessary growth and increase vigor. This is therefore still in its youth as a metaphor. Arguably, *reap* in (23) is at a later stage of assimilation into the language: the evocation of harvesting is relatively weak; the expression *reap benefits* also shows a degree of frozenness – one cannot reap anything other than benefits – and by some definitions this would count as an idiom. (The deadness of *reaped* can be felt if it is contrasted with *harvested* in the same context.) When we come to (24), a normal speaker will probably not activate the PLANT domain at all, although if the connection is pointed out they will assent to the connection. The word *branch* has become the normal literal term for a local office, shop or other premises forming part of a larger organization. In this sense *branch* has developed a completely independent set of syntagmatic and paradigmatic relations that have nothing to do with the source domain. For instance, *branch office* contrasts with *head office*, rather than, say, *trunk office*; one *opens* a new branch (one does not *grow* one) and one *closes it down* (one does not *cut it off*); there is typically *a branch manager*. In (25), although the historical origin of *flourish* is undoubtedly the French verb *florir*, it is hard to believe that any contemporary speaker habitually makes the connection (according to the Compact Oxford English Dictionary, *flourish* came into English ca. 1300 with both literal and metaphorical meanings). Most people probably think of the literal meaning of *flourish* as having to do with businesses, or perhaps families, and may even feel, for example, *a flourishing garden* to be an extension from this. (The Oxford Advanced Learners Dictionary gives 'be successful, very active or widespread; prosper' as the first definition of *flourish*, with *No business can flourish in the present economic climate* as an example.)

The point of these examples is that one cannot expect to learn much about the mechanism of metaphor by studying cases such as *branch*, *flourish* or even *reap*, although *prune* might be more rewarding. Lakoff argues that it is precisely because metaphors such as ARGUMENT IS WAR have become fixed in the language (and because they are so widespread) that they are so significant, and reflect fundamental properties of the human mind. This is undoubtedly a valid point, but it does not reveal the basic mechanism of metaphor. All these established metaphors must have started life as novel ones. At the very least, there is a separate and worthwhile study to be done on novel metaphors, and that is what is being attempted here.

8.3.2 How do we recognize metaphors?

Lakoff is very much against the view that an essential property of a metaphorical expression is deviance. Basically, Lakoff asks how something so widespread and natural as metaphor can possibly be described as deviant. However, there are two different ways of interpreting 'deviance.' The argument of those who claim that anomalousness is a necessary feature of a metaphorical expression is not that the use of metaphor is an unnatural or deviant practice, it is that if a literal interpretation of an utterance is anomalous, that is normally a signal that we need to apply a different interpretive strategy. The metaphorical interpretation that we end up with is not deviant at all. A valid attack on the 'anomalist' position would have to show that there are perfectly normal metaphors whose literal interpretations are not anomalous. No such examples that bear close scrutiny have yet been proposed.

A common line to take is to quote examples of metaphors whose literal interpretations are *true*. A famous example is that of Max Black (1979), who first puts forward the metaphor:

(26)   Man is a wolf.

He admits that this is literally untrue, and thus seems to support the anomalist position. However, he then goes on to point out that (27) is true:

(27)   Man is not a wolf.

However, this, too, can bear a metaphorical reading, as in (28):

(28)   Man is not a wolf, he is a lion.

Does this undermine the anomalist case? Not really, because although *Man is not a wolf* may be true, it is nonetheless, in the sort of context in which a metaphorical reading would be normal, pragmatically or conversationally anomalous. Black himself effectively concedes this point. It is not obvious how a metaphor can function if there is nothing perceptibly odd whatsoever about its literal construal (Eco 1996 gives a concise account of this argument).

8.3.3   *Blending Theory and novel metaphors*

Lakoff's model does not capture what is perhaps the most characteristic feature of metaphor: a metaphor involves not only the activation of two domains, not only correspondences, but also a species of blending of two domains. This blending becomes weakened, eventually to disappear altogether, as a metaphor becomes established, but is a vital feature of a novel metaphor, whether it is totally fresh, or is a revitalization of a conceptual metaphor by using original linguistic means. A model of metaphor that takes this on board is the one presented in Grady et al. 1999, which builds on the notion of blending presented in Fauconnier and Turner 1996. (Fauconnier and Turner say very little on the topic of metaphor as such.) Grady et al. (1999) claim that the blending model (henceforward BT, for 'Blending Theory') is not a rival to Lakoff's model (henceforward CMT, for 'Conceptual Metaphor Theory') but presupposes it.

Whereas CMT operates with two domains and correspondences between them, BT works with four mental spaces (see §2.6). However, while CMT domains are permanent structures, BT's spaces are partial and temporary representational structures constructed at the point of utterance: they are thus at least partially responsive to contextual factors. However, there is a strong element of conventional fixedness: as Fauconnier and Turner put it, 'Dynamically, input spaces and blends under construction recruit structure from more stable, elaborate, and conventional conceptual structures . . .' (1996:115).

Two of BT's spaces are like CMT domains: they parallel the target and source domains in CMT, except that they are more partial. They add to these, first, a **generic space**, which represents what the target and source domains have in common; second, and most importantly, there is the **blended space**, where selected conceptual material from source and target spaces is combined to form a new structure. This is expressed by Grady et al. as follows:

> In a metaphoric blend, prominent counterparts from the input spaces project to a single element in the blended space – they are 'fused'. A single element in the blend corresponds to an element in each of the input spaces. A ship in the blend

[as in *the ship of state*] is linked to a ship in the source space and a nation in the target, a surgeon is linked to both a surgeon and a butcher, and so forth. Intuitively speaking, the point of metaphors is precisely that one thing is depicted or equated with another. (Grady et al. 1999:114)

The two input spaces have different roles: the material in the target space functions as topic, whereas the material in the source space 'provides a means of re-framing the first [i.e. the material in the target space] for some conceptual or communicative purpose . . .' (Grady et al. 1999:117).

However, the blended space does not only contain a selection of properties drawn from the two input domains: it also contains new conceptual material that arises from an elaboration of the conceptual blend on the basis of encyclopedic knowledge. As an illustration of the model, consider the following metaphor:

(29)   This surgeon is a butcher.

Grady et al. point out that this expression carries a strong implication that the surgeon is incompetent, although incompetence is a normal feature neither of surgeons nor butchers. The contents of the four mental spaces are described in (30) (adapted from Grady et al. 1999):

(30)	*Generic space*:	Agent	
		Undergoer	
		Sharp instrument	
		Work space	
		Procedure: cutting flesh	
	Input space I (Target):	Role: Agent:	Surgeon
			(X) (i.e. some individual)
		Role: Undergoer:	Patient
			(Y) (a different individual)
		Instrument:	Scalpel
		Work space:	Operating theatre
		Goal:	Healing
		Means:	Surgery
	Input space II (Source):	Role: Agent:	Butcher
		Role: Undergoer:	Dead animal
		Instrument:	Butcher's knife etc.
		Work space:	Butcher's shop
		Goal:	Producing edible portions
		Means:	Cutting flesh
	Blended space:	Role: Agent:	Butcher
			(X)
		Role: Undergoer:	Patient
			(Y)
		Work space:	Operating theatre
		Goal:	Healing
		Means:	Butchery

According to Grady et al., the inference of incompetence arises through an elaboration of the basic elements of the blended space, that is, we imaginatively reconstruct a scene in which a butcher is in charge of an operation, and uses his normal butcher's techniques on the patient: there is a basic incompatibility between the goal and the means, which leads to the inference of X's incompetence.

The informal description of the metaphorical process given by Grady et al. and quoted above is acceptable as far as it goes, and is not particularly new (cf. I. A. Richards' 'interanimation of words' [Richards 1936]). But it is difficult to see how the mental spaces format throws any light on the process of blending. Phenomenologically, a metaphor is highly distinctive, and this distinctiveness is due in no small measure to the phenomenon of blending. Stern (1999) tries valiantly to get to grips with this notion. He refers to 'seeing as': in X is Y we are made to 'see X as Y.' He illuminatingly invokes the type of visual conceptual blending that one sees in cartoons.

It seems clear that any account of metaphor that ignores this phenomenon is seriously flawed. In this sense, BT is an advance on the original Lakoff model. However, a full explanation of it is still lacking. It is not clear how the process envisaged in BT gives rise to a blend in the sense of 'seeing one thing as another.' A simple combination of conventional features from one domain with conventional features from another gives no account of the experience of a novel metaphor. One important factor that is missing from the BT account is what is referred to in §8.4 as the openness of mapping between the source and target domains: the correspondences simply cannot be enumerated. This point is well illustrated by example (1), repeated in (31):

(31)   A myriad of ugly, dark thoughts clung to my reason and dug in with their claws.

Perhaps the 'seeing as' account of blending is the most illuminating suggested so far, except that it is not really explicit enough.

8.3.4   Context sensitivity

A characteristic of novel metaphors is that they involve domains that are construed in context. Of course, such construals are subject to conventional constraints, but context also has an important role. Furthermore, the correspondences between domains in a novel metaphor are also subject to construal, and in a sense are created by the metaphor, rather than being preexisting. This aspect of novel metaphor is not recognized in either CMT or BT. There is an element of context sensitivity in the BT model, in that the features that enter into the input spaces are constructed on-line. However, no account of how the features are selected is offered.

Stern (1999) makes the lack of context sensitivity the major plank of his critique of Lakoff. He argues that the aspects of a source domain that are relevant to a target domain are heavily dependent not only on the domains themselves, but on the whole context of the utterance, even of the discourse, and that any model that depends on fixed structures in the mind is doomed to failure. He points out that every context structures domains that are invoked in it in a characteristic way, in terms of what is salient and what is backgrounded, patterns of inference, and expressive or attitudinal factors. He illustrates his point by considering possible metaphorical interpretations of *the sun* (with literal reference to the center of our solar system). He begins with the following example uttered by Romeo in *Romeo and Juliet* 2.2:

(32)   But soft, what light through yonder window breaks?
          It is the East, and Juliet is the sun.

He offers the following characterization: '[S]he is exemplary and peerless, worthy of worship and adoration, one without whose nourishing attention another cannot live, one who awakens those in her presence from their slumbering, who brings light to darkness' (Stern 1999:9). Stern contrasts this with *Achilles is the sun*, where it 'expresses Achilles' devastating anger or brute force'; then with *Before Moses' sun had set, the sun of Joshua had risen* (The Talmud), 'where it expresses the uninterrupted continuity of righteousness, which, according to the Talmud . . . preserves the world'; and finally with *The works of great masters are suns which rise and set around us. The time will come for every great work that is now in the descendent to rise again* (Wittgenstein 1980), 'in which "sun" expresses the cyclicity and eternal recurrence of greatness, that things once great will be great again . . .' (ibid.).

8.3.5 Asymmetry of vehicle and target

An important aspect of a metaphor is the different roles of the participating domains in the blend. In *Juliet is the sun* we are talking about Juliet rather than about the sun, and in the Patricia Cornwell example, we are talking about thoughts rather than about creatures. At the same time, as a result of the blending process we create entities that are both, for instance, thoughts and creatures. The notion of 'seeing as,' although it is suggestive, might seem to allow a complete takeover of the target domain by the source domain, which, of course, does not happen. The puzzle is how to reconcile these two aspects of metaphor. It is stipulated in the version of BT presented by Grady et al. that the 'target' input domain forms the 'topic' and the 'source' domain provides 'framing.' However, this addresses only the first aspect. A satisfactory account of novel metaphor will have to be more explicit on this matter.

8.4   Metaphor and simile

8.4.1   *Two types of simile*

Most writers distinguish two sorts of expression of comparison: Glucksberg (1999) speaks of 'literal similes' and 'metaphorical similes.' Here, the two types will be referred to as similes proper (henceforward, simply **similes**) and **statements of similarity**. A simple diagnostic test is whether they transform readily into metaphors or not. For instance (33) transforms easily into (34) without a great change in meaning (it will be argued in a moment that there is a difference, but here it is not great):

(33)   John is like a lion.
(34)   John is a lion.

On the other hand, (35a) and (36a) are statements of similarity, and do not correspond to metaphors:

(35)   a. My house is like yours.
         b. *My house is yours.
(36)   a. Nectarines are like peaches.
         b. *Nectarines are peaches.

There is a different but related distinction between true similes and what might be called **speculations**. Both may have the same form. Take the example of *He sounds like someone with a severe cold*. Said of a person at the other end of a telephone line, this could be a speculation that they indeed are suffering from a severe cold. On the other hand, if it is said of someone known by speaker and hearer to be perfectly healthy, it is a simile.

8.4.2   *Theories of the relation between simile and metaphor*

8.4.2.1   **Metaphors are implicit similes**

This is what Glucksberg (2001) calls the 'classical' view. To understand a metaphor (which is prototypically false on a literal interpretation) we first transform it into the corresponding simile, which, if the metaphor is a valid one, will prototypically be true. On this view, the simile gives a more direct picture of the semantic structure of the expression; the metaphor is to be seen as a kind of shorthand. Otherwise there is no substantive difference between the two.

8.4.2.2   Similes are implicit metaphors

Currently, this is the favorite position, held, among others, by Stern (2000) and Glucksberg (and attributed by him even to Aristotle). Glucksberg's position is as follows. We must first introduce Glucksberg's notion of 'dual reference.' Put simply, it is that all statements of the form *X is Y* are to be interpreted as class-inclusion statements, as in obvious cases such as *Dogs are animals*. A metaphor, on this view, is no different: it is a class-inclusion statement. *John is a lion* means that John is a member of the class of lions. However, words are systematically ambiguous, in that they can refer to a category (i.e. literally) or to a supercategory for which the literal category is a prototypical example. Since the lion is conventionally held to be representative, or emblematic, of the category of strong, courageous beings, then *John is a lion* simply means that John is a strong courageous being.

Every metaphor thus depends on our knowledge of what specific things are good examples of, and this more abstract category, or rather its defining features, tells us what we are to attribute to the subject. Every time we retrieve a word from the mental lexicon, we have equal access to the narrow meaning and the broad meaning (of course, an item may be an excellent example of more than one category): choosing the metaphorical reading over the literal one is no different in principle than choosing one reading of a (lexicographically) ambiguous word. Let us designate the literal meaning of a term as X and its supercategory X'. A metaphor then has the general form *A is X'*, while a simile has the general form *A is like X*. A simile is interpreted, on this view, by translating it into a metaphor, that is, interpreting X as X', reconstructing the supercategory, and applying its defining features to A.

8.4.2.3   Similes and metaphors are distinct

The position to be adopted here is that metaphors and similes are prototypically distinct, even though both involve two distinct domains. However, the difference in meaning between a metaphor and its corresponding simile (in cases where there is an equivalent) varies according to context and according to type of both simile and metaphor.

The first and most obvious difference is in propositional structure. An expression of the form *A is like B* asserts that there is a resemblance between A and B in some respect. An expression of the form *A is B*, on the other hand, predicates certain properties directly of A. In Langackerian terms, *A is like B* profiles the resemblance, while *A is B* profiles the properties predicated. This would be a difference even if there were no other. However, there are other differences.

There are two major differences between similes and metaphors. The first involves the scope of the correspondences between the two domains. Most of the discussion one encounters in the literature on the relation between metaphor and simile centers around examples of simile that are not prototypical. In fact, examples of simile of the form *X is like Y* are comparatively rare: in the vast majority of similes, there is a specification of the respect in which the resemblance holds, without which a proper interpretation is not possible. This feature will be called **restricted mapping** between the two domains. The following examples, taken from Patricia Cornwell's novel *Black Notice* (2000), will illustrate the point (the restrictions are in italic):

(37)   Marino *was breathing hard* like a wounded bear.
(38)   [The victim had been] shot and *dumped* somewhere like garbage.
(39)   Marino's voice *was soft and muted* like bourbon on the rocks.
(40)   And I know Anderson *follows her around* like a puppy.
(41)   . . . strong gusts of wind *pushed me* like a hand.

In contrast, in prototypical metaphors, the correspondences between the domains do not form a closed set, and cannot be exhaustively listed. This property will be referred to as **open mapping** between the two domains.

(42)   His sarcasm could have shred paper.
(43)   . . . his words grabbed her by the collar.
(44)   The mention of Lucy's name squeezed my heart with a hard, cold hand.
(45)   A myriad of ugly, dark thoughts clung to my reason and dug in with their claws.
(46)   Bray's self-confidence slipped just enough to unmask the evil coiling within.

The second major difference is that in a prototypical metaphor, what is presented is a blend of two domains, whereas in a simile, the two domains are presented as separate. In a simile, we are certainly invited to consider the two domains together, but they are presented as distinct.

(47)   Icicles bared long teeth from the eaves.
        (cf. *Icicles were like long teeth being bared.*)
(48)   The elevator has a mind of its own.
        (cf. *The elevator behaves like a being with a mind of its own.*)
(49)   Her eyes were dark holes.
        (cf. *Her eyes were like dark holes.*)
(50)   A headache began boxing with my brain.
        (cf.?? *My headache felt as if someone were boxing with my brain.*)

However, in addition to prototypical metaphors and prototypical similes, there are less prototypical examples of each. For instance, a characteristic of similes of the form *A is like B* is that they display open mapping (at least where the restriction is not latent). This makes them more 'metaphor-like' than the prototypical variety (although it does not make them into metaphors). But even some similes of the canonical form seem to have open mapping:

(51)   She was gone in a flash of red, like a vengeful queen on her way to order armies to march in on us.
(52)   Cameras were already on her like a storm of hurled spears.
(53)   It's like I'm on the wrong planet.
(54)   . . . now it's like he's a hunted animal with no place to go?
(55)   I felt as if I were inside cut crystal.
(56)   It was as if a wild animal had dragged her dying body off to its lair and mauled it.

Similarly, there are apparent metaphors, where the mapping is highly restricted – the motivation for the transfer can be reduced to one or a small number of features. In such cases, one can say that they are more simile-like than are prototypical metaphors. In fact, in certain cases, there appears to be no blending, either, which would make them almost indistinguishable from similes.

(57)   . . . her breath smoking out (= came out like smoke, because it was a cold day, and it condensed)
(58)   Grass was a thick, stiff carpet (because it was frozen) (change from metaphor to simile makes very little difference)
(59)   A computer mouse (any blending?)
(60)   A splinter of light glinted in the dark. (appearance only?)

There are many cases where there is a striking difference in interpretation between a metaphor and its corresponding simile:

(61)   . . . containers lined up at loading docks like animals feeding from troughs.
         (cf. *The containers were animals feeding from troughs.*)

Notice how this opens up the mapping possibilities: there is no obvious way of building in the mapping restrictions within the format of the metaphor. In (62), the meaning is changed completely:

(62)   Broken wooden packing cases littered the beach like the debris of a disordered mind. (J. G. Ballard: *Cocaine Nights*)
         (cf. *Broken wooden packing cases littered the beach, the debris of a disordered mind.*)

An interesting (and so far unanswered) question concerns what these have in common that distinguishes them from cases where the difference is slight.

In summary, we can recognize four types of expression:

(63)

	Mapping	Blending?
Prototypical metaphors	open	yes
Simile metaphors	restricted	yes
Prototypical similes	restricted	no
Metaphorical similes	open	no

8.4.3   Metaphor-simile combinations

Metaphor and simile very frequently combine, and the combination seems to have a unique function, that is, one cannot obtain the same effect in any other way. There are two major modes: metaphor within simile and simile within metaphor.

(a)   *Metaphor within simile*

What usually happens in these is that the simile serves to clarify the source domain, often because the key word in the metaphorical vehicle is one with a wide range of construals:

(64)   Bizarre, angry thoughts flew through my mind like a thousand starlings.

Here, the phrase *like a thousand starlings* gives a precise picture of the sort of *flying* that is to serve as the vehicle of the metaphor.

(65)   She was standing there, her eyes fastened to me like steel rivets.

Here, *like steel rivets* specifies the quality of *fastened*: rivets provide a particularly strong and rigid type of fastening.

(66)   Grief tumbled out of her like a waterfall.
(67)   This is really twisting my brain like a dishrag.

There are many different sorts of 'twisting' and 'tumbling,' but the similes function to narrow them down.

(b)   *Simile within metaphor*

These cases are in some ways more complex: in them, the second term of the simile is itself a metaphor. There are two varieties of this. In the first, the simile contains a complete metaphor, with topic and vehicle:

(68)   He looked tired, as if life had pushed him too far.
(69)   Rose looked dejected and somewhat embarrassed, as if afraid that her being so upset had sent her spinning threads of truth into tapestries of conviction.

In the second type, the second term of the simile appears completely literal in itself, but is only metaphorical when the comparison is made with the first term:

(70)   Talley made love as if he were starving.
(71)   Bray's tone had the effect of a metal box slamming shut.

8.5   Metaphor and metonymy

Just as an examination of the relations between metaphor and simile throws light on the nature of both, a consideration of the relations between metaphor and metonymy is similarly illuminating. This is in two ways: first, a comparison of the two highlights the special nature of each, and second, they can be shown to interact in significant ways. However, since the focus of this chapter is on metaphor, no attempt will be made to explore the further reaches of metonymy. (A fuller account can be found in Kövecses and Radden 1998.)

8.5.1   Characterizing metonymy

The term 'metonymy' is sometimes interpreted very broadly, to include, for instance, the relation between form and meaning within a sign, the relation between a linguistic sign and its referent, the relation between, for instance, an acronym and its full form, and the special relation between a prototype and the category it represents. For present purposes, we shall construe metonymy more narrowly. First of all, we shall say that metonymy involves the use of an expression E with a default construal A to evoke a distinct construal B, where the connection between B and A is inferable by general principles (i.e. is not a private prearranged code between individuals). In novel uses, there is normally an intuitive violation of conventional constraints.

This characterization covers metaphor as well as metonymy. Metonymy is distinguished by the fact that (i) A and B are associated in some domain or domain matrix,[1] (ii) any correspondences (in the Lakoffian sense) between A and B are coincidental and not relevant to the message and (iii) there is no blending between A and B. In chapter 5 we treated cases where A and B are unified separately, as facets; however, whether facets are considered distinct from metonymy, or a special variety of metonymy, has no serious theoretical consequences.

---

[1] While identity of domain does seem to be a factor, we agree with Feyaerts (2000) and Riemer (2001) that on its own it remains an unreliable criterion in the absence of independent means of delimiting domains.

This narrower characterization still covers a wide range of types in terms of the sorts of association that are operative. No attempt will be made to provide an exhaustive list (it is not clear that this is possible, even in principle); the following is to be taken merely as illustrative. We can divide the associations that support metonymy roughly into 'intrinsic associations,' which are either inherent, or at least relatively permanent, and 'extrinsic' associations, where A and B are associated contingently and non-inherently. The following are examples of intrinsic associations:

(a)   *Part-whole*
    Part for whole: *I noticed several new faces tonight.*
    Whole for part: *Do you need to use the bathroom?*
(b)   *Individual-class*
    Individual for class: *He's no Heifetz.*
    Class for individual: *Postman, this letter is covered in mud!*
(c)   *Entity-attribute*
    Entity for attribute: *Shares took a tumble yesterday.*
    Attribute for entity: *He's a size ten.*
(d)   *Different values on same scale*
    Hyperbole: *It's practically absolute zero in here – shut the window!*
    Understatement: *I'm feeling a bit peckish – I haven't eaten for three days.*
(e)   *Opposites*
    Irony: *Now let's move on to the small matter of the £30,000 you owe us.*

Extrinsic associations in metonymy are exemplified by (72)–(76):

(72)   Room 23 is not answering.
(73)   I'm parked out back.
(74)   The french fries in the corner is getting impatient.
(75)   Sperber and Wilson is on the top shelf.
(76)   England are all out for 156 runs.

8.5.2   *Metaphor–metonymy relations*

In this section we look at relations between metaphor and metonymy, in particular, the question of whether they can be sharply distinguished from one another. According to Radden (2000), prototypical cases of metaphor and metonymy are situated at opposite ends of a continuous scale, with no clear dividing line between them. This would make the distinction analogous to the traditional one between homonymy (no motivated relation between senses) and polysemy (motivated relation). Before considering cases that might support this position, we consider cases where there is interaction between metonymy and metaphor, but where their distinct identities are not compromised, and that arguably do not therefore support Radden's position.

Although the Lakoffians distinguish between metaphor and metonymy, they nonetheless emphasize that metonymy can play a vital role in the genesis of metaphorical expressions (§8.2.2). Take the ANGER IS HEAT metaphor. At the heart of this is a metonymy: an angry person subjectively feels hot, so one can refer indirectly to anger by way of mentioning heat. At this level, one could say that there are no correspondences, only the holistic one. The typical Lakoffian correspondences arise only when the basic metonymy is elaborated, for instance, in the idea of anger pictured as a liquid in a closed container undergoing a heating process, or as a fire. Another, more basic, example is the MORE IS UP metaphor. This, too, originates in a metonymy. If we take a pile of sand, say, and add more sand, the top of the pile rises, or if we add more books to a pile of books. Thus there is a real-life, literal correlation between 'more' and 'greater height,' which justifies us in saying *The pile is higher now*, meaning that there are more books. This metonymy can then be metaphorically extended to any case of 'more,' such as higher prices, higher temperature and so on. This kind of cooperation between metonymy and metaphor does not make them any less distinct.

A different type of case concerns what Goossens (1990) calls, somewhat inelegantly, **metaphtonymy**. This is when both metaphorical and metonymic processes are recruited in the construal of an interpretation. Different types can be distinguished. In one type, the elements that undergo metaphoric and metonymic transfer, respectively, are different. One example of this is the following, from Goossens:

(77)   She caught the minister's ear and persuaded him to accept her plan.

A plausible account of this is that we construe *ear* metonymically for 'attention,' which forces a metaphorical construal of *caught*; *catch X's attention* is interpreted as 'make X attend.' Another similar example (from Patricia Cornwell) is (68):

(78)   He stopped on the sidewalk and looked into my eyes as people flowed around us and light from shops unevenly shoved back the night.

In this case, *night* is first interpreted metonymically as 'area of darkness,' then *shoved back* is metaphorically interpreted as 'illuminated.'

In another variety of metaphtonymy, it is the same expression that undergoes successive metaphorical and metonymic construal. Take the case of (69):

(79)   My lips are sealed.

A literal interpretation of this can be metonymically understood to indicate that the speaker is physically unable to speak. This metonymy can then be metaphorically extended to a situation where the speaker is non-physically constrained. The metonymic construal of the expression thus precedes a metaphorical construal of the same expression. Another example is (80) (from Patricia Cornwell):

(80)   Anger slipped out of hiding.

The context makes clear that this refers to someone who has been trying to conceal her anger, but has lost control, and has allowed it to be perceptible. A possible interpretation of this is that *slipped out of hiding* is first metonymically interpreted as 'become visible,' which is then metaphorically extended to apply to someone's anger, that is, 'become perceptible (not necessarily visually).' In all these cases, metaphor and metonymy, although both present, can be seen to make separate contributions.

8.5.3   Types of indeterminacy

In the above cases, although both metaphor and metonymy can be shown to be operative, we can nonetheless easily separate the effects of the two processes and their distinctness is not compromised. But there are cases where there is arguably a genuine indeterminacy between metaphor and metonymy.

The first type may be labeled 'etymological indeterminacy.' These cases arise because a now conventionalized extended meaning could have been reached by either route. Claimed examples of this phenomenon are *head of the bed* and *back of the chair*. What is the motivation for these terms? Is it because a person's head normally rests near that part of the bed, or a person's back rests on that part of a chair? Or is it because of some resemblance between a bed and a supine person, or between a chair and a standing or sitting person? This is a question of historical fact, and is probably unresolvable. It is also possible that different speakers have different conceptions of the relationship between, say, a human head and the head of a bed. However, this is unlikely to lead to any observable difference in synchronic usage.

A more immediate type of indeterminacy can be observed in certain expressions. Consider, first, (81):

(81)   The car stopped in front of the bakery.

Of course it is possible that the car had been left with the brakes off, and had rolled down an incline on its own, coming to a stop in front of the bakery. This would be a fully literal construal of (81). But in the normal course of events, we would interpret this as referring to a car that was being driven, and that the agent of the stopping action was the driver. This could then be taken as an example of metonymy – *the car* is used to refer indirectly to 'the driver of the car' (whether this would be a case of noun transfer or verb transfer is not relevant here). But there is a third possible interpretation, which is that we are metaphorically attributing animacy to the car. The question then arises of whether the metonymic and metaphorical interpretations can really be separated.

The question is perhaps thrown into greater relief in (82):

(82)   A yellow Porsche drew up in front of the bakery.

The action of drawing up is not something the car can do on its own, so any interpretation must involve the driver. But (82) undoubtedly describes the motion of the car and the driver may not have been visible to the speaker. In this case, perhaps because of the specificity of the description of the car, it is easier to see this as a humanization of the car. But a pure metaphor account would not give full credit to the role of the driver.

A more revealing explication of (82) might be that *a yellow Porsche* denotes a single entity that represents a kind of fusion of car and driver (notice that this is different from the 'unity' observed with facets). If this were true, it would be neither pure metonymy nor pure metaphor, nor would it be part metonymy, part metaphor – it would be something intermediate. Another example is (83):

(83)   Britain declares war on Iraq.

It is very hard to specify exactly what *Britain* refers to on a pure metonymic construal (and on a facet analysis, it would be hard to pinpoint the facet involved). It does not seem to be 'the government,' because, although (84) is possible (in British English), (85) is not:

(84)   The government have decided to restrict immigration.
(85)   ?Britain declare war on Iraq. (cf. England win the World Cup.)

Once again, we seem to have a fusion – this time of country, government, final decision-taker, monarch (perhaps) and so on, forming a single, semi-animate agent, by a process that is neither pure metonymy nor pure metaphor. In one sense these examples would seem to support Radden's contention in the sense that *expressions* can be placed on a scale of metaphoricity-metonymicity. In another sense, however, the distinction between metaphor and metonymy *as processes* arguably remains intact.[2]

8.6   Conclusion

Much work remains to be done on metaphor and its relationship with metonymy and simile. Some facts about metaphor are well established. Metaphor

---

[2] Riemer (2001) comes to a similar conclusion, but by a different route.

essentially involves the use of an expression to elicit a construal whose content is the result of an interaction between two construed domains. One of these domains is a construal on the basis of the expression's conventionally associated purport; the other domain is construed on the basis of an alien region of purport. The interaction between the domains is a species of blending, whereby one domain, the target, is modified under the influence of the other domain, the source. The result is a unique semantic confection, unobtainable by any other means.

This summary conceals a multitude of mysteries: for instance, the role of contextual and other constraints and the mechanism by which they produce their effects; but most notably of all, the exact nature of the blending process, and the nature of the resultant blend. Most metaphors studied by cognitive linguists have been relatively simple. A further challenge is presented by more complex metaphors. Even a small increase in complexity is daunting. The reader is invited to unravel the interplay between metaphors and metonymies in one last example from Patricia Cornwell:

(86)   The temperature in my house slowly dropped, hours slipping deeper into the still morning.

PART III

Cognitive approaches to grammatical form

9

From idioms to construction grammar

9.1   Introduction

The cognitive linguistic approach to syntax goes under the name of **construction grammar**. It is not an exaggeration to say that construction grammar grew out of a concern to find a place for idiomatic expressions in the speaker's knowledge of a grammar of their language. The study of idioms led to calls for a rethinking of syntactic representation for many years before construction grammar emerged, and some of this work will be referred to in this chapter. At least partly independently of construction grammar, a number of researchers have emphasized the need to represent linguistic knowledge in a construction-like fashion. But in cognitive linguistics, these concerns led to a grammatical framework in which all grammatical knowledge is represented in essentially the same way. This chapter presents the arguments for a construction grammar.

Construction grammar, like any other scientific theory, did not arise in a theoretical vacuum. Construction grammar arose as a response to the model of grammatical knowledge proposed by the various versions of generative grammar over the period from the 1960s to at least the 1980s, and other syntactic theories that emerged as direct offshoots of generative grammar. (These models in turn represented extensions of the organization of a traditional descriptive grammar of a language, albeit with significant changes in terminology.)

In most theories of generative grammar, a speaker's grammatical knowledge is organized into **components**. Each component describes one dimension of the properties of a sentence. The phonological component, for example, consists of the rules and constraints governing the sound structure of a sentence of the language. The syntactic component consists of the rules and constraints governing the syntax – the combinations of words – of a sentence. The semantic component consists of rules and constraints governing the meaning of a sentence. In other words, each component separates out the specific type of linguistic information that is contained in a sentence: phonological, syntactic and semantic. In addition, all versions of Chomskyan generative grammar have broken down the syntactic component further, as **levels** or strata (such as 'deep structure,' later 'D-structure,' and 'surface structure,' later 'S-structure'; Chomsky 1981) and **modules** or theories (such as Case theory, Binding theory etc.; Chomsky 1981).

Further components have been proposed by other linguists. Some have argued that morphology, the internal formal structure of words, should occupy its own component (e.g. Aronoff 1993). Others have suggested that information structure, that is, certain aspects of discourse or pragmatic knowledge, should have its own component (Vallduví 1992). However many components are proposed, the general principle remains: each component governs linguistic properties of a single type: sound, word structure, syntax, meaning, use.

From our point of view, the number of different components is not as crucial as the fact that each type of linguistic knowledge is separated into its own component. We may describe this as a 'horizontal' model of the organization of grammatical knowledge, following its typical diagrammatic representation:

(1)   phonological component

            syntactic component

            semantic component

In addition to these components, there is the lexicon, which characterizes the basic units of syntactic combination. The lexicon differs from these components in that the lexicon gives, for each word, its sound structure, its syntactic category (which determines how it behaves with respect to the rules of the syntactic component) and its meaning. Thus, a lexical item combines information from the three components in (1) (and can include information from other components, such as its morphological structure and its stylistic pragmatic value). It represents a 'vertical' component as against the 'horizontal' components:

(2)

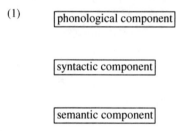

The components are intended to be highly general rules that apply to all structures of the relevant type. Thus the rules of the phonological component apply to all word forms and all phonological phrases (for prosodic and other phrasal phonology); the rules of the syntactic component apply to all sentences and sentence types; and the same applies to rules for other components.

Of course, there must be some general way to map information from one component onto another; for instance, there must be a way to map the syntactic structure of a sentence onto the semantic structure of the meaning conveyed by the sentence. These rules are called **linking rules**, and are also intended to be highly general, applying to all sentences of the language. One might ask at this point, why are the linking rules just a bunch of rules that link components, while the components define the way that grammatical knowledge is divided up in the speaker's mind? As we will see, that is essentially the question that construction grammar asks. The response of the generative grammarians is that the rules inside each component are so highly intertwined and self-contained that they represent a cohesive structure relative to the linking rules (and if they are not so highly intertwined, the components are broken down further into levels, modules etc.).

In sum, the final model of the organization of grammatical knowledge in the sorts of syntactic theories prevalent from the 1960s to the 1980s will look something like the diagram in (3):

(3)

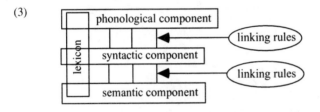

One of the crucial characteristics of this model is that there are no idiosyncratic properties of grammatical structures larger than a single word. Phrases and sentences are governed by the highly general rules of the syntactic component and their counterparts in the semantic and phonological components, and the equally highly general linking rules. On the other hand, words represent an arbitrary and idiosyncratic joining of form (phonological and syntactic) and meaning. The restriction of arbitrariness in grammar to the lexicon is a central principle of generative grammar, reiterated in recent versions of generative grammar (e.g. Chomsky 1993:3, 4).

One of the consequences of this model is the rejection of the concept of **construction** in the traditional grammar sense of that word. In traditional grammar, one describes a syntactic structure such as is found in the sentence in (4a) as 'the passive construction':

(4)   a. Janet was promoted by the company.
        b. [Subject *be* Verb-PastParticiple *by* Oblique]

The passive construction would be described as necessarily possessing the combination of syntactic elements given in (4b), including the subject noun phrase, the passive auxiliary verb *be* in some form, a verb in the past participle form, and (optionally in the case of English) a prepositional phrase with the preposition *by*. In addition, a traditional characterization of the passive construction would indicate that the agent of the action is expressed by the object of the prepositional phrase, and the undergoer is expressed by the subject.

In the generative model, as many of these properties of the passive construction as possible would be described by the general rules of the various components, and any idiosyncratic properties would be placed in the lexicon. For example, the fact that the subject precedes the verb is true of a large class of constructions in English (see [5]); the fact that the auxiliary follows and is in a finite form in contrast to the verb is also true of a large class of constructions (see [6]), and the fact that the prepositional phrase follows the verb (and also a noun) it modifies, and the preposition governs the object form of the noun phrase, is also true of a large class of constructions (see [7]):

(5)   a. Active: **John** ate.
        b. Relative Clause: the tart that **John** ate . . .
        c. Adverbial Clause: before **John** ate the tart . . .
        d. Conditional: If **John** ate a tart, then **I** will have a tart as well.
        e. Comparative: **John** ate a bigger tart than I did.

(6)   a. Perfect: John **has** eaten the tart.
        b. Progressive: John **is** eating a tart.
        c. Future: John **will** eat [**INFINITIVE**] a tart.
        d. Modal: John **might** eat [**INFINITIVE**] a tart.

(7)   a. Oblique Adjunct Phrase: John ate the tart **with a fork and spoon**.
        b. Prepositional Complement Phrase: John put the tart **in the refrigerator**.
        c. Circumstantial Phrase: John ate the tart **in the living room**.
        d. Nominal Prepositional Phrase Modifier: the tart **on the table** . . .

The logical conclusion of this process of analysis is the hypothesis that all properties of syntactic constructions – that is, a grammatical structure larger than just a single word – can be captured with the general rules of the grammatical components and their interfaces, and thus there is no need for constructions in grammatical analysis. Chomsky makes this claim explicit:

> a central element in the work discussed here, as in recent work from which it evolves, is the effort to decompose such processes as "passive", "relativization", etc., into more fundamental "abstract features". (Chomsky 1981:121)

> UG provides a fixed system of principles and a finite array of finitely valued parameters. The language-particular rules reduce to choice of values for these parameters. The notion of grammatical construction is eliminated, and with it, construction-particular rules. (Chomsky 1993:4)

Chomsky's position on the generality of syntax and the irrelevance of constructions to the analysis of grammar is the complement of his view that all arbitrary and idiosyncratic aspects of grammar should be restricted to the lexicon.

The componential model of grammatical organization given above is characteristic of the generative grammar and its offshoots. As we noted, in Chomskyan theory the syntactic component is internally complex, beginning with levels in the earliest versions and a further subdivision into modules in Government and Binding theory (Chomsky 1981). The most recent version, Minimalist theory (Chomsky 1993, 1995), apparently ends the internal organization of the syntactic component and recasts the phonological component as an 'articulatory-perceptual interface,' which links the language faculty to the perceptual-motor system and the semantic component as a 'conceptual-intentional interface,' which links the language faculty to other human conceptual activity. Nevertheless, it appears that the broad division into the three components in (3) remains, even if two components are now thought of in terms of their embedding in the cognitive system as a whole, and the third (syntactic) component is now the whole language system in between. Likewise, the notion of the lexicon as the repository of idiosyncratic information remains, and as such provides information linking the three components together (Chomsky 1993:3; 1995:235–36).

Other syntactic theories that diverge from Chomskyan theory also retain the organization into components. Earlier offshoots such as Relational Grammar (Perlmutter 1983) and its offshoot Arc-Pair Grammar (Johnson and Postal 1980) included multiple levels in the syntactic component but retained the separation of components. Later offshoots, such as Lexical-Functional Grammar (Bresnan 1982), Generalized Phrase Structure Grammar (Gazdar, Klein, Pullum and Sag 1985; see also Pollard and Sag 1993) and Categorial Grammar (Wood 1993), reject the concept of multiple levels but still retain the separation of components. In more recent theories of non-Chomskyan syntax, there is a shift in emphasis from separation of components to their interaction. But the development of construction grammar marks a more direct break from the componential view of grammatical organization.

9.2   The problem of idioms

Certain exceptions to the principle of the generality of rules governing larger grammatical structures have been made in the history of generative grammar. For example, the different syntactic structures required by different verbs, such as those illustrated in examples (8)–(9), must be represented somewhere in the grammatical model in (3):

(8)   a. Tina slept.
        b. *Tina slept bananas.
(9)   a. David consumed the bananas.
        b. *David consumed.

Until at least recently (e.g. Haegeman 1994:40–42), generative grammar has accounted for this pattern of distribution by **subcategorization frames** associated with lexical items in the lexicon, as in (10a–b):

(10)   a. *sleep*: V, [–]
        b. *consume*: V, [– NP]

The effect of this device is to include phrasal syntactic information in the lexicon, under the lexical entry for each verb. However, this way of handling the distributional patterns in (8)–(9) is consistent with the general principle that idiosyncratic information is to be found in the lexicon.

There is another class of syntactic phenomena that poses a much greater problem for the componential model of grammar and the principle that all grammar above the word level can be explained by highly general rules. These are **idioms**. Idioms are, by definition, grammatical units larger than a word which are idiosyncratic in some respect. Some examples of idioms are given in (11):

(11)   a. It takes one to know one.
        b. pull a fast one
        c. bring down the house
        d. wide awake
        e. sight unseen
        f. all of a sudden
        g. (X) blow X's nose
        h. Once upon a time . . .

It is difficult to give a precise definition of the category of idioms, for reasons that will soon become clear. Nunberg, Sag and Wasow (1994:492–93) offer a prototype definition of idioms with one necessary feature and a number of typical features. The necessary feature is **conventionality**: 'their meaning or use can't be predicted, or at least entirely predicted, on the basis of a knowledge of the independent conventions that determine the use of their constituents when they appear in isolation from one another' (492). The other, typical, properties of idioms they list are:

(12)   a. Inflexibility: restricted syntax, as in *shoot the breeze* vs. **the breeze is hard to shoot*
        b. Figuration: figurative meaning, as in *take the bull by the horns, lend a hand*
        c. Proverbiality: description of social activity compared to a concrete activity, as in *climb the wall, chew the fat, spill the beans*

    d. Informality: typically associated with informal speech styles or registers
    e. Affect: usually have an evaluation or affective stance towards what they describe

It is the necessary property of idioms that Nunberg et al. identify – their conventionality – which is the relevant property of idioms with respect to the componential model of grammar. If expressions such as those listed in (11a–h) are conventional, then they must somehow be stored as such in a speaker's mind. If so, then idioms are part of a speaker's grammatical knowledge. However, at least some aspects of an idiom cannot be predicted by the general rules of the syntactic and semantic components and their linking rules (we will leave out the phonological component for the time being). Hence they pose a problem for the componential model. It is possible to make certain sorts of stipulations to handle the conventionality of idioms (cf. Nunberg et al. 1994:507). However, a more general treatment would be preferable to such stipulations, if such a general treatment were available.

The linguists who ended up proposing the original construction grammar (in Fillmore, Kay and O'Connor 1988) approached the problem of idioms from the opposite direction. Instead of treating idioms as a problematic phenomenon from the point of view of the componential model of grammar, they analyzed the wide variety of idioms, and their analysis became the basis for a new model of grammatical organization. The remainder of this chapter will take the reader from idioms to construction grammar.[1]

Idioms can be characterized in many different ways. The description and classification that we will begin with is drawn from Fillmore et al. 1988, who used their analysis to argue for a construction grammar. Fillmore et al. begin with three features that can be used to classify idioms. The first feature they describe, drawn from Makkai 1972, is the distinction between encoding and decoding idioms.

An **encoding idiom** is one that is interpretable by the standard rules for interpreting sentences, but is arbitrary (i.e. conventional) for this expression with this meaning. Examples given by Fillmore et al. are *answer the door*, *wide awake* and *bright red*. These are all expressions that a hearer could figure out upon hearing them. However, a speaker would not have guessed these expressions are the natural-sounding English way to describe 'open the door in response to someone knocking,' 'completely awake' and 'intense color.' Another way of looking at

---

[1] Fillmore et al. were not the first linguists to analyze idioms in a systematic way. There is a vast literature on idioms, particularly in Europe where the study of idioms is called 'phraseology.' Another important line of research on idiomatic expressions is the Firthian research on collocations. Nor were Fillmore et al. the first to perceive the problem of idioms for a componential model of grammar, and to propose an alternative; one such antecedent is Becker (1975). However, as in the case of many scientific ideas, variants of the idea are proposed independently but commonly only one variant is propagated through the scientific community (Hull 1988).

encoding idioms is from the point of view of someone learning a foreign language. For instance, an English learner of Spanish would not be able to give the correct way of asking 'how old are you?', if s/he did not know it already; but if s/he heard a Spanish speaker say *Cuantos años tiene?* (lit. 'how many years do you have?'), s/he would very likely figure out what the speaker meant.

A **decoding idiom** is one that cannot be decoded by the hearer: a hearer will not be able to figure out the meaning of the whole at all from the meaning of its parts. Fillmore et al. give the examples of *kick the bucket* and *pull a fast one.* Any decoding idiom is also an encoding idiom: if as a hearer you cannot figure out what it means, then you are also not going to be able to guess that it is a conventional way to express that meaning in the language. One of the reasons that a decoding idiom is a decoding idiom is because there are not any correspondences between the literal and idiomatic meaning of the parts of the decoding idiom. For example, *kick the bucket* is a transitive verb phrase, but its idiomatic meaning is the intransitive 'die,' and there is nothing that corresponds even metaphorically to a bucket.

The encoding/decoding idiom distinction corresponds rather closely to Nunberg, Sag and Wasow's distinction between idiomatically combining expressions and idiomatic phrases respectively (Nunberg, Sag and Wasow 1994:496–97). **Idiomatically combining expressions** are idioms where parts of the idiomatic meaning can be put in correspondence with parts of the literal meaning. For instance, in *answer the door*, *answer* can be analyzed as corresponding to the action of opening, and of course *the door* denotes the door. In an idiomatically combining expression such as *spill the beans*, meaning to divulge information, *spill* can be analyzed as corresponding to 'divulge' and *the beans* to 'information.' In contrast, no such correspondences can be established for *kick* and *the bucket* in *kick the bucket* ('die'). Nunberg et al. call the latter **idiomatic phrases.**

The encoding/decoding distinction is not the same as the idiomatically combining expression/idiomatic phrase distinction, however. Some idioms, such as *spill the beans*, are encoding idioms even though they are idiomatically combining expressions. The encoding/decoding distinction is rather vaguely defined: it refers to how clever (or lucky) the hearer is in decoding an expression of the language. For this reason Nunberg et al.'s distinction is preferable.

The encoding/decoding distinction, as well as the idiomatically combining expression/idiomatic phrase distinction, characterizes idioms in contrast to regular syntactic expressions with respect to the interpretation rules linking the syntactic component to the semantic component. With idiomatic phrases such as *kick the bucket*, the interpretation rules cannot apply because the parts of the syntactic phrase do not correspond to parts of the semantic phrase at all. With idiomatically combining expressions such as *spill the beans*, the parts of the syntactic phrase correspond to semantic elements, but only in an interpretation that is unique to the idiomatically combining expression (*spill* does not mean 'divulge' except in the idiom *spill the beans*). Thus, the idiomatic meaning of idiomatically combining expressions cannot be determined from the general rules of semantic interpretation for the words or for the syntactic structure.

The second distinction that Fillmore et al. offer for defining idioms is between grammatical and extragrammatical idioms. **Grammatical** idioms are parsable by the general syntactic rules for the language, but are semantically irregular (i.e. they are encoding or decoding idioms). Examples include those discussed so far, such as *kick the bucket* and *spill the beans*, and also examples such as *(X) blows X's nose*. All of these idioms follow the general English syntactic rule that direct objects follow the verb, and that a possessive modifier precedes the noun it modifies.

Extragrammatical idioms are idioms that cannot be parsed by the general syntactic rules for the language. Fillmore et al. give as examples of extragrammatical idioms *first off, sight unseen, all of a sudden, by and large* and *so far so good*. One might think that extragrammatical idioms are rare, but Nunberg et al. suggest that they may not be particularly rare. Nunberg et al. provide a sampling of extragrammatical idioms, which are given here (Nunberg et al. 1994:515; note there is only one idiom overlapping with Fillmore et al.'s list):

(13)   by and large; No can do; trip the light fantastic; kingdom come; battle royal; Handsome is as handsome does; Would that it were . . .; every which way; Easy does it; be that as it may; Believe you me; in short; happy go lucky; make believe; do away with; make certain

The grammatical/extragrammatical distinction characterizes idioms in contrast to regular syntactic expressions with respect to the rules of the syntactic component. Grammatical idioms conform to the syntactic rules, but are idiomatic in some other fashion. Extragrammatical idioms do not conform to the syntactic rules, and for that reason alone are idiomatic.

Fillmore et al.'s third distinction is between substantive and formal idioms. A **substantive**, or lexically filled, idiom is one in which all elements of the idiom are fixed. For example, the idiom *It takes one to know one* is completely fixed; one cannot even alter the tense (**It took one to know one*). A **formal**, or lexically open, idiom is one in which at least part of the idiom can be filled by the usual range of expressions that are syntactically and semantically appropriate for the slot. For example, with the idiom *(X) blows X's nose*, the expressions I have described as X can be filled by a noun phrase (and a corresponding coreferential possessive pronoun) that refers to a person possessing a nose: *I blew my nose, Kim blew her nose, They all blew their noses* and so on. Fillmore et al.'s use of the term 'formal' corresponds to Langacker's term **schematic** to indicate a more general category (see §3.2), and we will use the term 'schematic' here.

Fillmore et al. note that one potential confusion with respect to the substantive/schematic distinction is that there may be a substantive idiom that fits the pattern of a counterpart schematic idiom. For example, they posit a schematic construction which they loosely describe as *The X-er, the Y-er*. Examples of this schematic construction are given in (14a–c):

(14)   a. The more you practice, the easier it will get.
        b. The louder you shout, the sooner they will serve you.
        c. The bigger the nail is, the more likely the board is to split.

There is also a substantive idiom that fits the pattern of the *The X-er, the Y-er* schematic idiom:

(15)   The bigger they come, the harder they fall.

The existence of the schematic idiom *The X-er, the Y-er* does not preclude the existence of a substantive idiom like (15), just as the existence of a general syntactic rule where the direct object follows the verb does not preclude the existence of an idiom such as *kick the bucket*.

The substantive/schematic distinction characterizes idioms in contrast to regular syntactic expressions on the one hand and the lexicon on the other. Both substantive and schematic idioms have parts that are lexically completely specified, although schematic idioms have parts that are specified in syntactic terms (that is, by a syntactic category such as 'noun phrase' or 'possessive pronoun'). In contrast, syntactic rules make reference only to general syntactic categories such as V (verb), NP (noun phrase) and so on, as in the phrase structure rules given in (16) for simple active intransitive and transitive sentences:

(16)   a. S → NP VP
        b. VP → V
        c. VP → V NP

The last distinction that Fillmore et al. give is for idioms with or without **pragmatic point** (Fillmore et al. 1988:506). Idioms with pragmatic point are idioms that, in addition to having a meaning in the usual sense of that term, also are specifically used in certain pragmatic contexts. Obvious examples of idioms with pragmatic point are idioms used for opening and closing conversations such as *Good morning* or *See you later,* and for other specialized discourse contexts such as telling a fairy tale (*Once upon a time . . .*; ibid.). Other idioms with pragmatic point are those that have a certain conventional pragmatic content, as with the schematic idiom illustrated by *Him be a doctor?!* On the other hand, many other idioms such as *all of a sudden* do not have any specific pragmatic point.

The with/without pragmatic point distinction characterizes idioms with respect to the 'information structure' or 'discourse' component that some linguists have argued for. They demonstrate that some idioms have conventional information-structure or discourse-contextual properties associated with them, which again cannot be predicted from general pragmatic or discourse-functional principles. For example, it may be a general pragmatic principle that in taking leave, one may make reference to a future meeting; but it cannot be predicted that the specific phrase *See you later* is conventionally used in English for that purpose, whereas in Spanish *Hasta luego* (lit. 'until later') is used for the same function.

Fillmore et al.'s analysis demonstrates that idioms are quite varied in their syntactic, semantic and pragmatic properties, ranging from completely fixed expressions to more general expressions, which may be semantically more or less opaque and may not even correspond to the general syntactic rules of the language. The distinctions discussed above are summarized in (17):

(17)   a. encoding vs. decoding
          b. idiomatically combining expressions vs. idiomatic phrases
          c. grammatical vs. extragrammatical
          d. substantive vs. schematic (formal)
          e. with pragmatic point vs. without pragmatic point

Fillmore et al. use the features given above for a final, three-way categorization of idioms. Their first category of idioms are **unfamiliar pieces unfamiliarly arranged**. The new aspect of this definition is the fact that certain words occur only in a idiom. Examples of (substantive) idioms with unfamiliar pieces are *kith and kin* 'family and friends' and *with might and main* 'with a lot of strength.' In other words, such idioms are lexically irregular as well as syntactically and semantically irregular. Unfamiliar words are by definition unfamiliarly arranged: if the words do not exist outside the idiom, then they cannot be assigned to a syntactic category in terms of a regular syntactic rule. Also, unfamiliar words unfamiliarly arranged are by definition semantically irregular.

However, an idiom containing unfamiliar pieces unfamiliarly arranged does not imply that it is an idiomatic phrase; such an idiom can be an idiomatically combining expression. This point is made clearer by the schematic idiom of this type given by Fillmore et al., the idiom *The X-er, the Y-er* illustrated in (14) above. The unfamiliar pieces are the two occurrences of *the*, which are not definite articles (in fact, they come from the Old English instrumental demonstrative *þy*). The unfamiliar arrangement is the parallel syntactic structure, with a degree expression followed by a clause with a gap corresponding to the degree expression. In (14a) for example, the parallel gapped structures are *more . . . you practice___* and *easier . . . it will get___*). Nevertheless, this idiom is an idiomatically combining expression, in that the parts of the construction can be made to correspond with the parts of its meaning (roughly, 'the degree to which you practice determines the degree to which it gets easy').

Fillmore et al.'s second category of idioms are **familiar pieces unfamiliarly arranged**. These idioms do not contain unique words but are extragrammatical. In other words, such idioms are lexically regular, but syntactically and semantically irregular. Fillmore et al. give *all of a sudden* and *in point of fact* as examples of substantive idioms in this category. They give as an example of a schematic idiom of this category the phrase *Nth cousin (M times removed)*: this is a syntactically unique construction. Again, idioms made up of familiar pieces unfamiliarly arranged may be idiomatically combining expressions.

Fillmore et al.'s third and last category of idioms are **familiar pieces familiarly arranged**. Such idioms are lexically and syntactically regular but semantically irregular. Again, such idioms may be substantive or schematic; Fillmore et al. give examples of both types. The substantive idioms they list are in fact not entirely fixed expressions; they include *pull X's leg* (which can have any person-denoting noun phrase as *X*) and *tickle the ivories* 'play the piano' (which can be inflected for tense/mood). Fillmore et al.'s schematic idioms are even more schematic; they include what they call 'fate tempting expressions' such as *Watch me (drop it, slip etc.)*.

The types of idioms, and their comparison to regular syntactic expressions, are given in Table 9.1.

Table 9.1 *Types of idioms compared to regular syntactic expressions*

	Lexically	Syntactically	Semantically
Unfamiliar pieces unfamiliarly arranged	irregular	irregular	irregular
Familiar pieces unfamiliarly arranged	regular	irregular	irregular
Familiar pieces familiarly arranged	regular	regular	irregular
Regular syntactic expressions	regular	regular	regular

9.3   Idioms as constructions

Having presented their analysis and classification of idioms, Fillmore et al. argue that the proper way to represent speaker's knowledge of idioms is as constructions. For Fillmore et al., a construction is a schematic idiom. That is, some elements of the construction are lexically open on the one hand, and so the idioms fitting the description cannot simply be listed as 'phrasal lexical items.' In this respect, schematic idioms differ from substantive idioms. Fully substantive idioms, such as *It takes one to know one* or *The bigger they come the harder they fall*, can simply be listed as lexical items. Listing substantive idioms would require the allowance for multiword lexical items in the lexicon. But this concession to the linguistic facts does not conflict greatly with the principle of componential grammar that arbitrary and idiosyncratic linguistic knowledge is found in the lexicon (cf. the discussion of subcategorization frames in §9.2). Hence substantive idioms do not require any drastic departure from the componential model of the organization of grammar.

Schematic idioms, on the other hand, cannot simply be listed in the lexicon. And schematic idioms are idioms; that is, they are semantically and possibly also syntactically and lexically irregular. Syntactic, semantic and in some cases pragmatic properties of schematic idioms cannot be predicted from the general rules of the syntactic and semantic components (and the pragmatic component) or the general rules linking these components together. Instead, the syntactic, semantic (and in some cases pragmatic) properties must be directly associated with the construction. Such a representation would cut across the components in the componential model of grammatical knowledge, and hence represents a direct challenge to that model, at least for idioms.

Fillmore et al. make the case for constructions as units of syntactic representation by examining one construction in great detail, the construction containing the conjunction *let alone*, and demonstrating that it has syntactic, semantic and pragmatic properties that cannot be described by the general rules of the language, but is rule-governed within the context of the *let alone* construction and certain related constructions. The following discussion will present some of the more salient unique properties of the *let alone* construction.

The syntax of the *let alone* construction is complex. *Let alone* can be described as a coordinating conjunction; like other conjunctions, it conjoins a variety of like constituents (Fillmore et al. 1988:514; the emphasized elements represent prosody):

(18)   a. Max won't eat SHRIMP, let alone SQUID.
        b. We'll need shrimp and squid.
(19)   a. Max won't TOUCH the SHRIMP, let alone CLEAN the SQUID.
        b. I want you to cook the shrimp and clean the squid.

However, *let alone* fails in some syntactic contexts where *and* is fine, and vice versa (Fillmore et al. 1988:515–16; Fillmore et al. also discuss WH-extraction and *It*-clefts):

(20)   a. Shrimp and squid Moishe won't eat.
         b. *Shrimp let alone squid Moishe won't eat.
         c. *Shrimp Moishe won't eat and squid.
         d. Shrimp Moishe won't eat, let alone squid.

Example (20d) shows that *let alone* allows sentence fragments for the second conjunct. In this respect *let alone* is like certain other conjunctions, including comparative *than* (Fillmore et al. 1988:517, 516):

(21)   a. John hardly speaks RUSSIAN let alone BULGARIAN.
         b. John speaks Russian, if not Bulgarian.
         c. John speaks better Russian than Bulgarian.

However, unlike comparative *than* and ordinary conjunctions, *let alone* is impossible with VP ellipsis (deletion of the verb phrase excluding the auxiliary; Fillmore et al. 1988:516):

(22)   a. Max will eat shrimp more willingly than Minnie will.
         b. Max won't eat shrimp but Minnie will.
         c. *Max won't eat shrimp let alone Minnie will.

The *let alone* construction is a focus construction, like a number of other constructions of English (see Prince 1981b, discussed below), hence its characteristic prosody. In fact, *let alone* is a paired focus construction, like those given in (23b–c) (Fillmore et al. 1988:517):

(23)   a. He doesn't get up for LUNCH, let alone BREAKFAST.
         b. He doesn't get up for LUNCH, much less BREAKFAST.
         c. She didn't eat a BITE, never mind a WHOLE MEAL.

The *let alone* construction allows for multiple paired foci (see [19a]), and in such sentences allows multiple *let alone*s (Fillmore et al. 1988:520):

(24)   a. You couldn't get a poor man to wash your car for two dollars, let alone a rich man to wax your truck for one dollar.
         b. You couldn't get a poor man, let alone a rich man, to wash, let alone wax, your car, let alone your truck, for two dollars, let alone one dollar.

In this respect, *let alone* is similar to the construction *not P but Q* (illustrated in [25]) and to the *respectively* construction (illustrated in [26]); but Fillmore et al. argue that in other respects *let alone* differs from both of these constructions (1988:521–22):

(25)   Ivan sent not an album but a book, and not to Anna on her anniversary but to Boris on his birthday.

(26)   Fred and Louise hated their shrimp and squid respectively.

Let alone is a negative polarity item, not unlike *any*; it occurs in negative contexts and certain other contexts (Fillmore et al. 1988:518):

(27)   a. He didn't reach DENVER, let alone CHICAGO.
        b. He didn't reach any major city.
(28)   a. I'm too tired to GET UP, let alone GO RUNNING with you.
        b. I'm too tired to do any chores.

However, unlike these polarity items, *let alone* is allowed in certain contexts where other negative polarity items are disallowed (Fillmore et al 1988:519; example [29a] is attested):

(29)   a. You've got enough material there for a whole SEMESTER, let alone a WEEK.
        b. *You've got enough material for any semester.

The semantics as well as the syntax of *let alone* is complex and not entirely predictable from more general rules of semantic interpretation from syntactic structure. As mentioned above, the *let alone* construction has at least one paired focus (e.g. the pair *semester* and *week* in [29a]). The interpretation of a *let alone* sentence requires the following steps. First the interpreter must recognize or construct a semantic proposition in the fragmentary second conjunct that is parallel to the proposition in the full first conjunct. Second, the interpreter must recognize or construct a semantic scale underlying the elements in the propositions. This is not always easy. For instance, the scale for (18a) may have to do with the assumed degree of distastefulness of shrimp versus squid, or it may have to do with the relative cost of shrimp versus squid (and Fred's stinginess; Fillmore et al. 1988:524–25).

More specifically, the interpreter must perform the following semantic operations. The interpreter must construct a **scalar model**, which ranks propositions on a scale – for example, the scale of distastefulness of eating seafood or the cost thereof. The propositions in the two conjuncts must be from the same scalar model – in this case, 'Fred not eat shrimp' and 'Fred not eat squid.' The two propositions are of the same polarity (in this case, negative). Finally, the initial, full conjunct denotes the proposition that is stronger or more informative on the scale – Fred not eating shrimp is more informative than Fred not eating squid, on the assumption that people who would eat squid would also eat shrimp but not vice versa. This semantic analysis can be generalized to multiple paired focus versions of *let alone* (see Fillmore et al. 1988 for details). This whole semantic apparatus is required for the interpretation of the *let alone* construction, and is not necessary (as a whole) for other constructions.

Finally, there is a specific pragmatic context in which the utterance of a *let alone* construction is felicitous (Fillmore et al. 1988:532). First, the discourse context is one such that the weaker (less informative) proposition, that is, the underlying proposition of the fragmentary second conjunct, is at issue – for example, the issue of whether or not Fred eats squid. The weaker proposition accepts or rejects this context – in this case, *Fred doesn't eat squid* rejects it. But simply uttering the less informative proposition is not cooperative since the speaker knows that the strong proposition represented by the initial conjunct is true. So the speaker utters the *let alone* sentence. Fillmore et al. note that *let alone* is similar pragmatically to other conjunctions allowing sentence fragments, such as those illustrated in (21b–c) above. However, some of these conjunctions present the stronger proposition in the second, fragmentary conjunct, unlike *let alone*:

(30)   a. He didn't make colonel, let alone general.
         b. He didn't make general; in fact, he didn't even make colonel.

The preceding discussion has presented some of the evidence that the *let alone* construction has its own syntactic, semantic and pragmatic properties that cannot be predicted from more general rules of syntax, semantics and pragmatics. A number of other studies done in the emerging framework of construction grammar demonstrate that other constructions also have unique syntactic, semantic and pragmatic properties. A reading of these studies gives rise to two general observations.

First, the construction on which attention is focused by the researcher(s) turns out to be just one of a family of related constructions. For example, the *let alone* construction turns out to be just one of a family of coordinate constructions that allow certain kinds of sentence fragments in the second conjunct, two of which were illustrated in (21b–c). The *let alone* construction also turns out to be just one of a family of paired focus constructions, two of which were illustrated in (23b–c). Paired focus constructions are in turn related to a family of single focus constructions. The phrase *let alone* is itself related to other negative polarity items, and *let alone* is also related to a number of items that require a scalar model for their semantic interpretation, such as *even, almost, few* and *merely* (Fillmore et al. 1988:530).

Likewise, Lakoff's seminal study of the *There*-construction, as in *There's a fox in the garden*, uncovered a large family of related constructions with slightly different syntactic and semantic properties, which are illustrated in examples (31)– (32) (see Lakoff 1987, Appendix 3 for the analysis of the differences among *There*-constructions):

(31)   *Deictic* There-*Constructions*:
         a. *Central*: There's Harry with the red jacket on.
         b. *Perceptual*: There goes the bell now!
         c. *Discourse*: There's a nice point to bring up in class.
         d. *Existence*: There goes our last hope.
         e. *Activity Start*: There goes Harry, meditating again.

    f. *Delivery*: Here's your pizza, piping hot!
    g. *Paragon*: Now there was a real ballplayer!
    h. *Exasperation*: There goes Harry again, making a fool of himself.
    i. *Narrative Focus*: There I was in the middle of the jungle . . .
    j. *New Enterprise*: Here I go, off to Africa.
    k. *Presentational*: There on that hill will be built by the alumni of this university a ping-pong facility second to none.

(32)   *Existential* There-*Constructions*
    a. *Central*: There's a fox in the garden.
    b. *Strange [Event]*: There's a man been shot.
    c. *Ontological*: There is a Santa Claus.
    d. *Presentational*: Suddenly there burst into the room an SS officer holding a machine gun.

Michaelis and Lambrecht's (1996) study of Nominal Extraposition, illustrated in (33a), reveals a family of related exclamative constructions, illustrated in (33b–e):

(33)   a. It's AMAZING the amount I SPENT!
    b. I can't believe the AMOUNT I spent!
    c. The AMOUNT I spent!
    d. I can't BELIEVE how much I SPENT!
    e. It's INCREDIBLE how much I SPENT!

The Nominal Extraposition construction in (33a) is characterized by extraposition of the NP and a metonymic interpretation of the extraposed NP as referring to a scale, unique to exclamatives (the exclamative character of the sentence is due to the assertion of an excessive degree on the scale). The constructions in (33b–c) share the metonymic interpretation of (33a), but the NP is not extraposed (33b) or is an independent utterance on its own (33c). The exclamative constructions in (33d–e) directly express the scale (*how much*), unlike (33a–c). The construction in (33e) extraposes the degree expression, not unlike the extraposed (33a), while the construction in (33d) does not. All five constructions in this family are distinguished by the fact that they are a distinct speech act (expressed by the simple present tense), and they assert an affective stance, namely contravention of expectation (this fact restricts the main clause predicate to a gradable, contrary to expectation assertion).

    The second observation upon surveying these studies of particular constructions follows from the first. The number and variety of constructions uncovered in these studies imply that speakers possess an extraordinary range of specialized syntactic knowledge that goes beyond general rules of syntax and semantic interpretation on the one hand, and a list of substantive idioms on the other. The detailed analysis of such constructions is not the exclusive preserve of construction grammarians. Linguists working in a variety of approaches to syntax and semantics have examined schematic idioms/constructions and demonstrated that they represent rule-governed and productive linguistic behavior, albeit limited to the family of constructions analyzed.

One of the linguistic schools that calls itself 'functionalist,' which we will call 'autonomous functionalist' (cf. Croft 1995:496–99), identifies constructions that possess a specific discourse-functional or information-structural value. For instance, Prince (1978) argues that the constructions known as *It*-cleft (illustrated in [34]) and WH-cleft (35) each have their own discourse-functional value (Prince 1978:885):

(34)   It is against pardoning these that many protest (*Philadelphia Inquirer*, February 6, 1977)

(35)   What you are saying is that the President was involved (Haldeman, Watergate tapes)

Prince notes that WH-clefts and *It*-clefts differ syntactically, in that the former allow clefted adverbs or prepositional phrases as well as clefted noun phrases, and the latter commonly allow verb phrases or sentences as clefted items (Prince 1978:884). Discourse-functionally, WH-clefts can be used when the information in the subordinate clause is in the hearer's consciousness (Prince 1978:894). In contrast, Prince identifies at least two distinct 'sub-senses' for *It*-clefts, illustrated in (36)–(37) (1978:896, 898):

(36)   So I learned to sew books. They're really good books. It's just THE COVERS that are rotten. (Bookbinder in S. Terkel, *Working*, 1974)

(37)   It was just about 50 years ago that Henry Ford gave us the weekend. (*Philadelphia Bulletin*, January 3, 1976)

Example (36) illustrates what Prince calls a stressed focus *It*-cleft. In the stressed focus *It*-cleft, the subordinate *that*-clause is given but not assumed to be in the hearer's consciousness. The stressed focus *It*-cleft is interesting also in that it has a phonological property associated with it: only the focused part (in small capitals in [36]) has strong stress; the *that*-clause is weakly stressed. Example (37) is an informative-presupposition *It*-cleft: the *that*-clause presents information that is a general known fact, albeit not to the hearer and hence new to the hearer (and therefore also not in the hearer's consciousness). Informative-presupposition *It*-clefts have a normal rather than weak stress on the *that*-clause. These examples indicate that constructions may have phonological features associated with them as well as syntactic, semantic and pragmatic/discourse features.

Birner and Ward (1998) analyze a wide range of preposing constructions, such as Topicalization (illustrated in [38]; Birner and Ward 1998:51), postposing constructions, such as right-dislocation (as in [39]; Birner and Ward 1998:146) and argument reversal constructions, such as inversion (as in [40]; Birner and Ward

1998:159):

(38)   As members of a Gray Panthers committee, we went to Canada to learn, and learn we did. (*Philadelphia Inquirer*, June 16, 1985)
(39)   It's very delicate, the lawn. You don't want to over-water, really. (father in the movie 'Honey, I Shrunk the Kids')
(40)   Behind them, moving slowly and evenly, but keeping up, came Pa and Noah. (J. Steinbeck, *The Grapes of Wrath*, 1939)

Birner and Ward argue that, although there are commonalities among the different constructions with respect to the discourse status of the preposed element and the status of the postposed elements for syntactically similar constructions, each has its own unique discourse properties. In other words, the various preposing, postposing and inversion structures they discuss must each be analyzed as distinct grammatical constructions.

Wierzbicka has discussed the properties of several families of constructions in various publications (see the papers collected in Wierzbicka 1980, 1988, as well as the examples discussed here). For example, Wierzbicka argues that the schematic idiom *have a V* and the related types *give a V* and *take a V*, illustrated in (41)–(43), represent rule-governed constructions (Wierzbicka 1988:293, 338):

(41)   a. have a drink
       b. *have an eat
(42)   a. give the rope a pull
       b. *give the window an open
(43)   a. take a look at
       b. *take a look for

Wierzbicka argues that the item following the indefinite article is a verbal infinitive, not a noun, and hence differs from other *have* constructions that do take a noun, or more generally a noun phrase. For example, the phrase *have a cough* is nominal, in that one can also *have a headache/have pneumonia* and so on in which the word is indubitably a noun (Wierzbicka 1988:295–96). In this respect, the *have a V* construction is syntactically unique.

Semantically, Wierzbicka argues that *have a V* represents an action as limited in time but not punctual, lacking an external goal, and repeatable, and is of benefit to the agent/experiencer (1988:297–302). Wierzbicka argues that this semantic characterization is still incomplete, since it provides necessary but not sufficient conditions for the occurrence of verbs in this construction. Instead, she presents ten subtypes of the *have a V* construction, just as Prince offers two subtypes of the *It*-cleft. One of these types she describes as 'aimless objectless action which could cause one to feel good,' exemplified by *have a walk/swim/run/jog/lie-down* and so on. In this subclass, the verbs are intransitive but durative and atelic (Wierzbicka

1988:303), hence the unacceptability of (44b–c):

(44)   a. He had a walk.
        b. *He had a walk to the post office.
        c. *He had a get-up.

The verb cannot describe a purposeful action (one with an external goal), other than a recreational activity, hence the unacceptability of (45b–c):

(45)   a. He had a swim.
        b. *He had a work.
        c. *He had a pray.

One indicator of the conventional character of the interpretations of schematic idioms/constructions, particularly pragmatic ones, is the lack of translatability of the idiom. For example, it has been argued that the tautological statement in (46) is inferred to mean something like 'That's the kind of unruly behavior you would expect from boys' on general pragmatic principles (Levinson 1983:125):

(46)   Boys will be boys.

Wierzbicka (1987) points out that in fact, the literal translation of (46) in various languages (see examples [47]–[50]) does not have the same pragmatic meaning as (46). Instead, different constructions are used to obtain approximately the same pragmatic force (Wierzbicka 1987:96–97). In examples (47)–(50), the (a) sentence is the closest literal translation to (46), the (b) sentence the one with the closest pragmatic meaning to that of (46), and the (c) sentence is the literal translation of the (b) sentence:

(47)   *French*:
        a. *Les garçons sont les (des?) garçons.
        b. ?Les garçons seront toujours les (des) garçons. [still questionable]
        c. 'Boys will always be boys'

(48)   *German*:
        a. *Knaben werden Knaben sein.
        b. ?Knaben bleiben (immer) Knaben.
        c. 'Boys remain (always) boys'

(49)   *Russian*:
        a. *Mal'čiki budut mal'čiki.
        b. (Čego ty xočeš'?) oni že mal'čiki.
        c. '(What do you expect?) They are boys'

(50)   *Polish*:
        a. *Chłopcy będą chłopcy.
        b. (Jednak) co Paryż to Paryż.
        c. '(However) what (is) Paris this (is) Paris'

These examples indicate that the pragmatic interpretation in (46) is in fact conventionally associated with the equational tautology in which it occurs in English. In fact, Wierzbicka argues for several different equational tautological constructions in English, which cannot be substituted for each other (Wierzbicka 1987:104):

(51) $N_{abstract}$ *is* $N_{abstract}$.
     a. War is war.
     b. *Kid is kid.

(52) N_{plural} *are* N_{plural}.
     a. Kids are kids.
     b. *Wars are wars.

(53) N_{plural} *will be* N_{plural}.
     a. Boys will be boys.
     b. *Wars will be wars.

(54)   *An N is an N.*
     a. A party is a party.
     b. *A war is a war.

(55)   *The N is the N.*
     a. The law is the law.
     b. *The war is the war.

Wierzbicka argues that the semantic interpretations for the constructions exemplified in (51)–(55) can be characterized as follows: a 'sober' attitude toward complex human activities (51); tolerance for human nature (52–53), the future subtype indicating 'the willful and uncontrollable spontaneity' of the human type (1987: 107); obligation with respect to a human role, activity or institution ([54]–[55]; Wierzbicka argues that [54] has other readings as well). These semantic differences cannot be inferred either from general rules of semantic interpretation in English or general rules of the pragmatics of communication.

Even in the generative grammatical tradition, which is the theory most closely identified with the componential model, there have been studies of schematic idioms, in particular by Jackendoff (1990, 1997; see also Akmajian 1984 and Lambrecht's 1990 reanalysis in construction grammar terms). For example, Jackendoff (1997) analyzes the 'time'-*away* construction, illustrated in (56):

(56)   Bill slept the afternoon away.

Syntactically, the noun-phrase after the intransitive verb acts like a direct object complement, and normally cannot occur with a transitive verb ([57a–b]). In some cases the 'normal' direct object can appear in a *with* phrase, which it cannot do in an ordinary active construction ([57c–d]; Jackendoff 1997:535):

(57)   a. Fred drank the night away.
         b. *Fred drank scotch the night away.
         c. Fred drank the night away with a bottle of Jack Daniels.
         d. *Fred drank with a bottle of Jack Daniels.

Semantically, the 'time'-*away* construction appears to have the same interpretation as the durative adverbial with *for* (Jackendoff 1997:536):

(58)   Bill slept for the (whole) afternoon.

However, unlike the durative adverbial, the 'time'-*away* construction requires a volitional subject ([59a–b]) and an activity rather than a state ([60a–b]; Jackendoff 1997:537):

(59)   a. The light flashed for two hours.
         b. *The light flashed two hours away.
(60)   a. Celia sat for two hours.
         b. *Celia sat two hours away.

The particle *away* as an aspectual particle seems to have a meaning and behavior similar to *away* in the 'time'-*away* construction:

(61)   Bill drank away.
(62)   *Celia sat away.

But the particle *away* is atelic (unbounded), while the 'time'-*away* construction is telic, as indicated by the *It take* NP_{time} construction:

(63)   a. *It took a month for Lois and Clark to finally get to dance away.
         b. It took a month for Lois and Clark to finally get to dance two blissful hours away.

These properties indicate the uniqueness of the 'time'-*away* construction with respect to general syntactic and semantic rules. Jackendoff further argues that the 'time'-*away* construction's properties cannot be predicted from the properties of other semantically related constructions, such as the resultative construction (64) and the *way* construction ([65]; see Jackendoff 1997):

(64)   The river froze solid.
(65)   Dora drank her way down the street.

Jackendoff weighs two analyses of the 'time'-*away* construction, the construction-based account of the construction grammarians, and an account in which a lexical rule derives the relevant verb that governs this type of construction. Jackendoff concludes that the only substantive difference between the two accounts is that if one wants to 'preserve the assumption that the lexical verb's argument structure always determines the argument structure of the VP' (Jackendoff 1997:557), then one must commit oneself to the lexical rule analysis. Jackendoff himself inclines to the constructional analysis for the 'time'-*away* construction, since he believes that constructions are necessary in other contexts anyway (ibid.).

Jackendoff's inclination in his 1997 paper is another step away from the componential model of generative grammar toward a construction grammar model. Jackendoff's inclination is also a step toward the construction grammarian's bolder hypothesis. Since one must posit constructions in order to account for a substantial part of a speaker's grammatical knowledge, is it possible to generalize the concept of construction to account for all of a speaker's grammatical knowledge? The next section presents construction grammar's arguments for the bolder hypothesis.

9.4   From constructions to construction grammar

The preceding section presented a number of case studies that argue for the need to posit constructions as a unit of syntactic representation. A construction is a syntactic configuration, sometimes with one or more substantive items (e.g. the words *let alone*, *have a* . . . and *away*) and sometimes not (as with the focus constructions, the exclamative constructions and the resultative construction). A construction also has its own semantic interpretation and sometimes its own pragmatic meaning (as with the tautological constructions). Hence a construction as a unit cuts across the componential model of grammatical knowledge. The existence of constructions would require a revision to the componential model in (3) that we may represent as in (66):

(66)

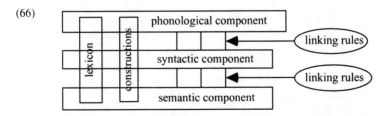

Constructions, like the lexical items in the lexicon, are 'vertical' structures that combine syntactic, semantic and even phonological information (for the specific words in a construction, as well as any unique prosodic features that may be associated with a construction). As more and more constructions are discovered and analyzed, construction grammarians came to argue that, in fact, grammatical organization is entirely 'vertical' (indeed, this approach is already suggested in Fillmore et al. 1988).

We begin with the syntactic structure of constructions. In §9.3, constructional analyses were proposed for schematic idioms. Schematic idioms were defined in §9.2 as idioms in which some element or elements are lexically open, indicated by a category label as in *have a V*. Schematic idioms were contrasted with substantive idioms such as *It takes one to know one*, in which there are no lexically open elements. Hence, substantive idioms can be listed in the lexicon without substantially altering the basic principles of the componential model.

But Fillmore et al. observe in a footnote that there is in fact a continuum from substantive to schematic (1988:505, n. 3). Although we described all idioms with any lexically open elements as schematic idioms in §9.2, in fact schematic idioms vary considerably in their schematicity. Some schematic idioms such as the verb-phrase idiom *kick the bucket* are fixed except for grammatical inflectional categories:

(67)   a. Jake kicked the bucket.
         b. Jake's gonna kick the bucket. [etc.]

Other schematic idioms have one or more open argument slots as well as inflectional flexibility, such as *give NP the lowdown* 'tell NP the news':

(68)   a. I gave/I'll give him the lowdown.
         b. He gave/He'll give Janet the lowdown. [etc.]

Still other schematic idioms have open classes for all 'content' words, leaving just a salient form such as the connective *let alone* as a substantive element:

(69)   a. She gave me more candy than I could carry, let alone eat.
         b. Only a linguist would buy that book, let alone read it.

Finally, a constructional analysis has been proposed for some schematic idioms in which all elements are lexically open, such as the resultative construction (Goldberg 1995:181; attested examples):

(70)   a. This nice man probably just wanted Mother to . . . kiss him unconscious.
            (D. Shields, *Dead Tongues*, 1989)
         b. I had brushed my hair very smooth. (C. Brontë, *Jane Eyre*, 1847)

Yet the resultative construction has no lexically specific element. It can be described only by a syntactic structure, in this case [*NP Verb NP XP*], with a unique specialized semantic interpretation.

It is a very short step from analyzing the resultative construction as a construction to analyzing all the syntactic rules of a language as constructions (Fillmore et al. 1988:501, 534; Langacker 1999:19). After all, a syntactic rule such as *VP → V NP* describes a completely schematic construction [*V NP*], and the semantic interpretation rule that maps the syntactic structure to its corresponding semantic structure is unique to that schematic construction. Indeed, Goldberg suggests that there is a transitive construction just as there are more specialized schematic syntactic constructions such as the resultative construction (Goldberg 1995:116–19). Reanalyzing general syntactic rules as the broadest, most schematic constructions of a language is just the other end of the substantive- schematic continuum for idioms/constructions.

Turning to semantic interpretation, one can also argue that constructions and compositional semantic rules differ only in degree, not in kind. As we noted in §9.2, Nunberg et al. (1994) argue that most idioms are idiomatically combining expressions. In an idiomatically combining expression, the syntactic parts of the idiom (e.g. *spill* and *beans*) can be identified with parts of the idiom's semantic interpretation ('divulge' and 'information'). Nunberg et al. argue that idiomatically combining expressions are not only semantically analyzable, but also semantically compositional.

Nunberg et al. observe that idiomatically combining expressions are only the extreme end of a continuum of conventionality in semantic composition. The other end of the continuum is represented by **selectional restrictions**. Selectional restrictions are restrictions on possible combinations of words which are determined only by the semantics of the concepts denoted by the word. For example, the restrictions on the use of *mud* and *car* in (71)–(72) follow from the fact that mud is a viscous substance and a car is a machine:

(71)   a. Mud oozed onto the driveway.
       b. ?*The car oozed onto the driveway.

(72)   a. The car started.
       b. ?*Mud started.

The restrictions on *mud* and *car* are not dependent on the conventional form in which the concepts are expressed. If one used the word *goo* instead of *mud* or *automobile* instead of *car*, the judgements in (71)–(72) would remain the same. The combinations in (71a) and (72a) are semantically compositional: the meaning of the whole can be predicted from the meaning of the parts.

An intermediate point on this continuum involves what are called **collocations**. Collocations are combinations of words that are preferred over other combinations that otherwise appear to be semantically equivalent. For example, Matthews argues that *toasted* and *roasted* describe essentially the same process, but are restricted in their acceptable combinations (Matthews 1981:5):

(73)   a. roasted meat
        b. toasted bread
(74)   a. ?*toasted meat
        b. ?*roasted bread

Most linguists would analyze (73a–b) as semantically compositional as well. In both cases, the meaning of the whole can be predicted from the meaning of the parts. It is just that speakers of English conventionally use *toasted* with *bread* and *roasted* with *meat*, but not the other way around. This convention does not affect the semantic compositionality of the expressions in (73a–b).

Typically, collocations are expressions that can be interpreted more or less correctly out of context, but cannot be produced correctly if the conventional expression is not already known to the speech community (Nunberg, Sag and Wasow 1994:495). In other words, collocations are encoding idioms. For example, the expressions in (75a) and (75b) are the American and British terms for the same type of object; each is compositional to the speakers of that dialect, but a speaker of the other dialect would not be able to know what conventional expression is used to refer to that type of object:

(75)   a. thumb tack (American English)
        b. drawing pin (British English)

Nunberg et al. argue that exactly the same reasoning applies to idiomatically combining expressions. Idiomatically combining expressions are largely fixed in their words; any substitution leads to ungrammaticality, as in (76b–c) and (77b):

(76)   a. Tom pulled strings to get the job.
        b. *Tom pulled ropes to get the job.
        c. *Tom grasped strings to get the job.
(77)   a. She spilled the beans.
        b. *She spilled the succotash.

However, given the meanings of the words in the idiomatically combining expression, the meaning of the whole expression is compositional:

> By convention . . . *strings* [in *pull strings*] can be used metaphorically to refer to personal connection when it is the object of *pull*, and *pull* can be used metaphorically to refer to exploitation or exertion when its object is *strings*. (Nunberg et al. 1994:496)

> When we hear *spill the beans* used to mean 'divulge the information', for example, we can assume that *spill* denotes the relation of divulging and *beans* the information that is divulged, even if we cannot say why *beans* should have been used in this expression rather than *succotash*. This is not to say, of course, that *spill* can have the meaning 'divulge' when it does not co-occur with *the beans*, or

that *beans* can have the meaning 'information' without *spill*. The availability of these meanings for each constituent can be dependent on the presence of another item without requiring that the meaning 'divulge the information' attach directly to the entire VP. Rather it arises through a convention that assigns particular meaning to its parts when they occur together. (Nunberg et al. 1994:497)

At first, Nunberg et al.'s analysis may look odd. To say that *pull* and *strings* each have a meaning found only in *pull strings*, and that those meanings are compositional in the idiomatically combining expression, seems ad hoc. The more natural description is the traditional one, that the meaning of the idiomatically combining expression is 'noncompositional.' In fact, it is sometimes said that one of the strongest pieces of evidence for constructions as independent syntactic objects is that there is some degree of 'noncompositionality' in the meaning of the construction. But there is evidence that Nunberg et al.'s analysis is the right one.

Some English words exist only in idiomatically combining expressions, such as *heed* in *pay heed*. It makes sense to say that *heed* has a meaning, that is of course found only in *pay heed*. It has been argued that *heed* is idiomatic, because it is essentially synonymous with *attention* in *pay attention*, and yet does not behave the same way (Radford 1988; see Nunberg et al. 1994:505):

(78)   a. You can't expect to have my attention/*heed all the time.
        b. He's a child who needs a lot of attention/*heed.

Nunberg et al. argue that *heed* does not in fact mean the same thing as *attention* does, when *attention* is the object of *pay* (Nunberg et al. 1994:505):

(79)   a. The children paid rapt attention/?*heed to the circus.
        b. I pay close attention/?*heed to my clothes.
        c. They paid attention/??*heed to my advice, but didn't follow it.

The semantic differences are related to the difference between the verbs *attend* and *heed*: 'we clearly attend to much that we do not heed . . . one can take heed but not attention, and . . . attention but not heed can wander' (Nunberg et al. 1994:506). In other words, *heed* in *pay heed* does have its own meaning even though it occurs (as a noun) in only that combination. Hence, it is reasonable to assume that other words have specialized meanings in idiomatically combining expressions, and that those meanings are compositional.

Another important line of evidence for the compositionality of idiomatically combining expressions is psycholinguistic. Speakers of English recognize the meanings of words in idiomatically combining expressions, and recognize them as figurative meanings, even though the figurative meanings are found only in the idiomatically combining expressions (Gibbs 1990). These two pieces of evidence point to Nunberg et al.'s conclusion that 'The dependency among the parts of idiomatically combining expressions is thus fundamentally semantic in nature' (Nunberg et al. 1994:505).

From a construction grammar perspective, Nunberg et al.'s analysis of idiomatically combining expressions looks more natural. An idiomatically combining expression such as *spill the beans* is a construction. As a construction, it has unique syntax: the verb must be *spill* and its object must be *the beans*. It also has a semantic interpretation, namely 'divulge information.' All Nunberg et al. are saying is that this construction has its own semantic interpretation rules, mapping *spill* onto 'divulge' and *the beans* onto 'information.' The constructional analysis is presented in the diagram in (80), using lowercase to describe form and uppercase to describe meaning, boxes to represent the construction and its parts, and dotted lines to indicate the syntax-semantics mapping (see §10.1):

(80)

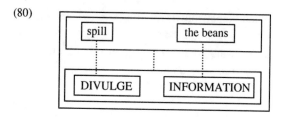

What Nunberg et al. have done is to dissociate **conventionality** from **noncompositionality**. Idiomatically combining expressions are not noncompositional. There exist truly noncompositional expressions; these are idiomatic phrases such as *saw logs* and *kick the bucket*. Idiomatically combining expressions differ from collocations and ordinary expressions only in that the conventional way of expressing the parts of its meaning are conventional and also relatively opaque, compared to collocations and ordinary expressions.

Earlier analysts have assumed that an idiomatically combining expression is 'noncompositional' because the meaning of the whole is not predictable from the meaning of the parts when those parts appear in other expressions than the idiom. More precisely, idiomatically combining expressions have been treated as 'noncompositional' because their meanings do not conform to the semantic interpretation rules of regular syntactic expressions such as [VERB OBJECT]vp in the case of *spill the beans*. But *spill the beans* is compositional in the sense that the parts of the syntactic expression can be mapped onto components of the meaning of the idiom, as in (80). The way that *spill the beans* differs from regular syntactic expressions is that there are rules of semantic interpretation associated with just that construction that are not derivable from the [VERB OBJECT]vp pattern of which *spill the beans* is an instance.

Thus, the common perception that a particular construction must be represented as an independent syntactic unit because it is 'noncompositional,' is technically incorrect. Constructions other than idiomatic phrases are compositional, that is, the meanings of the parts of the construction are combined to form the meaning of the whole construction. The reason that they must be represented as independent constructions is that semantic interpretation rules associated with the construction are unique to that construction, and not derived from another more general syntactic pattern, as construction grammarians carefully note (see, e.g., Goldberg 1995:13 and Michaelis and Lambrecht 1996:219).

Indeed, one can think of the general 'compositional' rules of semantic interpretation as being semantic rules associated with general (schematic) syntactic structures, just as specialized rules of semantic interpretation are associated with syntactically specialized extragrammatical idioms. Nunberg et al.'s analysis of idiomatically combining expressions can easily be extended to the general rules of semantic interpretation that link syntactic and semantic structures. Consider, for example, the English predicate adjective construction, illustrated in (81), and its semantic interpretation:

(81)   Hannah is smart.

The English predicate adjective construction has the form [*NP be Adj*]. It differs from the ordinary verbal construction in requiring the copula verb *be*. One can analyze the semantics of the predicate adjective construction as follows. The members of the Adjective category have a meaning that requires them to be combined with the copula *be* in order to be interpreted as ascribing a property to a referent (unlike verbs). The copula *be* has a meaning that requires combination with a member of the Adjective category in order to be interpreted as doing the job of ascribing (a property) to the subject NP. This analysis is in fact essentially the semantic analysis that Langacker argues for (Langacker 1987:214–22; 1991a:204–5). In Langacker's terminology (see §3.5), Adjective symbolizes an atemporal relation, and the copula *be* symbolizes a process that Adjective meanings must be combined with in order to be predicated.

In like fashion, semantic interpretation rules can be provided for any schematic construction describing the most general syntactic structures of the language. In other words, all syntactic expressions, whatever their degree of schematicity, have rules of semantic interpretation associated with them, although some substantive idioms appear to inherit their semantic interpretation rules from more schematic syntactic expressions such as [*Verb Object*] (see §10.2.1). Hence, the difference between regular syntactic expressions and idiomatically combining expressions is not that the former are 'compositional' and the latter are 'noncompositional.' Instead, the former's rules of semantic composition are more general and the latter's rules of semantic composition are more specialized. In semantics as well as syntax, the concept of a construction can be generalized to encompass the full range of grammatical knowledge of a speaker.

If syntax and semantics as a whole can be represented as constructions, what about morphology and the lexicon? Morphology, like syntax, represents complex grammatical units, made up of morphemes. From a structural point of view, the only difference between morphology and syntax is that morphemes are bound within a word, while words are morphologically free within a phrase or sentence. Interestingly, analogs to almost all of the peculiar phenomena of idioms can be found in morphology.

There are unfamiliar morphemes that exist only in single combinations, such as *cran-* in *cranberry* (cf. *kith and kin, pay heed*). Such morphemes caused problems for American structuralist analysis, because one had to assign a meaning (if any) to the unfamiliar morpheme only in that word. This is, of course exactly the analysis advocated by Nunberg et al. for their syntactic analogs.

There is also 'extragrammatical' morphology, that is, morphological patterns that do not obey the general morphological rules of the language. The general rule for plural formation in English is suffixation of an allomorph of *-s* to the noun stem. The ablaut plurals of English such as *feet, geese* and so on are outside the general plural formation rule. Arguably, the plural of *brother-in-law*, either *brothers-in-law* or *brother-in-laws*, is also outside the general rule. Such examples are common across languages. For example, the general rule for the position of agreement affixes in K'iche' Mayan is as a prefix immediately following the aspect prefix: *x-at-w-il-oh* 'I saw you [familiar].' However, the second person formal morpheme is a free word following the verb form, and hence is an 'extragrammatical' morpheme: *x-w-il alaq* 'I saw you [formal]' (Mondloch 1978:27).

Morphological expressions can be placed on a continuum of schematicity. A maximally substantive morphological expression is fully specified, as in *book-s*. Partially schematic morphological expressions include *book-NUMBER* and *NOUN-s*. Fully schematic morphological expressions include *NOUN-NUMBER*.

Finally, many words are what one might call 'idiomatically combining words,' where the meaning of a morpheme is specific to the stem it combines with (or a subclass of stems). For example, *-en* is the plural of *brother* only when it refers to a member of a religious community, and *brother* refers to a member of a religious community when it is combined with *-en*.[2] The derivational suffix *-er* refers to the agent of the event denoted by the verb stem when that verb stem is in a class including *write, run* and so on, but refers to the instrument if the verb stem is *clip, staple* and the like, or the patient if the verb stem is *fry, broil* and so on. All of

---

[2] We ignore here the fact that the plural stem for the plural in *-en* is distinct from the singular stem.

these observations suggest that in fact morphology is very much like syntax, and that a constructional representation is motivated for morphology as well.

Lastly, the lexicon differs only in degree from constructions. Words in the lexicon are pairings of syntactic form (and phonological form) and meaning, including pragmatic meaning. Constructions are also pairings of syntactic form (and phonological form, for the substantive elements) and meaning, including pragmatic meaning. The only difference is that constructions are **complex**, made up of words and phrases, while words are syntactically simple. Some words are morphologically complex, of course. But we have just argued that construction grammar would analyze morphologically complex words as constructions whose parts are morphologically bound. Morphologically simple words are **atomic**, that is, they cannot be further divided into meaningful parts. But a word is again just the limiting case of a construction (Fillmore et al. 1988:501).

The end point of this argument is one of the fundamental hypotheses of construction grammar: there is a **uniform representation of all grammatical knowledge** in the speaker's mind, in the form of generalized constructions. Table 9.2 compares the different types of grammatical entities found in the componential model of grammar and their analysis as constructions in construction grammar.

Table 9.2 *The syntax-lexicon continuum*

Construction type	Traditional name	Examples
Complex and (mostly) schematic	**syntax**	[SBJ *be-* TNS VERB *-en by* OBL]
Complex, substantive verb	**subcategorization frame**	[SBJ *consume* OBJ]
Complex and (mostly) substantive	**idiom**	[*kick-*TNS *the bucket*]
Complex but bound	**morphology**	[NOUN*-s*], [VERB-TNS]
Atomic and schematic	**syntactic category**	[DEM], [ADJ]
Atomic and substantive	**word/lexicon**	[*this*], [*green*]

Syntactic rules (and the accompanying rules of semantic interpretation) are schematic, complex constructions. The subcategorization frames required to handle verbal syntactic behavior are schematic constructions with a substantive verb. Idioms are complex and (at least partly) substantive constructions. Morphology describes complex constructions, but constructions of bound morphemes. Words in the lexicon are atomic substantive constructions, while syntactic categories are schematic atomic constructions. In other words, grammatical knowledge represents a continuum on two dimensions, from the substantive to the schematic and from the atomic to the complex. This continuum is widely referred to as the

syntax-lexicon continuum. Thus, construction grammar conforms to Langacker's content requirement for a grammar: the only grammatical entities that are posited in the theory are grammatical units and schematizations of those units (Langacker 1987:53–54).

The notion of a construction in construction grammar is much more general than the traditional notion of a construction. In construction grammar, a construction can be atomic or complex; it can have parts that are morphologically bound as well as free; and any or all of the parts may be substantive or schematic. All constructions in construction grammar, though, are pairings of a syntactic and morphological (and, where relevant, phonological) form with a meaning, including pragmatic meaning.

The model of grammatical knowledge in construction grammar is represented in (82):

(82)

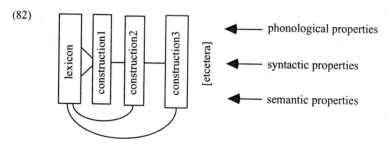

A construction grammar consists of a large number of constructions of all types, from schematic syntactic constructions to substantive lexical items. All of the constructions possess properties of form (syntactic and phonological) and meaning (semantic and pragmatic). All of these constructions are organized in a particular way in a speaker's mind. The next chapter describes how these generalizations are elaborated in various theories of construction grammar.

10

An overview of construction grammars

10.1   Essentials of construction grammar theories

In chapter 9, we presented the argument for representing grammatical knowledge as constructions. In this chapter, we will examine the structure of constructions and their organization in the grammatical knowledge of a speaker.

This section introduces fundamental concepts and descriptive terms for the analysis of the structure of a grammatical construction. The concepts in this section form the basis of any syntactic model, although they are combined in different ways in different syntactic theories. Any grammatical theory can be described as offering models of **representation** of the structure of an utterance, and models of **organization** of the relationship between utterance structures (presumably, in a speaker's mind). The latter are sometimes described in terms of levels of representation, linked by derivational rules. But construction grammar is a nonderivational model (like, for example, Head-driven Phrase Structure Grammar), and so a more general description of this aspect of grammatical theory is 'organization.'

Different versions of construction grammar will be briefly outlined in §10.2. We survey four variants of construction grammar found in cognitive linguistics – Construction Grammar (in capital letters; Kay and Fillmore 1999; Kay et al. in prep.), the construction grammar of Lakoff (1987) and Goldberg (1995), Cognitive Grammar (Langacker 1987, 1991) and Radical Construction Grammar (Croft 2001) – and focus on the distinctive characteristics of each theory.

10.1.1   Grammatical representation: the anatomy of a construction

Grammatical constructions in construction grammar, like the lexicon in other syntactic theories, consist of pairings of form and meaning that are at least partially arbitrary (but see §10.2.1). Even the most general syntactic constructions have corresponding general rules of semantic interpretation. Thus, constructions are fundamentally **symbolic** units, as represented in Figure 10.1 (compare Langacker 1987:60).

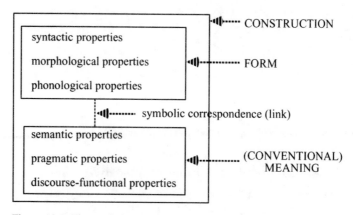

Figure 10.1 *The symbolic structure of a construction*

The term 'meaning' is intended to represent all of the **conventionalized** aspects of a construction's function, which may include not only properties of the situation described by the utterance, but also properties of the discourse in which the utterance is found (such as the use of the definite article to indicate that the object referred to is known to both speaker and hearer) and of the pragmatic situation of the interlocutors (e.g. the use of an exclamative construction such as *What a beautiful cat!* to convey the speaker's surprise). We will use the terms 'meaning' and 'semantic' to refer to any conventionalized function of a construction.

The central difference between componential syntactic theories and construction grammar is that the symbolic link between form and conventional meaning is internal to a construction in the latter, but is external to the syntactic and semantic components in the former (i.e. as linking rules). Figures 10.2 and 10.3 compare a componential syntactic theory and construction grammar on this parameter, highlighting in boldface the essential difference in the two models.

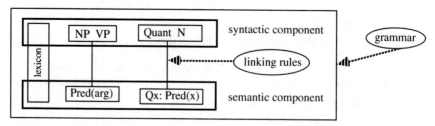

Figure 10.2 *The relation between form and function in a componential syntactic theory*

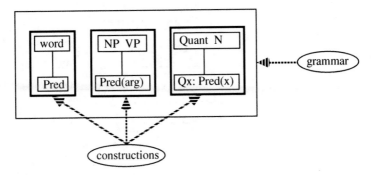

Figure 10.3 *The relation between form and function in construction grammar*

In the componential model, the various syntactic structures are organized independently of the corresponding semantic structures, as represented by the highlighted boxes in Figure 10.2. In construction grammar, the basic linguistic units are symbolic, and are organized as symbolic units, as represented by the highlighted boxes in Figure 10.3.[1] As a consequence, the internal structure of the basic (symbolic) units in construction grammar is more complex than that of basic units in the componential model.

The internal structure of a construction is the morphosyntactic structure of sentences that instantiate constructions. For example, a simple intransitive sentence such as *Heather sings* is an **instance** of the Intransitive construction. If we compare a simplified representation of *Heather sings* in generative grammar to a simplified representation of the same in construction grammar, we can see that they are actually rather similar except that the construction grammar representation is symbolic.

The box notation used in Figure 10.4b (on page 260) is simply a notational variant of the bracket notation used in Figure 10.4a (Langacker 1987; Kay and Fillmore 1999). Thus, we can see that both the generative grammar representation and the construction grammar representation share the fundamental part-whole or **meronomic** structure of grammatical units: the sentence *Heather sings* is made up of two parts, the Subject *Heather* and the Predicate *sings*.

The brackets in Figure 10.4a are labeled with syntactic category labels, while the corresponding boxes in the syntactic structure of Figure 10.4b are not labeled. This does not mean that the boxed structures in Figure 10.4b are all of the same syntactic type. Construction grammarians assume, of course, that syntactic units belong to

---

[1] Other theories that share construction grammar's basis in symbolic units are Head-driven Phrase Structure Grammar (HPSG; Pollard and Sag 1987, 1993), and Semiotic Grammar (McGregor 1997). However, these theories are not explicitly construction based, although HPSG and Fillmore and Kay's version of construction grammar have converged in many respects.

(a) Generative grammar: (b) Construction grammar:

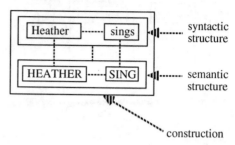

[[Heather]$_{NP}$ [sings]$_{VP}$]$_S$

Figure 10.4 *Simplified generative grammar and construction grammar representations of* Heather sings

a variety of different syntactic categories. The boxes have been left unlabeled because the nature of those categories is one issue on which different theories of construction grammar diverge. That is, we may ask the following question of different construction grammar theories:

(i)   What is the status of the categories of the syntactic elements in construction grammar, given the existence of constructions?

Beyond the meronomic structure of grammatical units, generative grammar and construction grammar diverge. First, as we have already noted, construction grammar treats grammatical units as fundamentally symbolic, that is, pairings of grammatical form and the corresponding meaning or **semantic structure**. As a consequence, the representation of a construction includes correspondence relations between the form and the meaning of the construction. We will call these correspondence relations **symbolic links**.

It will be convenient to use different names for the parts of a syntactic structure and the parts of a semantic structure. We will call the parts of the syntactic structure **elements** and parts of the semantic structure **components**. Thus, a symbolic link joins an element of the syntactic structure of a construction to a component of the semantic structure of that construction. There is also a symbolic link joining the whole syntactic structure to the whole semantic structure (the middle symbolic link in Figure 10.4b). This symbolic link is the construction grammar representation of the fact that the syntactic structure of the Intransitive construction symbolizes a unary-valency predicate-argument semantic structure. Each element plus corresponding component is a part of the whole construction (form + meaning) as well. We will use the term **unit** to describe a symbolic part (element + component) of a construction. That is, the construction as a symbolic whole is made up of symbolic units as parts. The symbolic units of *Heather sings* are not indicated in Figure 10.4b for clarity's sake; but all three types of parts of constructions are illustrated in Figure 10.5 (compare Langacker 1987:84, Fig. 2.8a; Figure 10.5 suppresses links between parts of the construction for clarity).

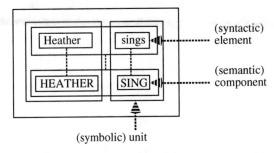

Figure 10.5 *Elements, components and units of a construction*

Figure 10.4b has two other relations apart from the symbolic relation: one joining the two syntactic elements and one joining the two semantic components. The link joining the two semantic components describes a **semantic relation** that holds between the two components, in this case some sort of event-participant relation. Thus, the semantic structure of a construction is assumed to be (potentially) complex, made up of semantic components among which certain semantic relations hold.

The link joining the two syntactic elements in Figure 10.4b is a **syntactic relation**. The syntactic relation does not obviously correspond directly to anything in the generative grammar representation in Figure 10.4a. This is because the representation of syntactic relations in most syntactic theories is more complex than a simple syntactic link. One layer is the syntactic relation itself, such as the subject-verb relation holding between *Heather* and *sings* in the construction grammar representation in Figure 10.4b. A second layer is the means of representing syntactic relations. Different syntactic theories use different means for representing abstract syntactic relations. For example, generative grammar uses constituency to represent syntactic relations, while Word Grammar (Hudson 1984) uses dependency. The third layer is the overt manifestation of syntactic relations, such as word order, case marking and indexation (agreement). We strip away the latter two layers in comparing construction grammar theories.

An important theoretical distinction is made regarding the internal structure of constructions (Kay 1997). The analysis of syntactic structure is unfortunately confounded by an ambiguity in much traditional syntactic terminology. We can illustrate this with the example of the term 'subject' in the Intransitive Clause construction in Figure 10.5, illustrated once again by the sentence *Heather sings*. The term 'subject' can mean one of two things. It can describe the **role** of a particular element of the construction, that is, a part-whole (meronomic) relation between the element labeled 'subject' in the Intransitive construction and the Intransitive construction as a whole. This is the sense in which one says that *Heather* is the 'subject of the Intransitive Clause' *Heather sings*. This part-whole relation is represented implicitly in (1) by the nesting of the box for *Heather* inside the box for the whole construction *Heather sings*.

(1)

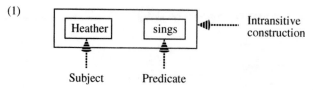

The subject role defines a grammatical category. But the term 'subject' can also describe a syntactic **relation** between one element of the construction – the subject – and another element of the construction – the Verb. This is the sense in which one says that *Heather* is the 'subject of the Verb' *sings*. In other words, the term 'subject' confounds two different types of relations in a construction: the role of the part in the whole, and the relation of one part to another part. The difference between the two is illustrated in (2):

(2)

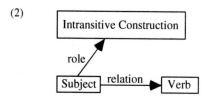

Different construction grammar theories develop different models of the internal relations between elements of constructions and components of constructions. These differences can be elucidated by answering question (ii):

(ii)   What sorts of syntactic relations are posited?

10.1.2   *The organization of constructional knowledge*

Constructions are not merely an unstructured list in construction grammar. Constructions form a **structured inventory** of a speaker's knowledge of the conventions of their language (Langacker 1987:63–76). This structured inventory is usually represented by construction grammarians in terms of a **taxonomic network** of constructions. Each construction constitutes a **node** in the taxonomic network of constructions.

A taxonomic relation describes a relationship of schematicity or generality between two constructions. For example, in §9.2 we noted the existence of a schematic idiom *The X-er, the Y-er*, and also of a substantive idiom *The bigger they come, the harder they fall*. We noted (following Fillmore et al. 1988) that the existence of the schematic idiom was not incompatible with the existence of the substantive idiom. A construction grammarian captures the fact that the substantive idiom is an instance of the schematic idiom by representing this relationship with a taxonomic link, as in (3):

(3)   [The X-er, the Y-er]

       |

    [The bigger they come, the harder they fall]

Any construction with unique idiosyncratic morphological, syntactic, lexical, semantic, pragmatic or discourse-functional properties must be represented as an independent node in the constructional network in order to capture a speaker's knowledge of their language. That is, any quirk of a construction is sufficient to represent that construction as an independent node. For example, the substantive idiom [SBJ *kick the habit*] must be represented as an independent node because it is semantically idiosyncratic. The more schematic but verb-specific construction [SBJ *kick* OBJ] must also be represented as an independent node in order to specify the verb's argument structure (or in older generative grammar terms, its subcategorization frame). Finally, the wholly schematic construction [SBJ TrVERB OBJ] is represented as an independent node.

These constructions are independent but related in terms of schematicity. For example, several levels of schematicity can be represented between the substantive idiomatic phrase *kick the habit* and the most schematic representation of the verb phrase in (4).

(4)   [VERBPHRASE]

       |

    [VERB OBJ]

       |

    [*kick* OBJ]

       |

    [*kick* [*the bucket*]]

Taxonomic relations between constructions allow construction grammarians to distinguish and yet relate the grammatical knowledge that is represented by different formal devices in the componential model of grammar. In (4), the top two levels in the taxonomy corresponds to the phrase structure rule VP → V NP in a componential model; the third level corresponds to the subcategorization frame *kick*: [_ NP]; and the lowest level an idiomatically combining expression *kick the habit*, which would be listed in the lexicon in the componential model. Thus, taxonomic relations complement the uniform representation of grammatical knowledge posited by construction grammar. Taxonomic relations allow a construction grammarian to distinguish different kinds of grammatical knowledge while acknowledging the existence of the syntax-lexicon continuum.

Of course, *kick the habit* has the same argument structure pattern as ordinary transitive uses of *kick*, and ordinary transitive uses of *kick* follow the same argument structure pattern as any transitive verb phrase. Each construction is simply an instance of the more schematic construction(s) in the chain [*kick the habit*] – [*kick* OBJ] – [TR VERB OBJ]. Thus, these constructions can be represented in a taxonomic hierarchy, as in (5):

(5)

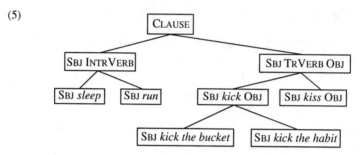

However, grammatical constructions do not form a strict taxonomic hierarchy. One of the simplifications in the hierarchy of constructions in (5) is the exclusion of tense-aspect-mood-negation marking, expressed by auxiliaries and verbal suffixes. If those parts of an utterance are included, then any construction in the hierarchy in (5) has multiple parents. For example, the sentence *I didn't sleep* is an instantiation of both the Intransitive Verb construction and the Negative construction, as illustrated in (6):

(6)

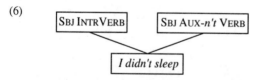

The sentence *I didn't sleep* thus has multiple parents in the taxonomy of constructions to which it belongs. This is a consequence of each construction being a **partial specification** of the grammatical structure of its daughter construction(s). For example, the Negative construction only specifies the structure associated with the subject, verb and auxiliary; it does not specify anything about a verb's object (if it has one), and so there is no representation of the object in the Negative construction in (6).

A construction typically provides only a partial specification of the structure of an utterance. For example, the Ditransitive construction [SBJ DITR VERB OBJ 1 OBJ 2], as in *He gave her a book*, only specifies the predicate and its arguments. It does not specify the order of elements, which can be different in different constructions: compare the Simple Declarative example just given above with the *It*-Cleft construction *It was a book that he gave her*. Nor does the Ditransitive construction specify the presence or position of other elements in an utterance, such as modal auxiliaries or negation, whether in a declarative sentence (where they are preverbal; see [7a]) or an interrogative sentence (where the auxiliary precedes the subject; see [7b]):

(7)   a. He **won't** give her the book.
        b. **Wouldn't** he give her the book?

Hence, any specific utterance's structure is specified by a number of distinct schematic constructions. Conversely, a schematic construction abstracts away from the unspecified structural aspects of the class of utterances it describes.

All versions of construction grammar employ taxonomic relations between constructions in the organization of grammatical knowledge. Constructions may be linked by relations other than taxonomic relations. A third question we may ask of different construction grammar theories is:

(iii)   What sorts of relations are found between constructions?

Finally, the taxonomic hierarchy appears to represent the same or similar information at different levels of schematicity in the hierarchy. For example, the fact that *the habit* is the direct object of *kick* in *kick the habit* is, or could be, represented in the idiom construction itself [*kick the habit*], or at any one or more of the schematic levels above the hierarchy, all the way up to [TR VERB OBJ]. Different theories of construction grammar have offered different answers to the question of how information is to be represented in the taxonomic hierarchy of constructions:

(iv)   How is information stored in the construction taxonomy?

In §10.2, the answers that various theories of construction grammar give to questions (i)–(iv) are presented.

10.2   Some current theories of construction grammar

This section surveys current theories of construction grammar in cognitive linguistics. All of the theories conform to the three essential principles of construction grammar described in chapter 9: the independent existence of constructions as symbolic units, the uniform representation of grammatical structures, and the taxonomic organization of constructions in a grammar. Of course, the exact means by which constructions and grammatical information are described in each theory, and the terminology used, varies. In each of the following subsections, the basic terminology used for the essential construction grammar features, and the approach to the four questions introduced above, will be presented for each theory. The different answers to the four questions bring out some current issues of debate in construction grammar. It should be noted that the different theories tend to focus on different issues, representing their distinctive positions vis-à-vis the other theories. For example, Construction Grammar explores syntactic relations and inheritance in detail; the Lakoff/Goldberg model focuses more on categorization relations between constructions; Cognitive Grammar focuses on semantic categories and relations; and Radical Construction Grammar focuses on syntactic categories and typological universals. Finally, the last three theories all endorse the usage-based model, which is described in chapter 11.

10.2.1 Construction Grammar (Fillmore, Kay et al.)

Construction Grammar (in capitals) is the theory developed by Fillmore, Kay and collaborators (Fillmore and Kay 1993; Kay and Fillmore 1999; Kay et al., in prep.). Construction Grammar is the variant of construction grammar (lower case) that most closely resembles certain formalist theories, in particular Head-driven Phrase Structure Grammar, which also calls itself a sign-based theory (i.e. a theory whose fundamental units are symbolic; Pollard and Sag 1993:15). Nevertheless, Construction Grammar conforms to the essential principles of construction grammar; Fillmore and Kay were among the first to articulate these principles (Fillmore, Kay and O'Connor 1988). Construction Grammar's distinguishing features are its elaborate, and still evolving, descriptive language for the internal structure of constructions, which can be only briefly sketched here (the version described here is essentially that of Kay and Fillmore 1999).

In Construction Grammar, there is a uniform representation of all grammatical properties, formal and functional, as **features** with **values**, such as **[cat v]** (syntactic category is Verb) and **[gf –subj]** (grammatical function is not Subject; Kay and Fillmore 1999). The value of a feature may itself be a list of features with their own values. The overall set of features with their values (including features) are more generally called **feature structures**. A simple example of a feature structure is the Verb Phrase construction (Kay and Fillmore 1999:8, Fig. 2). The Verb Phrase construction may be represented by brackets around the features and feature structures, as in (8), or by an equivalent box notation, as in (9):

(8)
$$\begin{bmatrix} [\text{cat v}] \\ \begin{bmatrix} [\text{role head}] \\ [\text{lex +}] \end{bmatrix} \\ \begin{bmatrix} [\text{role filler}] \\ [\text{loc +}] \\ [\text{gf } \neg\text{subj}] \end{bmatrix} + \end{bmatrix}$$

(9)

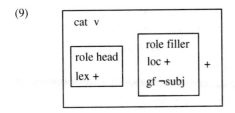

The equivalent diagrams in (8)–(9) are read as follows. The two inner boxes (feature structures) indicate the features of the verb and its complements (if any). The first box specifies that the first constituent of the VP construction is its head and that it must be lexical. For example, in *found her bracelet* the first constituent is the head of the VP and it is a word, not a larger constituent. The feature-value pair **[cat v]** above it is actually a simplification of a more complex feature structure (Kay and Fillmore 1999:9, n. 13), which specifies that the syntactic category of the head of the VP, in this case *found*, must be 'verb.' The second box specifies the complements, if any, of the verb. The + sign following the second box ('Kleene plus') indicates that there may be zero, one or more complements in the VP. In the VP *found her bracelet*, *her bracelet* is the one and only complement. In the VP construction, the complements are given the role value 'filler' (see below). The feature **[loc(al) +]** indicates that the complement is not extracted out of the VP. An example of an extracted, **[loc −]**, complement of *find* would be the question word *What* in the question *What did he find?*

The internal structure of a construction in Construction Grammar can be most easily understood by working from the parts to the whole. Minimal parts are words (or more precisely, morphemes; we will ignore this distinction for now). Each part has syntactic features, grouped under the feature **syn**, and semantic features, grouped under the feature **sem**. Construction Grammar separates the phonological features under a feature **phon** if the construction is substantive. The **syn** and **sem** features are themselves grouped under the feature **ss** (formerly **synsem**), which represents the symbolic structure of that part of the construction. The basic symbolic structure for Construction Grammar is given in (10):

(10)

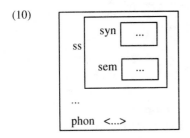

(i)   What is the status of the categories of the syntactic elements in construction grammar, given the existence of constructions?

The elements of constructions in Construction Grammar fall into a small set of atomic category types, such as **[cat v]** and **[gf sbj]**. That is, constructions in Construction Grammar can be described in terms of complex combinations of a set of primitive atomic units. This is a **reductionist** model of syntactic structure: the atomic units are primitive and the complex units are derived. Why are constructions not superfluous, then, in Construction Grammar? It is because specific constructions as a whole will contain syntactic and semantic information that is not found in the units of the construction that make up its parts. For example, the *What's X doing Y?* or WXDY construction (Kay and Fillmore 1999), illustrated by *What's this cat doing in here?*, possesses a number of syntactic and semantic properties not derivable from other constructions or the words in the construction. Its distinctive semantic property is the presupposition of incongruity of the event, which Kay and Fillmore argue cannot be derived by conversational implicature (1999:4). The WXDY construction is found only with the auxiliary *be* and the main verb *do* in the progressive (yet the progressive form here can be used with stative predicates), and excludes negation of *do* or *be*, all properties not predictable from the words, related constructions, or the constructional meaning (1999:4–7).

(ii)   What sorts of syntactic relations are posited?

The manner in which Construction Grammar assembles the parts of a construction into a whole uses three different sets of features: **role, val** and **rel**. The use of **role, val** and **rel** are illustrated in (11), based on the diagram contrasting roles and relations in (2) and using *Heather sings* as the example:

(11)

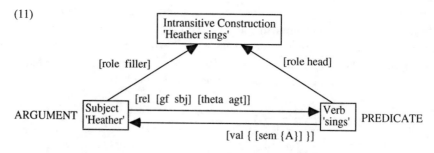

The **role** feature is used to represent the role of the syntactic element in the whole. The **role** feature is associated with each part of a complex construction and defines syntactic roles such as **mod**(ifier), **filler** and **head**. For instance, the subject-predicate (Intransitive) construction in (11), *Heather sings*, has the roles **head** for *sings* and **filler** for *Heather* (Kay and Fillmore 1999:13).

In addition to roles, each part of a complex construction has a relation to some other part of the construction in Construction Grammar. The relations between parts of a construction are all cast in terms of predicate-argument relations. For example, in *Heather sings*, *Heather* is the argument and *sings* is the predicate. The predicate-argument relation is symbolic, that is, both syntactic and semantic. Semantically a predicate is relational, that is, inherently relates to one or more additional concepts. In *Heather sings*, singing inherently involves a singer. The semantic arguments of a predicate are the concepts to which the predicate relates, in this case, Heather. Syntactically, a predicate requires a certain number of arguments in specific grammatical functions to it: *sing* requires an argument in the subject grammatical function. And syntactically, arguments are related to the predicate by a grammatical function: in this case, *Heather* is the subject of *sings*.

The remaining two features used to describe meronomic relations in Construction Grammar, **val** and **rel**, are used on predicates and arguments respectively. The **val** feature structure is used to indicate the relation of the predicate to its argument(s), and the **rel** feature structure is used to indicate the relation of each argument to its predicate. The **val** feature is found in the predicate's representation. The value of the **val** feature will be a set, indicated by the set notation {}; the **val** feature will be a set consisting of more than one member for predicates with multiple arguments. For the predicate *sings* in (11), the **val** set consists of just one member, namely the singer argument. Construction Grammar indicates the argument of a predicate by a cross-reference to the set of semantic arguments, which is part of the **sem** feature structure. In this example, we simply indicate that the singer argument corresponds to the argument A in the **sem** feature structure for *sings*.

The **rel** feature structure in the representation of the argument phrase indicates what grammatical function the argument is found in, and what semantic role it should have with respect to the predicate. The **rel** feature structure takes a syntactic feature, **gf** (for 'grammatical function'), and a semantic feature θ (for 'thematic role,' indicated as 'theta' in [11]).[2] In (11), the argument *Heather*'s **rel** feature structure has a grammatical function of 'subject' and a thematic role of 'agent.'

Finally, predicates and their arguments in a construction are matched with each other such that each argument's **rel** is matched up with one of the elements in the **val** list of its predicate. This is achieved through indexes on the relevant feature structures in the construction (not indicated in [11]). Kay and Fillmore call this matching principle the Valence Principle (Kay and Fillmore 1999:10).

---

[2] The version of the feature geometry given in Kay and Fillmore 1999:9, n. 10 includes another syntactic feature under **rel**, namely **case**.

Construction Grammar keeps distinct part-whole relations (**role**) and part-part relations (**val** and **rel**). Predicate-argument relations are independent of the role relations each predicate and argument has. For example, in both *The book is red* and *the red book*, *red* is the predicate and *(the) book* is the argument. However, in *The book is red*, *be red* is in the head role while in *the red book*, *book* is in the head role. Furthermore, Construction Grammar keeps distinct the **val** feature for predicates and the **rel** feature for arguments. The reason that **val** and **rel** are kept separate is that a single element in a construction can be a predicate taking arguments and at the same time be an argument for another predicate. For example, in *You should read this*, the element *read* is a predicate taking the argument *this*, but is itself an argument of the predicate *should* (Kay 1997).

The meronomic relations of a construction in Construction Grammar are analyzed in terms largely familiar from other syntactic theories (head, modifier, predicate, argument), although they are defined somewhat differently. In Construction Grammar, predicate-argument relations between elements are syntactic and semantic, and they are clearly distinguished from syntactic roles held by elements in the construction as a whole.

(iii)   **What sorts of relations are found between constructions?**

(iv)   **How is grammatical information stored in the construction taxonomy?**

We address both of these questions together because the answer to (iii) in Construction Grammar is dependent on the answer to (iv).

Construction Grammar, like all construction grammars, allows taxonomic relations between constructions. In examining a construction taxonomy such as those illustrated in (4)–(5), it can be noted that what is more or less the same information is represented at multiple levels in the taxonomy. For example, the taxonomy in (4) appears to represent the fact that the object follows the verb at each of the lower three levels. Redundant representation of information need not be the case, however. One can represent the fact that the object has the grammatical function **[gf obj]** just once, at the highest possible level in the taxonomy – in (4), the [VERB OBJ] level. The constructions at the lower taxonomic levels will then **inherit** this property by virtue of being an instance of (an instance of) the [VERB OBJ] construction. For example, the idiom *kick the habit* does not separately and redundantly represent the fact that *the habit* bears the object grammatical function to *kick*; it inherits this feature from the [VERB OBJ] construction.

Following Goldberg (1995:73–74), we will describe a model in which information is represented nonredundantly and is inherited as a **complete inheritance** model. Construction Grammar is a complete inheritance model (Kay and Fillmore 1999:7–8, 30–31). That is, Construction Grammar represents information only once in the construction taxonomy, at the highest (most schematic) level possible.

A consequence of the complete inheritance model is that some constructions may not be pairings of form and meaning, contrary to the general principle given in §10.1 that constructions are symbolic (Fillmore 1999:121, n. 11). Consider, for example, the following examples of constructions in English (Fillmore 1999:126, 122, 123, 121):

(12)	Did you understand what I said?	*Polarity question (positive)*
(13)	Boy, was I stupid!	*Subject-auxiliary inversion exclamation*
(14)	Don't you even touch that!	*Emphatic negative imperative*
(15)	May I live long enough to see the end of this job!	*Blessings-Wishes-Curses*

All of these constructions have in common the syntactic property that the auxiliary verb precedes the subject argument. In a complete inheritance model, one would posit a Subject-Auxiliary Inversion (SAI) construction possessing this syntactic property, which would be inherited by the constructions in (12)–(15) (Fillmore 1999). However, there is no common semantic property that is inherited in all of these constructions. Hence the schematic SAI construction will lack any semantic specification, and thus will be a purely syntactic construction. Nevertheless, this is only a limiting case in a model of grammar that is organized in terms of symbolic units.

In a complete inheritance model, a construction can inherit the feature structures of its parent constructions; this is the significance of the taxonomic relation between constructions in this model. Complete inheritance is an all-or-none relation, and so the categories defined by a construction taxonomy in Construction Grammar are classical (see chapter 4).

Kay and Fillmore also allow parts of a construction to inherit feature structures from another construction (Kay and Fillmore 1999:18; see also Fillmore 1999; Kay 2002). Kay and Fillmore argue that the nonsubject WH-question construction, instantiated in *Why did she leave him?*, is made up of a left-isolated (traditionally called 'fronted') WH question word and an inverted clause. Thus, the nonsubject WH-question construction as a whole inherits the feature structure of the schematic left-isolation (LI) construction, while the non-left-isolated part of the construction inherits the feature structures of the SAI construction:

(16) *Nonsubject WH-question construction*:

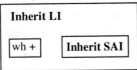

In other words, parts of constructions can be children of other constructions, whose feature structures they inherit. Thus, Construction Grammar models meronomic relations between constructions by taxonomic relations between a parent construction and the corresponding parts of other constructions.

10.2.2   Lakoff (1987) and Goldberg (1995)

Lakoff (1987) develops a variant of construction grammar in his important study of the *There*-construction in English. Lakoff's analysis emphasizes the complex, nonclassical structure of the category of *There*-constructions, in keeping with his interest in prototypicality and radial category structure. Lakoff's student Goldberg also adopts Lakoff's emphasis on constructional relations in her analysis of argument structure constructions (Goldberg 1995). Goldberg also addresses the other issues raised above, either explicitly or implicitly, in the context of analyzing argument structure constructions. But the chief distinguishing characteristic of Lakoff's and Goldberg's version of construction grammar is the exploitation of nonclassical categorization in the analysis of relations between constructions.

(i)   **What is the status of the categories of the syntactic elements in construction grammar, given the existence of constructions?**

Space prevents us from examining Goldberg's model of argument linking in detail; we touch only on those topics relevant to the representation of constructions. Goldberg argues that one should analyze participant roles in complex events as derived from the event itself, following the principles of frame semantics (see chapter 2). For example, the participant roles for *rob/steal* are 'robber' and 'victim' (Goldberg 1995:47–48). This analysis of participant roles is an example of a nonreductionist representation: the complex event or situation is treated as the primitive unit of semantic representation, and the definitions of the roles in the events are derived from the situation as a whole.

In contrast, Goldberg's analysis of syntactic roles and relations in argument structure constructions is reductionist. As in Construction Grammar, Goldberg employs a set of atomic primitive grammatical relations such as subject and object, and primitive syntactic categories such as verb.

(ii)   **What sorts of syntactic relations are posited?**

This question has not figured centrally in Lakoff's and Goldberg's theories. In Lakoff's study of *There*-constructions, he represents constructions with the following parameters of form (Lakoff 1987:489), which allow for relations between syntactic elements as well as relations between the elements and the construction as a whole:

- Syntactic elements (e.g. clause, noun phrases, verb etc.)
- Lexical elements (e.g. *here, there, come, go, be* etc.)
- Syntactic conditions (e.g. linear order of elements, grammatical relations such as subject and object, optionality of elements etc.)
- Phonological conditions (e.g. presence or absence of stress, vowel length etc.)

Goldberg's monograph analyzes argument structure constructions, focusing on relations between constructions (see immediately below), the semantics of argument structure, and the linking to syntactic roles. Because of the ambiguity of terms such as 'subject' between role and relation interpretations, Goldberg's representation of the syntactic structure of argument structure constructions (e.g. Goldberg 1995:50–55) is compatible with either interpretation.

(iii)   What sorts of relations are found between constructions?

Schematic constructions in taxonomies represent a categorization of utterances in accordance with certain of their grammatical and semantic properties. As such, it might be expected that construction taxonomies would display some of the same properties as conceptual categories, properties that we have discussed in chapters 4, 5 and 8. Two of the most central properties of category structure are polysemy and prototype-extension structure. Both of these properties are found in construction taxonomies.

Lakoff and Goldberg discuss a variety of relationships (links) among constructions, including taxonomic relations (Lakoff 1987, Appendix 3; Goldberg 1995:74–81). One of the links Goldberg discusses, the instance link (1995:79–81), corresponds to the taxonomic links described above. A second type of link, the subpart link, corresponds to a meronomic link: 'one construction is a proper subpart of another construction and exists independently' (1995:78). This formulation appears to represent the meronomic relation as a distinct type of link, unlike Construction Grammar where a proper subpart of one construction may be an instance of another construction. Elsewhere, Goldberg describes all links as inheritance links (1995:74–75), but the direction of inheritance in her diagrams is the opposite to that in Construction Grammar (see 1995:80).

Goldberg also proposes a third type of construction link, the **polysemy** link, for subtypes of a construction that are identical in syntactic specification but different in their semantics. For example, Goldberg argues that the ditransitive construction [S BJ VERB OBJ I OBJ 2] has a general meaning involving a transfer of possession of OBJ 2 to OBJ I. However, there are semantic variations on this syntactically unified construction (1995:38, Fig. 2.2):

(17)   *SBJ causes OBJ2 to receive OBJ1:*
        Joe gave Sally the ball.
(18)   *Conditions of satisfaction imply SBJ causes OBJ2 to receive OBJ1:*
        Joe promised Bob a car.
(19)   *SBJ enables OBJ2 to receive OBJ1:*
        Joe permitted Chris an apple.
(20)   *SBJ causes OBJ2 not to receive OBJ1:*
        Joe refused Bob a cookie.
(21)   *SBJ intends to cause OBJ2 to receive OBJ1:*
        Joe baked Bob a cake.
(22)   *SBJ acts to cause OBJ2 to receive OBJ1 at some future date:*
        Joe bequeathed Bob a fortune.

Goldberg treats the first sense (the one in [17]) as the central, prototypical sense and the other senses as extensions from the prototype. The extensions from the prototype inherit the syntactic construction schema from the prototype.

Goldberg does not explicitly argue for a schema subsuming all of the senses of the ditransitive construction. However, inheritance is a characteristic of taxonomic links, so Goldberg's analysis suggests that there is a schematic syntactic ditransitive construction, even if there is not a semantic schema (Goldberg does not propose a schematic meaning of the ditransitive). In other words, there is a syntactic construction schema that has as instantiations the six senses in (17)–(22), and the actual successful causation meaning in (17) is the prototype for the ditransitive construction.

In fact, however, the syntactic schemas for the six subsenses are all slightly different, because each sense has a distinct subclass of verbs associated with it (Croft 2003a). Thus, each subsense has associated with it a syntactic schema specifying the verbs or verb classes that each subsense applies to. In general, semantic differences in the grammatical constructions such as the ditransitive or the perfect are likely to have syntactic consequences, and so distinct constructional senses are likely to also have distinct syntactic schemas.

It is still possible to posit a superordinate ditransitive construction specifying what is common to all of the subordinate constructions. Such a construction would have a syntactic schema such as [SBJ DITR V OBJ1 OBJ2]. The DITR V category in the ditransitive construction would be a polysemous category, that is, there are no necessary and sufficient conditions to describe all and only the ditransitive verbs in the language. But as we saw in chapter 3, this is true of many linguistic categories, and so it is not surprising that a syntactic category turns out to be the same. Likewise, the semantics of the superordinate ditransitive construction would also be polysemous: although there would be a necessary condition that some modulated transfer of possession is involved (actual, intended, future etc.), this condition is not a sufficient condition defining the ditransitive construction's use.

The most important property of the polysemy analysis is that one construction sense is central and another is an extension from it. A clear case of extension from a central sense in constructions is a **metaphorical** extension, another type of link proposed by Goldberg, following Lakoff (1987) in his analysis of *There*-constructions.

Lakoff argues that many of the extensions of the central *There*-construction involve metaphorical extension. For example, the Perceptual Deictic *There*-construction, illustrated in (23), involves a number of metaphorical extensions from the Central Deictic *There*-construction illustrated in (24) (Lakoff 1987:511, 509):

(23)   a. Here comes the beep.
        b. There's the beep.

(24)   There's Harry.

The Perceptual Deictic describes the impending (23a) or just-realized (23b) activation of a nonvisual perceptual stimulus, for example an alarm clock that is about to go off. To express this meaning, the Presentational Deictic uses the metaphor of deictic motion of a physical entity in physical space. The extension of the Central Deictic to the Perceptual Deictic requires the following metaphorical mappings (Lakoff 1987:511):

(25)   *Perceptual Deictic domain*   *Central Deictic domain*
        NONVISUAL PERCEPTUAL SPACE   IS   PHYSICAL SPACE
        PERCEPTS   ARE   ENTITIES
        REALIZED   IS   DISTAL
        SOON-TO-BE-REALIZED   IS   PROXIMAL
        ACTIVATION   IS   MOTION

A metaphorical extension (or any other semantic extension, for that matter) need not establish a schema of which the basic construction and the metaphorical extension are both instantiations. Lakoff's based-on link, like Goldberg's polysemy link, involves inheritance of both syntactic and semantic properties, and so is not unlike a taxonomic link. Lakoff, however, does not posit a superordinate Deictic *There*-construction schema. On the other hand, Goldberg argues that there is a superordinate schema subsuming both a central construction and its metaphorical extension (Goldberg 1995:81–89).

(iv)   How is information stored in the construction taxonomy?

Goldberg and Lakoff differ from Construction Grammar in allowing **normal** (or **default**) **inheritance** (Goldberg 1995:73, citing Flickinger, Pollard and Wasow 1985). Normal inheritance is a method for accommodating the fact that much of what we know about a category is not true of every instance of a category. For example, we know that most birds fly, to the point that if we hear reference to 'a bird,' we will assume that it can fly. Of course, if we are further informed that the bird in question is an ostrich or a penguin, or that it has a broken wing or it is dead, we would cancel that assumption. One model for representing this information is to store the information FLIES with the category BIRD, instead of with the many instances of bird species and individual birds that can fly. The property FLIES is inherited in those cases, but inheritance can be blocked if it conflicts with information in the more specific case, such as penguins, ostriches, a bird with a broken wing, a dead bird and so on. This is normal inheritance.[3]

Lakoff uses normal inheritance in his analysis of *There*-constructions. Normal inheritance is part of Lakoff's based-on link between constructions (Lakoff 1987:508); so does Goldberg (1995:74). For example, Lakoff argues that the Presentational Deictic *There*-construction in (26) is based on the Central Deictic *There*-construction in (27) (Lakoff 1987:520, 482):

(26)   There in the alley had gathered a large crowd of roughnecks.
(27)   There's Harry with the red jacket on.

One of the properties of the Central Deictic is that the verb must occur in the simple present tense, because the semantics of the Central Deictic is to point out a referent in the speech act situation (Lakoff 1987:490–91). The Presentational Deictic is based on the Central Deictic but also specifies that the verb may appear in a variety of tenses as expressed in auxiliaries (Lakoff 1987:521). This specification blocks the inheritance of the simple present tense requirement from the Central Deictic.

Goldberg also allows for the representation of information at all levels in the taxonomic hierarchy of constructions. Goldberg describes such a model as a **full-entry** model (Goldberg 1995:73–74). She gives an example of a situation that virtually requires a full-entry representation, namely a conflict in multiple inheritance. If there are multiple parents, then there will be inheritance from multiple 'parents' in the taxonomic network. It may be that the multiple parent nodes have conflicting specifications of some properties, and this conflict has to be resolved for the specific instance. Normal inheritance cannot handle this problem. Normal inheritance adjudicates a conflict in specification between parent and child nodes in the taxonomy (the child always wins). In multiple inheritance the conflict is between the two parent nodes, and there is no principled way to choose which parent would win in a conflict.

---

[3] Construction Grammar eschews default inheritance; instead, default values are left unspecified and default constructions fill in unspecified values (Fillmore 1999:115, n. 3; Kay 2002:470).

Goldberg gives an example of a conflict in multiple inheritance with the resultative construction, illustrated in (28), and the verb-particle construction, illustrated in (29) (Goldberg 1995:97–98):

(28)   a. She hammered the metal flat.
        b. The metal was flat.

(29)   a. He cleaned the mess up.
        b. He cleaned up the mess.

Goldberg notes (following Bolinger 1971) that some resultatives allow for word order variation of the same type as is found in the verb-particle construction:

(30)   a. Break the cask open.
        b. Break open the cask.
        c. The cask is open.

Goldberg proposes that the class of resultatives illustrated with *break open* in (30) are instances of the verb-particle construction as well as of the resultative construction. However, the two parent constructions have conflicting properties. While the verb-particle construction allows word order variation (compare [29]), the resultative construction does not:

(31)   *She hammered flat the metal.

In this case, *break open* inherits the word order variation of the verb-particle construction, not the fixed word order of the resultative. Conversely, while the resultative allows for a simple predication (compare [28b]), the verb-particle construction does not:

(32)   *The mess is up.

In this case, *break open* inherits the predicability of resultatives, not the ungrammatical predication of the verb-particle construction.

The two parent constructions of (30) give conflicting specifications as to whether the word order change is acceptable or not, and whether the predication of the result phrase is acceptable or not. Goldberg suggests that, in this case, the information about the specific construction types is provided in the specific construction, even if it is redundant with the information contained in (one of) the parent constructions; then the problem of how to resolve the conflict of multiple inheritance does not arise. In other words, Goldberg argues that a full-entry model in this situation is desirable.

Is full entry plausible when the information could be represented nonredundantly by inheritance? It might appear to the reader that, a priori, the inheritance model is to be preferred over the full-entry model for reasons of parsimony.

However, most cognitive linguists argue that a cognitively based grammar should not be constructed in an a priori fashion, because grammatical knowledge is a psychological phenomenon. Clearly, speakers do not store a representation of every utterance they have ever used or heard. Speakers form schemas that generalize over categories of utterances heard and used. But it does not necessarily follow from this observation that speakers store every piece of grammatical knowledge only once. It does not even necessarily follow that actual speakers form a more schematic category for every linguistic generalization that clever linguists have found (see Croft 1998c and §11.2.5).

The principle that information should not be stored redundantly is motivated by the desire for parsimony in representation. But parsimony in representation simply pushes complexity to the processes of language use. A complete inheritance model maximizes **storage parsimony**, that is, it minimizes the redundant storage of information. A complete inheritance model thus requires maximum on-line processing in order to access and use the information in the production and comprehension of utterances (see Goldberg 1995:74; Barsalou 1992b:180–81). A full-entry model maximizes **computing parsimony**: as much information as possible is stored in multiple places, so that on-line computation is minimized during production and comprehension (Barsalou 1992b:180–81; see §§12.1, 12.2.5).

On the whole, the psychological evidence suggests that 'concepts and properties in human knowledge are organized with little concern for elegance and [storage] parsimony' (Barsalou 1992:180). This does not mean that full entry is to be preferred in all situations, however: such a model is just as a priori as the inheritance model. Instead, Goldberg, following Langacker (1987, chapter 10) and other cognitive linguists, advocates a **usage-based model**, in which patterns of language use are taken as evidence for the independent representation of grammatical information (see especially Goldberg 1995:133–39). In chapter 11, we will examine some suggested criteria for positing schematic constructions and the degree to which information is stored redundantly in the mind.

10.2.3 Cognitive Grammar as a construction grammar

Cognitive Grammar is a detailed, carefully worked out theory of syntax and semantics (Langacker 1987, 1991a, 1991b, 1999, inter alia; see also Taylor 2002). Langacker's seminal volume (Langacker 1987) gives an abstract exposition of the framework, and although the word 'construction' rarely appears there, and a completely different set of terms is used, Cognitive Grammar's model of syntactic representation is a construction grammar model. The distinguishing feature of Cognitive Grammar as a construction grammar is its emphasis on symbolic and semantic definitions of theoretical constructs traditionally analyzed as purely syntactic.

Langacker defines a grammar as a structured inventory of conventional linguistic units (1987:57). Most conventional linguistic units are symbolic units, with their two halves, form and meaning.[4] Like Construction Grammar, Cognitive Grammar assumes the symbolic character of the linguistic **sign** (to use the Saussurean term). Cognitive Grammar, also like Construction Grammar, nevertheless emphasizes a uniform representation of constructional form and function. Langacker argues that all semantic, pragmatic and discourse-functional properties are ultimately conceptual, a part of what he calls semantic space, which he describes as 'the multifaceted field of conceptual potential within which thought and conceptualization unfold' (1987:76; see chapter 1).

In the Cognitive Grammar representation of a construction, the symbolic unit itself must link the form (signifier) and meaning (signified) of the construction. Langacker describes the link as a **symbolic correspondence**. Langacker describes the functional structure (the signified) of the construction as the **semantic pole** of a symbolic unit, and its formal structure (signifier) as the **phonological pole**. The term 'phonological pole' may sound odd: syntax at least is not 'phonological,' particularly with respect to schematic constructions. However, Langacker argues that a schema such as NOUN in the description of a construction should be thought of as phonologically as well as lexically schematic: the schema ranges over possible nouns, and those nouns are all phonologically contentful, even if their exact phonological form cannot be specified schematically.[5]

(i)   **What is the status of the categories of the syntactic elements in construction grammar, given the existence of constructions?**

Cognitive Grammar argues that fundamental syntactic categories such as Noun, Verb, Subject and Object are abstract (schematic) semantic construals of the conceptual content of their denotations. Thus, fundamental syntactic categories

---

[4] Langacker also allows for independent phonological and semantic units, but not independent syntactic units.

[5] Cognitive Grammar and Construction Grammar, like Head-driven Phrase Structure Grammar (Pollard and Sag 1993), eschews the use of phonologically 'null' or 'empty' elements (see also Kay 2002). Construction Grammar replaces the concept of a null element with the concept of **null instantiation**, that is, some constructions have a feature that indicates that there is a (semantic) argument that is not formally instantiated (Fillmore 1986b; Fillmore and Kay 1993, chapter 7). Fillmore and Kay distinguish three types of null instantiation: definite (equivalent to null anaphora), indefinite (as in *The dog ate*) and free (corresponding to unspecified adjuncts). Fillmore and Kay argue that null instantiation is associated with either constructions or individual words; Croft (2001:275–80) argues that instantiation is associated with constructions only.

have an essentially semantic basis, but in terms of the construal of experience, not in terms of semantic classes. As described in chapter 3, Langacker has developed semantic construal analyses of a wide range of syntactic categories, including parts of speech, grammatical roles (subject and object), the count/mass distinction, various English tense/aspect inflections and auxiliaries, the English possessives -'s and *of*, ergativity, English complementizers and complement types, Cora locatives and the Yuman auxiliary (see Langacker 1987, 1991a, b, 1999).

One question that can be raised about the Cognitive Grammar analysis of grammatical categories is the relationship between the abstract semantic construal definitions and the variation in both formal distribution and semantic polysemy of such categories across languages. It has been suggested that cross-linguistic variation in putatively universal semantic categories can be accommodated in terms of conventionalized construal: the same semantic category is found everywhere, but the construal of specific experiences as belonging to the semantic category is language-specific:

> When we use a particular construction or grammatical morpheme, we thereby select a particular image to structure the conceived situation for communicative purposes. Because languages differ in their grammatical structure, they differ in the imagery that speakers employ when conforming to linguistic convention. (Langacker 1991b:12)

For example, the English root *sick* is construed as an adjective or atemporal relation, that is, summarily scanned (see §3.2), and requires a copula verb *be* for predication/sequential scanning; but the equivalent Russian root *bol(e)*- is construed as a verb (sequentially scanned) and requires an adjectival derivational suffix to be construed atemporally. But it is not clear that there is any difference between positing a universal semantic category plus language-specific conventionalized construal for specific cases on the one hand, and positing a polysemous category with a semantic prototype and language-specific semantic extensions on the other.

(ii)   What sorts of syntactic relations are posited?

Cognitive Grammar takes a more radical departure from the more familiar analyses of relations among parts of a construction (Langacker 1987, chapter 8). The Cognitive Grammar concept of **valence**, like that of Construction Grammar, is symbolic. Unlike valence in Construction Grammar, however, valence in Cognitive Grammar is gradient. We will begin by looking at a straightforward predicate-argument relation, where the Cognitive Grammar and Construction Grammar notions of valence coincide, and then examine the extension of valence in Cognitive Grammar to other semantic relations.

In a sentence such as *Heather sings*, *sings* is a predicate because it is relational. The relationality of *sings* is due to the fact that singing requires a singer. Hence, the semantic structure for *sings* includes a schematic singer as a **substructure**. In *Heather sings*, *Heather* is an argument: it is nonrelational and it fills the role of the singer for *sings*. *Heather* is nonrelational because the concept of a person does not presuppose another concept. Langacker's term for an argument filling the role of a predicate is that the argument **elaborates** the relevant substructure of the predicate. The substructure that can be elaborated by an argument is an **elaboration site** or **e-site** (Langacker 1987:304). These relations are illustrated in (33):

(33)

As we noted in §10.2.1, a unit in a construction may be simultaneously a predicate and an argument, as is *read* in *You should read this article*. How is this possible? It is because the event of reading elaborates a substructure of the modality expressed by *should*, and the thing read, *this article*, elaborates a substructure of the event of reading. Hence, predicate and argument status – valence – is relative: predicate and argument status depend on what two semantic structures are being compared.

Not only is valence relative, it is gradient. In a sentence such as (34), *I* and *what I am reading* are traditionally analyzed as **complements** of *read* while *on the train* is an **adjunct** to *read* (we ignore the progressive *be* in this example):

(34)   I was reading this on the train.

Complements are arguments of a predicate: reading inherently involves a reader and a thing read. Adjuncts are predicates and their head is the argument: *on the train* inherently involves a Figure (the event) whose location is described by the spatial relation. Hence, *read* elaborates a substructure of *on the train*.

But this description is an oversimplification. Reading is a localizable activity: reading takes place in a location, as well as involving a reader and a thing read. This is not true of all predicates; one cannot say for instance that **John was widowed on the train*. Hence the location of the reading event is a substructure of the semantic structure of *read*, and *on the train* also elaborates that substructure of *read*. The solution to this apparent paradox is that the substructure of *read* elaborated by *on the train* is much less salient in the characterization of the reading event than the substructures of *read* elaborated by *I* and *this*. Conversely, the substructure of *on the train* that is elaborated by *read* is highly salient in the characterization of the spatial relation. *On the train* is more of an adjunct of *read* than a complement because *read* elaborates a salient substructure of *on the train*, whereas *on the train* elaborates a not very salient substructure of *read*. The relative strength of the two relations is illustrated in (35):

(35)

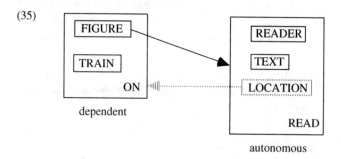

Langacker use the terms **autonomous** and **dependent** to describe the gradient reinterpretation of the predicate-argument distinction: 'one structure, D, is dependent on the other, A, to the extent that A constitutes an elaboration of a salient substructure within D' (1987:300). Conversely, A is autonomous relative to D to the extent to which it does not elaborate a salient substructure of D. In (35), *on the train* is dependent on *read* because *read* elaborates the highly salient figure role of the locative relation *on the train*. Conversely, *read* is autonomous relative to *on the train* because *on the train* elaborates only the not very salient substructure of the location of the reading event.

The Cognitive Grammar analysis of concepts of 'head,' 'modifier' and so on are both similar and different from the analysis in Construction Grammar. In Construction Grammar, the roles represent a relation between the parts of a construction and the whole, and are defined syntactically. In Cognitive Grammar, the analogous concepts also represent a relation between the parts of a construction and the whole, but they are defined semantically and symbolically.

Cognitive Grammar defines a semantic relation between part and whole as the **profile determinant**: the profile determinant is the part of the construction whose semantic profile the whole construction 'inherits' (Langacker 1987:289). The profile is the concept designated by the unit, against the background knowledge presupposed by that concept (see chapter 2). Langacker combines the concepts of profile determinacy and autonomy/dependence to define 'head,' 'complement' and 'modifier' in the intuitively expected way (1987:309). A head is a dependent predication that is a profile determinant; a complement is an autonomous predication that is not a profile determinant; and a modifier is a dependent predication that is not a profile determinant.

(iii)   What sorts of relations are found between constructions?

Langacker advocates what he calls a unified approach to categorization (1987, chapter 10). A category has a nonclassical structure, in that there is typically a prototypical member or set of members, and nonprototypical members are categorized by extension from the prototypical members. However, it is also possible for there to exist a schema subsuming both prototype and extension, which has a classical category structure, with necessary and sufficient conditions specifying its instances. Langacker's model of categorization is of course applied also to constructions. Hence, for Langacker, as for Lakoff and Goldberg, one may have both construction schemas and also nonclassical relations between constructions, such as prototype-extension relations, including metaphorical extensions.

(iv)   How is information stored in the construction taxonomy?

Cognitive Grammar is a usage-based model, in which the establishment of schematic constructions is the result of language use as described briefly in §10.2.2 and in more detail in chapter 11.

10.2.4 Radical Construction Grammar

Radical Construction Grammar (Croft 2001) was developed to account for typological variation in a construction grammar framework, and to address basic questions of syntactic argumentation. Radical Construction Grammar adopts the nonclassical category structure and the usage-based model of the Lakoff-Goldberg theory and Cognitive Grammar. Radical Construction Grammar takes a thoroughly nonreductionist approach to constructions, and rejects autonomous syntactic relations between elements in a construction. Radical Construction Grammar adopts the usage-based model, and brings in the semantic map model and the notion of a syntactic space from typological theory to provide organizing principles for constructions.

(i)   What is the status of the categories of the syntactic elements, given the existence of constructions?

The standard analysis of meronomic relations between syntactic structures is reductionist (§11.2.1): a construction such as the intransitive or transitive construction is made up of parts, and those parts are themselves defined independently of the constructions in which they occur. For example, various clausal constructions have verbs, which are analyzed as belonging to the same part of speech no matter what construction they occur in. This analysis is motivated in part because they have the same inflections (present in third person singular -*s* and non-third person singular zero, past in -*ed* or other allomorphs):

(36)   Present third singular:
     a. *Intransitive:* Toni dances.
     b. *Transitive:* Toni plays badminton.

(37)   Present non-third singular:
     a. *Intransitive:* We dance-Ø.
     b. *Transitive:* We play-Ø badminton.

(38)   Past:
     a. *Intransitive:* We danc**ed**.
     b. *Transitive:* We play**ed** badminton.

In other words, the same units occur as the parts of many different constructions. Ultimately, the decomposition of a construction will lead to a set of basic or primitive elements that cannot be analyzed further, and out of which constructions are built. These atomic elements include syntactic categories such as Verb or Noun and relations such as Subject or Object and so on. A model of grammatical structure of this type is a reductionist model: more complex structures are treated as built up out of primitive and ultimately atomic units. In the example given here, the atomic units are the basic categories and relations.

The reductionist model has a significant shortcoming: it does not capture certain empirical facts about the distribution of words. For example, while many English verbs occur in either the transitive or intransitive constructions, many others do not:

(39)   a. Judith danced.
     b. Judith danced a kopanica.

(40)   a. Judith slept.
     b. *Judith slept bed.

(41)   a. *Judith found.
     b. Judith found a 20 dollar bill.

One solution is to divide Verbs into Transitive Verbs and Intransitive Verbs. If so, then a decision must be made about verbs such as *dance*, which occur in both constructions: do they simultaneously belong to both subclasses? or do they form a third distinct class? One effect of dividing Verbs into Transitive Verbs and Intransitive Verbs is that one is essentially defining the categories in terms of the construction they occur in, Transitive or Intransitive. These problems are multiplied in cross-linguistic comparison, where the variation found is more extreme (Croft 2001).

One can deal with such problems in the reductionist model by adding syntactic features that prevent certain category members from occurring in the unacceptable constructions, as in (40b) and (41a). Again, the effect is that one is introducing a feature that specifies the category in terms of the construction it occurs in/does not occur in (in this case, Transitive and/or Imperative and/or VP Conjunction).

Radical Construction Grammar takes a different approach to the relations of constructions to their parts. It takes the constructions as the basic or primitive elements of syntactic representation and defines categories in terms of the constructions they occur in. For example, the elements of the Intransitive construction are defined as Intransitive Subject and Intransitive Verb, and the categories are defined as those words or phrases that occur in the relevant role in the Intransitive construction. In other words, Radical Construction Grammar rejects the existence of atomic schematic units (see Table 9.2 in §9.4), because atomic schematic units are defined independently of constructions. This differentiates Radical Construction Grammar from reductionist theories.

Radical Construction Grammar is a **nonreductionist** model because it takes the whole complex structure as basic and defines the parts in terms of their occurrence in a role in the complex structure. In effect, Radical Construction Grammar takes to its logical conclusion one of the strategies for handling these problems in reductionist theories, namely the subdividing of classes and the employment of syntactic features that essentially specify which constructions a particular word or phrase occurs in (see Croft 2001, chapter 1).

Constructions are individuated like any other conceptual object, by categorization. Constructions possess formal features, including word order, patterns of contiguity and specific morphemes (or very small classes of morphemes) in particular roles. Constructions are also symbolic units, and typically possess discrete meanings. Radical Construction Grammar assumes a nonclassical category model, and allows for prototypes and extensions of constructions, as well as the possibility of gradience between construction types.

(ii)   What sorts of syntactic relations are posited?

Radical Construction Grammar, like Construction Grammar and Cognitive Grammar, represents the role of a part of a construction in the whole construction. Radical Construction Grammar differs from Construction Grammar in that it defines relations between parts of a construction in purely semantic terms, that is, there are no syntactic relations in Radical Construction Grammar.

One motivation for the Radical Construction Grammar analysis is that relations between syntactic elements are not strictly necessary in a construction grammar framework, from the point of view of language comprehension. Consider the phrase *the song*, illustrated in (42) below with the semantic relation between [DEF] and [SONG] now indicated by a link (labeled **r**):

(42)

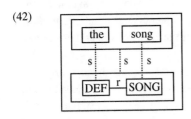

If a hearer recognizes the phrase *the song* as an instance of the construction [[DEF/*the*] [THING/*Noun*]] – that is, the hearer can retrieve the semantic structure of the whole construction, and identifies the elements of the construction (i.e. the words *the* and *song*), and can identify the corresponding components of the semantic pole (i.e. [DEF] and [THING]), then the hearer can identify the semantic relation **r** by virtue of the semantic relation between [DEF] and [THING] in the semantic pole of the construction. Hence the hearer need not rely on any syntactic relation between *the* and *song*.

In Radical Construction Grammar, the various morphosyntactic properties that are taken to express syntactic relations in other theories – case marking, agreement, adpositions, word order, contiguity and so on – are interpreted as expressing the symbolic links from the elements in the phonological pole of the construction to their corresponding components in the semantic pole of the construction. The evidence for this analysis of symbolic relations would take us too far afield (see Croft 2001, chapters 5–6). We mention here only two cross-linguistically widespread phenomena arguing against syntactic relations. The relationship between putative syntactic relations and semantic relations is noniconic in many cases (Croft 2001:206–20). This fact defeats attempts to construct general mapping relations between syntactic structures and semantic structures; if there are no syntactic relations, this problem disappears. More seriously, the absence of elements allegedly related syntactically, such as the absence of controllers of agreement, and the absence of the morphosyntactic expression of the alleged syntactic relation (Croft 2001:226–33), makes it impossible to represent syntactic relations without ad hoc devices. Again, if syntactic relations are abandoned, this problem disappears.

The morphosyntactic properties that appear to indicate syntactic relations in fact aid the hearer in identifying the role that construction elements fill in the meaning of the construction as a whole (Croft 2001:233–36). Also, the combination of morphosyntactic properties in an utterance taken as a whole aid the hearer in identifying a construction (Croft 2001:236–37). For example, the Gestalt combination of auxiliary *be*, the past participle form of the verb, and the preposition *by*, in the proper syntactic combination with the subject phrase, the verb and the oblique phrase, uniquely identifies the passive construction, while the individual elements identify the action (verb inflection and position after auxiliary), the agent (*by* plus oblique phrase) and patient (subject position). In other words, the syntactic properties that seemingly encode syntactic relations in fact encode symbolic relations, between individual elements and components of the construction and between the constructional form as a whole and its meaning.

Thus, in Radical Construction Grammar, concepts such as 'head,' 'argument' and 'adjunct' that are syntactically defined in other theories must be given semantic definitions, as in Cognitive Grammar (Croft 2001, chapter 7). Moreover, such definitions must ideally be defined relative to constructions, rather than individual components. For example, Croft argues that the Cognitive Grammar concept of profile determinacy (§10.2.3), which is defined in Langacker 1987 as the element whose profile determines the profile of the construction as a whole, is better defined as **profile equivalence**, that is, the element whose profile most closely matches the profile of the construction as a whole (Croft 1996:51–53; 2001:254–57). Profile equivalence allows for the cases where a construction has no profile determinant or more than one profile determinant. For example, a conjoined phrase such as *Bill and Tim* profiles a pair, but none of its elements has a profile matching that of the construction as a whole. Also, in the determiner-noun construction, the construction as a whole profiles the referent, but so do both elements. In *the song*, for example, *song* profiles the entity as an instance of a type or class, and *the* schematically profiles the entity as an entity in the shared knowledge of the interlocutors.

(iii)   What sorts of relations are found between constructions?

As a nonreductionist model, Radical Construction Grammar makes a radical shift in the conception of grammatical structure. Radical Construction Grammar does not posit a set of atomic primitive elements out of which constructions are built. Instead, complex constructions are the basic units of grammatical representation, and the categories defined by the parts of the construction are derived. However, the effect of the nonreductionist hypothesis on the organization of grammatical knowledge in the constructional network is minimal.

In Radical Construction Grammar, each part (unit) of a construction constitutes a category whose members are defined solely by their occurrence in that role in the construction. In order to differentiate categories, we append the name of the construction to the labels for each unit in the construction. A representation of the Intransitive and Transitive constructions is given in (43):

(43)

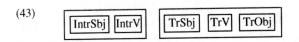

The establishment of a category Verb is a linguistic generalization over the categories IntrV and TrV. This generalization is thus a taxonomic relationship, with Verb superordinate to IntrV and TrV. However, any superordinate category, such as Verb, must be linguistically motivated. The motivation for a superordinate category such as Verb must be its occurrence as the category in some other construction. For example, the standard motivation for positing a category Verb is the ability of its members to be inflected with the tense/agreement suffixes. In a construction grammar, this linguistic fact is essentially another construction, the morphological construction [MVerb-TA]. We use the label MVerb to emphasize that this category is defined by a morphological construction, namely its occurrence with the tense/agreement suffixes (abbreviated TA):

(44)

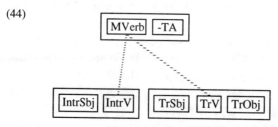

In other words, Radical Construction Grammar represents meronomic relations between constructions in a similar way to Construction Grammar (§10.2.1), namely as instances of a schema.[6] That is, the treatment of meronomic relations is not a distinctive characteristic of nonreductionist models. The primary difference between a nonreductionist model such as Radical Construction Grammar and a reductionist model such as Construction Grammar is that the latter uses syntactic features and values for roles that are defined independently of the constructions in which the units occur. (In addition, Radical Construction Grammar differs from Construction Grammar in allowing for nonclassical relations between constructions, as in the Lakoff-Goldberg and Cognitive Grammar theories.)

(iv)   How is information stored in the construction taxonomy?

Although Radical Construction Grammar is identical to Construction Grammar in its handling of part-whole relations between constructions, it is like Cognitive Grammar and the Lakoff-Goldberg model in that it allows for redundant representation of grammatical information in accordance with the usage-based model (see §10.2.2 and chapter 11).

One salient feature of Radical Construction Grammar's organization of grammatical knowledge is derived from typological theory but conforms to the usage-based model. This is the **semantic map** model. In the semantic map model, constructions are mapped onto a conceptual space according to their function, and thus constructions can be related to one another by virtue of having overlapping or neighboring functions in the conceptual space. The semantic map model is described in relation to the usage-based model in §11.3.3.

---

[6] More precisely, Radical Construction Grammar allows parts of constructions to be instances of a part of another construction (as in [44]), as well as allowing them to be instances of another whole construction. It does not appear that Construction Grammar allows the former possibility.

A second salient feature of Radical Construction Grammar, also inspired by typological research, is the introduction of the notion of a **syntactic space** (Croft 2001, chapters 8–9). Constructions that are functionally similar or identical across languages (and sometimes within a single language) vary considerably in their grammatical properties, so that, for example, one cannot posit a universal passive construction based on a fixed set of grammatical properties. The typical European passive has the grammatical properties of patient as Subject, agent as Oblique (or prohibited, in many languages), and a special passive verb form distinct from the active:

(45)   **The children** [patient = Subject] were taken [distinct verb form] to school **by their parents** [agent = Oblique].

This construction is by no means universal (even setting aside the problems of defining Subject etc. across languages): many structurally distinct voice constructions occur cross-linguistically, three of which are illustrated in (46)–(48) (examples from Croft 2001:292–94):

(46)   *Upriver Halkomelem: patient = Subject, agent not Oblique, distinct verb form*
tás   -l   əm   θúƛ'à   tə   swíyəqə
bump.into -ACCID   -3SG.PASS she   ART   man
'She was bumped into by the man'

(47)   *Bambara: patient = Subject, agent = Oblique, verb form not distinct:*
o   fo'ra   dugutigi   **fὲ**
3SG   greet'COMPL.INTR   chief   **with**
'S/he was greeted by the chief.'

(48)   *Maasai: patient not Subject, agent prohibited, distinct verb form:*
aa-   dɔl   **-i**
1SG.OBJ-   see   **-PASS**
'I am seen.'

Instead of representing constructions as discrete universal formal types that occur across languages, Radical Construction Grammar represents constructions as language-specific structures occupying positions in a syntactic space defined by the structural properties that vary across languages (in this case, patient coding, agent coding and verb form). The syntactic space allows one to formulate universals of the relationship between formal properties of constructions and their function, of the sort discovered by typologists. For example, the more 'passive-like' voice constructions are associated cross-linguistically with higher-animacy and higher-topicality patients, where distributional restrictions or structurally contrasting voice constructions exist (Croft 2001, chapter 8).

10.3   Conclusion

This chapter has presented the essential features of a construction grammar, and some of the different positions on basic representational issues found in different theories of construction grammar. Unfortunately space prevents us from describing analyses of more specific grammatical phenomena in the various theories, such as argument structure, so-called movement phenomena, information structure constructions, word order variation and so on; or specific grammatical constructions (other than those illustrated in chapter 9). There are also a variety of issues of representation and the processes that use that representation which have not been fully addressed by the construction grammar models at the time of writing. Nevertheless, there is a large and growing body of construction grammar analyses of a wide range of grammatical constructions, and a lively debate on basic issues of grammatical representation and process in a construction-based approach.

11

The usage-based model

11.1 Grammatical representation and process

Grammatical knowledge is not merely a representational structure in the mind of a speaker. In a recent survey of knowledge representation models in psychology, Markman argues that there are four basic elements to a model of knowledge representation (1999:5–10). One element is the representing world, that is, the domain of the representations themselves. In the cognitive linguistic approach to language, the representing world is of course the mind. A second element is the represented world. For grammatical knowledge, the represented world is utterances, that is, the form of utterances and their meaning in the discourse context. The third and fourth elements in Markman's analysis are some mechanism to link the representing world to the represented world, and processes using the representation. This last element is particularly important:

> It makes no sense to talk about representations in the absence of processes ... Only when there is also a process that uses the representation does the system actually represent, and the capabilities of a system are defined only when there is both a representation and a process. (Markman 1999:8)

The primary processes in which grammatical knowledge is involved are communication – the production and comprehension of utterances; the acquisition of grammatical knowledge by children and by adults; and the changes in grammatical knowledge of speakers over time. These processes link the representing world – the grammatical knowledge – and the represented world – the world of utterances and their meanings. These processes are the locus for the link between the representing and represented worlds, Markman's third element of a representation model.

Many cognitive linguists propose a **usage-based model** for language use, language acquisition and language change (§§11.2.2–11.2.4; see inter alia Langacker 1987, chapter 10; Barlow and Kemmer 2000; Bybee and Hopper 2001).[1] The

---

[1] Construction Grammar, on the other hand, is intended to be a competence model (Paul Kay, pers. comm., 1999).

usage-based model contrasts with the traditional structuralist and generative models of grammatical representation. In the structuralist and generative models, only the structure of the grammatical forms determines their representation in a speaker's mind. For example, the traditional models make a sharp distinction between **regular** and **irregular** word forms. Regular inflected word forms, such as the English plural form *boy-s*, are derived by a highly general **rule** forming the plural from the singular, because the structural relationship between *boy* and *boys*, namely addition of -*s*, allows this possibility. Irregular word forms, such as the plural form *feet*, do not have a straightforward structural relationship linking the singular and the plural. Since they cannot be derived by a general rule, irregular plural word forms are therefore **listed** in the lexicon.

In the usage-based model, properties of the use of utterances in communication also determine the representation of grammatical units in a speaker's mind. In particular, two usage-based properties are assumed to affect grammatical representation: the frequency of occurrence of particular grammatical forms and structures, and the meaning of the words and constructions in use. In §11.2, we discuss four hypotheses of the usage-based model derived from this assumption, and the evidence for those hypotheses in morphology, the area of grammar most intensively studied in the usage-based model (Bybee 1985, 1995, 2001). In §11.3, we discuss how the hypotheses of the usage-based model can be applied to the representation of syntactic constructions, their acquisition and syntactic change.

11.2   The usage-based model in morphology

11.2.1   *Entrenchment and representation of word forms*

The primary factor determining the independent storage of word forms in the usage-based model is the frequency of occurrence of the word form in language use, that is, the **token frequency** of the word form. The hypothesis is that each time a word (or construction) is used, it **activates** a node or pattern of nodes in the mind, and frequency of activation affects the storage of that information, leading to its ultimate storage as a conventional grammatical unit. A word form that occurs frequently enough in use to be stored independently is described as **entrenched** (Langacker 1987:59–60). Entrenchment comes in degrees, even beyond the minimum threshold required for independent storage.[2] In the usage-based model, the entrenchment of word forms is possible even if the word form is predictable from a more schematic grammatical representation. For example, the plural form *boys*

---

[2] Bybee has used the terms 'autonomy' and 'lexical strength' to refer to degree of entrenchment in her work (1985, 1995).

may be entrenched even though it is a regular instance of the noun plural schema [NOUN-*s*] because it has a high token frequency. In contrast, it is less likely that the plural form *cornices* is entrenched, because its low frequency of occurrence is probably insufficient to lead to the storage of this form independently of the base form *cornice* and the noun plural schema [NOUN-*s*]. This first hypothesis of the usage-based model is summarized in (1):

(1)   *Hypothesis 1*: the storage of a word form, regular or irregular, is a function of its token frequency.

It is clear that irregular forms must be independently stored in any model of morphology, since they are not entirely predictable from a more general schema. In the structuralist/generative models, irregular forms are simply listed in the lexicon. The usage-based model predicts that irregular word forms will be found among the more frequent words in the lexicon. The more frequent words are those more likely to be entrenched, and hence irregularities can survive in such forms. If an irregular form is not frequent enough, or declines in frequency of use, then it will be regularized: its representation will not be sufficiently entrenched and reinforced through use, and so the regular schema will take over in the production of the relevant inflection. The structuralist/generative model, in which there is no effect of frequency, predicts that there should be an even distribution of irregular word forms across the lexicon.

In this case, the evidence clearly favors the usage-based model. Irregular inflectional forms are consistently found among the higher frequency words in the lexicon. For instance, it is not surprising that the verb with the most irregular person forms in English is the extremely frequent verb *be* (*am, is, are; was* and *were* – the only past forms in English that distinguish person).

There is also evidence that low-frequency irregular inflected forms are regularized, while high-frequency irregulars resist regularization to a greater degree. For example, Bybee and Slobin examined the English verbs that form the past tense by changing the final stem consonant from *d* to *t*, as in *build/built* (Bybee and Slobin 1982:275). They compared the list of verbs in Jespersen's historical grammar of English (Jespersen 1942) to the same verbs listed in the *American Heritage Dictionary*; the verbs with the *American Heritage Dictionary* past tense forms are given in (2):

(2)
past in *t* only:	past in *ed* or *t*:	past in *t* or *ed*:
bend	*blend*	*rend*
lend	*geld*	past in *ed* only:
send	*gird*	*wend*
spend		not listed in *AHD*:
build		*shend* 'to shame'

Bybee and Slobin observe that the forms that retain the irregular past in *t* are all frequent, while the others are rare (in fact, one has dropped out of the language).

Further dynamic evidence that irregularity is correlated with frequency is the evidence that low-frequency irregular forms are more likely to be regularized in production. For example, Bybee and Slobin discovered that there was a significant rank order correlation between the likelihood of regularization of irregular past tense forms by preschool children and the token frequency of the verb in the adult caretaker's speech, such that lower token frequency correlated with a high regularization rate (Bybee and Slobin 1982:270). Bybee and Slobin found significant correlations between token frequency and regularization for some though not all irregular verb classes in experimental production tasks given to third-grade children and adults (1982:270–71).

A more indirect piece of evidence that regular forms are stored independently under some circumstances is that a regularly inflected word form, or a regularly derived word form, may diverge semantically from its parent word. For example, 'something can be *dirty* without involving real dirt at all . . . someone can *soil* an item without being anywhere near real soil' (Bybee 1985:88). Examples of divergence of a former inflectional form are *clothes*, formerly the plural of *cloth* (Bybee 1985:91) and *shadow*, formerly an Old English oblique case form of *shade* (Croft 2000:36). Presumably, semantic divergence presupposes the independent representation of the inflected form, which then is free to diverge in meaning.

This evidence regarding irregular word forms has led some generative linguists, including Pinker and colleagues, to accept that frequency effects associated with degree of entrenchment are found with irregulars. Hence, they accept that the usage-based model is valid for irregularly inflected word forms. However, Pinker and colleagues argue that regularly inflected word forms are not sensitive to frequency effects. Instead, regularly inflected word forms are represented by a grammatical rule based only on the structure of the word forms and not any properties of their use (Pinker and Prince 1994; Marcus et al. 1992). This model is called the **dual-processing model** of grammatical representation.[3]

Evidence from an experiment on the more regular third person present inflection in English indicates that low frequency regular forms are not stored in the lexicon, because they do not exhibit gang effects (Stemberger and MacWhinney 1988:111–12). Gang effects are effects on stored word forms of phonologically

[3] In fact, the traditional model, in which regularly inflected forms are generated by a structural rule and irregular forms are listed in the lexicon, is also a dual-processing model. The only innovation in the model proposed by Pinker and colleagues is that the irregulars conform to the usage-based model's predictions, instead of merely being listed in the lexicon.

similar stored word forms; if word forms are not stored, gang effects would not occur. The absence of gang effects has been taken to imply that regularly inflected forms are not stored (see, for example, Prasada and Pinker 1993). Other experiments, however, do suggest that high frequency regular inflected forms are stored. Stemberger and MacWhinney conducted an experiment in which subjects were required to produce past tense forms of regular verbs at high speed, and errors occurred significantly less often on high frequency regular past tense forms, implying that the high frequency regular past tense forms are stored (Stemberger and MacWhinney 1988:106). Bybee reports an experiment conducted by Losiewicz (1992) which provides some evidence of a frequency effect for regular forms (Bybee 1995:450–51). Losiewicz observed that the acoustic duration of word-final /t/ or /d/ is shorter if it is part of the word than if it is the regular past tense ending (e.g. *rapt* vs. *rapped*). If the difference in acoustic duration is due to storage of the word form, then high-frequency regulars should have shorter final /t/ or /d/ than low-frequency regulars. In a sentence reading task, subjects had an average 7 msec difference in duration between high-frequency and low-frequency final /t/ or /d/ duration, which was highly significant.

The evidence reported in the last paragraph is compatible with a model in which high-frequency regular word forms are stored but low frequency regular word forms are not. The results suggest that frequency affects the storage of regular word forms, and supports Hypothesis 1.[4]

11.2.2 Regularity, productivity and default status

In a structuralist/generative model, regularity is modeled by a **rule**. A rule is generally analyzed as an operation over strings, such as the phonological string of a word form or the syntactic strings of words and constituents of a construction. Affixation, such as the suffixation of the English past tense suffix allomorphs /t/, /d/ or /id/, is a relatively simple operation. Other rule-governed operations are more complex: they may involve internal changes to a word form, or other changes.

In a usage-based model, a simple rule such as the addition of the past tense would be represented by a **schema** of the sort used for the representation of constructions in chapter 10. The schema for the English past tense would be represented as something like [VERB-*ed*] (ignoring for now the three different allomorphs of

---

[4] It is possible that the absence of a frequency effect for regulars is what one would expect even in a usage-based model; activation network models trained on regular inputs do not display a gang effect (Daugherty and Seidenberg 1994).

the past tense). The representation of a generalization as a schema conforms to the principle that all grammatical knowledge is represented in a uniform fashion (§9.4).

There are some differences in what can be represented as rules vs. schemas, which will be discussed in §11.2.3. In this section, however, we will look at what determines regularity, rather than how regularity is to be represented.

One property of regular inflections is the **productivity** of the inflection. As the name implies, a productive inflection is one that is applied to almost any semantically and phonologically appropriate word form, including new forms coined or borrowed into the language. In the rule-based model, productivity is the open-ended scope of application of the rule, within the phonological and semantic constraints imposed by the inflection. As we will see, however, the interpretation of productivity in the usage-based model has led to the clarification of some hidden distinctions in the definition of regularity as productivity.

In a usage-based model, a productive inflection is one in which the schematic representation of the inflection is entrenched. The difference between the *-en* plural of *oxen* and the *-s* plural is that the only entrenched form in the former is [*oxen*], while in the latter case a schematic construction [NOUN-*s*] is entrenched. But the productivity of the regular plural form *-s* implies the existence of a general schema that can easily be combined with a particular noun to form a plural. From a usage-based point of view, then, the question is: what factors determine the entrenchment of a schematic morphological construction?

Bybee argues that the productivity of a schema is a function of **type frequency** (Bybee 1985:132–34; 1995):

(3)   *Hypothesis 2*: The productivity of a schema is a function of the type frequency of the instances of the schema.

Type frequency is the number of different word forms that are instances of a particular schema. The type frequency of the English past tense schema [VERB-*ed*] is thus the number of regular past tense verbs in English. The English past tense suffix *-ed* is highly productive under this account. There is a vast number of lower frequency verbs with the *-ed* past tense suffix which reinforce the past tense schema [VERB *-ed*]. In fact, of course, the past tense schema has three allomorphs, /t/, /d/ and /id/. But each of these phonologically defined schemas has a high type frequency of low token frequency instances, so each allomorph is highly productive for its phonologically defined class.

There is another important aspect of productivity: one must be able to form a coherent schema (Bybee 1995:430). That is, there must be enough resemblance between the types that contribute to the entrenchment of the schema that one can form a schema in the first place. The closer the resemblance, the more entrenched is the schema. Each allomorph of the English productive past tense is a coherent schema, that is, for the past tense suffix each allomorph defines a phonologically and semantically coherent category, namely [-t/PAST], [-d/PAST] and [-ɨSd/PAST]. Moreover, the three allomorphs possess a phonological family resemblance, reinforced by their complementary phonological distribution (in terms of the final segment of the verb stem) and identity of meaning. Because of the family resemblance a speaker may form a superordinate category, notated here [-*ed*/PAST] with the orthographic representation standing in for the phonological schema.

Bybee argues that instances of a schema that have a high token frequency will not contribute to the productivity of a schema (1985:132–34). Instances with a high token frequency are strongly entrenched (1995:434). Only the entrenched specific word form will be activated in language use and thus will not reinforce the superordinate schema. On the other hand, word forms with a low token frequency will not be as strongly entrenched (if they are entrenched at all; see §11.2.1). Bybee argues that low frequency word forms will contribute to the entrenchment of a schematic representation of the inflectional ending that applies across many different word forms, including new forms. However, the examples that Bybee gives in support of this hypothesis do not fully separate token frequency and type frequency. Instances of a productive schema with a high token frequency, such as the most common regular English past tense forms, are swamped by the number of instances with a low token frequency. One would have to find a conjugation class in a language where excluding the high token frequency instances results in too low a type frequency to make the schema productive, but including them would result in a high enough type frequency to make the schema productive. Hence, it is not clear that high token frequency instances in fact do not contribute to the productivity of a schema.

The usage-based definition of productivity is gradient, because type frequency is gradient. Thus, the usage-based model predicts that productivity might vary in degree. Forms for which there is a low type frequency may exhibit a minor degree of productivity. Evidence for this is found among the irregular English past tense forms. Most of the irregular English past tense forms involve an internal change to the stem, usually a change to the stem vowel. One particular class has a relatively high type frequency of relatively low token frequency verbs. This class is Bybee and Slobin's Class VI. Class VI verbs fall into two subclasses, those with a past tense form with /æ/ and a past participle with /ʌ/ (Class VIa in example [4]) and those with a past tense form with /ʌ/ (Class VIb; Bybee and Slobin 1982:288, Appendix).

(4)   Class VIa: Class VIb:

    m swim/swam/swum   *n* spin/spun

    n begin/began/begun   win/won

       run/ran   *ng* bring/brung* [dialectal]

    ng ring/rang/rung*   cling/clung

       sing/sang/sung   fling/flung*

       spring/sprang/sprung   hang/hung*

    nk drink/drank/drunk   sling/slung*

       shrink/shrank/shrunk   sting/stung*

       sink/sank/sunk   string/strung

                     swing/swung

                     wring/wrung

                nk slink/slunk

                k sneak/snuck* [dialectal]

                   stick/stuck*

                   strike/struck*

                   shake/shuck* [dialectal]

                g dig/dug*

                   drag/drug*

Class VI irregulars are relatively coherent as a phonological class: most of them have present tense vowel /I/ and end in a velar or nasal or nasal+velar. The past tense form of Class VIb in particular can be described as having a prototype pattern of present tense /CIŋ/ and past tense /CIŋ/, with extensions to velar and/or nasal final consonants and some variation in the stem vowel (cf. Bybee and Moder 1983 and §11.2.3). However, many of the Class VI verbs, particularly Class VIb verbs, are relatively low in token frequency (Bybee and Slobin 1982:278). Hence Class VI can be predicted to be mildly productive, although not nearly as productive as the *-ed* past tense allomorphs.

The evidence for the productivity of this schema is historical and psycholinguistic. The verbs asterisked in (4) were not part of this irregular class in Old English (Bybee and Slobin 1982:288, citing Jespersen 1942). In fact, three of the asterisked Class VIb forms are not standard English forms, but are used in nonstandard English dialects, suggesting a relatively recent shift of these verbs to Class VI. The asterisked forms were either irregular verbs of other classes, or even regular verbs to which the Class VIb vowel alternation was extended because of the phonological resemblance of their verb stems to the stems of Old English Class VI verbs, and the relative productivity of Class VI.

Bybee and Slobin also conducted experiments with children and adults: the children were asked to provide past tense forms in sentence completion tasks, and the adults were asked to provide past tense forms under extreme time pressure. Both tasks elicited novel past tense forms. Of these, the data for both children and adults indicated a mild degree of productivity of Class VI, such as *streak/struck* and *clink/clunk* (Bybee and Slobin 1982:278).

Advocates of the dual-processing model of morphological representation have argued that, while irregular verbs may display frequency-related patterns such as those found by Bybee and Slobin for the Class VI past tense verbs, regular inflections do not display any type frequency effects. Instead, regular inflections are productive because they impose the least phonological specificity on the verb stem (Prasada and Pinker 1993). For example, the allomorphs of the English regular past tense impose the least phonological specificity on their verb stems: verb stems are constrained only by certain phonological features of the final segment. In schema terms, the regular inflection provides a maximally **open** schema. The dual-processing hypothesis is given in (5):

(5)   *Hypothesis 2'*: productivity of a rule is determined by its being a (relatively) open schema.

English does not provide a good case to differentiate these two hypotheses for productivity, type frequency vs. open schema. The regular English past tense has both a much higher type frequency than any other past tense form and a very open phonological schema. Thus, both hypotheses predict (correctly) that the regular English past tense is highly productive. However, there are languages in which the open schema for an inflection does not have a high type frequency. Examples include the German plurals (Marcus et al. 1995) and Arabic plurals (McCarthy and Prince 1990).[5]

The German and Arabic plural cases both dissociate type frequency from open schema. Both German and Arabic have a range of plural formation processes, none of which has an overwhelmingly greater type frequency such as is found with the English plural -*s*. Both German and Arabic have an open schema plural, the German -*s* and the Arabic sound plural (a suffix instead of an internal stem change). Both German and Arabic open schema plurals are used as the plural schema with items other than standard common nouns, such as proper names, new borrowings and derived nouns and adjectives (Bybee 1995:440–42; Janda 1990:146–48). The open schema plurals are open schema precisely because they must be applicable to noncanonical nouns; but they are also of low type frequency for the same reason.

---

[5] Clahsen and Rothweiler (1992) argue that the German past participle ending -*t* has a lower type frequency than -*en* and yet is more productive. However, Clahsen and Rothweiler used only the first 1,000 verbs of a 4,314-verb frequency list of German verbs, thereby leaving out a very large number of regular verb types, and they counted the verb stems multiple times if they occurred with multiple productive prefixes, which again artificially increases the type frequency of -*en* (Bybee 1995:438).

Marcus et al. and Pinker and Prince argue that the applicability of the open schemas to noncanonical nouns is evidence of their high productivity. Bybee, on the other hand, argues that this is evidence only of their 'emergency' or **default** status by virtue of their open schema, and that investigating the full range of common nouns indicates that the default schema is no more productive than plural schemas with a high type frequency. For Arabic, the iambic broken plural has the highest type frequency, and is productive with any noun (including borrowed nouns) that fit its canonical phonological shape criteria. The iambic broken plural is overgeneralized by children as well as the default sound plural (Omar 1973, cited in Bybee 1995:442), indicating that both the iambic broken plural and the default sound plural are productive, the former especially so.

The German plural situation is more complicated. No single plural formation pattern is highly productive. However, the evidence for productivity apart from noncanonical nouns indicates some degree of productivity of several different plural endings, including -s (see Bybee 1995:440–41 and references cited therein). Children overgeneralize -en most frequently, and in nonce-probe tasks, different endings were preferred for different noun genders, particularly if the nonce forms were identified as common nouns. Even recent borrowings use -en and to a lesser extent -e especially for masculine nouns; -s is used about half of the time, and some loans have given up -s for -en upon integration into the language. Also, nouns ending in vowels favored -s in a nonce-probe task (Köpcke 1988) and in acquisition (Köpcke 1998:313–15). Among ordinary German common nouns -s is associated with nouns ending in a full vowel (Janda 1990:145–46). These facts suggest that -s is not truly a default schema.

A default schema does not require a high type frequency to arise. A default form can arise if the non-default forms form relatively narrow and phonologically well-defined classes, while the instances of the default schema are scattered across the remaining phonological space, even if those instances have a low type frequency (Hare, Elman and Daugherty 1995:626–27; they also simulate this effect in a connectionist network). The German and Arabic plurals conform to this pattern (compare Hare et al. 1995:608). If the phonological unity of the non-default classes breaks down through phonological change, as happened with the Old English past tenses, then the system becomes unstable, leading to a reorganization of the irregular forms around new phonological classes or survival by high token frequency (Hare and Elman 1995).

11.2.3 Product-oriented schemas

Up to this point, we have assumed that morphological generalizations such as the relationship between the present and past tense forms of English verbs can be equally well captured by rules deriving one form from another (or both forms from a common underlying form). Instead, we have focused on the fact that the usage-based model can capture generalizations about morphological patterns that are based on token frequency and type frequency, whereas rules in the dual-processing model do not imply the existence of any generalizations linked to frequency, at least for regular inflections. However, Bybee and others have argued that rules and schemas in fact make slightly different predictions about what sort of generalizations can be made over related word forms.

Structuralist and generative morphological rules are what Bybee calls **source-oriented**. Source-oriented rules specify the basic word form, such as the present tense of a verb like *wait*, and describe a single operation with a single set of conditions that produce the derived form, such as addition of /ɨd/ to a stem ending in *t* or *d* to form *waited*. In the usage-based model, a source-oriented schema is a schema with a systematic structural relationship to another schema (the source in a rule-based model). For instance the regular past tense schema [VERB-ɨd] contains the same stem as the present tense schema [VERB(-ɨz)], and so the past and present tense verb form schemas can be uniformly represented across all stems. The term 'source-oriented' is somewhat misleading in the usage-based model because there is no derivation of one schema from another by a rule in the usage-based model. The term 'source-oriented' simply indicates that the 'source' schema is as coherent, phonologically and semantically, as the 'product' schema.

Bybee argues (following Zager 1980) that in addition to source-oriented schemas, there also exist **product-oriented** schemas:

(6)   *Hypothesis 3*: In addition to source-oriented morphological rules/schemas, there also exist product-oriented schemas, which cannot be easily represented by derivational rules.

A product-oriented schema is a morphological schema that is coherent in terms of the phonological form and meaning of the 'derived' inflected form of the word, not in terms of a rule deriving the inflected form from a base form (Bybee 1995:443). In a morphological inflectional category with a product-oriented schema, the 'product' schema is more coherent phonologically than (and at least as coherent semantically as) its counterpart 'source' schema.

An example of a product-oriented schema is the schema for the Class VI irregular verb class illustrated in (4) above. Because of the variety of phonological shapes of the present tense forms of Class VI verbs, one cannot construct a single coherent rule to derive the past tense form from the base form. Instead, the past tense forms are more or less converging on the prototypical past tense shapes [. . . æŋ] (for Class VIa past tense forms) and [. . . ʌŋ] (for Class VIb past tense forms, and the Class VIa past participle forms).

Product-oriented schemas cannot be described in terms of a rule that converts a base form into a derived form. At best, one would have to have a different rule for each word (or small sets of words) deriving the product form from the source form. The reason for this is that product-oriented schemas are more coherent and unified categories than their so-called source schemas. Product-oriented schemas can best be described in terms of a prototype schema towards which the 'derived' forms converge, by whatever phonological means necessary (Bybee and Moder 1983). Since a purely structural description of a product-oriented schema is not possible (short of a 'rule' for each word), the structuralist/generative model predicts that product-oriented schemas should not exist.

The term 'product-oriented' is misleading in the usage-based model in the same way that 'source-oriented' is. In a usage-based model, 'product-oriented' schemas arise because they represent a schematic (taxonomic) generalization across the 'derived' forms, which are represented as independent units. The primary factor determining the existence of a schema, 'source'- or 'product-oriented', is a (relatively) high type frequency (§11.2.2). Hence, if a 'product-oriented' pattern in word forms is at least partially productive, then it provides evidence in favor of the usage-based model.

Such evidence is found with the English Class VI past tense schema. No single rule 'derives' the past tense form from the present tense form. But the past tense forms of Class VI can be described in terms of a family resemblance category, whose prototype is [. . . ʌŋ/PAST]. As we saw in §11.2.2, the schema is productive, demonstrated by performance by children and adults in psycholinguistic experiments, and in the extension of the Class VI past tense schema to other English verbs in the history of the language (see Bybee and Moder 1983 for a more detailed argument in favor of this schema).

Bybee cites further evidence from plural formation in Hausa (Bybee 1995:443–44). Haspelmath (1989) demonstrates that there is no set of general rules for forming the plural in Hausa, but the plural forms can be described in a set of product-oriented schemas which in turn can be subsumed under a more general product-oriented plural schema. Lobben (1991, cited in Bybee 1995) conducted nonce-probe experiments with Hausa speakers that indicate that the plural schemas were indeed productive.

11.2.4 Network organization of word forms

In chapter 10, we observed that in construction grammar, constructions are organized in a network in a taxonomy. However, in §10.1.2, we also observed that constructions can, and usually do, have multiple parents in the taxonomy. The description of the construction grammar of a language in any detail is going to lead to an extremely tangled network of construction taxonomies. Is there any evidence to determine which categories are more important in organizing multiple parent taxonomies?

Bybee proposes a model in which the essential organizing feature of the network of words is similarity. Similarities are connections or links between words. Bybee further makes a number of proposals regarding which similarities between words are more important. We may summarize Bybee's proposals in (7):

(7) *Hypothesis 4*: strength of connection between word forms, and thus forces influencing their phonological shape (among other things), is a function of similarity. Similarity is measurable by comparing words to each other in both meaning and form; similarity in meaning is much stronger than similarity in form.

Hypothesis 4 is part of the usage-based model of morphological representation in that the meaning of word forms, which is manifested in their use in communication, influences the organization of the knowledge of those word forms in a speaker's mind. In the structuralist/generative model, only structural properties determine the organization of word forms in a speaker's mind.

Words may be similar in form, meaning or both. Bybee describes similarity in form as implying a **phonological connection**, similarity in meaning a **semantic connection**, and similarity in both a 'morphological connection'; for the latter case, we will use the more general term **symbolic connection**.

Bybee argues that a solely phonological connection between words – in other words, homophony – is the weakest connection of all (Bybee 1985:118). Homophones such as the two most distinct senses of *bank* or *crane* have relatively little psychological effect. Homophony does give rise to a minor yet robust priming effect. In lexical decision and target naming tasks using homonyms, there is a priming effect of both the contextually appropriate meaning and the homonymous meaning within 0-200 msec of presentation of the stimulus; after 200 msec, only the contextually appropriate meaning is primed (Swinney 1979, 1982; Seidenberg et al. 1982). This priming effect indicates that there is a lexical connection based on mere phonological similarity, but not a strong one.

A solely semantic connection between words is much stronger. An example of a close semantic connection without a phonological connection is suppletive paradigms, as in English *go/went*. Bybee observes that suppletion is subject to regularization, as found in innovations in language use such as *goed* for *went* and the replacement of suppletive forms over time in languages. The semantic connection between GO+PRESENT and GO+PAST is so strong that one of the forms is changed (*went* > *goed*) in production so as to make it more similar to the other form with the similar meaning (*go*). In contrast, the existence of similarity in form in homonyms or near homonyms does not lead to one of the words changing meaning so as to make it semantically more similar to the other word with a similar form.

The strongest connection is a symbolic connection: similarity in form and meaning. Bybee argues that there are three factors that determine the strength of a symbolic connection: degree of semantic similarity, degree of phonological similarity and degree of entrenchment. Beginning with the last factor first: relative degree of entrenchment largely determines the direction of analogical changes in word paradigms. For example, one would predict that it is more likely that a speaker would produce *writed* in place of *wrote*, by analogy with *write(s)*, rather than *wrotes* in place of *writes*. The past tense is less entrenched because it is less frequently used than the present tense, and so is less resistant to being replaced by an analogical formation that results from activation of the more entrenched form.

As with solely phonological and solely semantic connections, in symbolic connections degree of semantic similarity is the more important factor. Bybee describes degree of semantic similarity as **relevance**. The notion behind relevance can be described by examining the inflectional categories that Bybee studied, those of the verb: aspect, tense, mood and person.

An inflectional semantic category that is highly relevant to the verb is one that makes the greatest change in the verb's meaning. For example, a change in aspect from, say, present meaning to habitual/generic meaning is a substantial change in meaning. The present time reference in (8a) describes a current state of affairs, true at the present moment but not long lasting. The habitual/generic meaning in (8b) describes a series of eating events over a long period of time (habitual), or an inherent property of mine that disposes me towards eating ice cream (or at least does not prevent me from eating ice cream):

(8)   a. I'm eating ice cream.
        b. I eat ice cream.

In contrast, changing the person who is doing the eating does not make a very substantial change in the nature of the eating event itself:

(9)   a. I'm eating ice cream.
        b. She's eating ice cream.

Relevance is inversely related to strength of semantic connection. Two different aspectual forms of a single verb are more weakly connected semantically, because the event types they describe are more different. Two different person agreement forms of a single verb are more strongly connected semantically, because the event types they describe are more similar.

On the basis of semantic argumentation, Bybee proposes the following ranking of verbal inflectional semantic categories, from most relevant to the verb/event to least relevant (see Bybee 1985:20–23 for the semantic argumentation):

(10)   valence changing < voice < aspect < tense < mood < person/number agreement

Bybee puts forward several types of typological and diachronic evidence for the ranking in (10). For example, more relevant inflectional categories of the verb occur closer to the verb stem. The reasoning behind this prediction is that the greater the meaning change, the more intimately associated with the stem meaning is the semantic category of the inflection. Bybee tested the hypothesis on the four most common verbal inflectional categories, aspect, tense, mood and person agreement, in a fifty-language sample (Bybee 1985:33–35). There were virtually no counterexamples to the ordering of aspect, tense and person/mood with respect to the other categories; mood and person agreement were more equivocal.

The notion of relevance is a further refinement of Hypothesis 4: that semantic similarity to different degrees influences formal similarity of word forms to different degrees. That is, greater semantic similarity will favor greater phonological similarity (and thus increase symbolic similarity). Semantic distinctions expressed lexically will be more phonologically different than semantic distinctions expressed inflectionally, on the whole. It should be remembered that other factors such as degree of entrenchment also affect phonological similarity: a higher degree of entrenchment weakens the connection between word forms and thus may lead to greater phonological differences.

Thus, another prediction from Hypothesis 4 is that, other things being equal, a stronger semantic connection between words will imply a greater phonological similarity of those words. Also, one would expect to find that phonological similarity can be increased through analogical change of semantically strongly connected words. There is considerable evidence for this prediction as well. Bybee reports that data from her survey and from Rudes (1980) indicate that suppletion in verbal paradigms is most likely along aspectual distinctions, then along tense, and least likely along mood. There is also some suppletion along person distinctions, but only in very high frequency forms; this can be explained by the principle given in the preceding paragraph, that a high degree of entrenchment weakens connections between words.

Finally, when paradigms are leveled analogically, they are most likely to be leveled among semantically closely related forms, in particular different person/number forms of the same tense-aspect-mood paradigm. Also, the direction of leveling will be most likely towards the most frequent form (third person singular, followed by first person singular), because forms with weak connections will give way to analogical formations from stronger forms. Bybee presents a number of examples of such leveling within person-number forms (Bybee 1985, chapter 3; see also Bybee and Brewer 1980 for Spanish). For example, the Old Provençal person-number forms for the preterite indicative in (11) were reformed analogically on the third person form including that form's -*t* person/number suffix, in a number of Modern Provençal dialects, such as the Charente dialect in (12) (Bybee 1985:55; Charente data from Meyer-Lübke 1923:352):

(11)   *Old Provençal preterite of* am- *'love':*
    am-éi   am-ém
    am-ést   am-étz
    am-ét   am-éren

(12)   *Charente preterites of* cant- *'sing':*
    cantí   cantét-em
    cantét-ei   cantét-ei
    cantét-Ø   cantét-en

In (12), the original third person singular stem *cantét* has become the base for the analogical reformation of the other person-number forms. The only form to resist the analogical change is the first singular form, which has the highest token frequency of the person-number forms after third singular.

Bybee and Pardo (1981) used a nonce-probe task with Spanish speakers to compare the effect of semantic connection on phonological production. Many Spanish verbs have a vowel stem alternation in the present vs. preterite forms, for example third singular present *comienza* 's/he begins' with a diphthong vs. third singular preterite *comenzó* 's/he began' with a simple mid vowel. Bybee and Pardo presented a third singular present form of a nonce verb with a diphthong followed by either the infinitive or the third singular preterite form with a mid vowel, and then asked subjects to produce a first singular preterite form. Subjects produced more mid vowel variants when presented with the semantically closer related third singular preterite than when presented with the more distant infinitive.

The evidence presented by Bybee and others (e.g. Andersen 1980) implies that semantic similarity of grammatical units such as words plays an important role in the organization of grammatical knowledge in a speaker's mind. Given a set of word forms, each of which can be subsumed under several more schematic categories (indicative, present, third person, singular), one can postulate a ranking of those schematic categories in terms of the network connections between words. One could go so far as to restructure the multiple-parent representation into a hierarchy, with the semantically most relevant (and hence most weakly connected) distinctions at the top of the hierarchy, as in (13) (compare the display of the Spanish verb paradigm in Bybee 1985:61, Table 1):

(13)

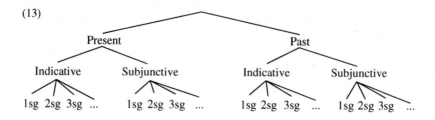

The hierarchy in (13) is still an oversimplification. The connections between members at the lowest level are not displayed, nor are the lowest levels (person and number) stratified. There remain semantic connections between the corresponding mood values (present indicative and past indicative etc.), and the corresponding person/number values (1sg present indicative, 1sg past indicative, 1sg present subjunctive, 1sg past subjunctive etc.). However, the hierarchy does indicate degree of semantic connection: one can heuristically measure degree of semantic connection by the number of connections that must be traversed in (13) in order to reach related forms. For example, only four connections need to be traversed to reach first singular present subjunctive from first singular present indicative, but six connections need to be traversed to reach first singular past indicative from first singular present indicative (for an alternative representation of degree of semantic connection, see §11.3.4).

11.2.5 Conclusion

The empirical data that we have discussed in support of the details of the usage-based model are drawn from the processes of language use (as tested in psycholinguistic experiments) and language change. These data provide evidence supporting four hypotheses about the effects of language use on grammatical representation. The independent representation of an inflected word form is a function of its token frequency in language use. The productivity of a rule/schema is a function of a high type frequency of low token frequency instances, not of the structural openness of the schema. Product-oriented schemas exist, that is, schemas can be formed from members of an inflectional category that cannot be described by rules deriving the members of the category from a source form. Finally, the organization of inflected word forms is influenced by the degree of semantic similarity between word forms.

The hypotheses of the usage-based model can be accounted for by an **interactive activation** network for the representation of knowledge (Elman and McClelland 1984). The storage of word forms is determined in part by patterns of activation of the network as a result of language use (§11.2.1). The phenomena described in Hypotheses 2–4 of the usage-based model are all analyzed in terms of the interaction of activation patterns, such that a schema activates an instance and vice versa, and a structure's activation can result from the activation of formally and especially semantically related structures. The result of the interactive activation is manifested not only in the conventional production and comprehension of word forms, but also in 'errors' in certain contexts, and innovations in language acquisition and language change.

The usage-based model contrasts with the complete inheritance model in two important respects. As we noted in §10.2.2, in the complete inheritance model information is stored only at the most schematic level possible. In the usage-based model information can be represented redundantly in less schematic constructions, if activation levels lead to entrenchment. The second contrast follows from the first. In the complete inheritance model, information flows down from the most schematic constructions in the processing of an utterance. In the usage-based model, processing involves activation of the entrenched construction(s) whose structure(s) most closely matches those of the utterance. Since more specific constructions match utterances more closely than more schematic constructions, the former are more activated than the latter. It is therefore possible that speakers will not have the most schematic constructions represented in their minds, if they are not activated sufficiently (Croft 1998c).

11.3   The usage-based model in syntax

In §11.2 we examined morphological representations of words, what they represent and the processes they are involved with. A number of concrete hypotheses and supporting evidence were put forward on the nature of word representations and processes, including the role of token frequency in entrenchment, the role of type frequency in productivity, the formation of schemas, phonological and semantic similarity in connections between words, and the emergence of generalizations in language acquisition. How many of these hypotheses might hold for syntax as well as morphology? In §9.4, we argued that the same types of phenomena found in the study of syntactic idioms are also found in morphology. In this section, we will examine the applicability of hypotheses about morphological networks to syntax.

11.3.1   Type/token frequency, productivity and entrenchment

In §§11.2.1–2, it was seen that type and token frequency play distinct roles in the empirical predictions of the usage-based model for morphology. In morphology, token frequency determines the degree of entrenchment of individual substantive word forms, and also implies that strongly entrenched words will have weak links to related forms (§11.2.4). Type frequency, and phonological coherence, determine the degree of entrenchment of a schema such as [VERB-*ed*] for the regular past tense.

However, all syntactic constructions, except for completely substantive idioms, are schematic to some degree. Even an idiomatic phrase like [*kick*-TNS *the bucket*] is schematic in that it can be used in different tense-aspect-mood forms, including auxiliaries:

(14)   a. He kick**ed** the bucket.
        b. He's **gonna** kick-**Ø** the bucket one of these days. [etc.]

In syntax, one would like to be able to differentiate between constructions at different levels of schematicity, such as [*kick the bucket*], [*kick* OBJ] and [TR VERB OBJ]. If we want to apply the generalizations of usage-based morphology to syntax, then we will have to find a more general description of frequency and the role it can play in morphology.

In the usage-based model, token frequency determines degree of entrenchment of a single word. A high token frequency for a word corresponds to a high number of specific usage events with that word. The network pattern for low vs. high token frequency is illustrated in (15) (boxes with rounded corners correspond to usage events, and a dashed box, a lower degree of entrenchment):

(15)
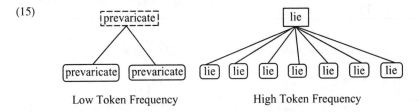

Low Token Frequency   High Token Frequency

Type frequency determines the degree of entrenchment of a schema. A high type frequency for a schema means that the schema is more deeply entrenched. The network pattern for low vs. high type frequency is illustrated in (16):

(16)
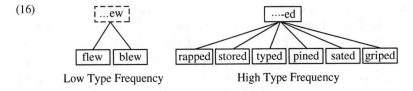

Low Type Frequency   High Type Frequency

The network structure for low vs. high token frequency (entrenchment) and low vs. high type frequency (productivity) is the same: the higher the number of instances, the more entrenched the superordinate category is. We may then formulate the following generalized definition of productivity:

(17)   *Generalized entrenchment/productivity*: entrenchment (productivity) of a construction is proportional to the number of instances of the construction at any level of schematicity, and to the degree of formal and semantic coherence of the instances of the construction.

Of course, two other factors have to be recognized in determining the degree
of entrenchment of the superordinate category (as were noted in §11.2.2). First,
the instances must be similar so that a category schema can be formed. Second,
instances that are themselves highly entrenched may not contribute as much to the
entrenchment of the superordinate category schema as instances that are not very
entrenched.

Proponents of the usage-based model have presented data supporting frequency
effects in syntax. Bybee and Thompson observe that the syntax of English auxiliaries is conservative, in that auxiliaries may invert with the subject in questions
and precede the negator *not* rather than follow it (Bybee and Thompson 1997):

(18)   a. Have you eaten?
         b. *Eat you?
(19)   a. I have not eaten.
         b. *I ate not.

In Middle English, all verbs had this ability, but it was lost in Modern English
(Bybee and Thompson 1997, from Mossé 1952):

(20)   Gaf ye the chyld any thyng?
         'Did you give the child anything?
(21)   a. My wife rose nott.
         b. cry not so

We will explain the analysis with the interrogative constructions; the same argument applies to the negative constructions. The auxiliary verbs have a very high
token frequency, compared to other verbs. In constructional terms, this means that
a construction schema such as [*Have* S BJ . . . ?] is much more entrenched than
was [*Eat* S BJ . . . ?]. That is, there are far more instances of the *have* constructions
(and other auxiliary constructions) than of the *eat* constructions (and other lexical
verb constructions). In early Modern English, the more schematic construction
[VERB SBJ . . . ?] declined, while [*Do* SBJ VERB . . . ?] spread and became
entrenched (see the account in Denison 1993, chapter 15). The (relatively) low
entrenchment of [*Eat* S BJ . . . ?] meant that [*Eat* S BJ ?] died out and was replaced
with [*Do* Sbj *eat*?]. However, [*Have* S BJ . . . ?] survived because of its high degree
of entrenchment.[6]

---

[6] This analysis is slightly different from Bybee and Thompson's. Bybee and Thompson argue that
this is a case of high token frequency, which is true for the individual auxiliary forms but not for
the auxiliary construction schema. The syntax of the auxiliary must be analyzed in terms of the
constructions in which it occurs. However, Bybee and Thompson's analysis is easily translatable into
the analysis presented here.

Readers may wonder why the construction schemas abstract away from arguments first, leaving
invariant the verbs and auxiliaries. Arguments in favor of this abstraction based on semantic relevance
and on language acquisition data are presented in §§11.3.3–4.

Bybee and Thompson also discuss a large scale corpus study of the French subjunctive by Poplack (1992, 1996). The French subjunctive form is disappearing from the spoken language, but is still variably used. However, the French subjunctive has survived largely in the complements of the highly frequent main clause verb *falloir* 'have to,' and/or in the most highly frequent complement verbs, including *avoir* 'have,' *être* 'be,' *aller* 'go' and *faire* 'make, do,' as predicted by the usage-based model.

The example of English auxiliaries in questions and negative sentences illustrates the maintenance of irregularity in more entrenched constructions that have resisted changes in the more schematic constructions of the language. Another respect in which more entrenched constructions are irregular is that they undergo changes that less entrenched constructions do not undergo. These changes commonly involve reduction, a typical concomitant of high frequency. In schematic constructions, reduction applies of course to the substantive unit(s) of the construction.

An example of reduction in a highly entrenched construction is the contraction of *not* with the auxiliary in the [SBJ AUX-*n't* . . .] construction. This contraction is recognized in written English, and includes the fused form *won't*. Of course, such reduction originated in the spoken language, and one would expect to find reduction of other negative-auxiliary contractions in the spoken language. Bybee and Scheibman (1999) investigate the reduction of one specific negative auxiliary form, *don't*, in spoken American English conversation. They demonstrate that the phonetic reduction of *don't* is strongly correlated with the frequency of the verb and of the subject with which *don't* is combined in the [SBJ *don't* VERB . . .] construction. The highest frequency subject is the first person singular *I*, and the highest frequency verb in this construction is *know*; in fact, this reduction is so salient that it is loosely represented orthographically as *I dunno*. But *I dunno* is only the extreme end of a continuum of phonetic reduction that spans the full range of verbs and subjects used in this construction. Bybee and Scheibman further note that the reduction applies across the substantive units in the constructions as a whole, regardless of their internal constituent structure.

In addition to syntactic irregularity as a consequence of high frequency, one would expect to find degrees of syntactic productivity. Of course, maximal syntactic productivity is the characteristic of the major, most schematic constructions of the language, such as the transitive construction [SBJ VERB OBJ]. The high productivity of this highly schematic construction is due to the very high frequency of instances of this construction, due to the high number of transitive verbs, the vast majority of which have a relatively low token frequency. However, even with completely schematic syntactic constructions, one can find varying degrees of productivity.

Bybee and Thompson (1997) cite an example of different degrees of productivity from the analysis of argument structure constructions by Goldberg (1995). Goldberg compares two constructions, the Caused Motion construction and the Ditransitive construction, illustrated in (22) and (23) respectively:

(22)   He told the news to the woman.
(23)   He told the woman the news.

The two constructions overlap in their distribution: some verbs allow both constructions, with approximately the same meaning, as in (22)–(23). The Ditransitive construction is used with many fewer verbs than the Caused Motion construction, and hence is much less productive than the Caused Motion construction (Goldberg 1995:124):

(24)   Sally whispered some terrible news to him.
(25)   *Sally whispered him some terrible news.

However, Goldberg notes that the prototypical ditransitive construction ('SBJ cause OBJ1 to receive OBJ2'; see §10.2.2) has the highest type frequency of any of the ditransitive subconstructions. And in fact the prototypical ditransitive has some productivity compared to the other ditransitive subtypes. The protoypical ditransitive is extended to new verbs, as in (26), but the subtype 'SBJ enable OBJ1 to receive OBJ2' is restricted to a subset of enabling verbs and does not extend to other verbs with that meaning (Goldberg 1995:129, 130):

(26)   Chris e-mailed/radioed/arpanetted him a message.
(27)   a. Sally permitted/allowed Bob one kiss.
        b. *Sally let/enabled Bob one kiss.

Finally, one must also differentiate between productive syntactic schemas and default syntactic schemas, used, for example, in borrowing. Many languages, particularly languages with complex verbal morphology, do not directly incorporate borrowed verbs into the productive native syntactic constructions of the language. Instead, they use a default construction, combining an invariant form of the borrowed verb with an inflected native verb (often meaning 'make, do') in a construction [BORRVERB 'make' . . .]. An example of this phenomenon can be found in K'iche' Mayan, which uses the verb *ban* 'make' with the infinitive form of borrowed Spanish verbs, as in (28) (Mondloch 1978:117):

(28)   x-   Ø-   im-   ban   engañar lē achi
        PST- 3SG.ABS- 1SG.ERG- make deceive the man
        'I deceived the man.'

The generalization of the notion of type/token frequency for constructions of varying degrees of schematicity allows us to make predictions about syntactic regularity and irregularity based on the usage-based model of morphology, and to seek evidence for those predictions.

11.3.2   Product-oriented syntactic schemas

In the usage-based model, word forms are not the output of rules but instances of schemas. In §11.2.3, it was noted that source-oriented schemas capture the same relationships between word forms as rules in the rule-based model. Evidence was presented there for product-oriented morphological schemas. Product-oriented morphological schemas are generalizations over word forms that would be analyzed as the output of a morphological rule in the rule-based model, but cannot be so analyzed because each word form would require a different 'rule' deriving the output. However, the 'outputs' have a phonological coherence that is greater than that of the 'input.' The example of a product-oriented morphological schema given in §11.2.3 is the [. . . ʌŋ] schema for the Class VIb irregular past tense verbs of English (Bybee and Slobin 1982). In this section, we will discuss possible cases of product-oriented syntactic construction schemas.

The classic rule-based model of syntactic representation is transformational generative grammar. In transformational grammar, a construction is describable as the product of general rules. The effect of these rules is to insert, move or (in earlier versions) delete syntactic elements from the source structure to yield a target structure. Although current generative theories use a variety of formal devices, and some theories eschew syntactic movement rules, a systematic relationship between constructions such as the active and passive voice is still recognized as a rule-based relationship.

In construction grammar, some construction schemas can be thought of as source-oriented. For example, the English active transitive and passive construction schemas can be described as in (29):

(29)   a. Active: [SBJ_i VERB$_k$-TNS OBJ$_j$]
        b. Passive: [SBJ_j *be*-TNS VERB$_k$-PP *by* OBJ$_i$]

In these constructions, systematic correspondences can be established between the elements of the two constructions (indicated by the indices on the elements), which can then be used to formulate a rule in the rule-based model that derives the product construction (the passive) from the source construction (the active, or some underlying structure from which both are derived).

Product-oriented syntactic construction schemas, on the other hand, would be construction schemas that have a coherent syntactic structure but would require different 'rules' for each type of 'input construction' in transformational-generative terms. Thus, a product-oriented construction schema is a schema subsuming the outputs of different 'rules' and 'input constructions.' Of course, since the syntactic constructions in question are themselves schematic, rules can be devised for each construction type. But this is no different than having a 'rule' for each word in morphology; it is the same phenomenon but at a higher level of schematicity. The crucial point is that there is a higher degree of structural coherence defining the product-oriented schema than its counterpart 'source' schema(s).

There are some strong candidates for product-oriented syntactic schemas in English. One is the pair of interrogative and negative construction types discussed in §11.3.1. A very general schema can be formed for each: [AUX SBJ . . . ?] and [SBJ AUX-*n't* . . .]. However, there would have to be at least two rules linking a source schema to the interrogative or negative product schema: a rule inserting the auxiliary *do* for sources without an auxiliary, and a rule applying to the (first) auxiliary for sources with an auxiliary. The different source-product correspondences are illustrated for the question schema in (30)–(32):

(30)   a. She found it.   b. Did she find it?
(31)   a. She will come.   b. Will she come?
(32)   a. She could have eaten already.   b. Could she have eaten already?

There is more structural coherence to the product constructions in (30b)–(32b) than to the 'source' constructions in (30a)–(32a). And of course, the product-oriented schema is productive.

Another relatively clear case of a product-oriented schema in English is the most general declarative construction. In the simple declarative construction, there must be a preverbal subject phrase; the schema must be something like [. . . SBJ (AUX) VERB . . .]. In this case, the 'sources' are varied, as well as the 'rules' that would produce the output constructions. In the canonical case, the subject argument occurs in preverbal position, as in (33a). In the case of certain verbs which are often analyzed as lacking a subject participant, such as weather verbs, a neuter subject *it* is put in preverbal position, as in (33b). In the case of certain constructions in which a subject argument is not in preverbal position, the neuter pronoun is put in preverbal position, leading to the appearance of two 'subject phrases,' as in (33c):

(33)   a. It's in the cupboard.
        b. It's raining.
        c. It is amazing how often it rains in Manchester.

Other analyses have been proposed for the constructions in (33b–c): some have argued that *it* in (33b) refers to the general ambience, and others have argued that there is only one 'surface' subject phrase in (33c), the 'underlying' subject having been extraposed to a different syntactic position. However, whatever rule-based analysis is proposed to derive (33a–c), the result is a coherent product-oriented construction schema for the constructions exemplified in (33a–c), in which there is a subject phrase in preverbal position. And this construction has been gradually spreading in the history of English, replacing constructions in which the subject could appear in different positions.

Another class of syntactic constructions that are easily analyzable as product-oriented schemas are the so-called extraction constructions, in which an extracted element, such as the question word in information questions, the head of a relative clause, or the clefted noun phrase in a focus cleft construction, is positioned at the beginning of the construction:

(34) a. Who (*did) met Jill yesterday?
      b. the man that/who/*Ø met Jill yesterday
      c. It was Ed that/who/*Ø met Jill yesterday.

(35) a. Who did Jill meet yesterday?
      b. the man (that) Jill met yesterday
      c. It was Ed that Jill met yesterday.

(36) a. Who did Jill talk to yesterday?
      b. the man (who) Jill talked to yesterday
      c. It was Ed that Jill talked to yesterday.

(37) a. What did Jill open the box with?
      b. the hammer (that) Jill opened the box with
      c. It was a hammer that Jill opened the box with.

The analysis of extraction constructions in rule-based models allows for movement (or the equivalent thereof) of the question word/relative clause head from any position in the sentence to initial position.[7] Syntacticians are accustomed to formulating a WH-movement rule as 'move from anywhere to a particular position': it is not generally observed that the movement rule is slightly different depending on the position from which it is moved; what the extraction constructions all have in common is the target structure, that is, the product of the different rules. In fact, the rule for English subject questions, relatives and clefts must be slightly different from the rule for the other types of extraction, since the subject question does not have an auxiliary (34a), and the subject relative and cleft prohibit deletion of the relative pronoun in most dialects (34b).

Moreover, other languages have substantially different 'rules' for the formation of information questions, relative clauses and focus (cleft) constructions for

---

[7] We disregard here the existence of constraints on the 'path of movement' (as it would be described in a rule-based transformational model). Although it is widely assumed that the constraints must be formulated in syntactic terms (beginning with Ross 1967), there are many counterexamples, and alternative accounts have been formulated in semantic/pragmatic terms (see Deane 1991 and references cited therein).

different arguments. In K'iche', for example, questions, relatives and focus constructions formed on the ergative (transitive subject) argument require the *-Vn* focus antipassive verb form (see example [38]; Mondloch 1978:74); those formed on the absolutive (intransitive subject or transitive object) argument retain the active voice verb form ([39]; Larsen and Norman 1979:357); those formed on the instrument require the *-bej* focus antipassive form ([40]; Norman 1978:462); and those formed on locative/directional phrases retain the active voice form but leave the demonstrative pronoun *wih* in the normal oblique position ([41]; Mondloch 1978:42):

(38)   jachin x- Ø- cun -**an**   lē   yawab?
        who   PF- 3SG- cure -antipass the   sick.one?
        'Who cured the sick one?'

(39)   jachin x- Ø-   u-   ch'ay -**Ø**   lē   achi
        who   PF- 3SG.ABS-   3SG.ERG-   hit   -ACT   the man
        'Who did the man hit?'

(40)   jas   x-   Ø-   u-   rami -**bej**   lē   achih
        what   PF- 3SG.ABS-   3SG.ERG- cut   -INST.PASS   the   man
        r-   ē   le   chē?
        3SG.POSS-   GEN the   tree
        'What did the man use to cut the tree?'

(41)   jawi? c-   at-   bē **wi**?
        where IMPF- 2SG.ABS-   go WI
        'Where did you go?'

Nevertheless, in K'iche' as in English, there is a coherent product-oriented schema such that the questioned, relativized or focused, phrase is put in initial position, whatever happens to the rest of the sentence. This generalization is also productive, and is another example of a product-oriented schema.

Another example of a product-oriented schema is the Japanese passive. The Japanese passive construction is characterized by: (i) a subject NP which may be marked with *ga* ('subject'), *wa* ('topic'), or may be absent altogether if highly topical; (ii) an oblique agent NP marked with *ni*, which is optional; and (iii) a verb form in *-(r)are*. The subject of a Japanese passive need not be merely the object of the corresponding active, as in (42) (Tsukiashi 1997:18; all examples are attested):

(42)   Dietrich ga   hangyakuzai de   jusatu   sareru
        Dietrich SBJ   treason   for shoot.to.death do:PASS
        'Dietrich is shot to death for treason.'

The subject of the passive construction may correspond to the indirect object of the active verb ([43]; Tsukiashi 1997:25), the possessor of the direct object of the active verb ([44]; 1997:30–31), the subject of the complement of the active verb ([45]; 1997:36), another NP somewhere in the sentence ([46]; 1997:38), or a referent that is not a participant in the event at all ([47]; 1997:39; note that *hiku* is intransitive only):

(43)   'neetyan beppin   dana'   to   iwareta
       girl   beautiful are   COMP say:PASS:PST
       'I was told, "you are a beautiful girl"'

(44)   watasi wa   sitagi   o   torarete-simatta
       I   TOP underwear OBJ   steal:PASS:PERF
       'I have had my underwear stolen.'

(45)   tamago wa zenmetu -ka   to   omowareta
       egg   sbj all.broken -QUES COMP think:PASS:PST
       'The eggs were thought to be all broken.'

(46)   ushiro-no seki de   wakarebanasi o   saretari suruto
       behind   table LOC   break.up.story OBJ do:PASS if
       'if I have people talking about their breaking up at the table behind me'

(47)   karako   no   sugata ni hikarete . . .
       Chinese.doll GEN figure NI attract:PASS:CONJ
       'I was attracted by the figure of the Chinese doll.'

As with the extraction constructions in (34)–(41), the product construction for the Japanese passives in (43)–(45) has a coherent structural schema, namely [(NP *ga/wa*) (NP *ni*) VERB-*(r)are* . . .]. A similar argument can be made for the Bantu passive-applicative patterns, as found in Kinyarwanda (Kimenyi 1980; see also Hawkinson and Hyman 1974). The various passive-applicative constructions in Kinyarwanda resemble the various K'iche' extraction constructions, in that a different applicative suffix must be added to the verb depending on the role of the oblique argument that is ultimately passivized. But all of them have in common a subject NP and a passive verb form.

All of these examples can be analyzed as product-oriented construction schemas in a usage-based model of construction grammar, in terms of their 'syntactic' or symbolic grammatical structure (see §11.2). There is also a plausible candidate for a product-oriented schema in English based on the phonological structure of a family of construction schemas. These are the so-called quasimodals, or recently grammaticalized constructions that have developed tense-aspect-mood functions but are syntactically distinct from the older auxiliary category of English. All of the quasimodal forms end in an alveolar consonant followed by schwa, although this ending represents the reduction of different source forms, as in (48):

(48)   a. She coulda done it.   [from *could have*; also *shoulda, woulda*]
       b. She oughta do it.   [from *ought to*; also *gotta, hadda, hafta, useta*]
       c. She oughta done it.   [from *ought to have*; also *gotta, hadda*]
       d. She's gonna do it.   [from *-ing to*; also non-third singular *wanna*]
       e. She betta do it.   [from *had better*]

We may describe the overall schema as [SBJ QUASIMODAL ... $C_{alv}ə$ VP]. This pattern seems to be mildly productive, in that almost all of the grammaticalizing quasimodals have reduced to forms ending in [. . . $C_{alv}ə$]; of course, there is a relatively low type frequency to this construction.

It should be pointed out that in the past two and a half decades of generative syntactic research, emphasis has shifted from the description of rules to the descriptions of constraints ('principles') on the output of rules (see, for example, Chomsky 1981:3–4; 1993:5). To the extent that the principles and constraints of generative grammar describe the structure of the 'product' schema, then generative grammar constraints are handling essentially the same kind of phenomena as product-oriented schemas in the usage-based model. However, current generative syntactic models utilize abstract syntactic structures and derivational processes, and generate a wide range of outputs, many of which are invalid ('crash'; Chomsky 1993:5) and only a few of which are actually occurring linguistic expressions ('convergence'; ibid.). In contrast, the usage-based model represents schemas abstracted inductively from actually occurring utterances; in syntax, as in morphology, the usage-based model does not posit underlying structures or nonexistent structures that are filtered out (see also footnote 7).

11.3.3   Relevance and the organization of construction networks

In the usage-based model of morphology, semantic connections are argued to be much stronger than phonological connections. Moreover, degree of semantic similarity predicts aspects of morphological structure, in particular the likelihood of suppletion and other morphophonological irregularities. The degree of relevance of semantic relations allows one to impose a roughly hierarchical structure on a taxonomic network (see the diagram in [13] above).

The notion of relevance (relative semantic similarity) allows us to construct hypotheses about the organization of syntactic knowledge as well. In this section, we will examine the hypothesis that the simple relevance hierarchy in (49) governs some aspects of the organization of syntactic knowledge of sentences (see Clausner 1991 for discussion of a more detailed hypothesis):

(49)   illocutionary force < predicate type < participant type

We first offer semantic arguments for the relevance ranking in (49). Relevance of sentences pertains to the meaning of the utterance in context. The illocutionary force of an utterance has the greatest semantic effect on the meaning of a sentence, since it alters the speaker's intention and the hearer's response to a proposition if it is presented as an assertion, question, command or other speech act. Predicate type is definable at two levels. At a general level, predicate type distinguishes predicating an action (verbal predication) vs. describing, classifying, locating or identifying a referent (various types of nonverbal predication). At a more specific level, predicate type distinguishes the different kinds of states of affairs described by different predicates (e.g. *run, talk, dance, sleep* etc.). Differences in predicate type effect the greatest semantic changes in a proposition since they alter the state of affairs; this is a more dramatic change to the semantic representation than merely changing the identities of the participants for a given state of affairs.

Evidence in favor of the relevance ranking in (49) would be a greater likelihood of significant differences in the phonological pole of a construction for semantically more distant – that is, less similar/less strongly connected – construction types. In morphology, evidence for semantic distance has been drawn from changes in the phonological substance of word forms. In syntax, we are dealing with largely schematic constructions, so evidence for distance will be drawn from the symbolic organization of grammatical form, that is, the syntactic elements of constructions, their presence/absence, and their order. Among the most significant structural differences between sentence types are changes of word order, insertion of additional units, and units positioned in first or last position, the two most salient positions of the word string (see Clausner 1991).

Differences in illocutionary force are associated with sentence types, such as the traditional categories of declarative, interrogative and imperative. Cross-linguistic surveys indicate that there are substantial syntactic differences in the order and presence/absence of syntactic units in different sentence types (Sadock and Zwicky 1985; Clausner 1991). Interrogatives typically involve the repositioning of the questioned element, either to sentence-initial or preverbal position, and the addition of a question morpheme. Imperatives typically lack the subject (addressee) element, and have a stripped-down verb form.

In contrast, differences in predicate type, that is, verbal vs. nonverbal predication, rarely involve any change in word order, although they may involve the presence of an additional element (the copula), and the reduction or absence of 'verbal' inflectional categories on the nonverbal element (Croft 1991, chapter 2; Stassen 1997). Finally, differences in the participants in events rarely involve a significant change in the structure of the sentence. The most common differences are the employment of special case markings for certain participant types found in many languages, such as the dative case for experiencers of mental state verbs (*I* in *I like Mozart*) and the instrumental case for inanimate forces (*the wind* in *The wind knocked down the tree*). And even these changes are more accurately described as dependent on the differences in the type of predicate (state of affairs) which requires special case marking of experiencers or inanimate forces.

Another sort of evidence for semantic distance in syntactic organization is ana-logical changes of syntactic constructions. One example from the history of English suggests that illocutionary force is more relevant than predicate type (and also that polarity is intermediate in relevance between illocutionary force and predicate type). This conclusion can be drawn by examining the constructional paradigm given in (50):

(50)

	Declarative	*Imperative*	*Prohibitive*
Verbal	a. He jumped.	c. Jump!	e. Don't jump!
Nonverbal	b. He is brave.	d. Be brave!	f. Don't be cruel!
			<g. Be not cruel!

English forms prohibitive (negative imperative) sentences from verbal predicates by preposing *Don't* to the bare verb stem, as in (50e); compare the imperative form in (50c). Among nonverbal prohibitives, the construction with *Be not*, as in (50g), gave way in the latter parts of the early Modern English period to a construction preposing *Don't* to *be*, as in (50f) (Denison 1998:252).

The construction [*Don't be* ADJ] is odd in the broader perspective of English syntax because a stative predicate normally does not take *do*, and *do* does not combine with *be* in any other construction, either declarative or (positive) impera-tive.[8] Yet the emergence of [*Don't be* ADJ] realigns the constructional paradigm in (50) so that the illocutionary force constructions are more distinct from each other and a single illocutionary force type is more uniform. The result of the change from (50g) to (50f) is that the new nonverbal prohibitive construction [*Don't be* ADJ] is now structurally more different from nonverbal declarative and imperative constructions than the old construction [*Be not* ADJ]; compare (50f–g) to (50c). However, [*Don't be* ADJ] is structurally more similar to the verbal prohibitive con-struction; compare (50f–g) to (50e). The constructions in (50e–f) are describable with a single coherent construction schema [*Don't* PRED]. In other words, the change has led to a greater similarity within a single illocutionary force type and greater differences between sentences of the same predicate type. This is what is predicted by the semantic distance hypothesis, since differences in predicate type are less relevant than differences in illocutionary force.

Additional evidence supporting the greater semantic distance between predicate types than between participant types is found in language acquisition. Children acquiring English tend to be very conservative in using verbs in different argu-ment structure constructions, but very liberal in substituting a range of nouns in argument position in a given verbal construction (see §11.3.4 and references cited therein). That is, a child learning the verb *break* will first learn to substitute dif-ferent participants in an argument position, such as *Mommy break, Daddy break*

---

[8] *Do* is sometimes found with the positive imperative as well (Denison 1998:252).

and so on; and only later will the child learn to use different arguments with the verb, such as *Break cup, Mommy break cup, Break with stick* and so on. These results imply that children generalize across different participant types quickly and early, but only later generalize across predicate types and the argument structure constructions that characterize them.

The evidence presented here, if it is borne out by further studies, would allow us to restructure the taxonomic organization of sentence-level constructions. Although a taxonomic organization for constructions must allow for multiple parents, we can use degree of semantic similarity to rank the syntactic distinctions and thus form a hierarchy, as was done in example (13) (§11.2.4) for morphological paradigms. Such an organization is illustrated in (51) for the Imperative half of the basic Declarative-Imperative split:

(51)

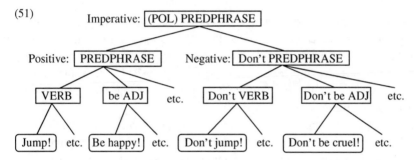

The diagram in (51) is a visual means to represent strength of connections or semantic distance between constructions. Another means to visually represent semantic distance between constructions is employed in typological theory and adopted by Radical Construction Grammar (§10.2.4). This is the **semantic map model** (see Croft 2001:92–98; 2003b:133–39; Haspelmath 2003, for references and general explication). In the semantic map model, semantic distance is represented in a multidimensional **conceptual space**, whose dimensions correspond to semantic properties. In the example in (50), the semantic dimensions are declarative-imperative, positive-negative and verbal-nonverbal (semantically defined as actions-properties etc.). Such a mapping is reduced by convenience to two dimensions. In this case, it corresponds roughly to the spatial arrangement of a morphological or constructional paradigm such as that in (50). For illustration, we will restrict ourselves to the imperative half of the paradigm in (50), that is, (50c–f).

Constructions in a single language (or across languages, for cross-linguistic comparison) are mapped onto the regions of the conceptual space according to their use. For example, one may map the English Copula construction, the prohibitive *Don't* construction, and the imperative Subjectless Clause construction on the conceptual space corresponding to the imperative paradigm in (50), as in (52):

(52)

Subjectless Clause	
positive action imperative	*Don' t* negative action imperative
positive property imperative	negative property imperative
	Copula

The lowercase labels 'positive action imperative' and so on designate points in conceptual space that can be expressed by constructions in a language such as English. The horizontal dimension of the space corresponds to positive-negative polarity and the vertical dimension to the action-property lexical semantic classes. The boxes map the occurrence of different English constructions in the conceptual space (compare the examples in [50c–f]).

The basic principle guiding the structure of conceptual space and semantic maps is formulated in the Semantic Map Connectivity Hypothesis: constructions must map onto a continuous region of conceptual space (Croft 2001:96; 2003b:134). This is one manifestation of the effect of semantic distance on formal structure: constructional uses must be semantically connected, at least historically. There is a dynamic hypothesis as well, namely that constructions are extended in use along connected paths in conceptual space (Croft 2001:101–2). In the example above, for instance, the *Don't* imperative was historically extended from the negative action imperative to the negative property imperative.

Typologists have applied this model cross-linguistically, so that the Semantic Map Connectivity Hypothesis is a universal hypothesis. Patterns of semantic maps across languages also suggest that the internal structure of grammatical categories, that is, relations among exemplars, is universal, while boundaries are language-specific (Croft 2001:103; compare chapter 4). Hence, the typological evidence indicates that at least the broad structure of the conceptual space is universal and therefore makes up part of human cognition, although boundaries are variable and hence less constrained by the nature of human cognition (Croft 2001:105; 2003b:138–39).

The semantic map model represents semantic relationships between constructions. Formal taxonomic relationships can be superimposed on the semantic map model. Relative semantic distances implied by the relevance hypothesis can be represented by relative distance in the conceptual space: (in [52], for example, the negative functions are closer to each other than either is to their positive counterparts). These relative distances impose constraints on the taxonomic organization of construction (in this case, requiring the positive and negative forms to be grouped together first in the taxonomy; compare [52] to [51]). Further structures must be imposed on conceptual space to allow for the formulation of constraints on the grammatical expression of conceptual structures (see, e.g., Croft 2001:160–61, 163–64, 169–70; 2003b:140–43).

The exploration of semantic relations between constructions and their constraints on formal properties of constructions is still in its infancy. Presumably, further research will allow construction grammarians to impose further structure on the network organization of syntactic as well as morphological knowledge.

11.3.4 The acquisition of syntax and syntactic change

In §11.3.3, we referred to evidence from language acquisition on the organization of the construction network. More generally, recent research in child language development offers evidence for a usage-based, inductive model of the acquisition of syntax.

Evidence from very detailed longitudinal studies of early language development demonstrates that children are in fact extremely conservative language learners (Braine 1976 is an early important study along these lines; for more recent studies, see Tomasello 2000, 2003 and references cited therein). Children's earliest multiword utterances demonstrate that children use verbs and other predicates in only one construction at a time (Tomasello 1992; Lieven, Pine and Baldwin 1997; Tomasello et al. 1997; Pine, Lieven and Rowland 1998).

In other words, children do not utilize schematic categories such as [VERB] or schematic constructions such as the transitive construction [SBJ VERB OBJ] in their early acquisition, whether these schematic structures are innate or not. Instead, children begin with very low-level generalizations based around a single predicate and a single construction in which that predicate occurs, and only later in acquisition learn more schematic categories and constructions.

The main exception to this highly specific acquisition process is that, as noted in §11.3.3, children do substitute different object names in a single participant role in a construction from early on. Tomasello (1992) proposes the Verb Island Hypothesis, namely that verbs and other predicates form 'islands' of a single verb plus a single construction, before joining together the 'islands' into a construction network such as that illustrated in (50) above.

Although children substitute object names or 'nouns' early in acquisition, it does not appear that this implies that children acquire a schematic [NOUN] or

[DETERMINER NOUN] noun phrase category early on. Pine and Lieven (1997) found that at the earliest stage of learning nouns and determiners, children also proceed in a piecemeal fashion. In their study, Pine and Lieven found that, although children use a variety of nouns with both *a* and *the*, the nouns they use with *a* and the nouns they use with *the* overlap very little at first. Instead, it appears that children learned nouns with one determiner, or that the determiner use was associated with larger structures in which the noun and determiner occur, such as [*in the* X] or [*That's a* X].

Pine, Lieven and Rowland (1998) studied the first six months of twelve children's multiword speech and found evidence that children begin with lexically quite specific constructions, but that it was not always verbs that functioned as the 'islands' around which utterances were learned. For example, children produced utterances with the auxiliaries *can, do, be* and *have*, constituting an average 90.3% of all children's utterances (Pine et al. 1998:818). However, there was very little overlap between the verbs used with each auxiliary for each child (only one child with one pair of auxiliaries had an overlap significantly different from zero; 1998:819). This suggests that the children are learning lexically specific auxiliary-verb combinations and have not yet developed a productive [AUX] or [VERB] category in their utterances.

A still more fine-grained study confirms that early acquisition begins piecemeal and indicates that acquisition is sensitive to token frequency in the input. Rubino and Pine (1998) conducted a longitudinal study of a child learning Brazilian Portuguese, and argued that the acquisition of sentence constructions with subject-verb agreement began in a piecemeal fashion, with the acquisition of singular and plural agreement beginning independently (in fact, in succession). Later, the child began to overregularize the third singular agreement affixes at the time that the child began to produce the third plural agreement affixes (Rubino and Pine 1998:51). This developmental sequence suggests that an initial stage of rote learning was followed by 'joining the islands' of singular and plural agreement to induce a system of number agreement in the third person.

The overall average of errors produced by the child was quite low, which is what one would expect in a model of conservative, inductive language learning. A breakdown of error rates by person and number indicated that frequency of forms in the input defined the course of acquisition of subject-verb agreement. The child acquired correct subject-verb agreement for the most frequent agreement forms in the input first, and the first correct productions of the less frequent subject-verb agreement combinations appeared with high frequency verbs in the input (Rubino and Pine 1998:53). However, frequency in the input does not appear to be the only factor determining acquisition. Gathercole, Sebastián and Soto (1999) examined the acquisition of Spanish verbal forms in two children, and observed the same piecemeal, incremental acquisition process, and some correlation with frequency of the form in the input. However, it appeared that morphological complexity of the verbal form also played a role in the order of acquisition of verbal forms by the children studied.

These and other language acquisition studies suggest that a careful, detailed examination of the actual course of development of children's language acquisition conforms to the predictions of the usage-based model. Children begin with very narrow construction types, even specific to individual verbs and nouns, and gradually build more schematic grammatical constructions over time. The rate of learning and generalization is influenced by the relative frequency of the constructions in the caregivers' input. The order of acquisition is also sensitive to the semantic distance between constructions, as described in §11.2.4 and §11.3.3.

Similar results are found in the detailed examinations of the paths of syntactic change. As many historical linguists have observed in detailed studies, the birth and growth of a construction proceeds in an incremental fashion, not unlike the expansion from 'islands' of highly specific constructions as in child language acquisition.

One example of a syntactic change, cast in a cognitive linguistic framework, is Israel's analysis of the development of the *way* construction, illustrated in (53) (Israel 1996:218):

(53)   a. Rasselas dug his way out of the Happy Valley.
        b. The wounded soldiers limped their way across the field.
        c. ?Convulsed with laughter, she giggled her way up the stairs.

All of the *way* construction examples given in (53) use a possessed direct object *way* and require a complement describing the path of motion. Example (53a) describes a means of achieving the motion along the path; (53b) describes a manner of motion along the path, and example (53c) describes an incidental activity of the subject as she travels along the path. The *way* construction is also syntactically and semantically idiosyncratic: the verbs in the *way* construction are normally intransitive, and their meaning does not normally entail motion.

Using data from the Oxford English Dictionary and the Oxford University Press corpus of contemporary English, Israel argues that the modern *way* construction grew gradually from two different, more narrowly used *way* constructions, the means and manner constructions (a third source, the acquisition or continued possession of a path, shrank rather than expanded, although it remains in certain common instances such as *find one's way*; Israel 1996:221, n. 3). The manner construction began as a special case of the Middle English [*go one's* PATH] construction, and was originally found with only the most common general motion verbs, no more than sixteen verbs before 1700 (Israel 1996:221). Verbs encoding manner and path of motion began to be used with the manner *way* construction, and in the nineteenth century, expanded particularly in the domain of laborious motion (*plod, scramble, fumble*) and tortuous path (*thread, worm, insinuate*). At the end of the nineteenth century, the manner *way* construction expanded to verbs expressing noise accompanying motion (*crunch, crash, toot*).

The means *way* construction does not emerge until around 1650, and began with verbs describing path clearing (*cut, furrow out*) and road building (*pave, smooth*), as well as forcible motion (*force out*; Israel 1996:223). Expansion begins with the cutting verbs and extends to fighting verbs starting around 1770. In the nineteenth century, progressively more indirect means of reaching the goal, as in *He . . . smirked his way to a pedagogal desk* (Israel 1996:224, from *New Monthly Magazine* VII.386, 1823). At this point the means and manner *way* constructions appear to merge, and in the late nineteenth century one finds the first examples of incidental activity, which is quite distantly related to motion, as in *He . . . whistled his way to the main front door* (Israel 1996:225, from Blackmore, *Cradock Nowell* xvi, 1866).

At the same time that the class of verbs in the *way* construction is expanding, the overall syntactic form of the construction becomes narrower, from allowing other nouns than *way* and an optional path expression to obligatory *way* and path expression (Israel 1996:221, 226). This (common) pattern in syntactic change illustrates how a new construction emerges from an often highly specific instance of an existing construction schema and then expands in its own direction. A usage-based model can account for this pattern in that it allows for the entrenchment of specific instances of construction schemas, which function as 'islands' from which a new construction expands, establishing and generalizing a new construction schema with its own syntactic and semantic peculiarities.

11.4 Conclusion

In this chapter, the construction grammar model of the representation of grammatical knowledge was linked to the processes that use that knowledge, and to the relationship between the representations and what is represented (utterances in discourse). The relationship between representations and what is represented is essentially one of categorization: categorization of the experience to be communicated and the utterance that is used as instances of the grammatical category of known constructions, symbolizing experiences of the same category. The categorization relation between language use and grammatical knowledge is also sensitive to frequency of use of grammatical constructions at different levels of schematicity, that is, the process of language use influences the structure of the representation. This model of grammatical representation and the processes that use it is the usage-based model. The formal representation of the usage-based model is as an activation network, in which activation corresponds to the process of language use, and entrenchment (or decay) is the effect of the process on the representation.

A number of general hypotheses about grammatical representation and process have been proposed by researchers into the usage-based model (in addition to those proposed in chapters 9–11). Productivity is hypothesized to emerge from a high type frequency, which can be generalized as the hypothesis that entrenchment of schematic constructions is proportional to the number of discrete instances of that construction. Generalizations are defined as schemas rather than rules producing an output structure from an input structure. In addition to source-oriented schemas that can be modeled by rules, there is evidence for product-oriented schemas in morphology and syntax, which cannot be easily modeled by rules. The organization of constructions is sensitive to their relative semantic distance from each other (relevance/semantic connections), which imposes further structure on the taxonomic network of constructions with multiple parents. This organization can be represented as semantic maps of constructions on conceptual space, the structure of which appears to be universal in large part. Finally, recent research on language acquisition indicates that both morphology and syntax are acquired in a gradual, piecemeal, inductive fashion. Although many of these hypotheses are recent and hence the evidence supporting them is fragmentary, the cognitive linguistic model of grammatical knowledge is an important and expanding strand of cognitive linguistics research.

12

Conclusion: cognitive linguistics and beyond

The contemporary movement of cognitive linguistics began largely as an approach to the analysis of linguistic meaning and grammatical form in response to truth-conditional semantics and generative grammar. In this book, we have focused on the analyses of syntax and semantics in cognitive linguistics, based on the three fundamental hypotheses presented in chapter 1: language is not an autonomous cognitive faculty; grammar is conceptualization; and knowledge of language emerges from language use. However, these basic hypotheses have consequences beyond the narrow confines of linguistics, and also the narrow confines of the mental representation of linguistic knowledge. A number of cognitive linguists have pushed the boundaries of cognitive linguistics; conversely, a number of critics have challenged cognitive linguistics to go beyond its boundaries. We conclude our survey by pointing out some of the ways cognitive linguistics has gone, and should go, beyond its boundaries.

The hypothesis that language is not an autonomous cognitive faculty has implied that conceptual structures and processes proposed for language should be essentially the same as those found in nonlinguistic human cognition. At first, this meant that cognitive linguists drew on the results of cognitive psychology (and, to a lesser extent, philosophy) in developing cognitive linguistic analyses. It also led to the analysis of conceptual structure using linguistic evidence, as described in Part I of this book. More recently, the reverse has taken place: cognitive linguists have applied the conceptual analyses of cognitive linguistics to other cognitive domains. The cognitive linguistic models of metaphor have been applied to literary analysis (Turner 1987; Lakoff and Turner 1989), philosophy and ethics (Johnson 1987, 1993; Lakoff and Johnson 1999; for a sympathetic but critical review, see Neisser 2001), politics (Lakoff 1996) and mathematics (Lakoff and Núñez 2000). Blending theory has been applied to a general theory of mind, human culture and the evolution of humankind (Turner 2001; Fauconnier and Turner 2002). These forays outside of linguistics are ambitious and highly controversial, but if the first hypothesis is valid, then there should be some implications from the results of cognitive linguistic analysis for nonlinguistic cognition.

The hypothesis that grammar is conceptualization, as well as the other two basic hypotheses, implies a close relationship between cognitive linguistics and cognitive psychology. Indeed, research on categorization was inspired by the work of psychologists such as Rosch (chapter 4), and research on construal operations was inspired by the work of the Gestalt psychologists (chapter 3). More recently, cognitive psychologists have been influenced by cognitive linguistic research (e.g. Gibbs 1994; see also Tomasello 1998, 2000, 2003), and construction grammar in particular has dovetailed with research in language acquisition (see §11.3.4). Also, there has been considerable mutual interest between cognitive linguists and those advocating activation network and parallel distributed processing models of language (see, for example, Elman et al. 1996). Unfortunately, space has prevented us from discussing the many experimental studies in psychology whose results are relevant to cognitive linguistics. Nevertheless, there is considerable scope for further interaction between cognitive psychology and cognitive linguistics, in particular for critical experimental testing of cognitive linguistic hypotheses, and a refinement of the linguistic assumptions behind the experimental designs of cognitive psychologists.

Finally, the hypothesis that knowledge of language emerges from language use reveals both a weakness and an opportunity for cognitive linguistics to respond to its own critics, who look at language from a different perspective than either cognitive linguists or the generative grammarians and truth-conditional semanticists that cognitive linguists were originally responding to. These critics attack all of the latter approaches to language for being focused exclusively on the mind of the speaker or hearer, and ignoring the central function of language as communication and the role of social interaction ('discourse') and the social structures it presupposes in understanding why language is the way it is.

It is true that cognitive linguistics, as its name implies, has focused its attention on mental representations and cognitive processes, and has only recently begun to respond to the discourse and functionalist approaches to language (see, for example, Langacker 1999, chapters 4 and 12; 2002). The hypothesis that knowledge of language emerges from language use provides an opportunity for cognitive linguistics to engage with the social-interactional nature of language. Usage events are of course acts of social interaction. Speakers construe their experience for the purpose of communicating that experience to others, which in turn has broader social-interactional purposes; and hearers likewise invoke a construal of the utterance for those broader purposes. In sum, cognitive linguistics has the potential to make a contribution to a theory of language that goes beyond cognition, as well as a theory of cognition that goes beyond language.

References

Akmajian, Adrian. 1984. Sentence types and the form-function fit. *Natural Language and Linguistic Theory* 2:1–23.

Allan, Keith. 1986. Interpreting English comparatives. *Journal of Semantics* 5:1–50.

Andersen, Henning. 1980. Russian conjugation: acquisition and evolutive change. *Papers from the 4th International Conference on Historical Linguistics*, ed. Elizabeth Closs Traugott et al., 285–302. Amsterdam: John Benjamins.

Ariel, Mira. 1990. *Accessing noun phrase antecedents*. New York: Routledge.

Armstrong, Sharon Lee, Lila R. Gleitman and Henry Gleitman. 1983. What some concepts might not be. *Cognition* 13:263–308.

Aronoff, Mark. 1993. *Morphology by itself: items and inflectional classes*. Cambridge, Mass.: MIT Press.

Atran, Scott. 1990. *Cognitive foundations of natural history: towards an anthropology of science*. Cambridge: Cambridge University Press.

Barlow, Michael and Suzanne Kemmer (eds.). 2000. *Usage-based models of language*. Stanford: Center for the Study of Language and Information.

Barsalou, Lawrence W. 1983. Ad hoc categories. *Memory and Cognition* 11: 211–27.

1987. The instability of graded structure: implications for the nature of concepts. *Concepts and conceptual development: ecological and intellectual factors in categorization*, ed. Ulric Neisser, 101–40. Cambridge: Cambridge University Press.

1992a. Frames, concepts, and conceptual fields. *Frames, fields and contrasts: new essays in semantic and lexical organization*, ed. Adrienne Lehrer and Eva Feder Kittay, 21–74. Hillsdale, N.J.: Lawrence Erlbaum Associates.

1992b. *Cognitive psychology: an overview for cognitive scientists*. Hillsdale, N.J.: Lawrence Erlbaum Associates.

Becker, Joseph. 1975. The phrasal lexicon. Bolt, Beranek and Newman Report No. 3081, Artificial Intelligence Report No. 28.

Berlin, Brent and Paul Kay. 1969. *Basic color terms: their universality and evolution*. Berkeley: University of California Press.

Berlin, Brent, Dennis E. Breedlove and Peter H. Raven. 1973. General principles of classification and nomenclature in folk biology. *American Anthropologist* 75:214–42.

Birner, Betty J. and Gregory Ward. 1998. *Information status and noncanonical word order in English*. (Studies in Language Companion Series, 40.) Amsterdam: John Benjamins.

Black, Max. 1993[1979]. More about metaphor. *Metaphor and thought* (2nd ed.), ed. Andrew Ortony, 19–41. Cambridge: Cambridge University Press.

Bolinger, Dwight. 1971. *The phrasal verb in English*. Cambridge, Mass.: Harvard University Press.

1980. *Language, the loaded weapon*. London: Longmans.

1992. About furniture and birds. *Cognitive Linguistics* 3:111–18.

Braine, Martin D. S. 1976. *Children's first word combinations*. (Monographs of the Society for Research in Child Development 41, no. 1.) Chicago: University of Chicago Press.

Bresnan, Joan (ed.). 1982. *The mental representation of grammatical relations*. Cambridge, Mass.: MIT Press.

Brown, Cecil H. 2002. Paradigmatic relations of inclusion and identity I: Hyponymy. *Lexicology: an international handbook on the nature and structure of words and vocabularies* (Handbooks of Linguistics and Communication Science, 21), ed. D. Alan Cruse, Franz Hundsnurscher, Michael Job and Peter Lutzeier, ch. 47. Berlin: Walter de Gruyter.

Brown, Roger. 1958. How shall a thing be called? *Psychological Review* 65:14–21.

Bybee, Joan L. 1985. *Morphology: a study into the relation between meaning and form*. Amsterdam: John Benjamins.

1995. Regular morphology and the lexicon. *Language and Cognitive Processes* 10:425–55.

2001. *Phonology and language use*. Cambridge: Cambridge University Press.

Bybee, Joan L. and Mary Alexandra Brewer. 1980. Explanation in morphophonemics: changes in Provençal and Spanish preterite forms. *Lingua* 52:271–312.

Bybee, Joan and Paul Hopper. 2001. *Frequency and the emergence of linguistic structure*. (Typological Studies in Language, 45.) Amsterdam: John Benjamins.

Bybee, Joan L. and Carol Lynn Moder. 1983. Morphological classes as natural categories. *Language* 59:251–70.

Bybee, Joan L. and Elly Pardo. 1981. On lexical and morphological conditioning of alternations: a nonce-probe experiment with Spanish verbs. *Linguistics* 19:937–68.

Bybee, Joan L. and Joanne Scheibman. 1999. The effect of usage on degrees of constituency: the reduction of *don't* in English. *Linguistics* 37:575–96.

Bybee, Joan L. and Dan I. Slobin. 1982. Rules and schemas in the development and use of the English past tense. *Language* 58:265–89.

Bybee, Joan L. and Sandra A. Thompson. 1997. Three frequency effects in syntax. *Proceedings of the 23rd Annual Meeting of the Berkeley Linguistics Society*, ed. Matthew L. Juge and Jeri O. Moxley, 378–88. Berkeley: Berkeley Linguistics Society.

Chafe, Wallace. 1994. *Discourse, consciousness and time: the flow and displacement of conscious experience in speaking and writing*. Chicago: University of Chicago Press.

Chafe, Wallace (ed.). 1980. *The pear stories*. New York: Ablex.

Chomsky, Noam. 1981. *Lectures on government and binding*. Dordrecht: Foris.

1993. A minimalist program for linguistic theory. *The view from Building 20*, ed. Kenneth Hale and Samuel Jay Keyser, 1–52. Cambridge, Mass.: MIT Press.

1995. *The minimalist program*. Cambridge, Mass.: MIT Press.

Clahsen, Harald and M. Rothweiler. 1992. Inflectional rules in children's grammar: evidence from the development of participles in German. *Yearbook of Morphology 1992*, 1–34.

Clark, Eve V. and Herbert H. Clark. 1979. When nouns surface as verbs. *Language* 55:767–811.

Clark, Herbert H. 1996. *Using language.* Cambridge: Cambridge University Press.

Clark, Herbert H. and Susan Haviland. 1977. Comprehension and the given-new contract. *Discourse production and comprehension,* ed. R. Freedle, 1–40. Norwood, N.J.: Ablex.

Clausner, Timothy C. 1991. Sentence types and salience. *University of Michigan working papers in linguistics,* ed. William Croft, 1–11. Ann Arbor: Department of Linguistics, University of Michigan.

Clausner, Timothy C. and William Croft. 1997. The productivity and schematicity of metaphor. *Cognitive Science* 21:247–82.

1999. Domains and image-schemas. *Cognitive Linguistics* 10:1–31.

Coleman, Linda and Paul Kay. 1981. Prototype semantics. *Language* 57:26–44.

Collins, Allan M. and M. Ross Quillian. 1969. Retrieval time from semantic memory. *Journal of Verbal Learning and Verbal Behaviour* 8:240–47.

Cornwell, Patricia. 2000. *Black notice.* London: Warner Books.

Coseriu, Eugenio. 1975. Vers une typologie des champs lexicaux. *Cahiers de Lexicologie* 27:30–51.

Coulson, Seana. 2000. *Semantic leaps: frame-shifting and conceptual blending in meaning construction.* Cambridge: Cambridge University Press.

Croft, William. 1991. *Syntactic categories and grammatical relations: the cognitive organization of information.* Chicago: University of Chicago Press.

1993 [2002]. The role of domains in the interpretation of metaphors and metonymies. *Cognitive Linguistics* 4:335–70. Revised version printed in *Metaphor and metonymy in comparison and contrast,* ed. René Dirven and Ralf Pörings, 161–205. Berlin: Mouton de Gruyter, 2002.

1995. Autonomy and functionalist linguistics. *Language* 71:490–532.

1998a. The structure of events and the structure of language. *The new psychology of language: cognitive and functional approaches to language structure,* ed. Michael Tomasello, 67–92. Mahwah, N. J.: Lawrence Erlbaum Associates.

1998b. Event structure in argument linking. *The projection of arguments: lexical and compositional factors,* ed. Miriam Butt and Wilhelm Geuder, 1–43. Stanford: Center for the Study of Language and Information.

1998c. Linguistic evidence and mental representations. *Cognitive Linguistics* 9:151–73.

2000. *Explaining language change: an evolutionary approach.* London: Longman.

2001. *Radical construction grammar: syntactic theory in typological perspective.* Oxford: Oxford University Press.

2003a. Lexical rules vs. constructions: a false dichotomy. *Motivation in language: studies in honour of Günter Radden,* ed. Hubert Cuyckens, Thomas Berg, René Dirven and Klaus-Uwe Panther, 49–68. Amsterdam: John Benjamins.

2003b. *Typology and universals* (2nd ed.). Cambridge: Cambridge University Press.

In preparation. *Verbs: aspect and argument structure.* Oxford: Oxford University Press.

Croft, William and Esther J. Wood. 2000. Construal operations in linguistics and artificial intelligence. *Meaning and cognition: a multidisciplinary approach,* ed. Liliana Albertazzi, 51–78. Amsterdam: John Benjamins.

Cruse, D. Alan. 1977. The pragmatics of lexical specificity. *Journal of Linguistics* 13:153–64.

1979. On the transitivity of the part-whole relation. *Journal of Linguistics* 15:29–38.

1986. *Lexical semantics.* Cambridge: Cambridge University Press.

1990. Prototype theory and lexical semantics. *Meanings and prototypes: studies in linguistic categorization*, ed. Savas L. Tzohatzidis, 382–402. London: Routledge.

1992a. Antonymy revisited: some thoughts on the relation between words and concepts. *Frames, fields and contrasts: new essays in semantic and lexical organization*, ed. Adrienne Lehrer and Eva Feder Kittay, 289–306. Hillsdale, N. J.: Lawrence Erlbaum Associates.

1992b. Cognitive linguistics and word meaning: Taylor on linguistic categorization. (Review article on John R. Taylor, *Linguistic categorization: prototypes in linguistic theory.*) *Journal of Linguistics* 28:165–83.

1994. Prototype theory and lexical relations. *Rivista di Linguistica* 6:167–88.

2000a. Lexical "facets": between monosemy and polysemy. *Sprachspiel und Bedeutung: Festschrift für Franz Hundsnurscher zum 60. Geburtstag*, ed. S. Beckmann, P. P. König and T. Wolf, 25–36. Tübingen: Max Niemeyer Verlag.

2000b. Aspects of the micro-structure of word meanings. *Polysemy: theoretical and computational approaches*, ed. Yael Ravin and Claudia Leacock, 30–51. Oxford: Oxford University Press.

2002a. Microsenses, default specificity and the semantics-pragmatics boundary. *Axiomathes* 1:1–20.

2002b. Hyponymy and its varieties. *The semantics of relationships: an interdisciplinary perspective*, ed. Rebecca Green, Carol A. Bean and Sung Hyon Myaeng, 3–21. Dordrecht: Kluwer.

Cruse, D. Alan., Franz Hundsnurscher, Michael Job and Peter Lutzeier (eds.). 2002. *Lexicology: an international handbook on the nature and structure of words and vocabularies*. (Handbooks of Linguistics and Communication Science, 21.1.) Berlin: Walter de Gruyter.

Cruse, D. Alan and Pagona Togia. 1995. Towards a cognitive model of antonymy. *Lexicology* 1:113–41.

Daugherty, K. and Mark Seidenberg. 1992. Rules or connections? The past tense revisited. *Proceedings of the 14th Annual Meeting of the Cognitive Science Society* 259–64. Hillsdale, N. J.: Erlbaum.

1994. Beyond rules and exceptions: a connectionist modeling approach to inflectional morphology. *The reality of linguistic rules*, ed. Susan D. Lima, R. L. Corrigan and Gregory K. Iverson, 353–88. Amsterdam: John Benjamins.

Deane, Paul D. 1988. Polysemy and cognition. *Lingua* 75:325–61.

1991. Limits to attention: a cognitive theory of island phenomena. *Cognitive Linguistics* 2:1–63.

DeLancey, Scott. 1981. An interpretation of split ergativity and related patterns. *Language* 57:626–57.

Denison, David. 1993. *English historical syntax*. London: Longman.

1998. Syntax. *The Cambridge history of the English language*, vol 4: *1776–1997*, ed. Suzanne Romaine, 92–329. Cambridge: Cambridge University Press.

Dreyfus, Hubert L. 1991. *Being-in-the-world: a commentary of Heidegger's* Being and Time, *Division I*. Cambridge, Mass.: MIT Press.

Eco, Umberto. 1996. Metaphor. *Philosophy of language: an international handbook of contemporary research* (Handbooks of Linguistics and Communication Science, 7.2), ed. Marcelo Dascal, Dietfried Gerhardus, Kuno Lorenz and Georg Meggle, 1313–23. Berlin: Walter de Gruyter.

Elman, Jeffrey L., Elizabeth A. Bates, Mark H. Johnson, Annette Karmiloff-Smith, Domenico Parisi and Kim Plunkett. 1996. *Rethinking innateness: a connectionist perspective on development.* Cambridge, Mass.: MIT Press.

Elman, Jeffrey L. and James L. McClelland. 1984. Speech perception as a cognitive process: the interactive activation model. *Speech and language,* vol. 10, ed. Norman Lass, 337–74. New York: Academic Press.

Fauconnier, Gilles. 1985 [1994]. *Mental Spaces* (2nd ed.). Cambridge: Cambridge University Press.

1986. Quantification, roles, and domains. *Versus* 44/45:61–80.

1997. *Mappings in thought and language.* Cambridge: Cambridge University Press.

Fauconnier, Gilles and Eve Sweetser (ed.). 1996. *Spaces, worlds and grammar.* Chicago: University of Chicago Press.

Fauconnier, Gilles and Mark Turner. 1996. Blending as a central process in grammar. *Conceptual structure, discourse and language,* ed. Adele E. Goldberg, 113–30. Stanford, Calif.: CSLI Publications.

1994. Conceptual projection and middle spaces. San Diego: University of California, Department of Cognitive Science Technical Report 9401 (available at http://www.blending.stanford.edu).

2002. *The way we think.* New York: Basic Books.

Feyaerts, Kurt. 2000. Refining the inheritance hypothesis: interaction between metaphoric and metonymic hierarchies. *Metaphor and metonymy at the crossroads: a cognitive perspective,* ed. Antonio Barcelona, 59–78. Berlin: Mouton de Gruyter.

Fillmore, Charles J. 1975. An alternative to checklist theories of meaning. *Proceedings of the First Annual Meeting of the Berkeley Linguistics Society,* ed. Cathy Cogen et al., 123–31. Berkeley: Berkeley Linguistics Society.

1977a. Scenes-and-frames semantics. *Linguistic structures processing* (Fundamental Studies in Computer Science, 5), ed. Antonio Zampolli, 55–81. Amsterdam: North-Holland.

1977b. The case for case reopened. *Grammatical relations* (Syntax and Semantics, 8), ed. Peter Cole and Jerrold M. Sadock, 59–82. New York: Academic Press.

1982a. Frame semantics. *Linguistics in the morning calm,* ed. The Linguistic Society of Korea, 111–37. Seoul: Hanshin.

1982b. Ideal readers and real readers. *Analyzing discourse: text and talk,* ed. Deborah Tannen, 248–70. Washington, D. C.: Georgetown University Press.

1985. Frames and the semantics of understanding. *Quaderni di semantica* 6:222–54.

1986a. ≪U≫-semantics, second round. *Quaderni di semantica* 7:49–58.

1986b. Pragmatically-controlled zero anaphora. *Proceedings of the Twelfth Annual Meeting of the Berkeley Linguistics Society,* ed. Vassiliki Nikiforidou et al., 95–107. Berkeley: Berkeley Linguistics Society.

1999. Inversion and constructional inheritance. *Lexical and constructional aspects of linguistic explanation,* ed. Gert Webelhuth, Jean-Pierre Koenig and Andreas Kathol, 113–28. Stanford, Calif.: CSLI Publications.

Fillmore, Charles J. and Beryl T. Atkins. 1992. Toward a frame-based lexicon: the semantics of RISK and its neighbors. *Frames, fields and contrasts: new essays in semantic and lexical organization,* ed. Adrienne Lehrer and Eva Feder Kittay, 75–102. Hillsdale, N. J.: Lawrence Erlbaum Associates.

Fillmore, Charles J. and Paul Kay. 1993. *Construction grammar coursebook, chapters 1 thru 11 (reading materials for Ling. X20).* Berkeley: University of California.

Fillmore, Charles J., Paul Kay and Mary Kay O'Connor. 1988. Regularity and idiomaticity in grammatical constructions: the case of *let alone*. *Language* 64:501–38.

Fillmore, Charles J., Paul Kay, Laura A. Michaelis and Ivan A. Sag. In preparation. *Construction Grammar*. Stanford, Calif.: CSLI Publications.

Flickinger, Daniel, Carl Pollard and Thomas Wasow. 1985. Structure-sharing in lexical representation. *Proceedings of the 23rd Annual Meeting of the Association for Computational Linguistics*, 262–67. Chicago: Association for Computational Linguistics.

Gadamer, Hans-Georg. 1989. *Truth and method*, trans. William Glen-Doepel, ed. John Cumming and Garrett Barden, translation rev. Joel Weinsheimer and Donald G. Marshall. London: Sheed & Ward.

Gathercole, Virginia C. Mueller, Eugenia Sebastián and Pilar Soto. 1999. The early acquisition of Spanish verbal morphology: across-the-board or piecemeal knowledge? *International Journal of Bilingualism* 3:133–82.

Gazdar, Gerald, Ewan Klein, Geoffrey Pullum and Ivan Sag. 1985. *Generalized Phrase Structure Grammar*. Oxford: Basil Blackwell.

Geckeler, Horst. 1971. *Strukturelle Semantik und Wortfeldtheorie*. Munich: Fink.

Geeraerts, Dirk. 1993. Vagueness's puzzles, polysemy's vagaries. *Cognitive Linguistics* 4:223–72.

Geertz, Clifford. 1973. *The interpretation of cultures*. New York: Basic Books.

Gentner, Dedre. 1983. Structure-mapping: a theoretical framework for analogy. *Cognitive Science* 7:155–70.

1988. Metaphor as structure mapping: the relational shift. *Child Development* 59:47–59.

Gibbs, Raymond W., Jr. 1990. Psycholinguistic studies on the conceptual basis of idiomaticity. *Cognitive Linguistics* 1:417–51.

1994. *The poetics of mind: figurative thought, language and understanding*. Cambridge: Cambridge University Press.

Gibbs, Raymond W. and J. O' Brien. 1990. Idioms and mental imagery: the metaphorical motivation of idiomatic meaning. *Cognition* 36:35–68.

Glucksberg, Samuel. 2001. *Understanding figurative language*. Oxford: Oxford University Press.

Goldberg, Adele E. 1995. *Constructions: a construction grammar approach to argument structure*. Chicago: University of Chicago Press.

Goossens, Louis. 1990. Metaphtonymy: the interaction of metaphor and metonymy in expressions of linguistic action. *Cognitive Linguistics* 1:323–40.

Grady, Joseph E. 1997. THEORIES ARE BUILDINGS revisited. *Cognitive Linguistics* 8:267–90.

1998. The "conduit metaphor" revisited: a reassessment of metaphors for communication. *Bridging the gap: discourse and cognition*, ed. Jean-Pierre Koenig, 205–18. Stanford, Calif.: Center for the Study of Language and Information.

Grady, Joseph E., Todd Oakley and Seanna Coulson. 1999. Blending and metaphor. *Metaphor in cognitive linguistics*, ed. Raymond W. Gibbs Jr. and Gerard J. Steen, 101–24. Amsterdam: John Benjamins.

Gundel, Jeannette K., Nancy Hedberg and Ron Zacharski. 1993. Cognitive status and the form of referring expressions in discourse. *Language* 69:274–307.

Haegeman, Liliane. 1994. *Introduction to government and binding theory* (2nd ed.). Oxford: Basil Blackwell.

Hahn, Ulrike and Nick Chater. 1997. Concepts and similarity. *Knowledge, concepts and categories*, ed. Koen Lamberts and David Shanks, 43–92. Hove: Psychology Press.

Haiman, John. 1980. Dictionaries and encyclopedias. *Lingua* 50:329–57.

Hampton, James. 1991. The combination of prototype concepts. *The psychology of word meanings*, ed. P. Schwanenflugel, 91–116. Hillsdale, N. J.: Lawrence Erlbaum Associates.

1997. Psychological representation of concepts. *Cognitive models of memory*, ed. Martin A. Conway, 81–107. Hove: Psychology Press.

Hare, Mary and Jeffrey L. Elman. 1995. Learning and morphological change. *Cognition* 56:61–98.

Hare, Mary, Jeffrey L. Elman and Kim G. Daugherty. 1995. Default generalization in connectionist networks. *Language and Cognitive Processes* 10:601–30.

Haspelmath, Martin. 1989. Schemas in Hausa plural formation: product-orientation and motivation vs. source-orientation and generation. *Buffalo Working Papers in Linguistics, 89–01*, 32–74.

2003. The geometry of grammatical meaning: semantic maps and cross-linguistic comparison. *The new psychology of language*, vol. 2, ed. Michael Tomasello, 211–42. Mahwah, N. J.: Lawrence Erlbaum Associates.

Hawkinson, Annie and Larry Hyman. 1974. Natural hierarchies of topic in Shona. *Studies in African Linguistics* 5:147–70.

Hayes, Victoria. 2001. A comparative analysis of antonymy and hybrid anto-complementarity in English and German within a cognitive framework. Ph.D. thesis, University of Manchester.

Heidegger, Martin. 1927 [1962]. *Being and time*, trans. John Macquarrie and Edward Robinson. New York: Harper and Row. (*Sein und Zeit*. Tübingen: Neomarius Verlag.)

Heider, Eleanor. 1971. Focal color areas and the development of color names. *Developmental Psychology* 4:447–55.

1972. Universals in color naming and memory. *Journal of Experimental Psychology* 93:10–20.

Herskovits, Annette. 1986. *Language and spatial cognition*. Cambridge: Cambridge University Press.

Hudson, Richard. 1984. *Word grammar*. Oxford: Basil Blackwell.

Hull, David L. 1988. *Science as a process: an evolutionary account of the social and conceptual development of science*. Chicago: University of Chicago Press.

Husserl, Edmund. 1948 [1973]. *Experience and judgement*, trans. James S. Churchill and Karl Ameriks. Evanston, Ill.: Northwestern University Press. (*Erfahrung und Urteil*, ed. Ludwig Landgrebe. Hamburg: Claassen & Goverts.)

Israel, Michael. 1996. The *way* constructions grow. *Conceptual structure, discourse and language*, ed. Adele E. Goldberg, 217–30. Stanford: Center for the Study of Language and Information.

Jackendoff, Ray. 1983. *Semantics and cognition*. Cambridge, Mass.: MIT Press.

1990. *Semantic structures*. Cambridge, Mass.: MIT Press.

1997. Twistin' the night away. *Language* 73:534–59.

Jackendoff, Ray and David Aaron. 1991. Review of George Lakoff and Mark Turner, *More than cool reason: a field guide to poetic metaphor*. *Language* 67:320–38.

Janda, Richard D. 1990. Frequency, markedness and morphological change: on predicting the spread of noun-plural -*s* in Modern High German and West Germanic. *Proceedings of the Eastern States Conference on Linguistics (ESCOL '90)*, 136–53. Columbus: The Ohio State University.

Jespersen, Otto. 1942. *A modern English grammar on historical principles*, vol. 6. London: Allen & Unwin.

Johnson, David E. and Paul M. Postal. 1980. *Arc pair grammar*. Guildford, N. J.: Princeton University Press.

Johnson, Mark. 1987. *The body in the mind*. Chicago: University of Chicago Press.

1993. *Moral imagination: implications of cognitive science for ethics*. Chicago: University of Chicago Press.

Jolicoeur, Pierre S., Martin A. Gluck and Stephen M. Kosslyn. 1984. Pictures and names: making the connection. *Cognitive Psychology* 19:31–53.

Kant, Immanuel. 1790 [1952]. *The critique of judgement*, trans. J. C. Meredith. Oxford: Clarendon Press. (*Kritik der Urteilskraft*. Berlin: Bey Lagarde und Friederich.)

Katz, Jerrold J. and Jerry A. Fodor. 1963. The structure of a semantic theory. *Language* 39:170–210. (Reprinted in *The structure of language: readings in the philosophy of language*, ed. Jerry A. Fodor and Jerrold J. Katz, 479–518. Englewood Cliffs, N. J.: Prentice-Hall, 1964.)

Kay, Paul. 1997. Construction grammar feature structures (revised). Available at http://www.icsi.berkeley.edu/~kay/bcg/FSrev.html.

2002. English subjectless tagged sentences. *Language* 78:453–81.

Kay, Paul and Charles J. Fillmore. 1999. Grammatical constructions and linguistic generalizations: the *What's X doing Y?* construction. *Language* 75:1–33.

Kimenyi, Alexandre. 1980. *A relational grammar of Kinyarwanda*. (University of California Publications in Linguistics, 91.) Berkeley: University of California Press.

Kleiber, Georges. 1996. Cognition, sémantique et facettes: une "histoire" de livres et de . . . romans. *Les formes du sens*, ed. Georges Kleiber and Martin Riegel, 319–31. Louvain: Duculot.

Koffka, Kurt. 1935. *Principles of Gestalt psychology*. New York: Harcourt, Brace & World.

Köpcke, Klaus-Michael. 1988. Schemas in German plural formation. *Lingua* 74:303–35.

1998. The acquisition of plural marking in English and German revisited: schemata versus rules. *Journal of Child Language* 25:293–319.

Kövecses, Zoltán. 2002. *Metaphor: a practical introduction*. Oxford: Oxford University Press.

Kövecses, Zoltán and Günter Radden. 1998. Metonymy: developing a cognitive linguistic view. *Cognitive Linguistics* 9:37–77.

Kuno, Susumu. 1987. *Functional syntax: anaphora, discourse and empathy*. Chicago: University of Chicago Press.

Kuno, Susumu and Etsuko Kaburaki. 1977. Empathy and syntax. *Linguistic Inquiry* 8:627–72.

Labov, William. 1973. The boundaries of words and their meanings. *New ways of analyzing variation in English*, ed. Joshua Fishman, 340–73. Washington D. C.: Georgetown University Press.

Lakoff, George. 1973. Hedges: a study in meaning criteria and the logic of fuzzy concepts. *Journal of Philosophical Logic* 2:458–508.

1987. *Women, fire and dangerous things: what categories reveal about the mind*. Chicago: University of Chicago Press.

1990. The Invariance Hypothesis: Is abstract reason based on image-schemas? *Cognitive Linguistics* 1:39–74.

1993. The contemporary theory of metaphor. *Metaphor and thought*, ed. Andrew Ortony, 202–51. Cambridge: Cambridge University Press.

1996. *Moral politics*. Chicago: University of Chicago Press.

Lakoff, George and Mark Johnson. 1980. *Metaphors we live by*. Chicago: University of Chicago Press.

1999. *Philosophy in the flesh*. New York: Basic Books.

Lakoff, George and Rafael Núñez. 2000. *Where mathematics comes from*. New York: Basic Books.

Lakoff, George and Eve Sweetser. 1994. Foreword to Gilles Fauconnier, *Mental Spaces*, ix–xlvi. Cambridge: Cambridge University Press.

Lakoff, George and Mark Turner. 1989. *More than cool reason: a field guide to poetic metaphor*. Chicago: University of Chicago Press.

Lambrecht, Knud. 1990. "What, me worry?" – 'Mad Magazine' sentences revisited. *Proceedings of the Sixteenth Annual Meeting of the Berkeley Linguistics Society*, ed. Kira Hall, Jean-Pierre Koenig, Michael Meacham, Sondra Reinman and Laurel A. Sutton, 215–28. Berkeley: Berkeley Linguistics Society.

1994. *Information structure and sentence form: topic, focus and the mental representations of discourse referents*. Cambridge: Cambridge University Press.

Langacker, Ronald W. 1976. Semantic representations and the linguistic relativity hypothesis. *Foundations of Language* 14:307–57.

1987. *Foundations of cognitive grammar*, vol. 1: *theoretical prerequisites*. Stanford, Calif.: Stanford University Press.

1988. An overview of cognitive grammar. *Topics in cognitive linguistics*, ed. Brygida Rudzka-Ostyn, 3–48. Amsterdam: John Benjamins.

1991a. *Foundations of cognitive grammar*, vol. 2: *descriptive application*. Stanford, Calif.: Stanford University Press.

1991b. *Concept, image, and symbol: the cognitive basis of grammar*. Berlin: Mouton de Gruyter.

1998. On subjectification and grammaticization. *Bridging the gap: discourse and cognition*, ed. Jean-Pierre Koenig, 71–89. Stanford, Calif.: Center for the Study of Language and Information.

1999. *Grammar and conceptualization*. Berlin: Mouton de Gruyter.

2002. Discourse and cognitive grammar. *Cognitive Linguistics* 12:143–88.

Larsen, Thomas W. and William M. Norman. 1979. Correlates of ergativity in Mayan grammar. *Ergativity*, ed. Frans Plank, 347–69. New York: Academic Press.

Levinson, Stephen C. 1983. *Pragmatics*. Cambridge: Cambridge University Press.

Lewis, David. 1969. *Convention*. Cambridge, Mass.: MIT Press.

Lieven, Elena V. M., Julian M. Pine and Gillian Baldwin. 1997. Lexically-based learning and early grammatical development. *Journal of Child Language* 24:187–219.

Lobben, M. 1991. Pluralization of Hausa nouns, viewed from psycholinguistic experiments and child language data. M. Phil. dissertation, University of Oslo, Norway.

Losiewicz, B. L. 1992. The effect of frequency on linguistic morphology. Ph.D. dissertation, University of Texas, Austin.

Lyons, John. 1963. *Structural semantics*. Cambridge: Cambridge University Press.

1968. *Introduction to theoretical linguistics*. Cambridge: Cambridge University Press.

Makkai, Adam. 1972. *Idiom structure in English*. The Hague: Mouton.

Marcus, G., U. Brinkmann, H. Clahsen, R. Wiese, A. Woest and S. Pinker. 1995. German inflection: the exception that proves the rule. *Cognitive Psychology* 29:189–256.

Markman, Arthur B. 1999. *Knowledge representation*. Mahwah, N. J.: Lawrence Erlbaum Associates.

Matthews, Peter H. 1981. *Syntax*. Cambridge: Cambridge University Press.

McCarthy, John and Alan Prince. 1990. Foot and word in prosodic morphology: the Arabic broken plural. *Natural Language and Linguistic Theory* 8:209–83.

McCawley, James D. 1981 [1993]. *Everything that linguists have always wanted to know about logic (but were ashamed to ask)* (2nd ed.). Chicago: University of Chicago Press.

McGregor, William B. 1997. *Semiotic grammar*. Oxford: Clarendon.

Meyer-Lübke, W. 1923. *Grammaire des langues romanes*. New York: Stechert.

Michaelis, Laura A. and Knud Lambrecht. 1996. Toward a construction-based theory of language functions: the case of nominal extraposition. *Language* 72:215–47.

Mondloch, James L. 1978. *Basic Quiché grammar*. (Institute for Mesoamerican Studies, Publication 2.) Albany: Institute for Mesoamerican Studies.

Moore, Terence and Christine Carling. 1982. *Understanding language: towards a post-Chomskyan linguistics*. London: Macmillan.

Mossé, Fernand. 1952. *A handbook of Middle English*, transl. James Albert Walker. Baltimore: The Johns Hopkins University Press.

Murphy, Gregory L. and Mary E. Lassaline. 1997. Hierarchical structure in concepts and the basic level of categorization. *Knowledge, concepts and categories*, ed. Koen Lamberts and David Shanks, 93–132. Hove: Psychology Press.

Murphy, Gregory L. and Douglas L. Medin. 1985. The role of theories in conceptual coherence. *Psychological Review* 92:289–316.

Neisser, Joseph Ulric. 2001. Review of George Lakoff and Mark Johnson, *Philosophy in the flesh*. *Language* 77:166–68.

Norman, William M. 1978. Advancement rules and syntactic change: the loss of instrumental voice in Mayan. *Proceedings of the Fourth Annual Meeting of the Berkeley Linguistics Society*, ed. Jeri J. Jaeger, Anthony C. Woodbury, Farrell Ackerman, Christine Chiarello, Orin D. Gensler, John Kingston, Eve. E. Sweetser, Henry Thompson and Kenneth W. Whistler, 458–76. Berkeley: Berkeley Linguistics Society.

Nunberg, Geoffrey. 1995. Transfers of meaning. *Journal of Semantics* 12:109–32.

Nunberg, Geoffrey, Ivan A. Sag and Thomas Wasow. 1994. Idioms. *Language* 70:491–538.

Omar, M. 1973. *The acquisition of Egyptian Arabic as a native language*. The Hague: Mouton.

Perlmutter, David M. (ed.). 1983. *Studies in relational grammar 1*. Chicago: University of Chicago Press.

Pine, Julian and Elena V. M. Lieven. 1997. Slot and frame patterns and the development of the determiner category. *Journal of Child Language* 18:123–38.

Pine, Julian, Elena V. M. Lieven and Caroline F. Rowland. 1998. Comparing different models of the development of the English verb category. *Linguistics* 36:4–40.

Pinker, Stephen and Alan Prince. 1994. Regular and irregular morphology and the psychological status of rules of grammar. *The reality of linguistic rules*, ed. Susan D. Lima, R. L. Corrigan and Gregory K. Iverson, 353–88. Amsterdam: John Benjamins.

Pollard, Carl and Ivan A. Sag. 1993. *Head-driven Phrase Structure Grammar*. Chicago: University of Chicago Press and Stanford: the Center for the Study of Language and Information.

Poplack, Shana. 1992. The inherent variability of the French subjunctive. *Theoretical analyses in Romance linguistics*, ed. Christiane Laeufer and Terrell A. Morgan, 235–63. Amsterdam: John Benjamins.

1996. The sociolinguistic dynamics of apparent convergence. *Towards a social science of language: papers in honor of William Labov*, vol. 1: *variation and change in language and society*, ed. Gregory Guy, John Baugh and Deborah Schiffrin, 295–309. Amsterdam: John Benjamins.

Prasada, Sandeep and Steven Pinker. 1993. Generalization of regular and irregular morphological patterns. *Language and Cognitive Processes* 8:1–56.

Prince, Ellen F. 1978. A comparison of WH-clefts and *it*-clefts in discourse. *Language* 54:883–906.

1981a. Toward a taxonomy of given-new information. *Radical pragmatics*, ed. Peter Cole, 223–56. New York: Academic Press.

1981b. Topicalization, Focus-movement and Yiddish-movement: a pragmatic differentiation. *Proceedings of the Seventh Annual Meeting of the Berkeley Linguistics Society*, ed. Danny K. Alford et al., 249–64. Berkeley: Berkeley Linguistics Society.

Pulman, Steven G. 1983. *Word meaning and belief*. London: Croom Helm.

Pustejovsky, James. 1995. *The generative lexicon*. Cambridge, Mass.: MIT Press.

Quine, Willard van Orman. 1951 [1961]. Two dogmas of empiricism. *From a logical point of view* (2nd ed.), 20–46. New York: Harper. (Originally published in *Philosophical Review* 60:20–43, 1951.)

Radden, Günter. 2000. How metonymic are metaphors? *Metaphor and metonymy at the crossroads: a cognitive perspective*, ed. Antonio Barcelona, 93–108. Berlin: Mouton de Gruyter.

Reddy, Michael J. 1979 [1993]. The conduit metaphor – a case of frame conflict in our language about language. *Metaphor and thought* (2nd ed.), ed. Andrew Ortony, 164–201. Cambridge: Cambridge University Press.

Reinhart, Tanya. 1984. Principles of gestalt perception in the temporal organization of narrative texts. *Linguistics* 22:779–809.

Richards, I. A. 1936. *The philosophy of rhetoric*. London: Oxford University Press.

Ricoeur, Paul. 1978. The metaphorical process as cognition, imagination and feeling. *On metaphor*, ed. Sheldon Sacks, 141–57. Chicago: University of Chicago Press.

Riemer, Nick. 2001. Remetonymizing metaphor: hypercategories in semantic extension. *Cognitive Linguistics* 12:379–401.

Rosch, Eleanor H. 1973. Natural categories. *Cognitive Psychology* 4:328–50.

1978. Principles of categorization. *Cognition and categorization*, ed. Eleanor Rosch and Barbara Lloyd, 27–48. Hillsdale, N. J.: Lawrence Erlbaum Associates.

Rosch, Eleanor H. and Carolyn B. Mervis. 1975. Family resemblances: studies in the internal structure of categories. *Cognitive Psychology* 7:573–605.

Rosch, Eleanor H., Carolyn B. Mervis, Wayne Gray, David Johnson and Penny Boyes-Braem. 1976. Basic objects in natural categories. *Cognitive Psychology* 8:382–439.

Ross, John R. 1967. Constraints on variables in syntax. Ph.D. dissertation, Massachusetts Institute of Technology.

Rubino, Rejane B. and Julian M. Pine. 1998. Subject-verb agreement in Brazilian Portuguese: what low error rates hide. *Journal of Child Language* 25:35–59.

Rudes, Blair A. 1980. On the nature of verbal suppletion. *Linguistics* 18:655–76.

Sadock, Jerrold M. and Arnold Zwicky. 1985. Speech act distinctions in syntax. *Language typology and syntactic description*, vol. 1: *clause structure*, ed. Timothy Shopen, 155–96. Cambridge: Cambridge University Press.

Schank, Roger C. and Robert P. Abelson. 1977. *Scripts, plans, goals and understanding*. Hillsdale, N. J.: Lawrence Erlbaum Associates.

Searle, John. 1979. Literal meaning. *Expression and meaning*, ed. John Searle, 117–36. Cambridge: Cambridge University Press.

Seidenberg, Mark S., Michael K. Tanenhaus, James M. Leman and Marie Bienkowski. 1982. Automatic access of meanings of ambiguous words in context: some limitations of knowledge-based processing. *Cognitive Psychology* 14:489–532.

Slobin, Dan I. 1991. Learning to think for speaking: native language, cognition, and rhetorical style. *Pragmatics* 1:7–26.

Smith, Edward E., Edward J. Shoben and Lance J. Rips. 1974. Structure and process in semantic memory: a featural model for semantic decisions. *Psychological Review* 81:214–41.

Smith, Linda B. and Larissa K. Samuelson. 1997. Perceiving and remembering: category stability, variability and development. *Knowledge, concepts and categories*, ed. Koen Lamberts and David Shanks, 161–95. Hove: Psychology Press.

Sperber, Dan and Deirdre Wilson. 1986. *Relevance: communication and cognition*. Oxford: Basil Blackwell.

Stassen, Leon. 1997. *Intransitive predication*. Oxford: Oxford University Press.

Stemberger, Joseph P. and Brian MacWhinney. 1988. Are inflected forms stored in the lexicon? *Theoretical morphology*, ed. Michael Hammond and Michael Noonan, 101–16. San Diego, Calif.: Academic Press.

Stern, Joseph. 2000. *Metaphor in context*. Cambridge, Mass.: MIT Press.

Sweetser, Eve. 1990. *From etymology to pragmatics: metaphorical and cultural aspects of semantic structure*. Cambridge: Cambridge University Press.

Swinney, David A. 1979. Lexical access during sentence comprehension: (re)consideration of context effects. *Journal of Verbal Learning and Verbal Behavior* 18:645–69.

1982. The structure and time-course of information interaction during speech comprehension: lexical segmentation, access and interpretation. *Perspectives on mental representation: experimental and theoretical studies of cognitive processes and capacities*, ed. Jacques Mehler, Edward C. T. Walker and Merrill Garrett, 151–67. Hillsdale, N. J.: Lawrence Erlbaum Associates.

Sylestine, Cora, Heather K. Hardy and Timothy Montler. 1993. *Dictionary of the Alabama language*. Austin: University of Texas Press.

Talmy, Leonard. 1972. Semantic structures in English and Atsugewi. Ph.D. dissertation, Department of Linguistics, University of California, Berkeley.

1976. Semantic causative types. *The grammar of causative constructions* (Syntax and Semantics, 6), ed. Masayoshi Shibatani, 43–116. New York: Academic Press.

1977. Rubber sheet cognition in language. *Papers from the Thirteenth Regional Meeting, Chicago Linguistic Society*, ed. Woodford A. Beach et al., 612–28. Chicago: Chicago Linguistic Society.

1978. The relation of grammar to cognition: a synopsis. *Proceedings of TINLAP-2: theoretical issues in natural language processing*, ed. David Waltz, 14–24. Urbana: University of Illinois Coordinated Science Laboratory.

1983. How language structures space. *Spatial orientation: theory, research and application*, ed. Herbert L. Pick, Jr. and Linda P. Acredolo, 225–82. New York: Plenum Press.

1988a. The relation of grammar to cognition. *Topics in cognitive linguistics*, ed. Brygida Rudzka-Ostyn, 165–205. Amsterdam: John Benjamins.

1988b. Force dynamics in language and cognition. *Cognitive Science* 12.49–100.

2000. *Toward a cognitive semantics, vol. 1: concept structuring systems*. Cambridge, Mass.: MIT Press.

Taylor, John R. 1989 [1997]. *Linguistic categorization: prototypes in linguistic theory* (2nd ed.). Oxford: Oxford University Press.

2002. *Cognitive grammar*. Oxford: Oxford University Press.

Togia, Pagona. 1996. Antonyms in English and Modern Greek: a cognitive approach. Unpublished Ph.D. thesis, University of Manchester.

Tomasello, Michael. 1992. *First verbs: a case study of early grammatical development*. Cambridge: Cambridge University Press.

2000. Do young children have adult syntactic competence? *Cognition* 74:209–53.

2003. *Constructing a language: a usage-based theory of language acquisition*. Cambridge, Mass.: Harvard University Press.

Tomasello, Michael, Nameera Akhtar, Kelly Dodson and Laura Rekau. 1997. Differential productivity in young children's use of nouns and verbs. *Journal of Child Language* 24:373–87.

Tsukiashi, Ayumi. 1997. A usage-based analysis of the Japanese passive construction. M.A. dissertation, University of Manchester.

Tuggy, David. 1993. Ambiguity, polysemy and vagueness. *Cognitive Linguistics* 4:273–90.

Turner, Mark. 1987. *Death is the mother of beauty: mind, metaphor, criticism*. Chicago: University of Chicago Press.

1990. Aspects of the invariance hypothesis. *Cognitive Linguistics* 1:247–55.

2001. *Cognitive dimensions of social science*. Oxford: Oxford University Press.

Ungerer, Friederich and Hans-Jürgen Schmid. 1996. *An introduction to cognitive linguistics*. London: Longman.

Vallduví, Enric. 1992. *The informational component*. New York: Garland.

Wertheimer, Max. 1923 [1950]. Laws of organization in perceptual forms (abridged and translated by Willis D. Ellis). *A source book of Gestalt psychology*, ed. Willis D. Ellis, 71–88. New York: Humanities Press. (Untersuchungen zur Lehre von der Gestalt. *Psychologische Forschung* 4:301–50.)

Whittlesea, Bruce W. A. 1997. The representation of general and particular knowledge. *Knowledge, concepts and categories*, ed. Koen Lamberts and David Shanks, 335–70. Hove: Psychology Press.

Wierzbicka, Anna. 1980. *Lingua mentalis: the semantics of natural language*. New York: Academic Press.

1985. Oats and wheat: the fallacy of arbitrariness. *Iconicity in syntax*, ed. John Haiman, 311–42. Amsterdam: John Benjamins.

1987. Boys will be boys. *Language* 63:95–114.

1988. *The semantics of grammar*. Amsterdam: John Benjamins.

1996. *Semantics: primes and universals*. Oxford: Oxford University Press.

Wilson, Deirdre. 1975. *Presuppositions and non-truth-conditional semantics*. New York: Academic Press.

Wittgenstein, Ludwig. 1953. *Philosophical investigations*. New York: Macmillan.
   1980. *Culture and value*, trans. P. Winch. Chicago: University of Chicago Press.
Wood, Mary McGee. 1993. *Categorial grammars*. London: Routledge.
Zager, David. 1980. A real-time process model of morphological change. Ph.D. dissertation, State University of New York at Buffalo, New York.

Author index

Aaron, David 201, 203
Abelson, Robert P. 7, 17
Akhtar, Nameera 323
Akmajian, Adrian 245
Allan, Keith 176
Andersen, Henning 306
Ariel, Mira 51
Armstrong, Sharon Lee 88
Aronoff, Mark 226
Atkins, Beryl T. 11–12
Atran, Scott 86

Baldwin, Gillian 323
Barlow, Michael 291
Barsalou, Lawrence W. 87, 92, 96, 278
Bates, Elizabeth A. 329
Becker, Joseph 231
Berlin, Brent 81, 82, 83
Bienkowski, Marie 303
Birner, Betty J. 242–43
Black, Max 203, 206
Bolinger, Dwight 85, 277
Boyes-Braem, Penny 82, 84
Braine, Martin D. S. 323
Breedlove, Dennis E. 82, 83
Bresnan, Joan 229
Brewer, Mary Alexandra 305
Brinkmann, U. 294, 299–300
Brown, Cecil H. 86, 87, 162
Brown, Roger 77
Bybee, Joan L. 291, 292–94, 296–306, 310–12, 313

Carling, Christine 97
Chafe, Wallace 46, 50
Chater, Nick 76
Chomsky, Noam 226, 227–29, 318
Clahsen, Harald 299
Clark, Eve V. 47
Clark, Herbert H. 13, 18, 47, 60, 102–3

Clausner, Timothy C. 22–23, 44–45, 68, 198–99, 318–19
Coleman, Linda 31–32
Collins, Allan M. 76
Cornwell, Patricia 193, 210, 213, 218, 219, 221
Coseriu, Eugenio 141
Coulson, Seana 38, 207–9, 210
Croft, William 4, 22–23, 26, 44–45, 57–58, 59, 64, 66, 68, 70–71, 73, 97, 102, 198–99, 242, 257, 274, 278, 279, 283, 285–87, 289, 294, 319, 321–23
Cruse, D. Alan 4, 79, 80, 83, 84, 109, 116, 117, 120, 130, 136, 141, 142, 143, 147–50, 152, 154, 156, 158, 159, 160–61, 165, 173–74, 182, 187

Daugherty, K. 295, 300
Deane, Paul D. 109, 315
DeLancey, Scott 62
Denison, David 310, 320
Dodson, Kelly 323
Dreyfus, Hubert L. 59

Eco, Umberto 207
Elman, Jeffrey L. 300, 307, 329

Fauconnier, Gilles 33–39, 71, 123, 207, 328
Feyaerts, Kurt 216
Fillmore, Charles J. 7, 8–14, 15, 16, 17–20, 28, 30, 60, 76, 95, 231–40, 248–49, 255, 257, 259, 263, 266–71, 276, 279
Flickinger, Daniel 275
Fodor, Jerry A. 76

Gadamer, Hans-Georg 21
Gathercole, Virginia C. Mueller 324
Gazdar, Gerald 229
Geckeler, Horst 141
Geeraerts, Dirk 109
Geertz, Clifford 21

Gentner, Dedre 195
Gibbs, Raymond W. 199, 251, 329
Gleitman, Henry 88
Gleitman, Lila R. 88
Gluck, Martin A. 96
Glucksberg, Samuel 195, 201, 211, 212
Goldberg, Adele E. 248, 249, 253, 257, 266,
   270, 271–78, 283, 288, 312
Goossens, Louis 218
Grady, Joseph E. 198, 200, 204, 207–9, 210
Gray, Wayne 82, 84
Gundel, Jeannette K. 51

Haegeman, Liliane 230
Hahn, Ulrike 76
Haiman, John 30
Hampton, James 81–82, 88, 89, 91, 144
Hardy, Heather K. 20
Hare, Mary 300
Haspelmath, Martin 302
Haviland, Susan 13
Hawkinson, Annie 317
Hayes, Victoria 183, 190
Hedberg, Nancy 51
Heidegger, Martin 58–59
Heider, Eleanor 81
   see also Rosch, Eleanor H.
Herskovits, Annette 64–65, 69, 70
Hopper, Paul 291
Hudson, Richard 261
Hull, David L. 231
Husserl, Edmund 54, 63
Hyman, Larry 317

Israel, Michael 325–26

Jackendoff, Ray 153, 201, 203, 245–47
Janda, Richard D. 299, 300
Jespersen, Otto 293, 298
Johnson, David 82, 84
Johnson, David E. 229
Johnson, Mark 24, 44–45, 55, 63, 69, 194–96,
   198–204, 328
Johnson, Mark H. 329
Jolicoeur, Pierre S. 96

Kaburaki, Etsuko 61
Kant, Immanuel 54
Karmiloff-Smith, Annette 329
Katz, Jerrold J. 76
Kay, Paul 31–32, 81, 231–40, 248–49, 255, 257,
   259, 261, 263, 266–71, 276, 279, 291

Kemmer, Suzanne 291
Kimenyi, Alexandre 317
Kleiber, Georges 123
Klein, Ewan 229
Koffka, Kurt 56, 63
Köpcke, Klaus-Michael 300
Kosslyn, Stephen M. 96
Kövecses, Zoltán 205, 216
Kuno, Susumu 61

Labov, William 87
Lakoff, George 3, 15, 16, 24, 28, 31, 32,
   44–45, 55, 63, 72, 79, 80–81, 89, 95, 97, 142,
   151, 194–204, 205, 209–10, 218, 240–41,
   257, 266, 271–76, 283, 288,
   328
Lambrecht, Knud 61, 241, 245, 253
Langacker, Ronald W. 7, 14–15, 16, 18, 22,
   23–24, 25–26, 29, 40, 43–44, 48–50, 51, 52,
   53, 54–55, 58, 59, 60, 62–63, 64, 67–68, 69,
   72–73, 89, 131, 133, 149, 157, 249, 253, 256,
   257, 258, 259, 261, 262, 278–83, 291, 292,
   329
Larsen, Thomas W. 316
Lassaline, Mary E. 82, 84, 86
Leman, James M. 303
Levinson, Stephen C. 59
Lewis, David 102
Lieven, Elena V. M. 323, 324
Lobben, M. 302
Losiewicz, B. L. 295
Lyons, John 88, 141, 143, 158

MacWhinney, Brian 294–95
Makkai, Adam 231
Marcus, G. 294, 299–300
Markman, Arthur B. 291
Matthews, Peter H. 134, 249–50
McCarthy, John 299
McCawley, James D. 37
McClelland, James L. 307, 329
McGregor, William 259
Medin, Douglas L. 17
Mervis, Carolyn B. 77, 82, 84
Meyer-Lübke, W. 305
Michaelis, Laura A. 241, 253, 257, 266
Moder, Carol Lynn 298, 302
Mondloch, James L. 254, 312, 316
Montler, Timothy 20
Moore, Terence 97
Mossé, Fernand 310
Murphy, Gregory L. 17, 82, 84, 86

Neisser, Joseph Ulric 328
Norman, William M. 316
Nunberg, Geoffrey 48–50, 70, 230–31, 232, 233,
    249–54
Núñez, Rafael 194, 328

O'Brien, J. 199
O'Connor, Mary Kay 231–40, 248–49, 255, 263
Oakley, Todd 207–9, 210
Omar, M. 300

Pardo, Elly 306
Parisi, Domenico 329
Perlmutter, David M. 229
Pine, Julian 323, 324
Pinker, Stephen 294, 295, 299–300
Plunkett, Kim 329
Pollard, Carl 259, 275, 279
Poplack, Shana 311
Postal, Paul M. 229
Prasada, Sandeep 295
Prince, Alan 294, 299–300
Prince, Ellen F. 13, 238, 242
Pullum, Geoffrey 229
Pulman, Steven G. 79
Pustejovsky, James 137

Quillian, M. Ross 76
Quine, Willard van Orman 30

Radden, Günter 216, 217, 220
Raven, Peter H. 82, 83
Reddy, Michael J. 200
Reinhart, Tanya 59
Rekau, Laura 323
Richards, I. A. 209
Ricoeur, Paul 203
Riemer, Nick 216, 220
Rips, Lance J. 88, 89
Rosch, Eleanor H. 77, 82, 84
Ross, John R. 315
Rothweiler, M. 299
Rowland, Caroline F. 323, 324
Rubino, Rejane B. 324
Rudes, Blair A. 305

Sadock, Jerrold M. 319
Sag, Ivan A. 229, 230–31, 232, 233, 249–54,
    257, 259, 266, 279
Samuelson, Larissa K. 92–93
Schank, Roger C. 7, 17

Scheibman, Joanne 311
Schmid, Hans-Jürgen 79, 86
Searle, John 29
Sebastián, Eugenia 324
Seidenberg, Mark S. 295, 303
Shoben, Edward J. 88, 89
Slobin, Dan I. 73, 293–94, 296–99, 313
Smith, Edward E. 88, 89
Smith, Linda B. 92–93
Soto, Pilar 324
Sperber, Dan 100
Stassen, Leon 319
Steen, Gerard J. 199
Stemberger, Joseph P. 294–95
Stern, Joseph 209–10, 212
Sweetser, Eve 33, 67, 97
Swinney, David A. 303
Sylestine, Cora 20

Talmy, Leonard 34, 44, 51, 53, 56–57, 58, 59,
    63, 66, 67 69–70
Tanenhaus, Michael K. 303
Taylor, John R. 3, 15–16, 79
Thompson, Sandra A. 310–12
Togia, Pagona 173–74, 180
Tomasello, Michael 323, 329
Tsukiashi, Ayumi 316–17
Tuggy, David 131
Turner, Mark 38–39, 44–45, 63, 194–95, 202–3,
    207, 328

Ungerer, Friederich 79, 86

Vallduví, Enric 226
Vamling, Karina 20

Ward, Gregory 242–43
Wasow, Thomas 230–31, 232, 233, 249–54, 275
Wertheimer, Max 63
Whittlesea, Bruce W. A. 92
Wierzbicka, Anna 147, 243–45
Wiese, R. 294, 299–300
Wilson, Deirdre 13, 100
Wittgenstein, Ludwig 77, 98, 210
Woest, A. 294, 299–300
Wood, Esther J. 45
Wood, Mary McGee 229

Zacharski, Ron 51
Zager, David 301
Zwicky, Arnold 319

Subject index

Bold page numbers indicate definitions or major discussions. Category values ('future') are found under category entries ('tense').

ablaut 254
abstraction 4, 44, 52
   see also scalar adjustment, qualitative
access node 30
Access Principle 35
accessibility 46, 50
acquisition 1, 84, 291, 292, 294, 300, 307, 308, 320–21, 323–25, 327, 329
activation 46, 292, 295, 304, 307–8, 327, 329
   see also interactive activation model
active zones 48–49, 137, 138, 140, 156
   see also metonymy
adjective 53, 67–68, 118, 121, 142, 167–92, 253, 299
adjunct 228, 281
adposition 286
adverb 71, 242
adverbial clause 228
affectedness 66
agreement 11, 254, 261, 286, 287–88, 304–5, 324
Alabama 20
ambiguity 118, 138, 140
analogical change 304, 305–6, 320
antagonism **112–13**, 115, 116, 121
anthropological linguistics 86
antonyms 3, 165–66, 172–92
   committed 176, 177–81, 182, 183, 184, 187
   (im)partial 175–76, 177–81, 182, 183, 184, 187, 190
   polar 172–81, 190, 191
   see also monoscalar antonym
   see also biscalar antonym/system; construal, absolute; construal, committed; construal, hybrid; inherentness (in antonyms); monoscalar antonym/system; sub; supra

antonymy 104, 141, 162, 165–66, 167, 168, **169–92**
applicative constructions 317
Arabic 299–300
Arc-Pair Grammar 229
argument (grammatical) 49, 53, 70, 137, 195, 264, 280–82, 310, 314, 320–21
argument structure constructions 66, 263, 264, 269–70, 273, 312, 320–21
argument reversal constructions 242
argumentation, syntactic 283
articles 11
   definite 13–14, 258
   indefinite 243
artifacts 17, 152
artificial intelligence 8, 17, 28
aspect 64, 71, 254, 280, 304–5, 317
   atelic 243, 246
   habitual/generic 71, 304
   progressive 41, 52, 64, 228, 268
   punctual 243
   simple (nonprogressive) 41, 52, 241, 276
   telic 246
assertion 61
atemporal relations 253, 280
attachment 156–58
attention 3, 43, **46–54**, 62, 68, 100, 101, 112
autonomous (grammatical structure) 282
autonomy of cognitive faculty 1, 2, 3, 328
autonomy of senses 109, **112–14**, 116–20, 121–22, 126, 127, 128, 131, 138, 140
   attentional autonomy **112–13**, 119–20
      see also antagonism
   compositional autonomy **114**, 118, 138
   relational autonomy **113–14**, 117, 126, 128, 137
   truth-conditional autonomy 128–29, 133, 134

auxiliary 228, 238, 264, 265, 268, 271, 276, 280, 286, 310, 311, 315, 317, 324

background 59
background assumptions 29–30
Bambara 289
Bantu 317
base 7, **15–16**, 19, 25, 132
based-on link 275
Being-in-the-world 58–59
binarity 164–65, 166
biological kinds 17, 86
biscalar antonym/system **170**, 172, 174, **181–85**
   disjunct **170**, 172, 182
   equipollent **170**, 172, 174, **181–83**, 188, 191
   overlapping **170**, 172, **183–85**, 188, 190
   parallel **170**, 182–83
blending 38–39, 193, 213–15, 216, 221
   see also space, mental
Blending Theory (BT) 38–39, 203, 207–9, 210, 328
'Blessings-Wishes-Curses' construction 271
borrowing 296, 299, 300, 312
boundary (of category/sense) 75, 76, **89–91**, 93–95, 97, 102, 104, 105, 109–15, 122, 143, 146, 151, 153, 155–56, 159, 168, 322
   see also fuzziness (of boundaries)
bounded/unbounded 64, 70, 71
bridging 13

calibration 171–72, 178, 179, 180, 184, 191–92
case (marking) 261, 286, 319
Categorial Grammar 229
categorical 61
categorization/category 3, 17, 46, 53, **54–55**, 74–106, 282–83, 285, 326
   ad hoc category 92
   see also boundary (of category); classical model; dynamic construal model; frame, semantic; levels (categories); prototype model
Caused Motion construction 312
change *see* language change
circumstantial phrase 228
classical model (categorization) **76–77**
   see also categorization
clause 273
coercion 43
cognitive abilities/capacities 2, 3, 45
Cognitive Grammar 72, 257, 266, **278–83**, 285, 287, 288

cognitive linguistics 1, 40, 42, 45, 105, 225, 291, 325, 327, 328–29
cognitive psychology 3, 7, 17, 28, 30, 45, 46, 54, 75, 86, 328, 329
collocations 12, 18, 249–50, 252
common ground 60–61, 102–3
communication 19, 74, 99, 103, 193, 291, 326, 329
comparative 177–79, 183, 186, 228
   quantified comparative 178–79, 183
comparison 44, **54–58**, 68
complement 267, 281, 325
complement constructions 280, 316
complementaries 165–66, **167–69**, 185, 188
complementizer 280
componential model (of a grammar) 225–29, 231, 232, 237, 245, 247, 248, 255, 258–59, 263
component, semantic (of a construction) 138–40, 260, 286
compositionality, semantic 105, 120, 177, 179, 249–54
compound 31
comprehension 99, 100, 278, 285, 307
concepts 7, **14–15**, 24–27, 30, 37, 47, 48, 88, 92–93
   generic concepts 74–75
   individual concepts 74–75
Conceptual Metaphor Theory (CMT) **194–204**, 207, 209
conceptual space 109, 288, **321–23**, 327
conceptual structure 2, 3, 15, 30, 34, 39, 46, 197, 328
conceptualization *see* construal
conditional 228
conjunction 237–38
connection 303–4
   see also phonological connection; semantic connection; symbolic connection
consciousness 46, 75
constituency (syntactic) 261, 311
constitution *see* Gestalt
constraints (conceptual) 100–1, **101–3**, 109
constraints (syntactic) 225, 315, 318
construal 1, 19, 28, 40–69, 75, 79, 80, 93–98, 103–4, 109–10, 122, 127, 138, 140, 144, 145, 150, 151, 153, 155, 158, 160, 161, 164–65, 167–68, 169, 182, 185–92, 216, 218, 221, 279–80, 328, 329
   absolute construal (antonyms) 177, 178, 179–81, 185–89

default construal **71–72**, 83, 102, 103–4, 126, 140, 144, 146–47, 158, 159, 166, 168, 185, 189, 190, 191, 216
  hybrid construal (antonyms) 186–87
  relative construal (antonyms) 175, 177, 179–81, 184, 185–89
construal operations 40–73
  interaction of 69–70
construction grammar 4, 76, 225, 227, 229, 231, 240, 245, 247–48, 252, 255–56, 257–90, 302, 313, 317, 326, 329
Construction Grammar (FIllmore, Kay et al.) 257, **266–72**, 279, 280, 282, 285, 288, 291
Construction Grammar (Lakoff, Goldberg) 257, 266, **272–78**, 283, 288
constructions, grammatical 4, 8, 14, 34, 41–42, 53, 73, 177, 227–29, 236–49, 251–56, 257–90, 295, 302, 308, 313, 319, 321–27
container/containment image schema 80, 89, 104, 142, 151, 201
contextual constraints/pressure **102–3**, 109, 122–23, 127–28, 130, 131, 134, 135, 136, 150, 159, 164, 165, 182, 193, 204, 221
contextual modulation **128**, 129, 130, 135, 140
contextual pressure *see* contextual constraints
contiguity (syntactic) 286
controller (of agreement) 286
convention, conventionality 31, 43, 72–73, 156, 195–98, 199, 203–4, 230, 231, 249–52, 258, 279, 280
conventional constraints 102, 103–4, 109, 111–12, 114, 117, 131, 135, 139, 144, 159, 161, 164, 166, 193, 209, 216
conventional imagery 72
conventional universalist position 73
conversational implicature *see* implicature
conversion 43
conversive 166
coordinate construction 240
copula 253, 319, 321–22
Cora 280
core (intensional) 150
correspondence *see* metaphorical correspondence; symbolic correspondence
countability (count/mass) 71, 280
  see also noun
counterfactual 36, 38, 39

declarative sentence construction 264, 265, 314, 319–21
default construal *see* construal, default
default schema *see* schema, default
default specificity **127**, 129–33, 134, 135, 158
degree of membership (DOM) **79–81**
deictic center 60
deixis 10–11, 44, 46, 58, **59–62**, 63
  epistemic deixis 46, **60–61**, 63
demonstrative 51, 235
dependency 261
dependent (grammatical structure) 282
derivation, grammatical 40, 41–42
determiner 324
diachrony 111, 305
dictionary meaning 30
dimension 25, 69
direct object *see* object
discourse function *see* information structure
disjunction 34
ditransitive construction 264–65, 273–74, 312
domain, semantic **15–16**, 17–32, 39, 44, 47, 65, 68–69, 70, 79, 131–32, 164–66, 167–69, 172, 194–216, 221
  abstract domain 24
  basic domain 24, 25, 26
  image-schematic domains 68–69
  source domain 55, 195–204, 207, 210, 215, 221
  target domain 55, 195–204, 207, 210, 221
domain, social
domain matrix **25**, 27, 31, 47, 69, 122, 132, 216
domain structure 26
dominion 46, **51–52**
dual-processing model 294, 299
durative adverbial 246
dynamic construal model (categorization) 4, 75, **92–104**, 141
  see also categorization

economy 74
elaboration 281–82
elaboration site (e-site) 281
element (syntactic) 260, 264, 285, 286, 287
embodiment 44
empathy 46, **61**, 62, 63
emphatic negative imperative construction 271
encyclopedic knowledge/meaning 30, 86, 148, 196, 204, 208
English (Modern) 14, 21, 24, 41, 42, 64, 72, 90–91, 110, 178, 181, 228, 235, 253, 280, 293, 310, 314, 316, 320–22

English (Modern) (*cont.*)
  Middle English 310
  Old English 235, 294, 300
entailment 13, 104, 143, 145–46
entity/interconnection 44, **67–68**
entrenchment 111–12, 131–33, 135, 136, 139,
    292–95, 296, 297, 304, 305, 308–11, 327
epistemic correspondences 196–97, 201
epistemic deixis *see* deixis
equality/inequality constructions 179–80
ergativity 280, 316
  split ergativity 62
e-site *see* elaboration site
evaluative terms 18–19
event 57–58, 70
evolution of humankind 328
exclamative constructions 241, 247, 258
experience 19, 24, 28, 44, 45, 54, 63, 68, 69,
    71–73, 74, 101, 172, 195, 201, 203–4,
    326
expert systems 86
explicature 100
exposure 177–81
extraction constructions 237, 315–16, 317

facets 47–48, 101, **116–26**, 131, 132, 137, 138,
    140, 216, 220
familiarity 78
family resemblance 78, 82, 85
feature
  grammatical 266–70, 284, 285
  semantic 7, **8–10**, 76, 78, 87, 88, 91, 100, 148,
    150
feature structure 266–67, 269, 271
fictional situations 33
fictive motion 46, **53**, 54
figurative meaning 193, 230, 251
figure/ground 44, 46, **56–58**, 59, 62, 71, 101, 281
filler 268
focal adjustments 43–44, 47, 58, 59
focal orientation 149–50
focus antipassive 316
focus constructions 238, 240, 247, 315–16
folk classification 86
force dynamics 43, 46, **66–67**, 69
foreground 59
frame, semantic **8–22**, 34, 37, 39, 46, 47, 53, 55,
    87, 91–92, 95–96, 167, 272
French 20, 72, 90–91, 136, 178, 180–81, 311
frequency 78, 80, 133, 292, 304, 305, 309
  token frequency 292–95, 301, 306, 307, 308,
    309–10, 324–25

type frequency 296–300, 301, 307, 308, 309,
    312, 327
full-entry model 276–78
functionalism (linguistics) 242, 329
fuzziness (of boundaries) 77, 91, 94, 95

games 33
gang effects 294–95
gender (grammatical) 300
Generalized Phrase Structure Grammar 229
generative grammar 1, 2, 225–29, 259–60, 261,
    263, 292, 293, 294, 302, 313, 317, 328,
    329
geometric structure 63, **64–65**, 70
German 10, 20, 21, 53, 183–84, 299, 300
Gestalt 46, **63–69**, 75, 100, 101, 115, 116, 175,
    286
Gestalt psychology 56, 63, 329
goodness of exemplar (GOE) **77–79**, 80–81, 92,
    153, 166
Government and Binding theory 229
gradability 71
graded centrality 3, 32, 75, **77–81**, 88, 91
grammar/grammatical knowledge 1, 3, 12,
    106, 225–27, 229, 231, 247, 254,
    255–56, 257, 263–65, 271, 278, 279,
    287, 288, 291, 292, 296, 306, 326–27,
    328, 329
  see also Arc-Pair Grammar; Categorial
    Grammar; componential model (of a
    grammar); construction grammar;
    Construction Grammar (Fillmore, Kay et
    al.), Construction Grammar (Lakoff,
    Goldberg); generative grammar;
    Generalized Phrase Structure Grammar;
    Government and Binding theory;
    Head-driven Phrase Structure Grammar;
    Lexical-Functional Grammar;
    Minimalist theory; organization,
    grammatical; Radical Construction
    Grammar; Relational Grammar;
    representation, grammatical; rules;
    schemas; Semiotic Grammar;
    usage-based model; Word Grammar
grammaticalization 63, 317–18
granularity 52
Greek, Modern 162, 172, 178, 180–81, 182
ground *see* figure/ground

have a X constructions 243–44, 247, 248
head 267, 268, 270, 282, 282
hearer 100, 286, 318, 329

Head-driven Phrase Structure Grammar 259, 266, 279
Hebrew, Modern 72
historical linguistics 1
   see also change, language; diachrony
holonym 160
homonymy 100, 111, 217, 303
homophony 303
hyperonym 84, 114, 117, 120, 121, 127, 128, 129, 130, 131–32, 133, 134, 135, 148, 149, 158
hyponym 14, 117, 120, 121, 127, 128, 132, 143, 144, 146, 147, 148, 152, 175
hyponymy 3, 7, 104, **141–50**, 159, 162

iconicity 175, 286
ideal 80
Idealized Cognitive Model (ICM) **28–32**, 92, 95
   cluster ICM 31, 92, 95
identity 36
idiom 199, 205, 225, 2300–37, 270
   decoding idiom 231, **232**, 235
   encoding idiom **231–32**, 235, 250
   extragrammatical idiom **233**, 235, 236
   formal idiom **233**, 235
      see also idiom, schematic
   grammatical idiom 232, 235
   schematic idiom **234**, 235, 236–37, 241, 243, 244, 247, 262–63
   substantive idiom **233**, 234, 235, 236, 237, 247, 253, 262–63
   see also pragmatic point
idiomatic phrase **232**, 235, 252, 253
idiomatically combining expression **232–33**, 235, 236, 249–53, 263
illocutionary force 318–20
image 44
image nouns 33
   see also picture nouns
image schemas **44–46**, 62, 64–65, 68, 80, 104, 167, 169, 172, 201–4
imaging systems 43
immediate scope, *see* scope of predication
imperative constructions 319–22
implication 8
   see also entailment
implicature 10, 185, 268
incompatibility 104, 117, 126–27, 133, 141, 145, 147, 152, 162
individuation **64**, 70
induction 4, 323–25, 327
infinitive 247

inflections, grammatical 40, 41–42, 293–307, 324–25
information structure 61, 226, 235, 242
inherentness (in antonyms) 184–85, 189
inheritance 76, 270–72, 273, 274, 275–78
   complete inheritance 270–71, 278, 308
   default inheritance *see* inheritance, normal
   multiple inheritance 264, 276–77
   normal inheritance 275–76
   see also full-entry model
innate capacity for language 2–3
instance (of a construction) 259
instrument 316
integration (of components of a meaning) 125–26
intention 88
interactive activation network 307
interconnection *see* entity/interconnection
interface (grammatical) 228, 229
interpretation 98–100, 101, 109–10
interrogative constructions 265, 310, 314, 319
   see also questions
intransitive construction 234, 259, 260–62, 264, 268, 283–85, 287
Invariance Hypothesis 201–2
inversion constructions 242–43
irregularity *see* regularity
It-cleft construction 237, 242, 265, 315
iteration 70

Japanese 316–17
Javanese 21
judgement *see* comparison

K'iche' Mayan 254, 312, 316, 317
Kinyarwanda 317
knowledge of language 1, 2, 3–4, 225, 328, 329

landmark 58
language 2, 71–73, 99, 328–29
language change 291, 292, 293–94, 298, 307, 325–26
language use 1, 2, 3–4, 278, 307, 326, 328, 329
latency 134–37
learning 74, 78, 325
   see also acquisition
left isolation (LI) construction 271
let alone construction 237–40, 247, 248
levels (categories) 75, **82–87**, 96–97, 130
   basic 82, **83–84**, 96, 97, 130, 148, 175
   generic *see* level, basic
   subordinate 82, 84, **85–86**, 96, 130
   superordinate 82, **84–85**, 96, 97, 130, 175

levels (syntax) 225–26
lexical decision task 78–79, 303
  see also priming
lexical field theory 10–11
Lexical-Functional Grammar 229
lexical rules 246–47
lexical semantics *see* semantics, lexical
lexicon 97, 205, 212, 226, 227, 229, 230, 234, 237, 247, 255, 257, 263, 293, 294
linking rules 227, 231, 258
links (between constructions) 273–75
list 292, 294
literary analysis 194, 328
locative 50–51, 280

Maasai 289
mapping (between domains) 194, 198–99, 201–4
  open mapping 213–15
  restricted mapping 213–15
  see also epistemic correspondences; metaphorical entailments; ontological correspondences
mathematics 194, 328
maximal scope *see* domain structure
meaning 30, 97–98
  word meaning 4
memory 3, 101
mental spaces *see* space, mental
meronomic structure (of a construction) 259, 260, 262, 269–70, 273, 283, 288
meronomy 3
meronym 114–26
meronymy 7, 104, 141, 150–51, **159–63**
metalinguistic 133–34, 164
metaphor 3, 39, 44, 46, **55–56**, 70, 83, 119, 133, **193–221**
  conventional metaphors 194–204
  deviance in metaphors 206–7
  image metaphors 195, 203
  novel metaphors 204–11
  see also blending; Blending Theory; Conceptual Metaphor Theory; domain, semantic; epistemological correspondences; Invariance Hypothesis; mapping; ontological correspondences; substitution theory of metaphor; target; target domain override; vehicle
metaphor within simile 215
  see also simile within metaphor
metaphorical correspondence 193, 213, 218
metaphorical entailments 197, 201

metaphtonymy 218–19
metonymy 46, **48–49**, 70, 126, 193–94, **216–20**
  see also active zone
microsenses 101, 116, **126–37**, 138, 140, 158, 161
  microsense complexes 129, 131–33, 136
mind 2, 24, 72, 291, 292
Minimalist theory 229
modal 67, 228
modifier 53, 54, 268, 282
modulation, contextual *see* contextual modulation
module 1, 226
  see also autonomy
monoscalar antonym/system 170, 171–81
  see also antonym, polar
mood 304–5, 306–7, 317
morphology 1, 4, 226, 254–55, 292–307, 313, 318, 319, 321, 327
motor activity 2
movement rule 313–15

negation 13, 33, 36, 139, 239, 265, 269, 311
negative constructions 264, 310, 311, 314, 321–23
negative polarity item 239, 240
network 30
  neural network 46
node 262, 263, 292
Nominal Extraposition 241
nonreductionist model 272, 283, 287, 288
nonrelational *see* relationality
nonsubject WH-question construction 271
nonverbal predication 319–22
noun 12, 41, 42, 53–54, 67–68, 137, 141, 243, 254, 279, 284, 299, 323–24
  count noun 24, 41, 42, 43, 64, 85
  mass noun 24, 41, 42, 43, 48, 64, 85
  noun phrase 233, 242, 243, 273, 324
  null instantiation 279
  number 206–7
  plural 48, 254, 292–93, 294, 296, 299–300, 302, 324
  singular 48, 254, 292, 324
numeral 178

object (grammatical) 42, 62, 66, 134, 228, 270, 273, 279, 280, 284, 316, 325
objectivity *see* subjectivity/objectivity
oblique 42, 66, 228, 286, 289, 294, 316
odd number paradox 88

ontological correspondences 196–97
ontological type 122, 126, 133, 153
open schema *see* schema, open
oppositeness 164–67, 170, 185–87
organization, grammatical 257
orientation 46, 59, 63, 65

paired focus construction *see* focus constructions
paradigm (grammatical) 304–5, 321–22
paragon 80
parallel distributing processing 329
parsimony 277–78
    computing parsimony 278
    storage parsimony 278
part 83, 120, **151–59**, 160–63
    core part 156
    extrinsic construal of part 160
    integral part 156–57
    intrinsic construal of part 160
    segmental part 154, 162
    spare part 152, 160
    systemic part 154, 162
    ultimate part 155
partial specification 264
partiality
    scale-partiality 181, 183, 184
    system-partiality 181, 183, 184
    see also antonym, committed; antonym,
        impartial
participant type 318–21
partonymy *see* meronymy
parts of speech 40, 41, 280
passive construction *see* voice, passive
perception 2, 3, 88
person (grammatical) 11, 254, 293, 304–7, 324
perspective 30, 43, 44, 46, **58–63**, 68
phenomenology 45, 58, 63
philosophy 28, 54, 194, 328
phonological connection 303, 304, 318
phonological pole 279, 286, 319
phonology 1, 4, 225, 226–27, 242, 255, 294,
        296–97, 298, 301–2, 319
phrase structure rule 263
'picture' nouns 33, 62
    see also image nouns
piece 151–53
planning 74
pluralia tanta 64
polarity question construction 271
politics 194, 328
polysemy 3, 19, 97, **109–40**, 217, 273–75, 280

portion **151**, 152
Portuguese, Brazilian 324
possessive constructions 23–24, 51, 62, 73, 280
possible worlds 33
postposing constructions 242–43
pragmatic point (of idiom) 234
pragmatics 12–13, 34, 50, 61, 127, 132, 136,
        226, 239–40, 244–45, 255
pre-meaning **103**, 104, 105, 110, 112, 114, 117,
        138, 140, 143, 159, 162
predicate 259, 262, 264, 269–70, 280–82
predicate adjective construction 253
predicate transfer 49–50, 219
predicate type 318–21
prefix 254
preposing constructions 242–43
preposition 41, 52, 286
prepositional phrase 228, 242
presentational sentence 41, 61
presupposition 13, 24, 27, 37, 61, 139, 268, 281
    presupposition float 38
priming 78–79, 93, 303
process (cognitive) 291
process (semantic) 53, 54, 253
production 2, 278, 294, 307
productivity 199, 296–300, 302, 308–9, 311–12,
        314
profile **15–16**, 17–23, 46, 47–50, 53, 92, 132,
        149, 150, 196, 212–13
    configurational profile 22–23
    locational profile 22–23
    profile shift 47–50
profile determinant 282, 287
profile equivalence 287
prohibitive constructions 320–22
pronoun 36, 51, 59–60, 62, 233, 316
proper name 299
prototype 3, **77–92**, 120, 152, 216, 272, 273–74,
        283, 285, 302
    prototype effects 32
    prototype model **77–92**
    see also categorization
Provençal 305–6
psycholinguistics 251, 298–99, 302, 307
psychology *see* cognitive psychology
purport 1–2, **100–1**, 104, 109–10, 127, 147, 161,
        162, 193, 221

qualia roles 137
    see also ways-of-seeing
quantification 34

quantifier 48
quasimodals 317–18
questions 311, 314, 315–16
  How X is it? 173–74, 176, 179, 180, 183, 184
  Is it X? 181–82
  What is its NOM? 173, 176, 179–82, 184
  see also interrogative constructions

radial category structure 272
Radical Construction Grammar 257, 266,
  283–89, 321
range congruence 160
reality 101–2
reductionism 1
reductionist model 268, 272, 284–85
reference 35–36, 54
reference point 51
referential opacity 35–36
referential/attributive 36
regular syntactic expressions 232, 233, 234, 236,
  252
regularity/irregularity (grammatical) 292–300,
  303, 311, 313, 318
relation *see* semantic relation; symbolic relation;
  syntactic relation
Relational Grammar 229
relationality 46, 48, 58, **67–68**, 195, 269, 281
  see also entity/interconnection
relative clause 315–16
relativity (semantic/linguistic) 72–73
relevance 304, 318–19, 322, 327
  see also similarity
Relevance Theory 100
representation, grammatical 2, 257
representation, knowledge 291, 326
resultative construction 246, 247, 248, 249, 277
reversive 165–66, 169
right-dislocation construction 242–43
roles (in mental spaces) 34–36
roles, syntactic *see* syntactic roles
rules 225, 229, 237, 246, 292, 294, 295–96,
  300–2, 313–18, 327
Russian 42–43, 280

salience 47
  see also attention
sanction 55
scalar adjustment 46, **51–53**, 64, 65
  qualitative 46, 52–53, 64
  quantitative 46, 51–52, 64
scalar model 239, 240

scale 22–23, 46, 65, 69, 104, 166, 167, 169–92,
  201
scale-committedness *see* partiality,
  scale-partiality
scale-impartiality *see* partiality, scale-partiality
scale-schema 173
  absolute scale-schema 173, 175
  relative scale-schema 173
  see also construal, absolute; construal, hybrid;
  construal, relative
scanning 44, 46, **53–54**, 67, 280
  sequential scanning 46, 53–54, 67, 72, 280
  summary scanning 46, 53–54, 67, 280
schema 295–302, 207, 308–11, 314, 317, 327
  default schema 300, 312
  open schema 299–300
  product-oriented schema 301–2, 307, 313–18,
  327
  source-oriented schema 301, 313, 327
schematic relation 24, 26–27
schematic systems 43
schematicity 175, 198–201, 202, 253, 254, 263,
  265, 309, 312
schematization 4, 44, 52–53
scope of attention 46
scope of predication 23–24, 46, 154
script 8, 17
search domains 50–51
selection 44, 46, **47–50**, 65
selectional restrictions 249
semantic connection 303, 304, 307, 318, 321,
  327
semantic interpretation rules 232–33, 237, 245,
  249, 252, 253, 254, 257
Semantic Map Connectivity Hypothesis 322
semantic map model 283, 288, **321–22**, 327
semantic pole 279, 286
semantic relation 261, 286
semantics 1, 2, 4, 12–13, 34, 40, 226, 297, 301,
  328
  frame semantics **8–32**
  lexical semantics 3
  semantics of understanding 4, 8, 13, 99
  structural semantics 7, 76
  truth-conditional semantics 1, 2, 7, 8, 12, 33,
  38, 40–43, 64, 328, 329
  see also lexical field theory
semelfactive 43
Semiotic Grammar 259
sense unit 109
  full sense unit 112, 115

sign, linguistic 266, 279
  see also symbolic unit
similarity 82, 303–6, 308
  see also relevance
simile 211–16, 220
simile within metaphor 215–16
  see also metaphor within simile
situatedness *see* perspective
situational use (adpositions)
social interaction 329
sociology 17
sounds 2
space, mental **32–39**, 71, 207–9
  base space 33, 34, 35, 36
  blended space 39, 207–9
  generic space 39, 207–8
  input space 39, 207–8, 209
  space builders 33
  see also blending; Blending Theory
Spanish 232, 235, 324–25
spatial relations 56, 58
specificity, default *see* default specificity
speculation 211
speech act 241, 318
speech act situation 10–11, 60, 276
speech community 17–18, 77, 103, 197, 204
state 53, 64
state of affairs 319
stereotypicality 80–81
structural schematization 43, 46, **63–65**, 69
structuralism 254, 292, 293, 302
structured inventory 262, 279
  see also taxonomic network; taxonomy
sub **173**, 174, 177, 179, 181, 182, 183, 188, 189,
    190
subcategories 75, 81
subcategorization frame 230, 237, 255, 263
subject 62, 66, 228, 259, 261, 262, 264, 265,
    269, 271, 273, 279, 280, 284, 286, 289,
    314, 316, 319, 325
subject-auxiliary inversion (SAI) construction
    271
subject-auxiliary inversion exclamation
    construction 271
subjectivity/objectivity 44, 46, **62–63**
subjunctive 311
subordination 57–58, 59
substitution theory of metaphor 194
suppletion 177, 303, 305, 318
supra **173**, 174, 177, 181, 183, 189, 190, 191
Swedish 20

symbolic connection 303, 304
symbolic correspondence/link 260, 279
symbolic relation 286
symbolic unit 2, 258, 259, 266, 271, 279, 285
synonym 146
synonymy 8
syntactic category 259–60, 268, 272, 274,
    279–80, 283–85
syntactic relation 262, 263, 268–70, 272–73,
    280–82, 285–87
syntactic role 261–62, 268–70, 285
syntactic space 283, 289
syntax 1, 2, 4, 225, 226, 229, 240, 241, 254, 255,
    278, 279, 308, 319, 327, 328
syntax-lexicon continuum 255–56, 264
system-committedness *see* partiality,
    system-partiality
system-impartiality *see* partiality,
    system-partiality

target 193
  see also domain, target
target domain overrides 201
target naming task 303
tautological constructions 244–45, 247
taxonomic network 262, 302, 318, 327
taxonomic relation 3, 24, 26–27, 262–64, 265,
    270–72, 273, 275, 322
taxonomy/taxonomic hierarchy 117, 128,
    147–50, 199–200, 264, 265, 271, 273,
    302, 306, 321–23
taxonym 148–49
taxonymy 147
temporal expressions 33
tense 276, 287–88, 304–5, 317
  future 228
  past 10, 283, 293–99, 304
  perfect 228
  present 241, 276, 283, 304
  preterite 306
text 13–14
  text coherence 14
thematic role 269
theory theory 18
There-constructions 240–41, 272, 275, 276
thetic 61
thought 71–73
'time'-*away* construction 245–46, 247
token frequency *see* frequency, token
topic 316–17
Topicalization construction 242–43

topic-comment 61
topological structure 63, **64–65**
'Tough-movement' 49
trajector 58
transformational grammar *see* generative
  grammar
transitive construction 234, 249, 283, 284, 287,
  323
transitivity (category) 232, 243, 316
transitivity (relation) 144–45
translation 19–21
truth-conditional semantics *see* semantics,
  truth-conditional
type frequency *see* frequency, type
typicality 80
typology 283, 288, 89, 305, 321, 322

unbounded *see* bounded
unification of senses 113, 115, 116–22, 131,
  132
Upriver Halkomelem 289
usage-based model 4, 199, 278, 283, 288,
  291–327
use *see* language use
utterances 2, 12, 33, 60, 62, 258, 265, 278, 291,
  318, 326

valence 280–82
valence-changing (morphology)
Valence Principle 269
values (in mental spaces) 34–36

values (grammatical) 266
vantage point 46, **59**, 63, 69
vehicle 193, 215
  see also domain, source
verb 12, 53, 66, 67–68, 137, 142, 169, 228, 254,
  261, 264, 267, 268, 270, 273, 274, 279,
  283, 284, 286, 287, 289, 293–99, 304,
  310, 312, 314, 323, 324, 325–26
Verb Island Hypothesis 323
verb phrase 238, 264, 266–67
verb-particle construction 277
Vietnamese 42
viewpoint 46, **59**
voice 66
  active 41, 61, 313, 316
  passive 41, 61, 227–28, 286, 289, 313, 316–17

way construction 247, 325–26
ways-of-seeing (WOS) 137–38
WH-cleft construction 242
whole 151, 160
  ultimate whole 155–56
word 8, 14, 34, 53, 98, 109, 251, 254–55, 267,
  268, 279, 292–307
Word Grammar 261
word order 261, 264, 277, 286, 319

Yuman 280

zeugma 49, 113, 118, 119–20, 121, 134, 136,
  139, 168, 191